AN ILLUSTRATED HANDBOOK
AND PRICE GUIDE

AN ILLUSTRATED HANDBOOK
AND PRICE GUIDE

KEN ARMKE

Wallace-Homestead Book Company
Radnor, Pennsylvania

I dedicate this book with love to

Brenda Lea Abney Armke,

my wife and my friend, my confidante and my partner,
the person in my life who offers unfailing affection and loyalty.

_____

Copyright © 1995 by Ken Armke

All Rights Reserved

Published in Radnor, Pennsylvania 19089, by Wallace-Homestead, a division of Chilton Book Company

No part of this book may be reproduced, transmitted or stored in any form or by any means, electronic or mechanical,
without prior written permission from the publisher.

Designed by Ken Armke
Cover design by Anthony Jacobson

The word Sieglinde® in signature and/or block letters is a registered trademark of Smith & Schoen, Inc.

The words M.I. Hummel®, Hummel® and M.I. Hummel Club® in signature and/or block forms are registered trademarks of
W. Goebel Porzellanfabrik, Germany.

M.I. Hummel® figurines, plates and bells are copyrighted products of W. Goebel Porzellanfabrik, Germany. ©Goebel

Illustrations of M.I. Hummel® original art and M.I. Hummel® figurines are printed under License by ARS AG

© ARS AG, Zug/Switzerland.

Hummel® and M.I. Hummel® are used under License from Goebel

**Neither ARS AG nor W. Goebel Porzellanfabrik are responsible for any general information or
price information contained in the guide**

Manufactured in the United States of America

Armke, Ken.
    Hummel : an illustrated handbook and price guide / Ken Armke.
       p.   cm.
    Includes bibliographical references and index.
    ISBN 0-87069-728-5 (hardcover)
    1. Hummel figurines—Collectors and collecting—United States—
    Catalogs. 2. Hummel plates—Collectors and collecting—United
    States—Catalogs. 3. Hummel, Maria Innocentia, 1909–1946.
    I. Title.
    NK4660.A68   1995
    738.8'2'094331—dc20
                                      94-24211
                                         CIP

1 2 3 4 5 6 7 8 9 0   4 3 2 1 0 9 8 7 6 5

Contents

SIDEBARS

Throughout the text chapters of the book, the author has included miscellaneous information in box form. The following index is designed to help locate the individual boxes.

ACKNOWLEDGMENTS

A work such as this cannot be completed without the guidance, assistance and encouragement of others. The problem in compiling a list of *thank yous*: Who have you overlooked?

To those instrumental in the completion of this work whom I have neglected to mention, I'll apologize in advance. My memory is far from being a faultless one.

Among those whom I have not forgotten, I'll begin with Melanie Moss, my executive assistant at Opa's Haus. Not only did Melanie guide me through my various computer problems, she also put together most of the indexing for this book and was equal to every unusual task I asked of her.

I have also not forgotten the encouragement of great friends Jacques and Marcel Nauer, without whom the venture would not have been begun. And the staff of the ARS AG offices in Zug, Switzerland, especially the ready help there of Bernadette Galliker.

Ken LeFevre, a close business friend for almost two decades, not only offered his services and that of his staff at the M.I. Hummel Club, but agreed to guest author the chapter on the club at my request. Among his staff, Beth Baer, Gwen Toma, Linda Famula and Trudy Williams were always only a phone call away from answering literally hundreds of my questions. I'll not forget their help nor the cheerful manner in which it was given. Ditto for Joan Ostroff on the occasions when I called her for technical advice. A lot of information for the book was gleaned from Joan's articles in early issues of *INSIGHTS*.

The contributions of W. Goebel Porzellanfabrik itself certainly must be mentioned. The company's helpfulness in answering technical questions was greatly appreciated. And, of course, without Goebel and its high standards of excellence, there would have been no reason to write a book such as this.

Among prominent secondary market dealers, John Hobe, Rue Dee Marker and Dick Hunt were not only cooperative, but also freely giving of their time.

I am indebted to Alfred Hummel, the nephew of Sister Hummel, and to The Hummel Museum of New Braunfels, Texas, for photographs depicting Berta Hummel in her youth.

I think I owe thanks, too, to authors Eric Ehrmann, Robert Miller and Carl Luckey, whose books on Hummel figurines not only made my task easier, but also have helped sustain the immense interest in Sister Hummel's art.

There must be a very special tribute reserved here for Sieglinde Schoen Smith and her husband, Bill. I count both as close friends and strong supporters. Sieglinde, too, was talked into writing a guest chapter. Read her chapter on Sister Hummel and you'll know why I coerced her into doing it.

I feel sincere appreciation for my new friends at Chilton Book Co. Everyone there was agreeable and pleasant and helpful from the beginning of this project to the end. I extend special thanks there to Susan Clarey and Troy Vozzella, with whom I worked personally, and to an anonymous proofreader who saved me from multitudes of insufferable errors.

(If you are an English teacher and have already suffered through some of my incomplete sentences and my paragraph structure which divides topic sentences from supporting statements, blame not my proofreader nor copy editor for they tried in vain. I have stubbornly clung to the journalistic style which I was taught.)

For last, I have saved loving thanks to a couple of ladies—my mother, who taught me the patience to complete a project of this magnitude, and my wife, Brenda, whose faith in my abilities and unending encouragement in the face of any adversity may have been the most important ingredients of all.

Introduction

When Jacques and Marcel Nauer first suggested that I write this book and include "good color pictures," my first instinct was to run. My thoughts: I have a business to run, a family that sometimes enjoys my presence, and pursuits to pursue. Where do I fit in time for a book?

Rationalization set in. Encouraged, I began to think *it shouldn't take that long; after all, how much work can a little old book be that's mostly prices anyway?*

It was the devil at work! More than a year later as I was trying to finish the project, I could see that very clearly.

Two factors caused serious delays in completion of the book. One was other demands upon my time. The second was pride in the form of a desire to make the book much more than a carbon copy of whatever has already been done.

Considering that some good people have previously spent much time and effort in the chronicling the life and works of Sister Hummel, this was to be no mean feat.

Nevertheless—whether due to perseverance or stubbornness or luck—I feel I succeeded. With the active help of a publisher willing to go all out in terms of photo and reproduction quality and with the free-for-the-asking help and input from business friends and acquaintances, I think the book crosses new boundaries in relating Maria Innocentia (Berta) Hummel, the person and artist, to the line of M.I. Hummel figurines which have made her famous.

The sum of the parts is this: No matter what you have read before, I don't think you can read this book without gaining new appreciation for the person, for her work and for the figurines based upon her work. And if I am right about this, then I have succeeded in my endeavor.

Perhaps that is enough said, but there are some key elements of the book which beg for brief elaboration.

One has to do with goals. My first goal when I started this book was to build an easier-to-follow system of Hummel figurine identification.

On the day I wrote this, I received a letter from a perplexed lady who had been given the task of cataloging and disposing of a collection of old Hummel figurines owned by her elderly father. She said she didn't think six years of college had adquately prepared her for the difficulty of this job!

With this book, I've tried very hard to simplify the task for this lady and others like her. I hope I have succeeded.

I also tried hard to achieve a second goal, which was to correctly present Sister Hummel as an artist and to clarify the roles played by Goebel, ARS and the Convent Siessen in the reproduction of her orignal art.

Enormous blocks of time were devoted to the establishment of values in the pricing section. This was not because I thought they were that important—because I don't—but because I know how seriously people take these values in the various price guides. I tried my best, but I issue no warranties with these values.

Finally, there are regrets. I regret that time and other constraints prevented the depiction of all of the originals themselves. And I regret that the old Hummel prints and other two-dimensional products cannot be adquately covered. I've tried—in ways in which I was able—to compensate for these omissions.

Corrections and additions to this effort are welcomed. Correspondents expecting brief replies should include self-addressed stamped envelopes.

The author can be reached at the following address:

—Ken Armke

855 Laurel Lane
New Braunfels, Texas 78130

CHAPTER ONE

Sister M.I. Hummel and Her Art

(Guest author for this chapter is **Sieglinde Schoen Smith**, who modeled for Sister Hummel as a child and who has become an authority on Sister Hummel and her originals.)

It is very difficult for me, in writing this chapter, to know where to start this story. Sister M.I. Hummel. So many accomplishments, such a short life span. It seems almost impossible that this story is about a single, frail, ever-so-gentle lady.

Which Sister Hummel will I start with?

How will I explain this Berta Hummel, who was affectionately called *s'Hummele* or *Bertl* by her family? What do I say about a child, long gone, that was so alive and had so much zest for living?

Should I start with Miss Berta Hummel the artist, outstanding in her craft, with a bright future—a pretty young lady, so vibrant, always attentive to the needs of her fellow man and yet ready for a prank whenever the opportunity presented itself?

Should it be Maria Innocentia Hummel, the nun, the lady who gave up rich worldly promises for her religious belief?

Or, should it be the accomplished artist, the artist so extraordinary that entire museums have been dedicated to her life and creations?

And then, there is *the lady,* one so full of love, so full of caring that she kept on loving and caring even in times when the world only seemed to know hatred!

Little Princess. In the Hummel family album, Berta's father, Adolf, wrote those words under this photo. It's just one example of the family love with which Berta lived. The photo is courtesy The Hummel Museum via the Hummel family.

I do not favor third-person biographies because it is so difficult to do justice to the subject. But I was asked to do this, so I will attempt to share what I have learned and what I feel about this lady and her art. The lady, I must add, is one whom I have learned to admire and, yes, to love very much.

The only way I feel I can adequately perform this task is to let Sister Hummel's art assist me. I have found that it speaks well for its creator. Be reminded that I am not an accredited art critic nor historian, so if, in this attempt of sharing, I should make a mistake, I ask for forgiveness. It will have been an honest one.

THE EARLY YEARS

Bertl. Little Princess. s'Hummele. If you are of German heritage, you will recognize these as endearing nicknames given to one much loved. They were the names used for Berta after she was born May 21, 1909, in the small town of Massing in Lower Bavaria, Germany, the third of six children born to Adolf and Viktoria Hummel.

From what I have been told by her brother Adolf, this little girl was an individualist from the earliest days of her life. She was not easily controlled.

When I asked Adolf when his sister first started to draw, his answer came quite quickly: "She was born with a pencil in her hand!" When Berta was a mere toddler, he explained, she would find a way to get to her daddy's desktop and, pencil in hand,

---

SIGNIFICANCE OF THE BUMBLEBEE

It's such a simple thing if you know it, such a revelation if you don't—the fact that *Hummel* is the German word for bumblebee.

It explains why bumblebees abound both in Sister Hummel's original artwork and in the promotional support materials developed in behalf of her work.

The bumblebee was incorporated into Goebel's trademark circa 1948-50 and remained there in some fashion until 1979. One version says Goebel altered its traditional crown trademark as a memorial to Sister Hummel, who died in 1946.

"decorate" his work for him. She would "decorate" everything in the vicinity while she was at it!

On another visit to Adolf shortly before his death in 1992, I was allowed to look through the family album and spotted a picture of blonde little Berta seated on a chair as if on a throne. Under the photo, her proud father had written the words *Little Princess.*

In southern Germany and Bavaria, it is very common, in fact customary, to impart pet names to those for whom we deeply care. Ideally, the pet name reflects the personality of the individual. The nickname *Hummele* must have been perfect for young Berta. It means little bumblebee, and we can readily imagine that Berta was one busy little girl!

The nickname *Bertl* is also fitting. It's an endearing diminutive of Berta, a more informal way of addressing her.

By the time *s'Hummele* started school, her creations already showed much promise for the arts and the theater. Creating fashions for her dolls was yet another favorite pastime, and there was early passion for nature and religion. Mr. Hummel often took his children on field trips into the countryside to teach them about God's creations. Afterwards he would encourage them to recreate these experiences and discoveries on paper.

When World War I broke out in 1914, *s'Hummele* was stricken. Her father was called to serve in the German army, and he was terribly missed by this little six-year-old. His guidance, love, encouragement, understanding and discipline had been taken from her young life.

No child at such a tender age can understand chaos of this nature, and *Bertl* began to show signs of willfulness, often trying the patience of teachers at the convent school in her hometown. Despite this, one of the teachers saw something very special in the child, deciding to do what she could to foster the talents of this youngster.

Through the efforts of this lady, Berta was enrolled in a religious boarding school, the Institute of English Sisters, in the nearby town of Simbach. This took place on May 2, 1921, when Berta was 12 years of age.

Here I would like to interject and share a story that may add insight to what life was like for this little girl during the war. She was nine at the time, and she is in a photograph since donated by Adolf Hummel to The Hummel Museum. In the photo,

H 175: This is the now-famous original, Child with Bluebells, *executed by Sister Hummel of Sieglinde Schoen Smith in 1942 when Sieglinde was 16 months old. It is one of two originals of Sieglinde which she still retains; the other, in charcoal, is called* Sieglinde's First Tree.

Introducing Sieglinde

I asked Sieglinde to put together this chapter on Sister Hummel because I harbor the strong conviction that no one in this country—absolutely no one—has developed more understanding of who Sister Hummel was, both as a person and as an artist.

It wasn't always the case.

Until June 1987, Sieglinde gave little thought to Sister Hummel. Oh, in her home in Fort Worth, Texas, she had two "paintings" of herself as a small child which she knew had been finished by Sister Hummel.

She fondly called these two originals—one done in pastels and one sketched in charcoal—her "little babies." They had immigrated from Germany with her and were part of an almost forgotten past.

Until June 1987.

Sieglinde and her Texan husband, Bill Smith, were touring Germany—visiting her sisters and taking in the sights. They were in the part of Wuerttemberg near her birthplace and were approaching the Franciscan Convent Siessen.

she's dressed all in white, flowers in her hair, holding a candle.

It was *Bertl's* first holy communion picture—an important happening in her family. The photo had been used as a postcard which she had hand-addressed to her father on the reverse.

She tells him about this special day in her life that he was not able to attend. And there is a plea which touches me deeply. "Will you please be here for my confirmation in July? I would be so pleased." She was unable to comprehend that her daddy would be unable to attend the next important day in her life either.

The contrast between life then and now is shown in the confirmation gift from her father. Where children today receive expensive mementos, her gift in 1918 was a photo postcard showing her father in uniform and his written explanation: "Sorry, I will not be able to be there for this special day in your life either."

Then and in succeeding years at the convent school in Simbach, Berta wrote frequently to her family. Favorite course was art, in which she received great encouragement. Her letters were frequently embellished with special drawings. A memo-

H 193. Officially, this original is called Little Brother's Lesson, *but Sister Hummel titled it* Feldpost. *Sieglinde thinks it held sentimental significance for the famous artist.*

rable one from the Christmas season depicts a Santa figure carrying a bag of toys and a tree. Adolf Hummel lovingly cataloged this collection of early letters, and many are now on display in the family's Berta Hummel Museum in Massing.

These early memories must have greatly influenced such an impressionable child and stayed with Sister Hummel throughout life. For instance, I cannot help but be drawn to one of her originals which is cataloged as *H 193 Little Brother's Les-*

"Isn't this the convent where Sister Hummel lived?" asked Bill.

With effort, he finally convinced Sieglinde they should stop and visit the origin of the "babies."

Inside the convent, they were looking at the selection of Hummel postcards when Sieglinde exclaimed to Bill, "Look, this postcard is almost like my drawing!"

Behind her in a gentle voice the words: "Fraulein Schoen! Are you the daughter of Herr Director Schoen from Buchau?"

Sieglinde felt shivers. She had not been to the convent since she was a toddler; she had not been addressed by her maiden name for many years.

The sister who identified her is caretaker of Sister Hummel's art at the convent. In convent records, she had recently uncovered references to an "unknown" commissioned work:

Dir. Schoen Buchau org. Kind mit Enzian bez. 50.-m. (Dir. Schoen of Buchau original *Child with Bluebells* paid 50 marks.)

The sister had only the one entry from which to try to locate the original. She had tried to trace the Schoen family, but could not. So, she told Sieglinde, she prayed two weeks previously:

"God, if I am to find this drawing, it is up to you; I can not get any further by myself.

"And then you come from heaven!"

Sieglinde today cites the visit as the time her life was changed. From this point, she has said, she felt like she was being led, as if on a mission.

"For some time, I did not know what to do. Eventually, I came to the conclusion that Sister Hummel intends for me to share my drawings and convey her love to as many people as possible."

She uttered these words in 1989—years before she was to play a major role in bringing The Hummel Museum to Texas.

It was in 1989 that I first met Sieglinde. I had received a call from Bill earlier.

"My wife," he had said, "owns two Hummel originals which we are arranging to have printed. Your company, Opa's Haus, has been recommended to me to help us market the prints."

As calls of this nature are usually frivolous, I tried to discourage him on the phone, but he was personable and persistent. I determined that if he was willing to drive the 500-mile round trip from Fort Worth to New Braunfels to show me the originals and discuss the matter, the very least I could do was listen.

son, which in turn was interpreted into the figurine *Smart Little Sister*.

However, this was not Sister Hummel's name for it. She has the original clearly named *Feldpost*, for military postal service. The drawing, which seems to depict a young girl showing her little brother how to write, was done in 1942. Another vicious world war was in progress.

I believe with all my heart that Sister Hummel, remembering the terrible wartime in her early life, was moved when she once again saw young children writing letters to their fathers at remote military fronts. I think she is drawing her own memories in this original. I think she is showing her brother how to write their father.

In her teens, Berta was setting out on all manner of artistic endeavors. Her classmates had discovered her talent, and more than one would seek to be a subject in her drawings. She was introduced to watercolors and developed a love for landscape painting.

H 106: The artist called this original 's Hummele (It Is the Little Bumble-bee)—a portrait which illustrates Sister Hummel's readiness to poke fun at herself and other members of the Hummel family.

Germany is a country of folk tales and fairy tales. With her imagination, Berta found it simple to bring these characters to life on paper or on stage at school. At the same time, she was developing an individual style that was reflected even in her scenes and costume design.

Berta was known for her ready sense of humor, and it is evident throughout her drawings that she

---

The visit with Sieglinde and Bill not only initiated a business relationship, but a friendship and, for me, a lasting admiration for the will and determination of the lady.

As it transpired, Sieglinde and Bill made a trip to Switzerland to visit the ARS AG office of Jacques Nauer, overseer of his family's huge collection of Hummel originals.

During the visit, they learned of the Nauer family's desire to locate a museum home for the collection, and Sieglinde immediately began a campaign for New Braunfels, with which she had become acquainted through her visits with me at Opa's Haus.

Back home, she contacted me. I, in turn, contacted people involved in the leadership of the New Braunfels Chamber of Commerce.

The Hummel Museum, against long odds, came to be. And to help in the effort in every way possible, Sieglinde and Bill moved from Fort Worth to New Braunfels.

In the course of these efforts, Sieglinde has become not only an authority on, but a recognized spokesperson for Sister Hummel.

She frequently addresses gatherings to speak about Sister Hummel. "Sometimes," she has confided, "I don't know what I will say until I start talking. But I don't worry about it, because it always comes out. I think she is helping me."

Those of us who have attended Sieglinde's talks have often seen her leave adult audiences in tears. She feels what she says, and she is very adept at conveying this feeling.

Sieglinde is artistic herself. She can sculpt and paint well, and for an extended period she was a professional designer for a well-known line of western wear.

So, perhaps it shouldn't be surprising that she has so adapted to Sister Hummel's art that her opinions and advice on it are regularly sought by European sources, including those at ARS.

I wish to assure all who have met and heard of Sieglinde that she is what she seems, and that mostly what she is is a person who harbors a deep, intensive and completely unselfish love for Sister Hummel.

I have heard her criticized for calling herself a *Hummel model*. She didn't call herself that; I did, as her marketing agent. She *was* a child model for Sister Hummel.

I have heard her criticized for calling her originals the *lost* paintings. She didn't call them that; I did. And they were *lost* to the convent and everyone else but Sieglinde.

All I can say is this: If you like Sister Hummel's art, you will love it after you have met Sieglinde.

—Ken Armke

Clowning Around. *Another photo from the family album tells much about Berta Hummel— individuality, sense of humor, fondness for the theater, love of costuming. She's the clown in the foreground. (Photo courtesy The Hummel Museum via the Hummel family.)*

had much fun with her own last name, *Hummel.* Imagine what you might do if your last name was *Bumblebee* and you were a young artist filled with both talent and a sense of humor.

At age 16, she did a series of drawings with this *Hummel* theme. A brother is shown as a bumblebee running on his way to school, suggesting that he might have been late on occasion. Katharina, a sister, is a bumblebee dressed in a pink pleated skirt admiring herself in front of a mirror. Sister Viktoria is a bumblebee in a green pleated skirt positioned on a round piano stool playing the piano.

What of herself? There is a bumblebee seated, as if on a throne, atop a paint palette on wheels, behind which is a wagon filled with paint pots. The entire train is being pulled by a team of countless ants, while the bumblebee uses a paint brush like a whip to speed the team along, the paints spilling from the pots along the way. She called this memorable self-study *The Bumblebee's Happy Drive Into the New Year.*

Seeing it made it easier for me to understand yet another portrait—this one done much later in 1940 of a new addition to the Hummel family. Its catalog number is *H 106* and, again, the English title of *My Baby Bumblebee* does not do it justice. Her title, written in her own hand, was simply *s'Hummele,* which in the native Bavarian dialect I share with her literally means *This Is the Little Bumblebee.*

Perhaps when this latter work was done—when she was already at Convent Siessen, the war was on and she had to face so much that was ugly—she would sometimes wish and dream to be a little *Hummele* again, safe and protected by her parents just one more time!

She so enjoyed poking fun at her name and she so often used the images of bumblebees in her drawings that the bumblebee can logically be

thought of as her pictorial signature. With her bee, she might be trying to say *I was there, too* or *I'll protect you, little one,* or perhaps in some cases the little bumblebee was just so much fun for her to draw she could not resist.

(Oh my, I got myself sidetracked again. I warned you.)

Other than good educations, the schools where Catholic sisters reign are well known for one other ingredient: discipline! At these schools one will not only receive religious training, but, let's face it, the sisters can be very tough. One *will* learn restraint.

From what I have heard, this was also the case with Berta at the convent school in Simbach. The strict environment helped her develop into a well-adjusted and much-liked young lady, as well as a promising artist.

THE MIDDLE YEARS

It was a proud day for father Adolf when, in the spring of 1927, he accompanied his daughter to Munich to enroll her in the Academy of Fine Arts, where on April 25 she successfully completed her entrance exams and was accepted into this special school. To be in surroundings that were at least partially familiar, she took up residence off campus in a dormitory run by a religious order.

At the academy, Berta was now receiving extensive training in all the arts. She learned to paint with oils and to sketch live models, even nudes! She learned to design and weave fabrics, and she continued to grow in mind and soul.

Her teachers were very pleased with her as a talented and likable student, and they expressed the hope that she stay at the academy as a teaching assistant after completion of her final exams.

Self Portrait. *Executed in pencil, this is a rare serious self study by Berta Hummel. Done in 1928 when she was 19, it shows her serious and contemplative side. (Photo courtesy The Hummel Museum via the Hummel family.)*

She must, therefore, have been aware that not only the town, but the whole world, was opening up to her and recognizing her abilities. Somehow—and I doubt that anyone today really knows the exact reason—Berta made a decision that surprised everyone, including her own family.

While she was a student at the academy, Berta formed a friendship with two Franciscan nuns who were also students there. Did they convince this formidable young lady to become one of them? Was it her rural, loving and very religious upbringing that led her to her decision?

Whatever the reason, before graduation from the academy, Berta Hummel visited the Convent Siessen in the state of Wuerttemberg to ask for admission. That was on August 14, 1930.

On March 15, 1931, an excited Berta sent a telegram to her parents, informing them that she had passed her exams at the top of her class!

On April 22, 1931, Berta entered the Convent Siessen as a candidate. She was immediately put to work teaching art in the nearby town of Saulgau and creating liturgical church garments in the art

room at the convent. In her spare time, she was drawing children and working on art commissions.

Her works were published as early as 1932. The first Hummel postcards were printed by publishing houses in Rottenburg and Munich.

On August 30, 1934, Sister Maria Innocentia Hummel was ordained as a sister of the third order of Saint Francis in the Convent Siessen.

The first Hummel book (named *Hummel-buch*) was printed on November 4, 1934, by the printing house of Emil Fink in Stuttgart, Germany. Printing for the first edition was 5,000 copies.

HER LIFE AS A NUN

In retrospect, the years of 1933 and 1934 were important ones for Sister Hummel. Her art was on exhibit in Saulgau and soon thereafter captured the attention of both Franz Goebel, head of the Goebel porcelain factory, and principals from the printing firm ARS Sacra. Both were looking for fresh new ideas and were captivated by what they saw—drawings of children with bright faces, serene religious scenes, imaginative style. They found just what they had been looking for.

Goebel and ARS Sacra successfully sought permission to reproduce Sister Hummel's art, initiating business relationships that continue to exist today. A number of Goebel figurines based on her work were made and introduced as early as 1935.

These must have been happy times for Sister Hummel, but dark clouds were gathering over Germany. Hitler had taken full control of the country and was determined to destroy everything and everyone who did not conform to his wishes.

There was this sister in this convent who just would not see things his way. She had the audacity to draw these peasant children with shoes too large, dresses too small, hair uncombed and all the while

H 242: In English, it's called The Stargazer, *but Sister Hummel called it* Der neue Stern (The New Star). *Don't you agree she was referring to the boy—not to what he's viewing?*

Sister Hummel suddenly left the room, only to return shortly to surprise the sister with a drawing of a little yellow duck. The duck is paddling its feet as if for dear life, its little neck and head high in the air. Under it Sister Hummel has written: *Hold your head high....and swallow*! She posted the drawing on the outside of the door where the sisters were staying.

H 156: Sister Hummel's spunky little duck, titled Hold Your Head High....and Swallow, *helped cheer her fellow sisters during some of the more trying times of the world war.*

happy about it! Not at all the way he wanted the world to conceive of his *super race*!

In a March 20, 1937, edition of the Nazi publication *The SA Man*, Sister Hummel and her art is viciously and publicly attacked. Soon thereafter, the sisters at Siessen, to their total dismay, learn that the Nazi government is determined to close the convent.

In 1940, only about 40 sisters are allowed to stay at the convent. After much begging to remain, Sister Hummel is one of them. Convent Siessen itself is turned into a repatriation center for German nationals from other countries.

The sisters are no longer in charge. They are made to stay in the less desired parts of the convent, since the rest is overflowing with the humanity that the sisters have to take care of.

Sister Hummel, accustomed to a spacious studio of her own, is forced to move into new quarters serving as both bedroom and studio. The previous studio was made into an activity room for all of the remaining 40 sisters.

One can imagine how the sisters in these evening gatherings would lament what had befallen their beloved home, the convent. One day, one sister was especially upset over the conditions and expressed herself to Sister Hummel.

This is but one of many anecdotes about Sister Hummel which have been preserved. She was known as always positive, always supportive toward others. I have been told that even in the times when she was so physically frail, her heart and mind were strong and always full of cheer.

Many of her originals tell stories. Through them, she teaches even today what she believed to be right and wrong. These works of art also tell of sadness, hope and joy. Whatever the subject, one can feel the love of the creator, because somehow she had the ability to weave her heart and soul into her art.

HER LIFE ENDS PREMATURELY

It's sad that these terrible times took their toll on Sister Hummel. She contracted a lung infection which was probably the result of too little food and otherwise poor living conditions.

Her illness would be diagnosed as chronic tuberculosis. It created a debilitating and extended period of poor health. She tried hard to continue her work during her illness, but often to no avail. The war finally ended, but help came too late for this special human being.

Sister Maria Innocentia Hummel, OSF, died on November 6, 1946. She was put to rest in the graveyard of the Convent Siessen by the sisters of the order on November 9, 1946. She was only 37 years old.

One of the sisters who was there tells this story of the day this special lady was laid to rest:

"During her illness, Sister Maria *Innocentia* Hummel had wished that it should snow on the day she was to be buried.

"On November 9, 1946, while her body was carried to its final resting place, snow began to fall in big, happy flakes from a single cloud in an otherwise blue sky until the earth was covered with a white veil, representing a veil of *Innocence*."

(Footnote: I would like to thank everyone who is involved in The Hummel Museum, Inc., especially the Nauer family, the Convent Siessen and all who have helped in establishing the museum, for allowing me to work with the art that this great lady created so many years ago! Most of all, *Thank you, Sister Maria Innocentia Hummel*, for creating so much joy on earth!—Sieglinde Schoen Smith)

OVERSIZE SHOES AND THE SEARCH FOR LOVE

In her originals, Sister Hummel depicts many of her children in shoes which are obviously several sizes too large.

Sieglinde Schoen Smith, now famous as a child model for Sister Hummel, says this is not happenstance.

"During the war in Germany," she explains, "hand-me-downs were much the rule rather than the exception, and you were lucky to get those! The too-big shoes and other ill-fitting garments were part of being a child at this time. Sister Hummel simply drew what she saw."

Sieglinde can produce lots of childhood pictures of her and her four sisters to reinforce the point.

Sieglinde, incidentally, is convinced that the period in which Sister Hummel worked— the period in Germany before and during World War II—helped inspire the artwork which is so admired today.

"She was searching for love and innocence in her world," Sieglinde says convincingly, "and she found it in the little children around her. You don't need to be an art expert to see that in her work."

CHAPTER TWO

The Hummel Museum

True story:

When the long-awaited shipment of M.I. Hummel originals finally reached their destination at The Hummel Museum in New Braunfels, Texas, it was 2 a.m. on March 25, 1992.

The originals had been carefully packed and cataloged in Switzerland. Now they were safely inside the museum's large vault, and the laborious task of uncrating was begun.

The persons responsible for checking in the shipment of more than 300 originals were Sieglinde Smith, who had recently moved to New Braunfels to help with the museum, and Ude Muehlethaler from the ARS offices in Switzerland.

That afternoon, Sieglinde and Ude, approaching early stages of exhaustion, took a lunch break. They would return after the break to work on checking in the originals—a gargantuan task that would take six weeks to complete.

H 668 has message from Sister Hummel.

While they were gone, a museum employee, trying to be helpful, began unpacking the crates at random. He didn't know that he was undoing the careful order with which the originals had been packed to facilitate the check-in process. When Sieglinde and Ude returned, they were stunned but already too tired to be angry.

"Well," Ude said, "let's just start somewhere or we will never get finished."

"Okay," Sieglinde replied, grabbing one from the top of the nearest stack, "we'll begin with this one.

"H 668. *Divine Love.*"

It is a large, relatively unknown Hummel original of Christ holding his wounded heart. Ude turned it over and said, "This one has a message from Sister Hummel on the back."

On the reverse, Sister Hummel had written in her German script:

"Begun on Heart-Jesus-Friday in March.

"Finished on The Festival of St. Mary's Annunciation March 25, 1936.

"In all places, where this my favorite heart shall be kept in adoration, there will be blessings upon it many fold—Marg(areta) M(aria Alacoque)."

Sieglinde and Ude were shaken. They cried.

The painting had been completed 56 years before to the day. Without the mixup caused by the employee, it would not have been first in order in

the check-in process. Of the 300-plus originals, it's the only one which contains a personal message from Sister Hummel.

When Sieglinde later phoned the Convent Siessen in Germany to tell her of the incident, she was told by a sister in a matter-of-fact tone, "My dear child, don't be so vain. You didn't really think you could get this art to the United States all by yourself, did you?"

Coincidence? Perhaps. But there have been a number of such coincidences associated with the founding of The Hummel Museum. Sieglinde says she has now come to expect them.

The incident has earned the original H 668 *Divine Love* a place of honor at the museum. It is on continuous, special display with an abbreviated version of the story.

Display of the 300-plus originals is rotated so that about 50 are shown at any one time. Each exhibit runs about six months.

Art not on exhibit is stored inside the temperature- and humidity-controlled vault.

The variety, artistry and impact of the original works of art usually stuns those only familiar with the figurines. When Gerhard Skrobek, the great

*An **interior view** of The Hummel Museum showing the main gallery area.*

master sculptor of Hummel figurines, first viewed the museum's collection, tears came to his eyes. Most, he had never previously seen as originals.

To the figurine collector, the originals represent numerous familiar motifs. Often—but not always—they can be matched to the figurines they inspired. In many cases, the original has never been reproduced in commercial form.

The museum originals, representing the largest holding in the world of her convent art, are in the U.S. on a lease/purchase basis arranged between the Nauer family of Switzerland and the museum.

It is the only non-profit Hummel museum in the U.S. and, as such, is able to accept gifts which,

under normal circumstances, are tax-deductible to their donors.

Located in a large and attractive building in downtown New Braunfels, The Hummel Museum also offers a large M.I. Hummel figurine display in addition to the art exhibit.

Feature attractions of the figurine exhibit are rarities from a large and valuable collection donated to the museum by Elizabeth Pedder of California.

The famous rarity *Silent Night Candleholder* (Mold 31) is on display both with white child and with black child—the first a gift from Mrs. Pedder and the latter an earlier gift from Mr. and Mrs. James Pierce of Louisiana.

From the beginning, however, The Hummel Museum has strived to provide more than a static display of Sister Hummel's art or the famous figurines she inspired. There is a genuine attempt to look at Sister Hummel as a person and to understand her life and times.

A historical wall display—large and impressive—is an additional focus of attention. With pictures and captions, it chronicles the life of Sister Hummel and introduces her family and the entities which have been associated with her name.

These include, of course, the Goebel company, the Müller/Dubler/Nauer family that was ARS Sacra Printing House, the printing firm of Emil Fink and the Schmid firm of Randolph, Massachusetts.

BERTA HUMMEL MUSEUM

In Massing, Lower Bavaria, Germany, the Hummel family has created a museum in the house where Berta Hummel was born in 1909. It features her pre-convent art and accomplishments.

On display are some of her early originals, a selection of personal items from her childhood, and figurines, dolls and rarities made by W. Goebel Porzellanfabrik.

Address is Marktplatz 32, 84323 Massing. Phone number is {08724}960250. Fax number is {08724}960299.

There is a children's art room, created because museum founders thought that Sister Hummel would like the idea of children trying to actively emulate her art interests.

There is a video and presentation room, where a Goebel-produced video continuously details the life of Sister Hummel and the making of the famous M.I. Hummel figurines.

The video room is located in an upstairs mezzanine section that also houses the figurine displays and several vignette rooms. The vignette rooms are quite interesting.

One is a replica of Sister Hummel's art studio at the convent. The furniture for the studio was donated by the convent, but with the admonition, "You can't say this easel was actually used by Sister Hummel, because we aren't certain it was hers."

Later, in the process of cleaning the easel, Sieglinde uncovered a set of initials: *M.I.H.*

A second vignette room forms a reproduction of a German school room from Sister Hummel's time. The furnishings are authentic antiques donated by the Nauer family and exported from Germany.

**THE GOEBEL
AND M.I. HUMMEL® GALLERY
OF ROSEMONT**

The Hummel Museum in New Braunfels, Texas, is not the only major facility in the U.S. devoted in part to the artistry of Sister Hummel.

In 1994, the Goebel and M.I. Hummel Gallery opened in Rosemont, Illinois—the result of a joint venture between Goebel and the Village of Rosemont.

Rosemont, as a suburb of Chicago, is easily accessible and already owned a large and valuable Hummel figurine collection assembled by Donald E. Stephens, a former mayor and benefactor of the city.

Along with the Stephens collection, the gallery-museum offers a complete display of all current M.I. Hummel products, a display of other Goebel figurines, a Hummel figurine production display and special shows and exhibits.

All is housed in a 15,000-square-foot building which also offers an auditorium and retail store.

Small and intimate, a third depicts a prayer room with a kneeling rail. In it is her actual prayer bench that she used as a child. It was donated by a teaching order of nuns in Massing.

The rosary is a reproduction of the original stored in the museum's vault. The original was donated to the museum by Adolf Hummel, Sister Hummel's brother, shortly before he died in 1992.

There is also a room which depicts the repair and restoration of Hummel figurines.

The figurines on hand include a set of newly made Hummel figurines, furnished by Goebel, along with attractive, halogen-lighted display cases given by Schmid Co.

The museum offers a gift shop stocked with Hummel figurines and many of the two-dimensional M.I. Hummel products which are often difficult for consumers to locate.

On the museum's drawing board are improvements in all of the various rooms, plus additional displays and major modifications. All await funding. Since the museum is a non-profit organization, its success is dependent upon memberships, donations (monetary or material), and admissions.

New Braunfels itself is a Texas resort city of some 30,000 persons. It is a German-heritage suburb of San Antonio and is located on Interstate 35 less than a half hour from San Antonio International Airport.

Museum hours are 10 a.m. to 5 p.m. Monday–Saturday and 12–5 p.m. Sundays. There is an admission charge.

Various types of memberships are offered by the museum. Persons interested in joining the museum or in making a contribution are encouraged to contact the museum as follows:

The Hummel Museum, Inc.
199 Main Plaza
New Braunfels, Texas 78130

Phone numbers are 210-625-5636 or 800-456-4866. Fax number is 210-625-5966.

THEY'RE NOT PAINTINGS

Note that Sister Hummel's original works are not called *paintings*. It has been pointed out that few of Sister Hummel's *originals* were *painted* oils. Most were created with the use of other media.

CHAPTER THREE

The Making of the Figurines

Goebel has produced some beautiful videos on the production of M.I. Hummel figurines, and a little old text chapter like this just can't compete for effectiveness. However, the videos aren't always at our finger tips, and the subject needs to be covered, so...

THE ORIGINAL ART

This book is the first to attempt to link each Hummel figurine to the original work of art which inspired it. The relationship between the two-dimensional original and a three-dimensional figurine is the first step—the very foundation—of the creative process.

With input from the marketing department, it is up to the master sculptor to create a figurine based on one of Sister Hummel's original works—or at least a portion of it. His creation must meet the standards of Goebel itself plus the screening board at Convent Siessen, and it must pass the stringent tests of the production department and the buying public.

The initial sculpture is normally of clay; the master sculptor molds it to add the third dimension to the art he is interpreting. He will attempt to make the figurine an extension of the art original while allowing for the mold preparation procedures in the production department.

The process is so quick to word, so slow and painstaking to execute. The master sculptors, from Arthur Moeller and Reinhold Unger in the beginning to Gerhard Skrobek and Helmut Fischer today, are celebrated artists because of their interpretations of Sister Hummel's works.

Once the original clay model has been completed, it must receive the approval of Convent Siessen, which decides if it meets criteria related to the design and the spirit of the original artwork.

THE MOLD-MAKING PROCESS

After the actual modeling of the figurine and initial approval by the convent, the mold-making process begins with a dissection of the clay original. With a scalpel-type instrument, the mold maker

---

THE ROLE OF THE CONVENT

Experienced Hummel collectors are aware, for the most part, that the Convent Siessen continues to play a role in the creation of figurines, but few understand details of the relationship.

Through a three-dimensional licensing agreement with Goebel that dates to 1934, the convent retains artistic control of representations of Sister Hummel's original art.

A design for a new figurine is not finalized, not copyrighted, until a review board at the convent has given final approval to both the sculpture itself and the coloring to be used.

The approval process normally will include two or more visits to the convent and usually will include personal consultation with Goebel's master sculptor and master painter.

ARS AG of Switzerland, which holds the two-dimensional licensing rights, must go through similar steps to obtain approval prior to the marketing of any new two-dimensional product.

The convent gets a percentage of the income derived from the sale of all licensed M.I. Hummel products.

2-D, 3-D AND BAS-RELIEF

Elementary to those of us who work with art products on a day-to-day basis, the terms 2-D, 3-D and bas-relief are sometimes confusing to lay persons.

A two-dimensional (2-D) product portrays the artwork in flat form. Examples are paintings, prints, most decals and even your TV screen.

A three-dimensional (3-D) product portrays the artwork in depth. Best example is a freestanding figurine.

Bas-relief is between the two. The artwork is raised partially from a surrounding surface. Examples would be the Hummel annual plates and bells and most of the plaques.

A sculpture is being dissected.

the master sculptor can provide finishing touches to his work.

Once the first painted prototype has been given final approval—again by Goebel, its production department and the convent—the working molds can be made. Numerous working molds are needed, as they deteriorate rapidly with usage. Each work-

A mother mold is created.

cuts away sections of the sculpture—as many as 30 different sections in some complicated models—which are to be created independently of each other. This is essential so that the molds can be separated from the clay in the production procedures to come.

For each component of the sculpture, a plaster mother mold is prepared and, from that, a working model of synthetic resin is created. With this model,

ing mold will be divided into parts which can be separated to extract its clay component.

The walls of each working mold will be held together with a fastening device and there will be an

HOW MANY PARTS TO A HUMMEL?

The answer will vary according to figurine, but you are correct if you assume that a M.I. Hummel figurine can't be pulled intact from its plaster mold. Components are molded separately, inspected, cleaned of unsightly seams and assembled prior to firing.

Assembled?

This process involves the use of clay slip, a semiliquid material which has much the same ingredients as the clay parts it is holding together. The slip performs much the same function as glue in this situation, but, once in the kiln, it must expand and contract and harden in harmony with the parts it is bonding.

One can imagine that this job done well is painstaking and time-consuming. Indeed, it is part of the manufacturing process which bears heavily on the cost of individual figurines.

The complicated and expensive figurine, *Adventure Bound,* for example, is put together from 39 separate molded components.

WEIGHT VARIATIONS IN HUMMELS

Sometimes, one Hummel figurine will seem to be heavier than another, seemingly identical Hummel figurine. Sometimes, it will be heavier.

The reason lies in the manufacturing process. The figurines are made of fine earthenware, a ceramic material, and are cast.

Casting means that a liquid clay slip, roughly with the look and consistency of soft mud, is poured into a plaster mold. There, it dries from the outside in much the same manner that mud dries from the outside.

After a time interval, the slip is poured from the mold, leaving only that portion which has been able to dry to a leather-like hardness.

Depending upon this time interval, you see, one figurine may have a thicker ceramic "wall" and consequently weigh more than another, seemingly identical figurine.

A working mold is opened.

(1/8") shell on the inside wall of the mold. The thin shell forms as a result of the water in the clay slip being absorbed by the inside walls of the plaster mold.

When time has passed to permit the hardened clay to reach the desired thickness, the undried slip is poured from the mold. Later, the mold parts will be separated from the clay component.

After the component is "cleaned" (the resulting mold seams, etc., removed with a sponge or fretting tool), it will be ready to form its part of the figurine.

ASSEMBLING THE PARTS

opening to receive the semiliquid clay slip, which may resemble soft mud as it enters the mold.

In the casting process by which Hummel figurines are produced, the slip is allowed to form a thin

After molding, the various components must be assembled to complete each figurine. The parts are positioned manually and adhere to each other with the help of slip. More cleaning must take place, and it is at this point that a air hole is added to the figurine. The air hole, subject of many questions

Components from various working molds are assembled to create a figurine.

from novice collectors, allows gasses to escape from the hollow interior of the figurine during the kiln-firing process.

Without the air hole, the gasses are likely to cause the figurine to self-destruct in the kiln. The air holes are normally well disguised so as not to be evident on finished figurines, but they do show up. And people do wonder about them.

Paints *are being selected.*

which would prevent the finished figurine from passing final quality-control procedures.

THE PAINTING PROCESS

Paints for a Hummel figurine will have been pre-selected as part of the prototype approval process. Now it is time to use them.

A kiln firing *is in progress.*

THE FIRST FIRINGS

Before painting is begun, two preparatory firings are usually required—a bisque firing of 1140 degrees centigrade (about 2100 degrees Fahrenheit) and a glaze firing of 1020 degrees centigrade (about 1870 degrees Fahrenheit). The glaze is applied to the bisque figurine by spraying or dipping.

Within the general field of ceramics, these firings are at relatively high temperatures. Some common ceramic items are fired at 1000 degrees Fahrenheit or less. On the upper end, porcelain and stoneware are fired at approximately 2400 degrees Fahrenheit. Earthenware is a term often used for clay material which is fired just short of vitrification—the point at which some clays turn glass-like in hardness.

Inspections follow both preparatory firings, and many pieces must be discarded due to blemishes

SIZE DISPARITIES

There is a marked disparity in the sizes of many otherwise identical M.I. Hummel figurines produced during the 1930s, 1940s and early 1950s. The reason is mold deterioration.

During this earlier period, working models—the positive molds used to make the negative working molds—were made of plaster of paris, a material which wears with each succeeding use.

Through Goebel pioneering, the plaster of paris was replaced about 1954 with acrylic resin working models. After this time, figurine sizes were much more uniform than before.

However, the plaster working molds themselves create slight size differentiation. Each succeeding figurine produced within a single working mold tends to be slightly larger than the preceding figurine until the mold is discarded and replaced—or after about 20 pieces are made, in the case of Hummels.

Goebel painters at work.

Several quality-control inspections will have been made during and between the firing and painting processes. An individual figurine may be subjected to 25 or more such inspections before it finally reaches a retailer's shelf.

PRODUCTION TERMS

For persons wanting to delve a little deeper into the technical aspects of ceramic figurine production, we'll include here an abbreviated glossary of common terms so that information from reference sources can be used to better understand how Hummel figurines are produced. The order is loosely sequential.

Positive form. This is the form, for instance, of a finished figurine. The sculptor's original creation is nearly always a positive form.

Negative form. This can be described as the reverse image of a positive form. A hardened plaster of paris cast removed by a doctor from a broken arm will retain the *negative form* of the arm. Similarly, plaster of paris is usually used to capture the negative image of the master sculptor's original creation.

Through the years, a diverse palette of specially blended colors has been developed for use on M.I. Hummel figurines. In fact, more than 2000 color variations, made of a combination of metallic oxides, oil and turpentine, have been developed.

With the selected colors in hand and the master painter's samples to use as a visual guide, a professional hand-painter begins to decorate the glazed figurines.

Depending upon the colors used, at least one additional kiln firing at a lower temperature—about 1200 degrees Fahrenheit—will be required to fix the paints. If colors with incompatible firing requirements are used on one piece, multiple firings will be needed.

IS OLDER PRETTIER?

Many persons viewing older M.I. Hummel figurines for the first time will immediately note the difference in finish compared to their more modern counterparts.

The older figurines tend to have a more mellow appearance. Often they appear to have a matte finish in comparison to their newer, brighter counterparts. Colors tend to be more subtle.

In this way, the figurines are not so different from other antique items. Many have taken on the patina of age. In the mid-1950s, Goebel pioneered the development of paints resistent to the fading of time. Since then, the figurines have been relatively more uniform in color.

Which are more appealing—the older, mellow figurines or the newer, brighter ones? It's strictly a matter of taste, and many think the answer is a combination of the two.

Mother mold. This is the plaster of paris negative image from which the working models are made.

Working model. This is, in the case of Hummel production, an acrylic resin mold in positive form which has been made from the master mold.

Working mold. This is a plaster of paris, negative form mold which has been made from a working model. It is the last stage in the molding process and will produce a positive form ready for other production techniques.

Greenware. This is the name given to the hardened clay material after it is removed from a working mold but before it has been fired to ceramic (earthenware) consistency in a kiln.

Kiln. Kilns can be small and oven-like, or they can resemble long tunnels, or they can be something between. In all cases, they are used to heat wares to specific, high temperatures.

Bisque. Sometimes called biscuit, bisque is a name given to clay which has been fired unglazed in a kiln. Unless bisque materials have been fired to vitrification, they are able to absorb moisture.

Vitrification. This is the point at which certain clays—at specific high temperatures—spontaneously become glass-like in a kiln. Only certain clays can withstand these temperatures, which range from about 2250 to 2400 degrees Fahrenheit. Vitrification renders the clay relatively impermeable, even in bisque form. True hard-paste porcelain is always fired to vitrification. Certain other clays, when fired to vitrification, are called stoneware. The clay used to produce Hummel figurines is fired just short of vitrification to a point which lends itself to the famous decorating techniques.

Glaze. A coating of minerals applied in liquid form to a bisque figurine, then fired in a kiln to form a hard, impermeable, paintable surface on the figurine. Often the glaze will be tinted so that adequate and even coverage on the figurine can be readily judged.

Slip. This is clay in its semiliquid form. It is utilized in this fashion so that it can be poured into molds and so that it can be used to adhere greenware components, at which time it is sometimes called *slurry.* Slip used as an adhesive must be of the same material as the clay in the greenware due to changes, especially shrinkage, which occur in the clay during the kiln-firing process.

Plastiline. This is a compound made from clay and beeswax which is sometimes used by master sculptors to create a new original. It warms and becomes malleable to the artist's touch.

HINTS ON CARE AND PRESERVATION

M.I. Hummel figurines are manufactured by Goebel with remarkably high degrees of care and quality control seldom encountered in a similar industry.

The fact that so many of the figurines have now been around for 50-plus years speaks well not only of their appeal, but of their durability.

But even Hummel figurines are not indestructible.

And they are not completely problem-free.

The following is a compilation of some of the more common problems and how to prevent or cope with them:

Dirt. Over a period of time, it is very difficult to keep Hummel figurines from becoming dirty. Sooner or later, they need to be cleaned.

And problems await the unwary. There are a couple of things you should know about Hummel figurines before attempting to clean them.

1. M.I. Hummel figurines are made of fine earthenware, which is a non-vitrified ceramic. This means that any area of the figurine *not protected by a glaze* is able to absorb moisture.

2. M.I. Hummel figurines are created with an air hole, usually located in some hidden area so as not to be too conspicuous. The air hole is there to permit the escape of gasses which, if not allowed to escape during firing, can destroy the figurine.

The insides of the figurines are not glazed. If you immerse a figurine in water to clean it *without covering the air hole*, you run the risk of permitting entrapment of moisture which may gradually discolor the figurine from inside out.

If you cover the air hole, a short bath should not harm a figurine. Most mild soaps and shampoos can be used in combination with wiping or soft scrubbing to clean more soiled pieces. Use common sense.

A word of warning: A Hummel figurine is just slightly less slippery than solid ice when coated with soap and water. I advise cleaning over a well-cushioned surface while exercising great care in handling.

A stoic attitude helps, but is hard to maintain. An M.I. Hummel Care Kit is available through the M.I. Hummel Club.

Damage. If you drop and break a Hummel figurine, you've got problems. However, you've also got an accident, and we can't always avoid accidents no matter how hard we try.

More important, perhaps, is awareness of damage that can be avoided with reasonable care. Think of it as the four *C's*—chipping, cracking, crazing and (dis)coloration.

Chipping and cracking are nearly always the result of mishandling that could easily be avoided. A protrusion from a figurine comes in contact with a protrusion from a second—or any other solid object in the vicinity—and, *bingo!*, chips.

Ask any retailer. Hummel figurines are usually sold out of secured cabinets not so much to discourage shoplifting as to prevent handling damage.

Exercise care in displaying, dusting, cleaning and moving your figurines.

Crazing, which makes areas of figurines look like they have permanent spider webs attached to them, is probably a bigger problem than chipping, but it's less obvious. It sneaks up on you.

Crazing consists of hairline cracks in the glasslike glaze which was applied in the manufacturing process. It doesn't harm a figurine structurally, but it can make it unsightly.

There are various possible causes for crazing, but the primary culprits are temperature and humidity. To prevent crazing, avoid rapid and extreme temperature changes (and the resultant expansion/contraction). Avoid exposure to extremely high humidity conditions (moisture damage).

Discoloration, as you can imagine, can be caused by too long exposure to too intense light. Don't display a figurine on the windowsill of a west-facing window. Don't try to emulate this condition artificially. Okay?

Another piece of advice: Don't wrap and store Hummel figurines in newspaper pages. Printer's ink doesn't blend at all well with Hummel colors, but it sure tries! Pieces discolored in this fashion can be cleaned, but it's a project.

Improper storing and moving. There are too many improper possibilities to consider, so let's talk about what you should do.

Hopefully, you have extra space and have saved the original box and its cushioning contents for each figurine. Now you can simply return the figurine to the box for storage or moving.

If you haven't, then create as much of a likeness as you can. At the minimum, wrap each figurine well in accepted wrapping materials such as colorless foam or bubble wrap—and in an individual box, if at all possible.

(A nightmare is a collection of valuable Hummel figurines lightly wrapped and deposited together in a cardboard box as if they were dinner plates. This is disaster waiting to happen.)

If the wrapped and boxed figurines are to be stored, find a storage place that avoids the temperature extremes discussed earlier.

If they are to be transported in the family vehicle, be sure each figurine is adequately separated from the next, or any other object which could cause it damage.

If they are to be shipped, do not, do not, do not attempt shipping in a single box. Figurines should be well wrapped, individually boxed and then placed in a strong, well-cushioned shipping container for transport. In simpler words, there should be at least two boxes between the figurine and the outside world; three is even better.

And one final word: No matter how well they are packed for shipment, it is important that Hummels be adequately insured during transit.

OXIDATION DAMAGE

Once in a while an older Hummel figurine or group of figurines will be found with a detracting silvery sheen that cannot be removed with normal cleaning methods.

The sheen itself is caused by re-oxidation of the metallic oxide paint used by Goebel artists to hand-paint the figurines. The re-oxidation may be caused by excessively damp storage conditions or by wrapping the figurines in silk paper.

The prevention is to store the figurines in dry, cool places, avoiding any extremes, and to wrap them in colorless, commercial-grade wrapping materials.

And, happily, there is also a cure. Professional refiring can restore the figurines to original appearance.

CHAPTER FOUR

An Introduction to the Master Sculptors

When Gerhard Skrobek makes a personal appearance anywhere in the United States, it is an event. He has earned and has been given celebrity status by those who understand his role in bringing Sister Hummel's originals to them in the form of the popular figurines.

Skrobek, now semiretired as a Goebel master sculptor, has spent almost 40 years of his life in the creation of Hummel figurines, and he may leave a legacy of achievements which cannot be matched.

Helmut Fischer, long Skrobek's understudy at Goebel, assumed the mantle of master M.I. Hummel sculptor several years ago. He already has some remarkable achievements to his credit and has earned the right to be considered Skrobek's qualitative—if not quantitative—peer.

As you peruse the pricing section of this handbook, you will note that much effort has been expended in matching each Hummel figurine with its master sculptor creator.

The names of Skrobek and Fischer are prominent. So are those of Arthur Moeller and Reinhold Unger, the early masters.

It would be remiss not to offer at least a brief introduction to the Goebel masters who, for more than 50 years, have contributed mightily in an effort that has helped make *Hummel* a household name on both sides of the Atlantic.

HELMUT FISCHER

If you are serious—or even semi-serious—about the Hummel figurines of today and tomorrow, you'll want to acquaint yourself with Helmut Fischer. He is the talent who has stepped into the prodigious shoes of Gerhard Skrobek to serve as today's Goebel master sculptor.

How good is Fischer?

Check out some of his recent creations. Look at figurines such as *Rock-a-Bye* and *I'm Carefree*, then judge for yourself.

The company should be in excellent artistic hands for the next 20 years or more.

Fischer was only 14 years old when he began his apprenticeship at Goebel in 1964. After three years of intense training, he passed his exam and was designated a Goebel sculptor.

Helmut Fischer

Later, he would develop series for Goebel quite familiar to collectors of today. Included among these are the Serengeti animals, DeGrazia figurines and the Goebel-produced Walt Disney figurines.

In 1988, Fischer's talent was assigned to the development and sculpting of M.I. Hummel figurines. Prior to *Rock-a-Bye*, he had already created two of the famous century releases—*We Wish You the Best* from 1991 and *Welcome Spring* from 1993.

Maintaining a small art studio at home, Fischer is often creating even when not on duty, both in the form of sculpture and drawing. African wildlife and his cat are favored subjects.

Outside his studios, Fischer relaxes with mountainbike riding and kayaking.

GERHARD SKROBEK

Now in his 70s, but still quite active in his retirement, Gerhard Skrobek's tenure with Goebel dates to more than 40 years ago. He joined the company in 1951 and three years later sculpted his first M.I. Hummel figurine, *Bird Watcher* (M 300).

Altogether, Skrobek has accounted for something in the neighborhood of 150 original Hummel designs, plus numerous restylings, plus now-famous non-Hummel creations such as the *Bust of Sister Hummel,* the camels for the Hummel nativi

21

Gerhard Skrobek

Arthur Moeller

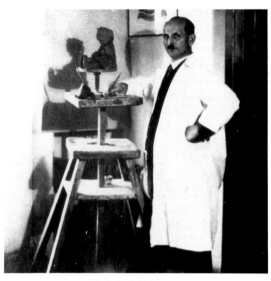

Reinhold Unger

ties, a magnificent full nativity set which bears his own name, and the Goebel Collectors' Club clown issues, *Oops!* and *In the Spotlight.*

In retrospect, it seems that Skrobek has had a hand in nearly all of the milestone achievements of the M.I. Hummel figurine line.

Are there more famous Hummel figurine creations than *Ride Into Christmas, Pleasant Journey* or *Valentine Gift*? All Skrobek creations.

Are there larger and more complicated figurines than *Land in Sight* or *Ring Around the Rosie*? Both Skrobek creations.

Was there ever a more ambitious Hummel sculpting project than the large *Hummel Mold 260 Nativity Set*? Skrobek.

The Skrobek legacy will continue to be evident in future years—probably into the new century—as more of his creations, now only in prototype form, are introduced to the marketplace and put into production.

ARTHUR MOELLER & REINHOLD UNGER

When the first M.I. Hummel figurines were made in 1935, the Goebel master sculptors were Arthur Moeller and Reinhold Unger. At the time, Moeller had worked for Goebel for almost 25 years and Unger for almost 20 years.

Both actively sculpted until the mid-1950s, and each is responsible for the creation of approximately 100 different Hummel figurine molds which are known today.

It could be said that their creativeness and artistry—with assistance and input from Sister

Hummel herself—not only set the standards for their successors, but laid the foundation for what became the most famous figurine line of all time.

Though their careers seem to closely parallel each other during the first 20 years of Hummel production, it seems evident that Unger specialized in the sculptured interpretations of Sister Hummel's religious works, while Moeller concentrated more on the secular interpretations.

Most of the angel and madonna figurines will show Unger as original sculptor. Among his credits are the *Hummel Mold 214 Nativity Set, Heavenly Angel, Worship, Forest Shrine* and *Saint George.* He was also responsible, however, for nonreligious motifs such as *Kiss Me, Stormy Weather, Skier* and *Playmates.*

Moeller's contributions are every bit as famous and include one of the best-known religious figurines, *Blessed Event.* Others immediately recognizable to most are *Apple Tree Boy, Apple Tree Girl, Umbrella Boy, Umbrella Girl, Goose Girl, Little Fiddler* and *Crossroads.*

Moeller also has the distinction of sculpting *Puppy Love,* the figurine which bears Hummel mold number 1, and *Merry Wanderer,* the figurine which ultimately became the symbol for the entire M.I. Hummel line.

Moeller died in 1972 at the age of 86, Unger in 1974 at the age of 94.

THE OTHER SCULPTORS

There have been master sculptors other than Fischer, Skrobek, Moeller and Unger. And, while none are as well-known individually, some of their creations have become quite famous.

Karl Wagner, for instance, is credited with sculpting less than a handful of surviving pieces, but these include *Artist,* the figurine which is the symbol for The Hummel Museum, and the ever-popular *Little Pharmacist.*

Theo R. Menzenbach and Helmut Wehlte are similarly credited with less than 10 original sculptures each.

However, Menzenbach was responsible for *Adventure Bound,* the most elaborate and expensive of all the Hummel figurines and one of the most fascinating.

Wehlte contributed two of today's most popular pieces, *Letter to Santa Claus* and *Honey Lover.*

CHAPTER FIVE

The M.I. Hummel Club

(Guest author for this chapter is **Ken Le Fevre**, president of Goebel Marketing Corp., the division of Goebel Art GmbH which administers the M.I. Hummel Club.)

For many, M.I. Hummel figurines have represented a collecting tradition passed down from generation to generation.

The spirit of carefree children so vividly captured in M.I. Hummel figurines, the memories they evoke, the beauty of each hand-crafted piece, and the intriguing history behind the artist all add to the timeless appeal and collectible interest associated with the figurines.

Whether one piece or a hundred pieces exist in a collection, each owner's passion is unique.

Yet, despite this uniqueness, there is an organization that strives to help each and every collector appreciate and enrich his or her individual M.I. Hummel interests to the fullest. One organization is dedicated to sharing the legacy of Sister Maria Innocentia Hummel and the history behind the world-famous figurines that bear her name.

This organization is the M.I. Hummel Club.

A CLUB IS BORN

The M.I. Hummel Club has been bringing joy to collectors since 1977. Proudly, the Club began as the first collector's club of its kind in the industry, starting as the Goebel Collectors' Club.

Providing information to meet the interest of the collectors was and remains its highest priority.

First, a quarterly newsletter was developed to answer questions and keep members informed of new pieces as they were created. Later, the Club created an M.I. Hummel figurine each year that would be available exclusively to Club members and sold only through participating dealers. Each piece reflects its exclusive status through the special Club backstamp on the base of the figurine.

In addition to these benefits, each member would also receive a ceramic bisque plaque to serve as a certificate of membership.

Because these treasures are never sold to the general public, they automatically became some of the rarest and most sought after exclusives in the world of collecting.

Kenneth G. Le Fevre *directs activities of the M.I. Hummel Club as part of his duties as president of Goebel Marketing Corporation, a division of Goebel Art GmbH headquartered in Pennington, New Jersey. In various capacities, Le Fevre's lifelong profession has centered around the sales and marketing of Hummel and other Goebel products.*

During its first year of operation, the Goebel Collectors' Club attracted more than 100,000 members.

The Club then experienced many positive changes. The Club newsletter, originally called the *Goebel Collectors' Club News*, was renamed *INSIGHTS*.

In addition to the news and information originally included, it began carrying profiles of various artists, hints on how to display figurines, contests awarding M.I. Hummel prizes, information on travel opportunities, invitations to artist demonstrations, insights into other collectors, and the history of some of the figurines.

By the late 1980s, it had grown from the original six-page newsletter into a magazine of 16 pages.

Club members would later be given a membership card and a handsome binder filled with a collector's log, a price list, and facts about M.I. Hummel history and production. Services expanded to include a research department and a Collectors' Market to match buyers and sellers of M.I. Hummel collectibles.

Local chapters emerged to help collectors broaden their friendships and learn even more about M.I. Hummel.

LOCAL CHAPTERS

For many M.I. Hummel collectors, the joy of collecting has been greatly enhanced by their experiences as part of an M.I. Hummel Club local chapter.

In August 1978 the first local chapter was founded in Atlanta, Georgia. Chapters grew by leaps and bounds over the years, finally reaching today's figure of 130-plus active chapters operated by M.I. Hummel Club members.

Local chapter membership provides members the chance to expand their knowledge of M.I. Hummel through meetings with those members who share their collecting interest. Over the years, local chapters developed into sessions of exploring the original art of Sister M.I. Hummel and comparing it to the finished figurine, appraising and insuring figurines, and discussing trademark variations of figurines.

NON-HUMMEL HUMMEL CLUB ITEMS

Confused? Don't be. The M.I. Hummel Club was the Goebel Collectors' Club until 1989, so some of the club's exclusive member editions bore no relation to the artwork of Sister Hummel.

Most recent of these were the *Mickey Mouse* and *Minnie Mouse* figurines of 1988-89. The 6.5-inch figurines were limited and originally sold for $275 per pair.

Other club editions included *Little Cocopah Indian Girl (1987-88)*, based on the artwork of Ted DeGrazia; *In the Spotlight* (1983) and *Oops!* (1986), both by Gerhard Skrobek; *Hush-a-Bye* and *Rise-and-Shine* (1985), both based on the artwork of Irene Spencer; *On the Alert* by Gunther Granget; *Awakening* by Laszlo Ispanky; and *Postilion*.

Local chapters have increasingly become more involved within their communities to help disadvantaged citizens through donations, service work and sharing collectible knowledge with interested civic groups.

In the midst of all the educating and sharing local chapter members do, they still find time for socializing and celebrating in M.I. Hummel fashion.

While local chapters operate mainly on their own, the M.I. Hummel Club supports their efforts without additional costs to the members. Some benefits provided include *Chapter & Verse*, a quarterly publication written exclusively for local chapter members; prior release of various M.I. Hummel news happenings; a local chapter patch; exclusive offers; special programs for meetings; giveaways at conferences; and membership incentive programs.

In 1981, the first of five annual national local chapter conventions took place. By 1986, the North American Convention was being held every other year, and inter-chapter conferences were introduced.

These conferences provide chapters with the opportunity to host and share informational meetings and seminars in their hometowns. Members have been known to travel great distances to meet and share their knowledge with other members.

Through M.I. Hummel Club support in the way of giveaways, Club representative appearances and promotional assistance, local chapters are encouraged to host these educational and social meetings.

Local chapter conventions later evolved into Club conventions open to all members. These provide local chapters with greater opportunities to meet and recruit additional members into their chapters while expanding their knowledge of M.I. Hummel figurines. Special programs or information are provided exclusively to local chapter members in the spirit of their convention history.

TRAVEL OPPORTUNITIES

The Goebel factory in Roedental, Germany, remains an exciting attraction for collectors throughout the world. To celebrate the 50th birthday of M.I. Hummel figurines, the Club initiated a travel program in 1985 which offers members the opportunity to travel throughout Europe with fellow collectors.

While the itineraries vary among the trips, each excursion includes a visit to the factory for a behind-the-scenes look at how M.I. Hummel figu-

The history of the M.I. Hummel Club is linked with the contributions of Joan Ostroff. She was the first executive director of the then Goebel Collectors' Club, serving in this capacity from 1975 until 1988. She was director of special projects for Goebel Marketing Corp. until January 1, 1995.

rines are hand-crafted. Only members traveling on an M.I. Hummel Club tour are privy to this special presentation of their favorite collectibles.

Also, on most trips members get to walk the beautiful grounds of the Convent of Siessen where Sister M.I. Hummel was inspired to create some of her most beloved and well known works of art.

At the convent, members may view original paintings and drawings, see the grave site of Sister M.I. Hummel, and visit the church where she worshipped. The convent remains a hallmark to the precious years Sister M.I. Hummel lived and worked within its confines.

THE CLUB BECOMES INTERNATIONAL

By 1989, the fascination with collecting was growing in other parts of the world. Several countries in Europe were showing an increase in sales, while other countries, including Japan and those in the Far East, began to display an interest in collectibles.

With this expanded interest, the International M.I. Hummel Club was begun on June 1, 1989.

European activity began in Germany, Austria and Switzerland, followed shortly thereafter by The Netherlands, Belgium, Sweden and Great Britain.

Today, the International M.I. Hummel Club has members from over thirty nations, and local chapters dot many of these countries as well.

Changes occurred simultaneously in North America. New members began to receive the exclusive member figurine, *I Brought You a Gift*, in place of the bisque plaque. The binder given to members to hold their copies of *INSIGHTS* magazine was redesigned, and valuable information was added in the form of handy inserts.

Renewal gifts presented to members when they rejoin for another year include an M.I. Hummel figurine or other Hummel-related treasure.

In 1994, the international group of the M.I. Hummel Club announced plans for the first convention in Roedental, Germany, inviting members from across the globe.

Through all of the changes and expansions that the M.I. Hummel Club has undergone since 1977, its focus remains uniform—to inform, educate and provide the best possible service to M.I. Hummel collectors throughout the world.

For it is the collectors' passion and desire to "know" that keeps the love of Sister M.I. Hummel alive in the hearts of many and is shared for generations that follow.

CONTACTING THE CLUB

Persons interested in participating in M.I. Hummel Club programs and activities are encouraged to visit an affiliated dealer or to contact the Club directly.

M.I. Hummel Club
Goebel Plaza
P.O. Box 11
Pennington, NJ 08534-0011

Phones: 609-737-8777
800-666-2582

CHAPTER SIX

The Trademarks and Their Kin

Because the subject of Goebel trademarks used on M.I. Hummel figurines can be either simple or complex, let's consider it that way.

Let's deal with it in two parts, which we'll call the *short course* and the *long course.*

But we'll preface both parts by repeating—again—that it's difficult to use this or any other price guide on Hummel figurines without a rudimentary knowledge of the trademarks (TM's) and how to identify them on a figurine.

Outside of condition, trademarks are the most important factor in determining values and prices on M.I. Hummel figurines. A figurine such as *Cinderella* (mold 337) may be worth up to *six times* more in TM4 (trademark 4) than it is in TM7, for instance.

If you have acquired an older *Cinderella*, this information won't help you unless you know how to identify which trademark was used on your figurine.

Many people seem to be intimidated by the prospect of having to learn the "Hummel marks."

Don't be one of them. It's really rather simple, and, if you don't already know the system, we're here to explain it.

THE SHORT COURSE

While Goebel has used numerous different marks to stamp its factory "brand" on M.I. Hummel figurines, these have been consolidated by common usage into seven distinctive TM eras, beginning with the very first Hummel figurines in 1935 and ending with the figurines leaving the factory in Germany as you read this.

These TM eras are what you will find referenced repeatedly in this book as TM1, TM2, TM3, TM4, TM5, TM6 and TM7. In the accompanying boxes, you will find the trademark most commonly associated with each of these TM eras.

If a figurine you are examining has a backstamp under the base matching one of these trademark designs, you should have no trouble identifying the TM era in which it was produced.

If we do a skin-deep examination of the TM eras, here's what we'll find.

TM1. This is the so-called *crown mark* era which identifies the earliest (and usually most valuable) Hummel figurines. The crown itself had been part of the company's trademark for decades, and the *WG* entwined initials honored William Goebel, a founder of the company.

The era extends from the beginning of production in 1935 through the World War II years to 1950, but...

The TM1 Era

1935-1949

Made in
U.S.-Zone
Germany.

1946-1948

In the 1946-1948 period after WWII, Hummel figurines were commonly marked simply with some sort of *U.S. Zone* mark, a postwar mark used to identify the items as coming from the U.S.-controlled region of divided Germany.

These *U.S. Zone* marked figurines, coming as they did within the crown era, are valued and priced as TM1 pieces.

TM2. In 1950, Goebel officially adopted its now-famous *full bee* mark in honor of Sister Maria Innocentia Hummel, who had died four years previously.

The TM2 Era

1950-1959

The bumblebee in the mark represents Sister Hummel, *Hummel* being the German word for bumblebee. The *V* in which the bee flies stands for *Verkaufsgesellschaft,* or distribution company.

The TM2 era extends through 1959. Through 1955, the bee is quite large in relation to the *V* and is easily identified. From 1956 through 1959, it was diminished in size, and its placement in relation to the *V* was changed several times.

Common to all TM2 era pieces, however, is a bumblebee that looks like a bee. That is contrary to...

TM3. The so-called *stylized bee* era begins about 1957 and ends officially in 1972. The bee now can be identified simply as a round dot with wings.

Though the trademark wasn't officially put aside until 1972, it wasn't used as often after 1964 as the concurrently running...

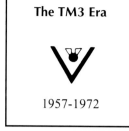

The TM3 Era

1957-1972

TM4. This is the so-called *three-line* mark—always easily identified on a figurine by the use of the *stylized bee inside V* mark in combination with three short lines of text to the right of the *V* as you view it.

The TM4 Era

© by
W. Goebel
W. Germany

1964-1972

The TM4 era officially extends from 1964 to 1972. The *three-line* mark is said to be the prevalent mark in the years its use overlapped that of the *stylized bee.*

In 1972, it gave way to...

TM5. This is sometimes called the *last bee* mark and at other times the *Goebel bee* mark. It was officially used from 1972 until 1979. It was adopted to help identify Goebel as the producer of the M.I. Hummel figurines, for the figurines had developed such a strong identity that many did not associate them with a maker.

The TM5 Era

Goebel
W.Germany

1972-1979

This trademark varied little in the era in which it was used and can be easily identified by the word *Goebel* decorated with a small *stylized bee in V* positioned above the letters *be,* and by the small text *W. Germany* centered beneath.

It represented the last use of the bee in any form, because in 1979 Goebel adopted...

TM6. In use from 1979 through 1990, this mark incorporates the text *Goebel* with its now-familiar registration symbol and, again, the small text *W. Germany* centered beneath.

The purpose for dropping the *bee with V* altogether hasn't been detailed, but I think it probably had to do with Goebel's desire to strongly promote other products it produced. By closely identifying Goebel with Hummel, it could be argued, the immense popularity of Hummel could be conveyed through the Goebel name to other Goebel-made figurines.

The TM6 Era

Goebel®
W Germany

1979-1990

The change also came at a period that may have been *the* heyday in Hummel/Goebel popularity. In the late 1970s and early 1980s, retailers were fighting over available product, as the company could not produce enough to meet demand.

In 1989, the Berlin Wall fell and West Germany subsequently became *Germany* again. The small line of text in the trademark needed to be altered, so why not just create...

TM7. For a combination of nostalgic and promotional reasons, Goebel in 1991 resurrected the *crown with WG initials* mark, but incorporated it as the bottom tier in a three-tiered trademark topped by the large word *Goebel*, under which is the smaller word *Germany* to indicate country of origin.

The TM7 Era

Goebel
Germany

1991-

This mark is found on figurines of contemporary production and is quite easy to identify.

TM1 and TM2 Eras

M.J.Hummel © 🐝

Though not grouped with the copyright marks, this mark was sometimes used on the side or top of a figurine base in a period beginning in 1935 and ending about 1955. As its use spans all of the TM1 and much of the TM2 era, it should not be confused with the *crown* marks.

THE LONG COURSE

Now, if the short course sounds a bit too simple to be true—if you think there might be a bit more to this trademark thing—you're right on. Here, we'll reexamine the TM eras to see how they relate to figurine values.

Warning: We'll deal somewhat in suppositions, so if you feel like you've been saturated with all the trademark data you can handle, it's time to tune out.

TM1

The *crown era*, as we have seen, begins with the first production of Hummel in 1935 and continues all the way through the decade of the 1940s.

It is documented that the earliest pieces were nearly always marked with what is

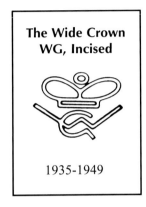

The Wide Crown WG, Incised

1935-1949

called the *wide crown WG* mark in its incised form. (The *WG* initials in the company of a copyright symbol can also sometimes be found on the side or top of the base of a model.)

The incised mark is usually colorless.

Soon thereafter—but we don't know exactly when—the company also began applying the mark with the use of a print under glaze (PUG) decal, commonly referred to as the *stamped crown* mark.

This printed or stamped crown mark will normally be either blue or black. (There is a very limited range of mineral colors which will print *under glaze.)*

Not infrequently,

The Wide Crown WG, Stamped

1935-1949

Hummel figurines will be found marked both with the incised and the stamped *wide crown WG* mark. These examples are referred to as "double crown" figurines. They are highly prized by advanced collectors and usually command a modest premium in price.

From 1937 to 1945, the *wide ducal crown with Goebel* mark (also called the *narrow crown* mark) became prominent for a while on certain Goebel

products. However, the products did *not* normally include figurines, and the mark is thought to be rare to nonexistent on Hummel figurines.

Before advancing beyond the World War II years, there are factors which should be considered. They help explain why early crown-marked Hummels in good condition are so rare and valuable today.

Wide Ducal Crown With Goebel

1937-1945

We can start with the supposition that, in the 1930s, Hummel figurines were not produced in anything resembling the abundance of later generations.

Produced by a major manufacturer and of obvious appeal, the figurines were no doubt well received. However, the prewar 1930s period was not one of voluminous export from Germany to the U.S., where the M.I. Hummel figurines would later find their greatest market.

Moreover, it can be assumed that production was abated in almost direct proportion to Germany's military buildup of the late 1930s. This may be reflected somewhat in the history of the molds themselves.

A quick, rough count shows some 33 new models were credited to the year 1938. In 1939, this figure is 17. In 1940, it is nine.

In 1941, it is six, two of which were never produced. In 1942, it is three. In 1943, it is 11, eight of which were never produced.

In 1944, a single new mold was produced, and it wasn't until 1948 that such production again hit double figures.

Figurines produced by Goebel during the World War II years bore the crown mark, but it's very unlikely they were produced in any abundance.

The point is that the M.I. Hummel figurines made between 1935 and 1946—never plentiful by today's standards—needed to survive the physical tumult of a world war, dislocations, shipping to the U.S., and more than 50 years of wear and tear in order to sit today on collectors' shelves looking new and fresh from the factory.

Not many did.

The remainder of the TM1 era—the postwar years of 1946-1949—formed a new, important epoch in the history of the Hummel figurine as a favorite American collectible.

Its mission to conquer Germany completed, the American military began the task of reconstructing its part of the country, which fortunately included the Coburg/Roedental area where the Goebel factory is located.

From 1946 to 1948, figurines intended for the U.S. market (for practical purposes, the *only* market of this period) were marked with one of the several *U.S. Zone, Germany* backstamps, usually with print under glaze decal but sometimes stamped over the glaze.

The *U.S. Zone, Germany* mark definitely dates any TM1 Hummel to postwar production. Quite often, however, it is accompanied by one of the crown marks. And, it is even known to be accompanied on one figurine by both the crown mark and the full bee mark (TM2)!

Only Some of the U.S. Zone Marks

1946-1948

The more important happening of the postwar period, however, was *discovery* of Hummel figurines by American servicemen and their families.

Oh, it wasn't just Hummels they discovered. With the war and the efforts to destroy Germany over, there came the time to study, appreciate and enjoy the country's treasures.

This seeking of treasures coincided with a time when the German people had little in mind except restoring order to their lives. To most Germans of the period, nonessential possessions held little importance.

Americans bought cheaply and bartered favorably for classic Black Forest clocks, for wonderful antique German steins, for exquisite Meissen porcelain, for original works of art, for woodcarvings and ivory carvings—and, of course, for M.I. Hummel figurines.

For the most part, this is how the bulk of the early Hummels came to America—in the company of or shipped by American servicemen in the years of 1946 through about 1972. During this extended period, Germany's finest goods were cheap, and the German people were more than willing to part with them.

(Today, there are literally caravans of German antiques dealers scouring the U.S. for these clocks and steins and Meissen pieces and art and carvings and Hummels to send them back to a rapidly growing German/European market.)

Before we leave the TM1 era, there are still other important things to note.

First, there was a period, say 1948-1950, when the crown mark was again used *without* the U.S. Zone mark. Surviving examples of this marking will likely be indistinguishable from the pre-1946 pieces if they were produced in both periods.

Second, we discover early on that there is a major overlap in the TM eras. Recall, we said, "In 1950, Goebel officially adopted its now-famous *full bee* mark in honor of Sister Maria Innocentia Hummel, who had died four years previously."

However, it has been verified that the *full bee* mark was used on at least some pieces as early as 1948, *two years before its supposed inception.*

A few paragraphs back we alluded to a figurine marked with the *crown, full bee* and *U.S. Zone* marks. Note this occurred even though, officially, the U.S. Zone mark was not used *after* 1948 and the full bee mark was not used *before* 1950.

In his book, *Luckey's Hummel Figurines and Plates,* Carl F. Luckey does a fine job in explaining the progression of trademarks, and he says: "The dates of the early trademark changes are approximate in some cases, but probably accurate to within five years or so." *Five years or so!*

Almost assuredly the crown mark appears on a number of figurines which were actually produced in 1950 or later. It appears frequently in combination with the full bee mark on a single figurine.

(Best rule of thumb for these TM1 + TM2 marked figurines: Price or value them on the TM1 scale as they are considered to be made during the crown era.)

Finally, you should understand that the TM1 era did not come to an abrupt end. At some point *around 1950,* Goebel was busy phasing in its full bee mark and shipping out the last supply of figurines bearing the crown mark. We do know that figurines *first introduced* after 1949 are not found with the crown mark.

A point made repeatedly in this book is that these phase-in periods—when one trademark was phased in to replace its predecessor—should be of great interest to advanced collectors because they created trademark scarcities and rarities.

In the TM1 era, for instance, it can be assumed that any figurine first introduced on the market in 1948 or later will fit somewhere between relatively scarce to quite rare in TM1.

After all, it could not have been in production long, and only so many pieces would have been manufactured before the total change to TM2, which we'll take up next.

(Footnote: The crown mark was used for an unspecified period and on an undetermined number of pieces both in 1960 and in 1969-1971 in conjunction with the prevailing mark in order to protect Goebel's copyright of the mark. Examples on Hummels must be few as they seldom turn up.)

TM2

Though the official onset of the TM2 era was 1950, we've already seen that the mark was used—perhaps infrequently—as early as 1948, at times accompanying the crown mark on the same piece. (See the foregoing treatise on TM1.)

It was used throughout the decade of the 1950s, but its use in the latter years—1957-1959—is thought to overlap again, this time with TM3.

There are no less than five distinct versions of what today we call the *full bee mark*. Additionally, the first and most identifiable of these had at least four sub-varieties.

In all its forms, the full bee mark is identified by the presence inside a *V* of a bumblebee that looks like a bee.

Through 1955, the bee was quite large and hovered with approximately half its body over the top edge of the *V*.

It was found incised into the base.

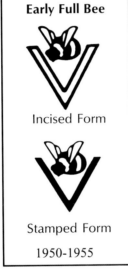

Early Full Bee

Incised Form

Stamped Form

1950-1955

The Full Bee With Goebel

Goebel Script

W. GOEBEL

Goebel Block

1950-1955

It was found printed under glaze via decal in the mineral colors of black, blue, green or manganese violet, with the first two colors by far prevalent.

It was found in the company of and centered below ©*W.Goebel* in script.

And it was found in the company of and centered above © *W.Goebel* in block letters.

Then, in 1956, Franz Goebel, who had designed the full bee mark, decided to alter it.

For 1956, the bee was downsized and inserted inside the *V* so that the top of its wings are even with the top of the *V*. This variation is called the *small bee*.

For 1957, Goebel changed its design again, creating what is now known as the *high bee*. The bee retained its diminished size from 1956, but was lifted to fly slightly above the *V* similar to its location in the pre-1956 period.

For 1958, the bee was further diminished in size and was dropped down well inside the *V*, its *rounded* wings well below the top of the *V*. This one is called the *baby bee*.

For 1959, the *full bee* made its farewell appearance in the form of yet another change. The 1959 bee is identical to the 1958 bee except that its wings have straight edges instead of being rounded. It's now called the *vee bee* because of the V shape created by its new angular wings.

The 1956-1959 variations were applied only with black or blue underglaze decals.

TM3

There seems to be a lot of confusion surrounding the use of this mark, which we can identify as the stylized bee (dot with wings) *inside the V*, but without the word *Goebel* used as part of the mark. I'd like to clear up this confusion. Unfortunately, I don't think I can.

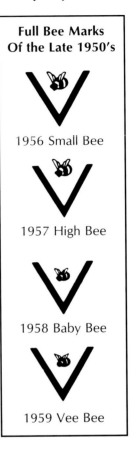

Full Bee Marks Of the Late 1950's

1956 Small Bee

1957 High Bee

1958 Baby Bee

1959 Vee Bee

I'm personally real confused, for instance, by the fact that all previous literature—including that produced by Goebel—says the mark was used until 1972, yet none of the Hummel figurines or plates sculpted in the late 1960s and early 1970s can be found with the mark.

Let's look at a few examples:

The figurine *Favorite Pet* (Mold 361) has been in production since 1964, but is considered rare in TM3.

So is the figurine *Mountaineer* (Mold 315), also introduced in 1964.

The *Angel Musician* figurines (Molds 238/A, B, C) have been abundantly produced since 1967, yet are unknown in TM3.

Not one of the 16 pieces—not even a prototype—of the large *Nativity Set 260* is known to exist in TM3, though they were sculpted in 1968.

To make sense out of this situation, I think it's best to acknowledge that the TM3 mark was *officially around* until 1972, but simply *wasn't used* after, say, the mid-1960s at the very latest.

The confusion doesn't end with when the mark was *last* used. Unfortunately, there's almost as much confusion about when it was *first* used.

Some existing literature says its was used beginning in 1960. Other says it was used as early as 1957, which would mean about a three-year overlap with the use of the full bee (TM2) mark.

I am inclined to go with the latter school of thought for a couple of convincing reasons.

Early TM3

Stamped Trademark
Inside Incised Circle

1957-1960

For one, Goebel, in some of its literature, refers to the 1957-1960 stylized bee as the *early stylized bee* mark with *incised circle*. (The incised circle is there as a guide into which workers could place the trademark decal.) This information, to me, seems too explicit to be false.

For another—and evenly convincing reason— the various figurines introduced in the mid-1950s all seem to be abundant in TM3 and fairly scarce in TM2. If the TM3 mark had been confined to use just for the period from about 1960 to 1965, it's hard to see how this could be the case.

Moreover, the TM3 mark seems to be more prevalent on older figurines than the TM4 mark.

And the TM4 mark was the dominant mark over an eight-year period from 1964 to 1972.

To summarize: If the TM3 mark went relatively unused after the mid-1960s, where did all of the surviving figurines with the mark come from? Either the early 1960s was a much more productive period for the M.I. Hummel brand than is realized,

Middle TM3

W. Germany

1960-1963

or the mark was already in common use before 1960...or both.

The two decades beginning with the late 1950s and ending with the late 1970s—a period that encompasses the TM3, TM4 and TM5 eras—is highly interesting for another reason.

There seem to be a number of "hidden" rarities during this time—that is, figurines much more uncommon in a given trademark than may have been thought. This is due to the fact that Goebel simply would not produce a given model over a period of years.

Late TM3

W. Germany

1960-1972

With Hummel collecting unsophisticated then in comparison to today, there was no reason for Goebel to announce these withdrawals, so, for the most part, they went unrecorded. Today, they can be traced sketchily through study of old price lists, which unfortunately seem to have been issued on an irregular basis.

At any rate, if you are the type who enjoys a stringent challenge—if it adds zest to your collecting enjoyment—you might want to see how many of the following models you can assemble that carry *either* the TM3 or the TM4 mark.

If you are the type who enjoys a challenge, but one somewhat less than stringent, you might want to try to assemble this group marked with *any type* of stylized bee, meaning TM3, TM4 or TM5. Though none of these are generally considered as rare, I think you'll still have your hands full.

The list:

Angel Serenade, M 83
Auf Wiedersehen, M 153/I
Birthday Serenade, M 218/0

Book Worm, M 3/III
Boots, M 143/I
Boy & Girl Wall Vases, M 360 (all)
Flitting Butterfly Plaque, M 139
Going to Grandma's, M 52/I & 52/0
Happy Birthday, M 176/I & 176/0
Happy Days, M 150/I & 150/0
Hello, M 124/I & 124/0
Little Fiddler, M 2/III
Lullaby Candleholder, M 24/III
Madonna with Halo, M 45/III
Meditation, M 13/II & 13/V
Merry Wanderer, M 7/III
School Boy, M 82/II
Standing Boy Plaque, M 168
Swaying Lullaby Plaque, M 165
Telling Her Secret, M 196/I
To Market, M 49/I
Tuneful Good Night Plaque, M 180
Volunteers, M 50/I & 50/0
Waiter, M 154/0
Whitsuntide, M 163
Worship, M 84/V

TM4

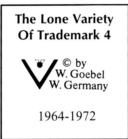

**The Lone Variety
Of Trademark 4**

© by
W. Goebel
W. Germany

1964-1972

This is the so-called *three-line mark*—so named after the three lines of type which always appear beside the stylized bee and V. Goebel's official charts show it was used beginning in 1964 and ending in 1972.

This seems to be fairly accurate. Research indicates that the mark was probably phased in during the 1964-65 period and that it was by far the prevalent mark after that time until it was phased out in 1972. The *1972 Annual Plate*, for instance, can be found with approximately equal effort in TM4 or in TM5.

Interestingly, there seem to be a number of M.I. Hummel models which were sparsely produced, or not produced at all, during the TM4 era. The mark, perhaps more than any other, has frustrated collector attempts to put together all-trademark collections of certain of the early figurines.

It's also interesting due to the array of important figurines which were first introduced during the 1971–72 period.

Encompassing some of Gerhard Skrobek's most memorable creations, and coming as they did at the very end of the TM4 era, these pieces range from somewhat difficult to almost impossible to find in TM4.

To assemble this complete group with the TM4 mark is another quest with which to challenge the most determined of collectors. If you don't mind frustration, try for the following:

A Fair Measure, M 345
Adventure Bound, M 347
Artist, M 304
Autumn Harvest, M 355
Bashful, M 377
Big Housecleaning, M 363
Chicken-Licken, M 385
Cinderella, M 337
Confidentially, M 314
Crossroads, M 331
Easter Greetings, M 378
Easter Time, M 384
Feathered Friends, M 344
Flower Vendor, M 381
Follow the Leader, M 369
Gay Adventure, M 356
Homeward Bound, M 334
Letter to Santa Claus, M 340
Little Tailor, M 308
Lost Stocking, M 374
Mischief Maker, M 342
On Secret Path, M 386
Ride Into Christmas, M 396
Run-a-Way (The), M 327
Visiting an Invalid, M 382

TM5

The transition in 1972 from TM4 to TM5 seems, in hindsight, to have formed a distinct division in the minds of many between the *old* Hummels and the *modern* Hummels.

I can think of a couple of reasons why it might thusly be considered. One is price. The other is familiarity.

Price. The year 1972 was also the last year for a fixed rate of exchange between the U.S. dollar and the German mark. Afterwards the dollar was free to float. From the 1972 exchange rate of four marks to one dollar, we have seen a more or less steady erosion of the dollar's relative value.

As this was being written, the exchange rate between the two currencies was a little more than 1.5 to 1.

The exchange rate itself accounts for a 250% price increase in an M.I. Hummel figurine compared to its 1972 price. Now, factor in a quarter century's worth of inflation and price increases on top of that, and you should readily see why the *1994 Annual Plate* had a list price of $225 and the *1971 Annual Plate* had a list price of $25.

Further, if you want to put a specific time-table or year to it, 1972 is as good a year as any with which to say the easy pickin's in Germany came to an end. Servicemen who were there will tell you that the early 1970s marked the end of the spectacular bargains in Hummels and antiques in Germany.

Familiarity. Hummel figurine fever reached a peak in our country in the late 1970s and early 1980s. Goebel, as a factory, responded to the best of its ability and cranked out figurines as fast as the equipment, people and quality-control procedures would permit.

Without an attempt to substantiate it, my guess would be that the total number of figurines produced by Goebel in the seven-year TM5 era—1972-1979—probably exceeded that of the 15 preceding years.

The TM5 era is especially noteworthy for still another reason. It was the era in which the Goebel Collector's Club (now M.I. Hummel Club) was initiated. Its maiden year was 1977, and it was so well conceived and so well received that it became a model for numerous other collector clubs in succeeding years.

All in all, I buy the idea that the onset of the TM5 era really does offer a dividing line between *antique Hummel* and *contemporary Hummel.*

TM6

Extending as it did from 1979 through the end of 1990, the TM6 era is too long and too recent to gain the respect of today's secondary market

The TM5 Varieties

Goebel
W. Germany
Symbol to Left

Goebel
W.Germany
No Symbol

Goebel
W. Germany
Symbol to Right

1972-1979

Hummel buyers. However, it was an era of experimentation, and it does have one distinction that will give it lingering importance. More M.I. Hummel items—figurines, plates, bells, etc.—bear the TM6 mark than any other.

Count them yourself. More than 600 different Hummel models were produced bearing Goebel's TM6 backstamp!

The trademark can be found on numerous pieces which are not in production during the current, TM7 period. These include a major-ity of the large models and a preponderance of the auxiliary pieces such as lamps, fonts, book-ends, plaques and vases.

The Lone Variety Of Trademark 6

Goebel
W Germany

1979-1990

It's also the only trademark which will ever appear on a number of the more important figurines—*Supreme Protection* and *Jubilee*, to name a couple outside the annual club pieces.

Through the 1980s, the U.S. collectibles market increasingly clamored for figurine issues which were special and unique, and Goebel responded by enlarging its range of club exclusives and by initiating the popular *Century Release* program.

Because so many different pieces were produced during this era and because so much attention was focused on relatively few pieces, I think there are many TM6 scarcities waiting to be unearthed. I've tried to call attention to the potential existence of some in the pricing chapter.

For the collector without the pocketbook or desire to pursue the early trademark rarities, these contemporary "sleepers" should hold strong appeal.

TM7

As the TM7 era is likely still in its infancy, it cannot be discussed in past-tense perspective. However, early emphasis remains clearly on the special pieces, and collectors should be alert for

Trademark 7

Goebel
Germany

1991-

Hummel offers available only for a limited, short period of time.

In the 1990s, there is definitely an emphasis on commemorative issues. Earliest examples included *Crossroads Berlin Wall Commemorative, Land in Sight* and the UNICEF pieces. I expect this trend to continue and possibly accelerate as Goebel strives to retain its share of the collectible figurine market.

It also would seem certain that the total number of different pieces will not approach that of the TM6 era. The 1990s market is very soft for the auxiliary pieces. And the large models have very limited markets due to high prices.

Experimentation will likely continue. Look for Goebel to seek ways to attract new collectors.

THE OTHER MARKINGS

There is, of course, more to the bottom of a Hummel figurine than its trademark. Goebel, from the very beginning and far better than most manufacturers, has been very diligent about imparting needed information with its markings.

This applies especially to contemporary figurines. The bottom and base of a figurine produced today may tell you—along with identifying trademark—the mold and model number, the country of origin (Germany), the signature of the master painter, the year in which it was painted, the name of the figurine, special circumstances surrounding the figurine if applicable, and whether it is either the first or the final year for the figurine.

In addition, you may find a small, incised, colorless, unexplainable number. This is a quality-control number which serves no purpose outside the factory except to confuse the novice.

M.I. Hummel

Somewhere on the base, if it exists, or in a comparatively inconspicuous spot, if there is no base, you will find the signature *M.I. Hummel* in script. On very small figurines, the signature will be shortened simply to *Hummel* for space reasons.

The signature is not used under the base and is not considered to be part of the backstamp. It is there as an affirmation of the authenticity of the piece and to protect copyright.

Very rarely in old, TM1-marked pieces, the signature appears only as *Mel.* Of the so-called *Mel* Hummels bearing this signature, the little candleholders, *Boy with Horse, Girl with Fir Tree* and *Girl with Nosegay* (molds 117, 116, 115), have been most often encountered. They command siz-able premiums in price when offered with the *Mel* signature.

Mold and Model Numbers

The incised mold number—or Hum number, if you prefer—is the single most important factor in positively identifying any M.I. Hummel figurine. Names have been known to change through the years (see appendix to this chapter). Mold numbers have not, but this statement requires an explanation.

Frequently, a Hummel figurine has been given a new *model* number when a new size variation has been introduced with an identical *mold* number.

The figurine *Ride Into Christmas*, for example, was introduced in 1972 as a 5.75-inch figurine bearing mold number 396. All pieces produced for the next decade are marked with the number 396.

In 1982, a smaller-size model of *Ride Into Christmas* was introduced as well. It is 4.25 inches in size and shares the 396 mold number. To avoid confusion, Goebel immediately began marking both models with a size suffix. The larger size was marked model 396/I and the smaller size was marked model 396 2/0.

When first introduced in 1935, the figurine *Meditation* (mold 13) was marked simply with an incised 13. In succeeding years, however, it became model 13/0 or model 13/II or model 13/V or model 13 2/0. Which of these models did the original mold 13 become? Well, that's how we sell books like this.

It's interesting, but not important, to understand Goebel's system for assigning size suffixes.

Through the design and introduction of the figurine *Serenade* (mold 218) in 1952, the *standard size* of a Hummel figurine was identified with the use of /0 as a size suffix to the mold number.

After *Serenade*, there has been no standard size. Instead, figurines marked with a Roman numeral-type suffix (sometimes Arabic numbers have been used) is considered to be *larger* than the previous standard. A size suffix which incorporates a *0* in its size suffix is considered to be *smaller* than the previous standard.

The accompanying charts show this clearly.

1952 and Before

mold # plus /V	
mold # plus /III	LARGER
mold # plus /II	THAN
mold # plus /I	STANDARD

mold # plus /0 = STANDARD SIZE	

mold # plus /0 1/2	SMALLER
mold # plus 2/0	THAN
mold # plus 3/0	STANDARD
mold # plus 4/0	

1952 and After

mold # plus /X	
mold # plus /V	LARGER
mold # plus /III	THAN
mold # plus /II	STANDARD
mold # plus /I	

mold # plus /0	
mold # plus /0 1/2	SMALLER
mold # plus 2/0	THAN
mold # plus 3/0	STANDARD
mold # plus 4/0	

In cases where Arabic numerals have been used in place of Roman numerals, they are never accompanied by the *0. Meditation*, for example, can be found marked 13/2 as well as 13/II, but the smaller size will be marked 13 2/0 or 13/2/0.

In some instances, letters are used as a mold suffix. These do not indicate size; rather, they normally indicate a pairing or grouping. Nativity figurines are a prime example of the use of letters; pieces of *Nativity Set 214* will each share the 214 mold number, but will be individually identified by an alpha character. *Joseph* is model 214/B, for example.

Similarly, *Umbrella Boy* (152/A) and *Umbrella Girl* (152/B) share a mold number, as do the paired figurines *Culprits* (56/A) and *Out of Danger* (56/B). Other examples exist.

Also infrequently, numbers are used *in front of* the mold number. These prefix numbers are *not* part of the mold or model number itself. Instead, they are there for a special purpose—to designate the size of candle to be used in a candleholder, for instance.

Country of Origin

Sooner or later, someone will inform you that the best way to tell a pre-WWII Hummel from one made after the war (until 1991) is by looking for the country of origin mark. If it says *Germany*, you will be told, that means the item was made during or before World War II. If it says *West Germany*, it will have been made after the war.

Don't believe it.

The *Germany* stamp appears on many figurines made well into the 1950s, and perhaps beyond.

The country of origin stamp is there to fulfill a U.S. Customs Service requirement that goods imported into the U.S. be labeled with their country of origin.

Before the reunification of West and East Germany, goods from East Germany were assessed at a much higher duty rate than those from West Germany.

However, I know from personal experience as an importer since the early 1970s that the country of origin mark on goods arriving from West Germany were acceptable if simply labeled *Germany*. Perhaps this was because goods from East Germany were always labeled *D.D.R.* (Deutsches Democratic Republik), avoiding possible confusion.

Painter's Signature

Most Hummel figurines have little black squiggly lines under the base that, once informed, a person can recognize as initials.

In fact, they are the initials of the painter who applied color to the face and eyes of the individual figurine. In company with the initials, one can (normally) find the actual year in which the individual figurine was made.

Actually, the practice of dating each figurine was not begun until 1979, and it is *not* something that is done without fail. (I determined this by simply examining a cross section of TM6 figurines; a good many bore no date.)

Wolfgang Schwatlo's *M.I. Hummel Collector's Handbook* (German-English) identifies the various Goebel master sample painters and depicts each's initial or symbol.

Last and First Issue Stamps

Beginning in 1990, Goebel began to use a special stamp—*Final Issue...Letzte Ausgabe...*then the year, all inside an oval—to designate the last year of production for a figurine being permanently retired. It's a means of paying homage to the creation and longevity of the piece before destruction of the molds.

Beginning in 1991, the company began using a similar looking stamp for all new figurines being put on the market for the first time. This stamp reads *First Issue...Erste Ausgabe...*then the year.

Other Marks

Other backstamp marks fall into the category of special and tend to be self-explanatory. The accompanying photo of the bottom of the *Crossroads Limited Edition* (mold 331) figurine of 1990 shows many of the markings that may be used on contemporary figurines.

Incised, Uncolored Mold Number *331*

Name of Figurine In German and English

Individual Numbering

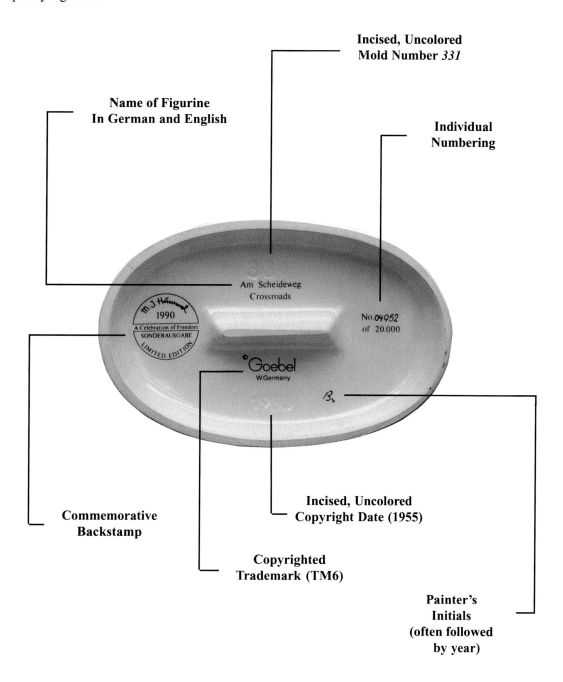

Commemorative Backstamp

Copyrighted Trademark (TM6)

Incised, Uncolored Copyright Date (1955)

Painter's Initials (often followed by year)

CHAPTER SEVEN

Preface to the Pricing Trends

This section, by necessity, will get tedious in places. Aside from passages dealing with condition and buying and selling, it's the part where I explain the following listings for all the M.I. Hummel products...how to read them, why I have done certain things the way I have, the causes and the effects, etc., etc.

It's sort of like reading the instructions for your new VCR. You won't want to look at this until you are totally confused or totally frustrated, or both. At least, that's the way I generally come to read similar passages in other books.

Just as in the instructions that came with the VCR, however, I'm going to make a fruitless plea for you to read and digest this information *before* attempting to analyze and use the following price guide pages. It will make those pages more useful and meaningful and no doubt answer a lot of questions.

BOOK TERMINOLOGY

Persons already accustomed to Hummel figurine resource materials will find that, while this work conforms to most existing terminology, it does make use of some notable departures.

These departures, based on a doctrine of "common sense," will hopefully make matters clearer for the novice while not offending the already informed.

We'll use the listing for the figurine *Going to Grandma's* to illustrate our brand of *"Hummelese."* You'll find the figurine in alphabetical sequence on the following pages. What you'll find is a listing that begins this way (numbers added):

1. **GOING TO GRANDMA'S**
2. Mold No.: 52
3. Copyright: 1936
4. Sculptor: R.Unger
5. 2-D Original: H 188

6. Model No.: 52/I
7. Ref. No.: 947
8. Approx. Size: 6.25"
9. 1995 Retail: T.W.

Model No.: 52/0
Ref. No.: 948
Approx. Size: 4.75"
1995 Retail: $260

Taking the numbers one-by-one, you'll see that, first and obviously, we've given you the English name for the figurine being discussed. In nearly all cases, the names conform to the official M.I. Hummel price list prepared by Goebel.

Line 2. Here, we have the first of the departures from norm.

Normal usage is to divide *Going to Grandma's* into two figurines called *Hum 52/I* and *Hum 52/0*, which, of course, are simply different size models of the same figurine. The *Hum* comes from old Goebel nomenclature to identify a mold or model based on the artwork of Sister Hummel—as opposed to that based on the artwork of some other artist.

Goebel's system is not common to many producers and tends to be misunderstood and confusing to novice collectors.

Primarily for this large group of people, I have chosen to use the more generic term *Mold*. With experience, I have learned that one can use the term *Hum number* with a novice collector and get a look of puzzlement. Use the term *Mold number*, and you are rewarded with a look of enlightenment.

In the case illustrated here, *Mold 52* identifies the figurine *Going to Grandma's*. Therefore and almost without exception, we can match one figurine to one mold number, and we can avoid the confusion that surrounds having one figurine with multiple *Hum* numbers.

Line 3. The copyright date normally appears on the figurine. It not only helps identify a particular figurine, it often provides clues as to the availability of figurines in the various trademarks.

Line 4. The original sculptor—in this case Reinhold Unger—is responsible for translating Sister Hummel's two-dimensional art into three-dimensional, figurine form. This information is a matter of interest only, and to date it has little affect on secondary market values.

Line 5. With most of Sister Hummel's original two-dimensional art now housed in the United States (see chapter on museums), it likely will be increasingly popular for collectors to match figurines with the original which inspired them. This book is the first of its kind to attempt to cross-index each figurine with its 2-D original. Elsewhere in the book, an index will give both the English and German titles for 2-D original number H 188.

Line 6. Goebel has produced *Going to Grandma's* in two sizes. For simplicity purposes, I have again resorted to the generic term *Model* for these size varieties which share a common mold number—in this case 52.

Now, about the */I* in the number *52/I*. I don't recall in my volumes of research literature seeing a name given to */I*. It is a size designator, used by Goebel to distinguish this size model of mold 52 from another size model of mold 52. What to call it? I decided on *size designator*, or commonly *size suffix*, and you will find both terms used with frequency in this work. Not original, but simple.

Line 7. With thoughts of the extra work involved, I nevertheless determined to include a *reference number* index as part of this work. Reference numbers are not found on the figurines themselves, but are frequently found on boxes of recent vintage. Plus, note that while models of figurines may share basic mold numbers and names, they never share reference numbers.

Where does the reference number come from? They are used as an order numbers for dealers to order product.

Why were reference numbers created when Hum numbers already existed? Hum numbers are too complicated for quick and easy reference.

Line 8. This line gives the approximate size of a size model. Be advised that most sizes given are for figurines of current or recent production. Very old figurines are quite likely to vary from the current norm.

Line 9. This line will provide either a) the *current, suggested retail price* of the model, if it is considered to be in current production, or b) the *current status* of the model, if it is not considered to be in current production. Here, the initials *T.W.* indicate that the model officially has been *temporarily withdrawn* from production by Goebel. This means it is not presently being produced at the factory, but may at some future time be put back into production. Other terms used on this line are usually self-explanatory.

Text. In the text accompanying *Going to Grandma's*, one can find this sentence: "In addition, *Variety II* model 52/I is difficult to locate in *TM5*, and, in *TM1*, this model commands a small premium if found without size suffix." (Italics added for emphasis.)

If there is any doubt in the reader's mind about what is meant by *TM5* and *TM1*, it will be important to review the section of this book on Goebel trademarks. A trademark (TM) period identifies the approximate date a given figurine was made and—in most but not all cases—is the most important factor in determining value.

The term *Variety* represents another of this book's departures from existing terminology. Borrowed from the much older coin and stamp collecting hobby, the term hopefully will be readily understood to represent an important deviation from the norm.

In the case of *Going to Grandma's*, major changes were made in the larger model of the figurine just as Goebel was switching from TM5 to TM6. As both the old type *(Variety I)* and the new type *(Variety II)* can be found stamped with TM5, it is important to distinguish between the two when listing estimated secondary market values.

As I had not found any consistent, existing terminology to fit this purpose, I determined to use that which exists for identical purposes in the coin/stamp field.

TRENDS IN SELLING

Throughout the pricing section, values—shown as *trends in selling*—are given within a range. This procedure is consistent with that used by authors such as Miller and Luckey, but is subject to criticism by some who would favor a single given value.

To such critics, I'll say that there is no such thing as a single, established value for a Hummel figurine, especially not one trading on a supply-and-demand basis in the secondary marketplace.

To place a single value on a figurine, I would argue, is an attempt to *set prices*, rather than to *reflect values*.

An admission: Even with the spread in values used in this book, I am certain that some of the value ranges are wrong, or soon will be wrong. On certain figurines, I adjusted the values *twice* (due to a volatile market) in the course of assembling this book.

This leads to an admonition that I'm sure every author of every price guide has intended: Prices quoted are meant to be used as a guide to prices prevailing at time of book preparation. They are not meant to be an inviolate listing of actual values.

PRICES AND VALUES

Let's pose—for thought-provoking purposes—a simple question. Is a *price* and a *value* the same thing, or can they be different?

Anyone who shops discount houses or bargain racks should know the answer. Yes, they can be different; the value of an item can exceed the price.

And, yes, you and I both know from unfortunate, personal experience that price can exceed value.

What we have in this work is a *price guide*, not a value guide. The prices given are approximately what are being charged by dealers specializing in the sale of M.I. Hummel figurines on the secondary market. (Quickie definition of *secondary market*: Nice, fancy term for *used*; a piece is being offered for retail sale *a subsequent time.*)

So all can understand what we're talking about, let's consider prices and values in terms of an appraisal. Appraisals of M.I. Hummel figurines can be performed at three levels.

At the top end, there is a *replacement cost appraisal* used to assign values. It is often used for insurance purposes. It's at the top end because an appraiser should assume there will be some difficulty replacing individual pieces, and allowance must be made for this.

At the bottom end, there is a *wholesale appraisal* used to ascertain quick cash value. This is the pricing level at which a dealer could be expected to make a cash purchase from an individual (or another dealer, etc.). This book does *not* address wholesale pricing; do not expect a retail dealer to be willing to pay prices reflected in this book.

Between, there is a *market value appraisal* used to determine the approximate market value at any given time.

It is these market values which are used in this book as prices. They will fluctuate with the rise and fall of demand in relation to supply. They will vary considerably from one part of the country to another—in fact, from one dealer to another. And, they are tremendously influenced by one factor not yet discussed....

CONDITION AFFECTS PRICE

The biggest shortcoming of this or any existing price guide on M.I. Hummel figurines is the lack of a formula relating price to condition of figurine. Prices given presume the figurines to be in flawless condition. Unhappily, many—perhaps most—aren't.

I have been in a position to see and handle many collections, large and small, that came directly from the collector or the collector's estate. What I found in these commercially untouched collections was just a little shocking.

This personal experience leads me to believe that, among surviving TM1 era figurines, *no more than 1 in 10 remains in flawless condition!* Perhaps less.

For the TM2 era, the figure is no more than *1 of 5.*

For the TM3 and TM4 eras, it is no more than *2 of 5.*

For the TM5 and TM6 eras, it is no more than *2 of 3.*

A good guess would be that at least 50% of all surviving M.I. Hummel figurines have either been repaired or exist with flaws serious enough to diminish full value.

Understand, the criteria being used here is not harsh. I'm not insisting upon figurines perfect in all respects that look as if they just left the factory.

No, I'm talking in terms of figurines which are blemished in the form of crazing or hairline cracks or small chips or breaks or reglued parts. Crazing, in particular, is a problem that makes even newer figurines difficult to find in pristine condition.

Believe me, it's amazing what a little soap and water will uncover in a typical group of older figurines. Remove the grime, and the gremlins of time appear.

Frequently, we have given a cursory inspection to a group of figurines and detected few problems. A bath and a detailed inspection then revealed multiple problems.

And, yes, we've seen what I think were outright attempts to defraud—groups of old figurines, each and every one with major breaks reglued, dirtied to the point where the breaks could not be recognized before the soap and water routine.

Seeing and therefore knowing all of this, I am amazed and more than a little suspicious when I see large numbers of older Hummel figurines offered for sale without defects or repairs noted. You should be, too. Ask why.

With the prices that good, older figurines bring today, professional repairs are now almost routine. Many of these repairs are essentially undetectable, especially to the novice.

There is no doubt in my mind that there are huge numbers of repaired M.I. Hummel figurines being sold today as flawless pieces. They are being sold both by unscrupulous dealers out to make a dishonest profit and by honest dealers who unknowingly have acquired repaired figurines.

In defense of the latter, I can say that I have on occasions minutely examined freshly repaired Hummel figurines without being able to locate or identify the repair even though I knew it was there.

If you purchase figurines or intend to purchase figurines from any but the most reputable of dealers, arm yourself with a good magnifying glass (lighted, preferably) and loads of suspicion. Then, be aware that you still might be "taken."

PRIME PRICES FOR PRIME PIECES

I have several other strong opinions relating to condition which I am determined to share.

First, I'll say that older figurines which are unblemished, absolutely fine, "mint-state" specimens should command premium prices. And you should be willing to pay them. These pieces are very, very difficult to come by if more than, say, 25 years old.

I foresee a time not too long off when these "mint-state" Hummels will be in strong demand and will fetch handsome premiums.

I see a time when premier specimens will be sold with certification.

I think the time will eventually come when all figurines will be graded, perhaps on a scale ranging from *damaged/unrepaired* to *damaged/repaired* to *fair* to *good* to *fine* to *excellent* to *mint*, which by common usage has come to mean *like new* throughout the collectible industry. I think the M.I. Hummel brand is a collectible ready for this type of sophistication.

If you've been really tuned in with me in this section, you may already realize that I'm saying that no more than 1 in 10 trademark 1 Hummels, and no more than 1 in 2 Hummels of any kind, will be worth the prices shown in this book.

The remainder of all M.I. Hummel figurines in existence are flawed or repaired, or both, and are worthy of prices less than those given.

How much less? That's a little question with a huge, variable answer. Nobody wants to address it, and I'm no exception.

Let's try to formulate an answer using some generalities and rules of thumb.

One of these is that there is less percentage deduction for a flaw in a rare figurine than there is for the same flaw in a more common figurine.

Another is that there is less percentage deduction for a flaw easily repaired than there is for one which can be repaired only with difficulty.

Still another is that there is less percentage deduction for a flaw in an obscure part of the figurine, such as the base, than there is for the same flaw in a prominent part of the figurine, such as the head or a limb.

Needless to say, the quality of repair on a repaired figurine affects price substantially. I've seen so-called repairs which were not only obvious, but almost grotesque.

I'll attempt here to list some of the more common flaws to look for in a figurine, listed more or less in order of severity. But first this preface: It's my opinion that, with very few exceptions, no figurine with flaw is worth more than 80-85% of the same figurine without flaw. Most are worth much less.

> *Paint flakes easily touched up.*
> *Minor craze lines under base.*
> *Small chips around bottom edge of base.*
> *Minor crazing shows on upper base.*
> *Small, easily repairable chip at end of some extremity.*
> *Multiple small, repairable chips.*
> *Clean, repairable break with no missing flakes.*
> *Semi-clean, repairable break.*
> *Large chip is evident.*
> *Crazing shows on face, limbs or major component of figurine.*
> *Figurine is discolored.*
> *Multiple breaks repairable.*
> *One or more pieces missing.*
> *Figurine looks unrepairable.*

For any of the above, figure a value somewhere between *worthless* and *less than full.* And now, you're on your own.

WHAT ABOUT ORIGINAL BOXES?

If you want to see a grown person cringe and gasp for air, bring up the subject of original boxes on your next visit to your secondary market dealer.

Every fellow dealer I've ever talked to decries the collector's fixation with original boxes. What do they want the boxes for, the dealers ask? Where did they come up with the idea?

I think I may have the answer to the last question.

I think it started in the 1970s—perhaps even earlier—when many advertisements in the antiques/collectibles industry began offering secondary market product *Mint in Box* or *New in Box*.

The intention, of course, is to convey the idea that the item has been unused and is still in original, fresh-from-the-factory condition regardless of age.

The terms are so fixed today that they appear in ads simply with the initials *MIB* or *NIB*.

Many knowledgeable collectors began retaining original boxes so that, if necessary, they could advertise their items as *MIB* or *NIB*.

Equally as many collectors—probably more—had no idea *why* they were retaining original boxes, except they had been advised by someone at some time to do so.

The original implication of *Mint or New in Box* has been defeated by common usage. The items being advertised can no longer be assumed to be unused. The collector, instead, routinely puts the new acquisition in one place for display and stores its box in another.

Secondary market retailer John Hobe tells the true story of a customer purchasing an expensive old Hummel figurine to add to her immense collection.

"I'll take it if you have a Hummel box for it," she said.

"None of the old pieces have boxes," he replied. "The only thing I could do is find a box from a new figurine."

"Fine."

It seems the lady had carefully acquired and labeled a box to match each and every piece in her large collection. These boxes had been broken down (folded) and were housed in a section of her garage which had been shelved especially to hold this box collection.

In the secondary market exchange that's part of my own business, we'll frequently have buyers pay $100, $200 and even $300 more for a collectible figurine (non-Hummel) *with* a box than for the same piece without a box. In one memorable instance, the buyer paid a full $1000 more!

Ridiculous, isn't it? Surely, *you're* not one of these box maniacs.

Actually, the M.I. Hummel brand is not as seriously infected with this original box disease as are some of the competing collectibles, but it is infected nonetheless.

Because of what I have actually seen happen, I must advise you that, if you harbor any thought of possibly reselling your new Hummel purchase in the future, you should try to retain the original box.

Try to obtain and retain original boxes for all annuals dating back to the *1971 Annual Plate* (it sells for $50-100 more with box than without), for all commemoratives and special editions, and, if possible, even for contemporarily produced figurines.

Don't expect to find boxes for the older figurines. Many of the older, original boxes were very nondescript and used for any figurine which would fit inside. Other original boxes were routinely tossed by dealers once the figurine was on display.

Don't be as silly as the prospective customer who not long ago turned down a good buy on a 1940s vintage Hummel she wanted because there was no original box to go with it.

So there is no misunderstanding, this price guide assumes that all M.I. Hummel figurines more than a decade old are *without* original box. Exceptions would be commemorative issues such as *Supreme Protection Madonna* and *Jubilee*, both of which came in special presentation boxes.

The various annual editions are priced in this guide *with* original boxes, but "no box" deductions from price should be quite small in most cases.

Goebel (now M.I. Hummel) Collector Club exclusive figurines should command small premiums if supplied with original boxes.

HOW AND WHERE TO BUY

Fifteen to twenty years ago, this would have been a simple little section. Buy your Hummels where and when you can find them—and hurry before someone else beats you to them!

For better or worse, this isn't 15 to 20 years ago, and the situation is much different today.

In 1979, the figurine *A Fair Measure* had a suggested retail price of $90. Fifteen years later the suggested retail price was $260.

In 1979, though, you might have had a very difficult time finding it, and, if you did find it, you might have had to fight your way through other collectors to buy it. It was definitely a seller's market, and many retailers sold at prices well above suggested retail.

Now, it's a buyer's market. There are less people who can afford to pay $260 for a figurine today than there were who could afford to pay $90 for a figurine in 1979. And the competition among dealers for this dwindled supply of customers is truly fierce.

There are basically only three ways a reputable dealer can successfully compete for your business as a retail Hummel buyer: *convenience, service, price.*

The convenience and service areas are completely noncontroversial. So, let's take up the matter of pricing, and explore this facet of today's Hummel market head-on.

Not many years ago the idea of discounting an authentic M.I. Hummel figurine—that is, selling it at a price *less* than suggested retail—was anathema. The guilty party was thought of in way less than complimentary terms by peers. *Legitimate* dealers—yours truly included—would curl their lips and bespeak of the devil.

But lo and behold, it wasn't long before some of the *legitimate dealers* joined the discounters.

Oh, in many cases these people didn't and don't announce up front, *We Discount Hummel Figurines*. Many still fear repercussions. In some cases, they give favored customer discounts—a favored customer being one who makes a purchase.

The point is that even the most loyal and ardent of M.I. Hummel retailers have had to find a way to compete successfully for the customer. A lower price, by whatever name, is more often than not a primary weapon.

This is quite likely the only book you will find which will suggest that you can buy Hummel figurines at less than suggested retail prices. Yet, one need only tune in to QVC to see brand-spanking-new Hummel figurines offered at discount prices on a week-in, week-out basis.

QVC is a fine, reputable mail-order retailer. There are other fine, reputable retailers now openly discounting Hummels from suggested price levels.

I have dealer friends who try to pretend that QVC doesn't exist, that the others are phantoms, that the only "discounters" out there are the "gray market" rogues who can't deliver anyway.

The problem with this view is that it's not factual.

I see the individual who is today's Hummel buyer, today's collector, as being a highly intelligent, well-informed consumer who knows quite well what his or her buying opportunities are. There is no pulling the wool over this person's eyes.

Luckily for many of today's retailers, this buyer is usually intelligent enough to know that the lowest possible price isn't always the best possible bargain.

For one thing, the matters of convenience and service are still there begging to be considered.

For another, risk and reliability should be carefully weighed.

Convenience, it seems to me, is a highly personal matter which I don't feel confident in addressing. What is convenient to one person may not be convenient to another, and vice versa.

Service, on the other hand, is fraught with tangibles and intangibles that are extremely important to the building of both a successful seller and a satisfied buyer.

There are the obvious matters of friendly and courteous service, prompt and efficient delivery, quick and careful paperwork. Simple. Easily understood. But difficult to achieve with consistency.

Let's take this discussion a step or two beyond the obvious.

In 1990, Goebel released a special version of the *Crossroads* figurine with *halt sign down* to commemorate the falling of the Berlin Wall. As the first-ever individually numbered limited edition Hummel figurine, public demand for the piece was incredible.

Long before the figurine was shipped and even before dealers received their very strict allocations, the issue was oversubscribed. That is, pre-orders exceeded available units.

Some people wanted to purchase three, six or even more of the piece. Others were openly willing to pay more than the $360 issue price.

As a dealer, how do you decide which customer gets the piece and which customer doesn't? Do you

---

DETECTING REPAIRS

For someone familiar with the product, poor repairs to broken Hummel figurines are easy to detect. But what about professional-quality repairs or restoration?

I had long heard of *detecting repaired breaks with a black light.* I wanted a black light; I thought I needed a black light. So, a number of years ago I finally bought a black light.

Almost useless!

Seems a black light is only useful for detecting old types of glue and almost-defunct types of paint. The newer materials cannot be detected with it.

The only consistent method of detecting a professional-quality repair is with an X-ray.

Anyone need a slightly used black light?

sell at issue price, or do you take the offers for more money? I can well remember having to address these questions.

The point of this narrative is this: How would your dealer address these questions as they relate to you? Would your dealer sell you a future equivalent of *Crossroads* at a price under the real market value because your everyday business is valuable to him?

Another, hypothetical question. A relative, knowing your interest in Hummels, decides to give you their possession—a rare old figurine that has an ugly chip in the hair. Can you take this figurine to your dealer and feel confident that, even though he didn't sell it, he will a) repair the figurine for you in a professional manner and at nominal cost, or b) see to it that someone else does? Or, will he simply say "sorry."

Let's try one more hypothetical question, and then we'll stop. You are missing the first club piece, *Valentine Gift*, from your collection, and you can't stand it. Can you go to your dealer and feel confident that he will a) have this figurine at a fair market price, or b) find it for you at a fair market price?

Do you see where I am heading? If lowest possible price becomes such an overriding factor with you that you do the bulk of your shopping at a large-scale discounter, you'll probably have to sacrifice the type of personal attention and service detailed above.

Now, if you've found a retailer who offers all three—price, service and convenience—count your blessings. Two of the three aren't bad.

If it's just one of the three—even if the one is price—you might want to search for a better primary source.

This section has thus far focused on a buying relationship with an authorized (or unauthorized, in some cases) retailer of M.I. Hummel products.

There are many other places one can buy Hummel figurines, and we'd be remiss to neglect them completely. Together, they account for a lot of sales.

There are classified ads in daily newspapers and hobby and collector publications where used Hummels can often be acquired from other individuals.

There are flea markets, garage sales and estate sales at which occasional bargains can be found at the expense of some time and effort in the search.

There are antiques dealers, some of whom like to deal in older Hummels.

Any of these offers the appeal of a possible *find,* either in terms of price or in terms of scarcity.

Any of these likewise offers the danger of a possible *waste*, both in terms of money and effort spent.

The danger, of course, is greatly lessened if you know and trust the seller.

If the trustworthiness of the seller is unknown to you, and you are determined to acquire Hummel figurines from these sources, go back and reread the section on condition versus price. Make yourself as knowledgeable as possible on Hummels, arm yourself with a strong magnifying glass and all the reference materials you can accumulate, and hope your lucky stars are aligned correctly.

I'm not saying this kind of search can't be fun. I'm just saying it is risky. And, there's seldom a money-back guarantee.

How and Where to Sell

I'd like to think that all the people reading this deeply into this book are avid Hummel buyers, each eagerly searching for just the right piece to add to a growing collection.

I'd like to think that, but I know it's not so.

There are a number of huge collections, lots of large collections, and countless small collections being broken up or disposed of today.

In many cases, these are collections begun in the decade after World War II and maintained faithfully through the 1960s, 1970s and into the 1980s. The figurines were bought for the most part when prices were unbelievably cheap by today's standards. And, they were bought by persons who, if still living, have reached the age where they are no longer much interested in accumulating.

Many people spending the money for this book will do so in an attempt to learn how to dispose of a collection of Hummel figurines. If you are among them, this, then, is for you.

First, understand this. If you are a collector offering your own collected pieces for sale, you are an active participant in the *secondary market.* Your problem is how to locate an active *secondary market buyer.*

For a dealer, this is not an easy task. For an individual, it can really be imposing.

Let me digress.

In early 1989, frustrated that there was no ready source for secondary market figurines (non-Hummel) to serve the wants of my customers, I assembled my staff and initiated a division of Opa's Haus Inc. called the OHI Exchange to provide just such a service.

The Exchange, first of its kind, was a success. It has now successfully matched thousands of secondary market sellers and buyers across the nation. It trades in Hummels and every other collectible figurine category in which demand exists.

But the Exchange deals with these collectibles *one piece at a time.*

It soon became apparent that, especially in the M.I. Hummel category, there was a huge need for selling assistance that went beyond what the Exchange could offer.

"I have inherited 60 Hummel figurines, and I need the money more than I need this collection," someone would call and say. "How can you help me?"

The Exchange was not a good option because of the numbers of pieces involved. Yes, I could offer to buy the collection outright, but there are many of these calls!

I assembled my staff again, and we devised the Opa's Haus HELP plan—the *Hummel Estate Liquidation Program.* It's a consignment-type program in which we actually take custody of a collection and market it in partnership with the seller. It's earned us the gratitude of a lot of people.

I relate this not to solicit further participation in our program, but as a means of introducing my foremost recommendation to a prospective seller.

Consignment. Find yourself a willing partner who you can trust, who has marketing skills, who knows the ins and outs of the M.I. Hummel brand, and who can reach nationwide if necessary. Unless you fit this description yourself, do what is necessary to enlist this partner's help.

The larger and more valuable your collection is, the more important this advice becomes. Your concern should be not only to find buyers, but to avoid pitfalls.

Which pitfalls?

We'll examine alternate means of liquidating a collection and try to identify the pitfalls within. And I don't mean to demean any of them. Each is tried and proven, and each is just right for someone.

We'll use the inheritor of the 60-figurine collection for our examples.

Direct sales. Our heir may decide the way to get the most money for the collection is to place a classified ad in the local metropolitan daily and perhaps a shopper publication or two. This way he might be able to get *full retail value* or something close to it.

He might be successful. People have been. More than likely, he will contend with an assortment of dealer types (antiques/Hummel) and bargain-seeking collectors who will have two things in common.

They both are looking in the collection for a valuable rarity overlooked by the seller, and they will want to "cherry-pick" the collection. That is, they will want to negotiate for the best 10% or so of the pieces, but be unwilling to buy the entire collection.

The problem with "cherry-picking," if allowed by the seller, is that it leaves him with no bargaining power to do much at all with the remainder of the collection. He will be at the mercy of other prospective buyers.

Try direct selling only if you consider yourself a shrewd negotiator. If you permit "cherry-picking," know that you are doing it for good reason.

You also need to be reminded that there is risk in revealing the inside of your home and its valuables to persons unknown to you. Be aware that there are criminals who plan break-ins and burglaries in just this way.

Wholesale sales. Wholesale means our heir is selling directly to a dealer who will want to resell the collection for a profit.

The advantages are that our seller can possibly make a quick sale of all 60 pieces in the collection, and he can do it with minimum effort. Circumstances often dictate such fast cash transactions.

The primary disadvantage is that, in nearly all cases, he is getting the lowest possible price for the collection. (The wholesale value of a Hummel figurine is much less in comparison to retail than the average person thinks. If you doubt this, carry a Hummel in to your favorite retailer and ask what he'll give you for it.)

There is another problem with wholesale selling. It is not in the dealer's interest to identify a rare or valuable piece that's part of the collection. Some will; some won't. It's a matter of conscience, not legality.

There seems to be a notion that a dealer should or will pay some flat percentage of what he intends to sell for. Well, there is such a percentage that the dealer considers a *maximum* that he will pay, but not a minimum.

Hey, it's human nature. Dealers like bargains every bit as much as the consumer. Unless they see a better than average bargain, few dealers will be willing to take on a 60-piece collection.

If the dealer spies a figurine or two in the group worth many times what he is allowing for it, his interest level will pick up. Commonly, a dealer will want to amortize the purchase of the entire collection with the sale of the top 10-25% of the pieces. It's just considered good business.

Auction sales. Hummel figurine auctions are much more common now than before. Our heir may decide this is the best way to go.

Pluses include the safety factor that the seller has formed a partnership with someone almost as interested as he in getting the highest possible value for the collection. And, any existing valuable rarities are likely to be discovered *before* sale.

Again, there is the opportunity to dispose of the entire collection fairly quickly. However, this only applies if the seller agrees to forego any reserve (minimum selling price).

The minuses center around risk of low prices. Auction-goers, by and large, are seeking bargains.

The spirited, high bidding of movie auctions, unfortunately, doesn't occur that frequently in reality—at least not in the ones I've attended.

If our heir does decide on the auction route, he'd best prepare himself for a few disappointments in hopes that, overall, he didn't fare too badly.

Consignment. Now we've come full circle back to consignment.

If the seller can get around the issue of trust and confidence in the selection of a marketing partner, a form of consignment offers many of the safeguards of auction selling with, in my experience, a much better return.

A word of advice: Before entering into a consignment relationship with a second party, be sure that the consignment agreement is in writing. Points can be spelled out in simplified form, but should certainly address concerns such as sales commission and fees, promptness and method of payment, and responsibility for loss or damage of the figurines

---

INSURING HUMMELS

With the help of this and other price guides on the market, it is not especially difficult to obtain insurance on your collection of M.I. Hummel figurines in the form of a rider on your homeowner's or renter's insurance. Consult your insurance agent.

Be aware, however, that most coverages protect only against such losses as theft, vandalism or damage due to natural disaster. Damage inflicted by handling—perhaps the most common form of damage—is normally not covered unless specifically provided for in the policy.

CHAPTER EIGHT

Pieces and Prices

**The Following Section
Provides
An Alpha-Numeric
Catalog
Of Important
M.I. Hummel Issues
With Current
Selling Values**

Note: An effort has been made in this chapter to relate each Hummel figurine
to the original piece of artwork which inspired it. However, not all Hummel figurines
can be related to the *H* numbers of the originals, as some original drawings are missing.
These, therefore, have not been listed.

1971 ANNUAL PLATE, HEAVENLY ANGEL
Mold No.: 264
Ref. No.: n.a.
Approx. Size: 7.5" diameter
2-D Original: H 425, F 215
1995 Retail: Closed Edition

Featuring the *Heavenly Angel* motif, the **1971 Annual Plate** is one of the best known and most coveted collector plates of all time. Issued at $25, the plate at one time (circa 1979) was trading regularly at around $1500. Its price has dropped and fluctuated since then, but it is always in high demand and never inexpensive. As 1971 was the 100th anniversary of W. Goebel Porzellanfabrik, each worker at the factory in Germany was presented with an example of this plate bearing a special, commemorative backstamp; these "workers' plates" command a premium of about one-third above prevailing prices.

Trends in Selling TM4: $750-950

1972 ANNUAL PLATE, HEAR YE, HEAR YE
Mold No.: 265
Ref. No.: n.a.
Approx. Size: 7.5" diameter
2-D Original: H 497
1995 Retail: Closed Edition

Knowing that it had vastly underestimated the market when it introduced its first annual dated plate in 1971, Goebel made the mistake of over-compensating in 1972. Bearing the *Hear Ye, Hear Ye* motif, the **1972 Annual Plate** was both over-produced and hoarded by dealers and collectors in hopes of a repeat of the bonanza of 1971. It didn't happen. Big stockpiles of the 1972 plate were still being released on the market by the hoarders up to 15 years later. While the value of this issue continues to be depressed, it is an interesting plate from the standpoint of being available both in TM4 and TM5. However, neither trademark appears to be especially scarce. Issue price was $30.

Trends in Selling TM4-5: $55-75

1973 ANNUAL PLATE, GLOBE TROTTER
Mold No.: 266
Ref. No.: n.a.
Approx. Size: 7.5" diameter
2-D Original: H 216
1995 Retail: Closed Edition

Recognizing that over-production of the 1972 plate had created a problem in the marketplace, Goebel greatly curtailed production of the **1973 Annual Plate** based on the *Globe Trotter* motif. The 1973 offering thus proved to be in short supply in comparison to demand and, of the first 10 plates in the series, has always ranked behind only the 1971 plate in value. Issue price was $32.50.

Trends in Selling TM5: $125-175

1974 ANNUAL PLATE, GOOSE GIRL
Mold No.: 267
Ref. No.: n.a.
Approx. Size: 7.5" diameter
2-D Original: H 155, F 220

1995 Retail: Closed Edition

Bearing one of the more popular Hummel motifs, the **1974 Annual Plate** has always enjoyed strong demand. Because of its popularity at issue, however, it is in relatively abundant supply. Issue price was $40.

Trends in Selling TM5: $70-90

1975 ANNIVERSARY PLATE, STORMY WEATHER
Mold No.: 280
Ref. No.: n.a.
Approx. Size: 10" diameter
2-D Original: H 288
1995 Retail: Closed Edition

As a first-issue Hummel plate introduced during a strong period, the **1975 Anniversary Plate** was destined for success. Issue price was $100.

Trends in Selling TM5: $145-185

Anniversary Plates: 1975, 1980, 1985

1975 ANNUAL PLATE, RIDE INTO CHRISTMAS
Mold No.: 268
Ref. No.: n.a.
Approx. Size: 7.5" diameter
2-D Original: H 316
1995 Retail: Closed Edition

Bearing one of the more popular Hummel motifs, the **1975 Annual Plate** has always enjoyed strong demand. Because of its popularity at issue, however, it is in relatively abundant supply. Issue price was $50.

Trends in Selling TM5: $65-85

1976 ANNUAL PLATE, APPLE TREE GIRL
Mold No.: 269
Ref. No.: n.a.
Approx. Size: 7.5" diameter
2-D Original: H 298
1995 Retail: Closed Edition

Bearing one of the more popular Hummel motifs, the **1976 Annual Plate** has always enjoyed strong demand. Because of its popularity at issue, however, it is in relatively abundant supply. Issue price was $50.

Trends in Selling TM5: $65-85

1977 ANNUAL PLATE, APPLE TREE BOY
Mold No.: 270
Ref. No.: n.a.
Approx. Size: 7.5" diameter
2-D Original: H 297
1995 Retail: Closed Edition

Bearing one of the more popular Hummel motifs, the **1977 Annual Plate** has always enjoyed strong demand. Because of its popularity at issue, however, it is in relatively abundant supply. Issue price was $52.50.

Trends in Selling TM5: $90-120

1978 ANNUAL BELL, LET'S SING
Mold No.: 700
Ref. No.: n.a.
Approx. Size: 6"
2-D Original: H 167, H 179
1995 Retail: Closed Edition

Remembering what had happened with the first edition annual plate after it was issued in 1971, collectors and speculators bought the **1978 Annual Bell** in quantity when it was released as the first edition in a new series. The bell has been in continuous high demand, but there seems to be a supply equal to the task. Issue price was $50.

Trends in Selling TM5: $50-70

Top row, left to right: 1978, 1979, 1980, 1981 Bells. ***Middle row, left to right:*** 1982, 1983, 1984, 1985 Bells. ***Bottom row, left to right:*** 1986, 1987, 1988, 1989 Bells.

1978 ANNUAL PLATE, HAPPY PASTIME
Mold No.: 271
Ref. No.: n.a.
Approx. Size: 7.5" diameter
2-D Original: H 306
1995 Retail: Closed Edition

When the **1978 Annual Plate** was released, U.S. collectors had begun a plate-buying frenzy that was to continue for the next several years. It is still relatively easy to find this plate in quantity. Issue price was $65.

Trends in Selling TM5: $50-65

1979 ANNUAL BELL, FAREWELL
Mold No.: 701
Ref. No.: n.a.
Approx. Size: 6"
2-D Original: H 310
1995 Retail: Closed Edition

Heavily purchased by speculators and hoarders, the **1979 Annual Bell** has always had the lowest secondary market value of any issue in the series. This was one of the last items produced before Goebel's conversion from TM5 to TM6; an example bearing TM6, if found, should bring a healthy premium. Issue price was $70.

Trends in Selling TM5: $35-50

1979 ANNUAL PLATE, SINGING LESSON
Mold No.: 272
Ref. No.: n.a.
Approx. Size: 7.5" diameter
2-D Original: H 305
1995 Retail: Closed Edition

With the 1971 plate selling for around $1500 and the 1973 plate for around $300 at the time the **1979 Annual Plate** was released, this issue was heavily purchased by speculators and hoarders. Consequently, it has always had the lowest secondary market value of any plate in the 25-year series. This was one of the last items produced before Goebel's conversion from TM5 to TM6; an example bearing TM6, if found, should bring a healthy premium. Issue price was $90.

Trends in Selling TM5: $35-50

1980 ANNIVERSARY PLATE, RING AROUND THE ROSIE
Mold No.: 281
Ref. No.: n.a.
Approx. Size: 10" diameter
2-D Original: H 204
1995 Retail: Closed Edition

Issued during the plate boom that was still on at the time, the **1980 Anniversary Plate** was purchased in multitudes. The market is still absorbing the extras originally bought by speculators. Issue price was $225.

Trends in Selling TM6: $85-115

1980 ANNUAL BELL, THOUGHTFUL
Mold No.: 702
Ref. No.: n.a.
Approx. Size: 6"
2-D Original: H 196
1995 Retail: Closed Edition

Bearing the *Thoughtful* motif, the **1980 Annual Bell** was issued at $85.

Trends in Selling TM6: $40-55

1980 ANNUAL PLATE, SCHOOL GIRL
Mold No.: 273
Ref. No.: n.a.
Approx. Size: 7.5" diameter
2-D Original: H 191
1995 Retail: Closed Edition

With the collector plate rush still on, the **1980 Annual Plate** received a reception little different from that of 1979. The plate, though wildly successful for Goebel at time of issue, has had a depressed secondary market value due to speculation and hoarding. It has begun to move some lately. Issue price was $100.

Trends in Selling TM6: $50-65

1981 ANNUAL BELL, IN TUNE
Mold No.: 703
Ref. No.: n.a.
Approx. Size: 6"
2-D Original: H 144
1995 Retail: Closed Edition

Bearing the *In Tune* motif, the **1981 Annual Bell** was issued at $85.

Trends in Selling TM6: $50-65

1981 ANNUAL PLATE, UMBRELLA BOY
Mold No.: 274
Ref. No.: 685
Approx. Size: 7.5" diameter
2-D Original: H 294
1995 Retail: Closed Edition

The plate fever in the country had begun to cool by 1981 and, despite the popularity of the *Umbrella Boy* motif, the **1981 Annual Plate** is in somewhat shorter supply than its predecessors. Issue price was $100.

Trends in Selling TM6: $65-85

1982 ANNUAL BELL, SHE LOVE ME, SHE LOVES ME NOT
Mold No.: 704
Ref. No.: 658
Approx. Size: 6"
2-D Original: H 126

1995 Retail: Closed Edition

Bearing the *She Loves Me...* motif, the **1982 Annual Bell** was issued at $85.

Trends in Selling TM6: $80-110

1982 ANNUAL PLATE, UMBRELLA GIRL

Mold No.: 275
Ref. No.: 684
Approx. Size: 7.5" diameter
2-D Original: H 296
1995 Retail: Closed Edition

In 1982, sanity returned to the collector plate market in the U.S. Even with a strong motif like *Umbrella Girl*, the **1982 Annual Plate** sold in more conservative numbers—as attested to by the less abundant availability of the issue in the secondary marketplace. Issue price was $100.

Trends in Selling TM6: $135-185

1983 ANNUAL BELL, KNIT ONE, PURL ONE

Mold No.: 705
Ref. No.: 657
Approx. Size: 6"
2-D Original: H 195
1995 Retail: Closed Edition

Bearing the *Knit One, Purl One* motif, the **1983 Annual Bell** was issued at $90.

Trends in Selling TM6: $70-90

1983 ANNUAL PLATE, POSTMAN

Mold No.: 276
Ref. No.: 683
Approx. Size: 7.5" diameter
2-D Original: H 246
1995 Retail: Closed Edition

In 1983, collector plates, having burned many speculators in prior years, were relatively unwanted in the marketplace. The **1983 Annual Plate** is in short supply today because Goebel read the market correctly and curtailed production of the plate. Issue price was $108.

Trends in Selling TM6: $200-275

1984 ANNUAL BELL, MOUNTAINEER

Mold No.: 706
Ref. No.: 656
Approx. Size: 6"
2-D Original: H 203
1995 Retail: Closed Edition

Bearing the *Mountaineer* motif, the **1984 Annual Bell** was issued at $90.

Trends in Selling TM6: $80-110

1984 ANNUAL PLATE, LITTLE HELPER

Mold No.: 277
Ref. No.: 682
Approx. Size: 7.5" diameter
2-D Original: H 340
1995 Retail: Closed Edition

Perhaps because the 1983 plate was immediately perceived as a hard-to-get plate likely to climb in the secondary market, sales were brisk for the **1984 Annual Plate**, based on the *Little Helper* decor. It consequently has been in plentiful supply. Issue price was $108.

Trends in Selling TM6: $90-120

1984 MINI PLATE, LITTLE FIDDLER

Mold No.: 744
Ref. No.: 466
Approx. Size: 4" d.
Sculptor: G.Skrobek
2-D Original: H 229,
    F 203
1995 Retail: Closed
    Edition

Bearing the *Little Fid-dler* motif, the **1984 Mini Plate** was issued at $30. It was the first of the four-year, four-plate *Little Music Makers Series* and was also the first of an eight-year series of mini plates.

Trends in Selling TM6: $35-50

**1985 ANNIVERSARY PLATE,
AUF WIEDERSEHEN**
Mold No.: 282
Ref. No.: n.a.
Approx. Size: 10" diameter
2-D Original: H 210
1995 Retail: Closed Edition

Burned by what happened with the 1980 issue, most speculators avoided the **1985 Anniversary Plate**, resulting in a diminished secondary market supply. Issue price was $225.

Trends in Selling TM6: $260-320

1985 ANNUAL BELL, SWEET SONG
Mold No.: 707
Ref. No.: 411
Approx. Size: 6"
2-D Original: Unknown
1995 Retail: Closed Edition

Bearing the *Sweet Song* motif, the **1985 Annual Bell** was issued at $90.

Trends in Selling TM6: $75-100

1985 ANNUAL PLATE, CHICK GIRL
Mold No.: 278
Ref. No.: 412
Approx. Size: 7.5" diameter
2-D Original: H 371
1995 Retail: Closed Edition

Decorated with the popular *Chick Girl* motif, the **1985 Annual Plate** is an easy find on the secondary market.
Issue price was $110.

Trends in Selling TM6: $100-140

**1985 MINI PLATE,
SERENADE**
Mold No.: 741
Ref. No.: 469
Approx. Size: 4" d.
2-D Original: H 342
1995 Retail: Closed
    Edition

Bearing the *Serenade* motif, the **1985 Mini Plate** was issued at $30.

Trends in Selling TM6: $35-50

1986 ANNUAL BELL, SING ALONG
Mold No.: 708
Ref. No.: 404
Approx. Size: 6"
2-D Original: H 146, H 178
1995 Retail: Closed Edition

Bearing the *Sing Along* motif, the **1986 Annual Bell** was issued at $100.

Trends in Selling TM6: $120-150

1986 ANNUAL PLATE, PLAYMATES
Mold No.: 279
Ref. No.: 405
Approx. Size: 7.5" diameter
2-D Original: H 372
1995 Retail: Closed Edition

Due to a weak economy and other reasons, sales of the **1986 Annual Plate**, based on the *Playmates* motif, were likely not up to the standards of the preceding issues, and it does not show up as commonly today. Issue price was $125.

Trends in Selling TM6: $160-200

1986 MINI PLATE, SOLOIST

Mold No.: 743
Ref. No.: 467
Approx. Size: 4" d.
Sculptor: G.Skrobek
2-D Original: H 284
1995 Retail: Closed
    Edition

Bearing the *Soloist* motif, the **1986 Mini Plate** was issued at $35.

Trends in Selling
    TM6: $45-60

1987 ANNUAL BELL, WITH LOVING GREETINGS

Mold No.: 709
Ref. No.: 397
Approx. Size: 6"
2-D Original: H 623
1995 Retail: Closed Edition

Bearing the *With Loving Greetings* motif, the **1987 Annual Bell** was issued at $110.

Trends in Selling TM6: $160-200

1987 ANNUAL PLATE, FEEDING TIME

Mold No.: 283
Ref. No.: 321
Approx. Size: 7.5" diameter
2-D Original: H 236
1995 Retail: Closed Edition

With a slow U.S. economy, Goebel was cautious in 1987, producing the **1987 Annual Plate** on a more limited basis while observing the market. Result was some under-estimation of the market. Almost since issue, this plate has ranked second only to the 1971 plate in secondary market demand and price. Issue price was $135.

Trends in Selling TM6: $300-400

1987 ARS CHRISTMAS PLATE, CELESTIAL MUSICIAN

Mold No.: n.a.
Ref. No.: n.a.
Approx. Size: 7.5" Ø

Sculptor: n.a.
2-D Original: H 441
1995 Retail: Closed
    Edition

Bearing the *Celestial Musician* motif, the **1987 ARS Christmas Plate** was issued at $35. The first plate in a four-year, four-plate series, it is referred to as the ARS Christmas plate because it features two-dimensional (ARS-licensed) artwork rather than the 3-D, bas-relief artwork featured on most other M.I. Hummel plates. It was, however, produced by Goebel and was limited to 20,000 pieces worldwide.

Trends in Selling TM6: $40-55

1987 MINI PLATE, BAND LEADER

Mold No.: 742
Ref. No.: 315
Approx. Size: 4" d.
Sculptor: G.Skrobek
2-D Original: H 248,
    H 285
1995 Retail: Closed
    Edition

Bearing the *Band Leader* motif, the **1987 Mini Plate** was issued at $40. It was the fourth and final in the *Little Music Makers Series*.

Trends in Selling TM6: $50-65

1988 ANNUAL BELL, BUSY STUDENT

Mold No.: 710
Ref. No.: 306
Approx. Size: 6"
2-D Original: H 193
1995 Retail: Closed Edition

Bearing the *Busy Student* motif, the **1988 Annual Bell** was issued at $120.

Trends in Selling TM6: $125-160

Top row, from left: 1990 & 1989 Ornaments. Bottom row, from left: 1988 & 1991 Ornaments.

1988 ANNUAL ORNAMENT, FLYING HIGH
Mold No.: 452
Ref. No.: 296
Approx. Size: 4.5"
Sculptor: G.Skrobek
2-D Original: H 452
1995 Retail: Closed Edition

Intended as a first-edition, annual, dated ornament when it was introduced in 1988, *Flying High* represents one of the few cases where Goebel just didn't have its act together. Pieces from the first production run were delivered without any special marking (Variety I). Those from the next production run were shipped with a decal reading "First Edition" under the skirt (Variety II). Not until the third try did the correct marking—the First Edition designation in combination with the 1988 date, both painted on back of the gown—finally appear (Variety III). Consequently, there are three distinct versions of one annual edition. Issue price was $75.

Trends in Selling TM6:
  Var. I: $125-160
  Var. II: $125-160
  Var. III: $100-130

1988 ANNUAL PLATE, LITTLE GOAT HERDER
Mold No.: 284
Ref. No.: 320
Approx. Size: 7.5" diameter
2-D Original: H 235
1995 Retail: Closed Edition

The **1988 Annual Plate**, based on the *Little Goat Herder* motif, usually commands the lowest price of any of the post-1985 plates. Issue price was $145.

Trends in Selling TM6: $140-180

1988 ARS CHRISTMAS PLATE, ANGEL DUET

Mold No.: n.a.
Ref. No.: n.a.
Approx. Size: 7.5" d.
Sculptor: n.a.
2-D Original: H 411
1995 Retail: Closed
  Edition

Bearing the *Angel Duet*
motif, the **1988 ARS
Christmas Plate** was is-
sued at $40. It is re-
ferred to as the ARS
Christmas plate because it features 2-D (ARS-
licensed) artwork rather than the 3-D, bas-relief
artwork featured on most other Hummel plates. It
was, however, produced by Goebel and was limited
to 20,000 pieces worldwide.

Trends in Selling TM6: $45-60

1988 MINI PLATE, LITTLE SWEEPER

Mold No.: 745
Ref. No.: 301
Approx. Size: 4" d.
Sculptor: G.Skrobek
2-D Original: H 234
1995 Retail: Closed
  Edition

Bearing the *Little
Sweeper* motif, the **1988
Mini Plate** was issued
at $45. It was the first
issue in the four-year,
four-plate *Little Homemakers Series*.

Trends in Selling TM6: $40-55

1989 ANNUAL BELL, LATEST NEWS

Mold No.: 711
Ref. No.: 279
Approx. Size: 6"
2-D Original: H 245
1995 Retail: Closed Edition

Bearing the *Latest News* motif, the **1989 Annual
Bell** was issued at $135.

Trends in Selling TM6: $140-175

1989 ANNUAL ORNAMENT, LOVE FROM ABOVE

Mold No.: 481
Ref. No.: 283
Approx. Size: 3.25"
Sculptor: G.Skrobek
2-D Original: H 142
1995 Retail: Closed Edition

Love From Above, the **1989 Annual Ornament**,
was issued at $75.

Trends in Selling TM6: $100-130

1989 ANNUAL PLATE, FARM BOY

Mold No.: 285
Ref. No.: 318
Approx. Size: 7.5" diameter
2-D Original: Unknown
1995 Retail: Closed Edition

Farm Boy adorns the **1989 Annual Plate**, which
commonly trades in the vicinity of its issue price,
which was $160.

Trends in Selling TM6: $155-195

1989 ARS CHRISTMAS PLATE, GUIDING LIGHT

Mold No.: n.a.
Ref. No.: n.a.
Approx. Size: 7.5" d.
Sculptor: n.a.
2-D Original: H 453
1995 Retail: Closed
  Edition

Bearing the *Guiding
Light* motif, the **1989
ARS Christmas Plate**
was issued at $47.50. It
is referred to as the ARS
Christmas plate because it features two-dimensional (ARS-licensed) artwork rather than the 3-D,
bas-relief artwork featured on most other M.I.
Hummel plates. It was, however, produced by
Goebel and was limited to 20,000 pieces worldwide.

Trends in Selling TM6: $45-60

1989 CHRISTMAS BELL, RIDE INTO CHRISTMAS

Mold No.: 775
Ref. No.: 270
Approx. Size: 3.25"
Sculptor: H.Fischer
2-D Original: H 316
1995 Retail: Closed
    Edition

Designed as the first in
a series of four annual
bas-relief Christmas
bells, the *Ride Into
Christmas* bell was well received. The original
series of bells ended with the 1992 issue, but was
immediately followed by another series of four bells
barely distinguishable from the first series. Result
is that most collectors and marketers now treat all
of the Christmas bells as one series. In either case,
the **1989 Christmas Bell** was the first issue. It
originally sold for $35.

Trends in Selling TM6: $65-80

1989 MINI PLATE, WASH DAY

Mold No.: 746
Ref. No.: 280
Approx. Size: 4" d.
Copyright: 1986
Sculptor: G.Skrobek
2-D Original: H 232
1995 Retail: Closed
    Edition

Bearing the *Wash Day*
motif, the **1989 Mini
Plate** was issued at $50.

Trends in Selling TM6: $50-65

1990 ANNUAL BELL, WHAT'S NEW?

Mold No.: 712
Ref. No.: 248
Approx. Size: 6"
2-D Original: H 199
1995 Retail: Closed Edition

Bearing the *What's New?* motif, the **1990 Annual
Bell** was issued at $140.

Trends in Selling TM6: $170-210

1990 ANNUAL ORNAMENT, PEACE ON EARTH

Mold No.: 484
Ref. No.: 243
Approx. Size: 3.25"
Copyright: 1987
Sculptor: G.Skrobek
2-D Original: H 434
1995 Retail: Closed Edition

Peace on Earth, the **1990 Annual Ornament**, was
issued at $80.

Trends in Selling TM6: $75-95

THE 'M.J.' HUMMELS

Anyone around M.I. Hummel parapherna-
lia long enough will eventually encounter a
logo, label or text which reads "M.J. Hummel".
The explanation is simpler than most realize. In the past, a capital *I* in German was
written like a capital *J* in English.

1990 ANNUAL PLATE, SHEPHERD'S BOY

Mold No.: 286
Ref. No.: 319
Approx. Size: 7.5" d.
2-D Orig.: H 293, F 204
1995 Retail: Closed
    Edition

The year 1990 was "soft" for collector plates, which meant lean sales for the **1990 Annual Plate** with the *Shepherd's Boy* motif. It now ranks as one of the six most pricey Hummel plates on the secondary market. Issue price was $170.

Trends in Selling TM6: $200-275

1990 ARS CHRISTMAS PLATE, TENDER WATCH

Mold No.: n.a.
Ref. No.: n.a.
Approx. Size: 7.5" d.
Sculptor: n.a.
2-D Original: H 410
1995 Retail: Closed
    Edition

Bearing the *Tender Watch* motif, the **1990 ARS Christmas Plate** was issued at $47.50. It is referred to as the ARS Christmas plate because it features two-dimensional (ARS-licensed) artwork rather than the 3-D, bas-relief artwork featured on most other M.I. Hummel plates. It was, however, produced by Goebel as the fourth and final plate in the series. It was limited to 20,000 pieces worldwide.

Trends in Selling TM6: $50-65

1990 CHRISTMAS BELL, LETTER TO SANTA

Mold No.: 776
Ref. No.: 247
Approx. Size: 3.25"
Sculptor: H.Fischer
2-D Original: H 318
1995 Retail: Closed
    Edition

Bearing the *Letter to Santa* motif, the **1990 Christmas Bell** was issued at $37.50.

Trends in Selling TM6: $55-70

1990 MINI PLATE, STITCH IN TIME

Mold No.: 747
Ref. No.: 249
Approx. Size: 4" d.
Sculptor: G.Skrobek
2-D Original: H 197
1995 Retail: Closed
    Edition

Bearing the *Stitch in Time* motif, the **1990 Mini Plate** was issued at $50.

Trends in Selling TM6: $45-60

MOLD NUMBERS AND HUM NUMBERS

Veteran Hummel chasers using this book will wonder what happened to the *HUM numbers*. This book, for instance, will tell you that the figurine *Botanist* is *mold 351*, while most previous works refer to *Botanist* as *HUM 351*.

I hope you'll bear with me in this regard. A HUM number is a mold number; it is simply part of Goebel's unusual numbering system whereby a portion of the artist's name is incorporated into the mold number for record-keeping purposes.

The Goebel system has a certain charm, but it does tend to confuse most beginners. The concept of a mold number is much more easily grasped, and that's why it is used here—with Goebel's blessings, by the way.

1991 ANNUAL PLATE, JUST RESTING
Mold No.: 287
Ref. No.: 317
Approx. Size: 7.5" d.
2-D Original: H 290
1995 Retail: Closed
   Edition

Decorated with the *Just Resting* motif, the **1991 Annual Plate** commonly trades near issue price. It is the first plate since the 1972 issue to be available with two different trademarks. Issue price was $196.

Trends in Selling TM7: $185-225
               TM6: $200-240

1991 ANNUAL BELL, FAVORITE PET
Mold No.: 713
Ref. No.: 207
Approx. Size: 6"
2-D Original: H 375
1995 Retail: Closed Edition

Bearing the *Favorite Pet* motif, the **1991 Annual Bell** was issued at $150. Examples bearing TM6 are known and command a premium when found.

Trends in Selling TM7: $150-190
               TM6: $175-215

1991 CHRISTMAS BELL, HEAR YE, HEAR YE
Mold No.: 777
Ref. No.: 206
Approx. Size: 3.25"
Sculptor: H.Fischer
2-D Original: H 497
1995 Retail: Closed
   Edition

Bearing the *Hear Ye, Hear Ye* motif, the **1991 Christmas Bell** was issued at $39.50. Examples bearing TM6 would command a premium.

Trends in Selling TM7: $40-55

1991 ANNUAL ORNAMENT, ANGELIC GUIDE
Mold No.: 571
Ref. No.: 202
Approx. Size: 4"
Sculptor: G.Skrobek
2-D Original: H 416
1995 Retail: Closed Edition

Angelic Guide, the **1991 Annual Ornament**, was issued at $95. Some of the ornaments were produced before Goebel had made the transition from TM6 to TM7. Examples bearing TM6 command a premium.

Trends in Selling TM7: $90-120
               TM6: $120-160

1991 MINI PLATE, CHICKEN LICKEN
Mold No.: 748
Ref. No.: 208
Approx. Size: 4" d.
Sculptor: G.Skrobek
2-D Original: H 376
1995 Retail: Closed
   Edition

The **1991 Mini Plate** was issued at $70. It was last in the *Little*

Homemakers Series and last of an eight-year series of mini plates. An example bearing TM6 would bring a healthy premium.

Trends in Selling TM7: $70-90

1992 ANNUAL BELL, WHISTLER'S DUET

Mold No.: 714
Ref. No.: 187
Approx. Size: 6"
2-D Original: H 145
1995 Retail: Closed Edition

Bearing the *Whistler's Duet* motif, the **1992 Annual Bell** was issued at $160. It was the 15th and final edition in the annual bell series.

Trends in Selling TM7: $145-185

1992 ANNUAL ORNAMENT, LIGHT UP THE NIGHT

Mold No.: 622
Ref. No.: 185
Approx. Size: 3.25"
Sculptor: G.Skrobek
2-D Original: H 384
1995 Retail: Closed Edition

Light Up the Night, the **1992 Annual Ornament,** was issued at $95.

Trends in Selling TM7: $85-115

1992 ANNUAL PLATE, WAYSIDE HARMONY

Mold No.: 288
Ref. No.: 316
Approx. Size: 7.5" d.
2-D Original: H 289
1995 Retail: Closed Edition

Despite its newness— or perhaps because of it—the **1992 Annual Plate** is not always an easy find. Issue price was $196.

Trends in Selling TM7: $200-275

1992 CHRISTMAS BELL, HARMONY IN FOUR PARTS

Mold No.: 778
Ref. No.: 186
Approx. Size: 3.25"
Sculptor: H.Fischer
2-D Original: H 284
1995 Retail: Closed Edition

Bearing the *Harmony in Four Parts* motif, the **1992 Christmas Bell** was issued at $45. It was the fourth and final edition in the original series of four bells.

Trends in Selling TM7: $50-65

A RINGING MISTAKE

Even with its excellent quality-control system, Goebel does make mistakes. Some examples of the *1989 Annual Bell, Latest News,* were released bearing the decal mold number 710. The 1988 bell was mold 710, and the 1989 bell should have been numbered mold 711. The mistake was soon remedied.

1992 FRIENDS FOREVER PLATE, MEDITATION
Mold No.: 292
Ref. No.: 188
Approx. Size: 7" diameter
Sculptor: G.Skrobek
2-D Original: H 345, F 201
1995 Retail: Closed Edition

Using the *Meditation* motif, Goebel issued in 1992 the first edition in a new four-year, four-plate grouping which it called the *Friends Forever Series*. Relatively obscure compared to most of the Hummel annuals, this plate will likely be in short supply if greater demand ultimately develops. Issue price was $195.

Trends in Selling TM7: $150-190

1993 ANNUAL ORNAMENT, HERALD ON HIGH
Mold No.: 623
Ref. No.: 153
Approx. Size: 4.5"
Sculptor: G.Skrobek
2-D Original: Unknown
1995 Retail: Closed Edition

Herald on High, the **1993 Annual Ornament**, was issued at $155. It was last in a six-year series based on new angel sculptures by Gerhard Skrobek. In the same year, Goebel started a new *mini ornament* series based on older, already familiar angel designs.

Trends in Selling TM7: $125-160

1993 ANNUAL PLATE, DOLL BATH
Mold No.: 289
Ref. No.: 157
Approx. Size: 7.5" d.
2-D Orig.: H 230, F 221
1995 Retail: Closed Edition

The **1993 Annual Plate** bears the *Doll Bath* motif. Like other special issues of 1993, the plate is a "sleeper" in the secondary market. Issue price was $210.

Trends in Selling TM7: $210-260

1993 CHRISTMAS BELL, CELESTIAL MUSICIAN
Mold No.: 779
Ref. No.: 155
Approx. Size: 3.25"
Sculptor: H.Fischer
2-D Original: H 441
1995 Retail: Closed Edition

The **1993 Christmas Bell** is either the first edition in a series of four annual editions, or it is the fifth in a series begun in 1989, depending upon viewpoint. Most collectors and marketers treat all of the Christmas bells as one series. The 1993–96 series does differ from the 1989–92 series in shape of bell (slightly), in the number of stars (four verus five), and in repetition of main design (repeated on the 1993–96 series, not on the 1989–92 series). Easiest distinction, of course, is the prominent date on the bell. Issue price of the 1993 bell was $50.

Trends in Selling TM7: $50-65

1993 FRIENDS FOREVER PLATE, FOR FATHER
Mold No.: 293
Ref. No.: 156
Approx. Size: 7" diameter
Sculptor: G.Skrobek
2-D Original: H 302
1995 Retail: Closed Edition

Bearing the *For Father* motif, the **1993 Friends Forever Plate** was issued at $195. Relatively obscure compared to most of the Hummel annuals, this plate will likely be in short supply if greater demand ultimately develops.

Trends in Selling TM7: $160-200

1994 ANNUAL PLATE, DOCTOR
Mold No.: 290
Ref. No.: 110
Approx. Size: 7.5" d.
2-D Original: H 256
1995 Retail: Closed Edition

The 24th and second-to-last in the famous series of M.I. Hummel annual plates features the bas-relief version of **Doctor**, a popular figurine created by Arthur Moeller in 1939. Issue price was $225.

Trends in Selling TM7: $200-250

1994 CHRISTMAS BELL, FESTIVAL HARMONY W/MANDOLIN
Mold No.: 780
Ref. No.: 108
Approx. Size: 3.25"
2-D Original: H 458
1995 Retail: Closed Edition

With the new, mini size *Festival Harmony with Mandolin* figurine and the *Festival Harmony with Mandolin* miniature ornament, the **1994 Festival Harmony with Mandolin Christmas Bell** completed the second in a series of four annual holiday groupings planned by Goebel. The first group in 1993 was based on the *Celestial Musician* motif. The bell is dated 1994. Issue price was $50.

Trends in Selling TM7: $45-60

1994 FRIENDS FOREVER PLATE, SWEET GREETINGS
Mold No.: 294
Ref. No.: 109
Approx. Size: 7" diameter
2-D Original: H 357
1995 Retail: Closed Edition

With the use of the *Sweet Greetings* motif, the third **Friends Forever Plate** had a Valentine's Day theme. The series began in 1992 and the concluding design in 1995 is *Surprise.* The four-year cycle for a collectible grouping has been standard for Goebel since the mid-1980s. Issue price was $205.

Trends in Selling TM7: $165-205

1995 ANNUAL PLATE, COME BACK SOON

Mold No.: 291
Ref. No.: 048
Approx. Size: 7.5" d.
2-D Original: H 210
1995 Retail: $250

The **1995 Annual Plate**, bearing the nostalgic title *Come Back Soon*, is the 25th and final in what, arguably, has been the most popular long-running collector plate series of all time. *Come Back Soon*, a figurine, was issued concurrently to match the plate.

Trends in Selling TM7: $200-250

1995 CHRISTMAS BELL, FESTIVAL HARMONY W/FLUTE

Mold No.: 781
Ref. No.: 046
Approx. Size: 3.25"
2-D Original: H 459
1995 Retail: $55

With the new, mini-size *Festival Harmony with Flute* figurine and the *Festival Harmony with Flute* miniature ornament, the **1995 Festival Harmony with Flute Christmas Bell** completed the third in a series of four annual holiday groupings planned by Goebel. The first group in 1993 was based on the *Celestial Musician* motif. The bell is dated 1995.

Trends in Selling TM7: $45-55

1995 FRIENDS FOREVER PLATE, SURPRISE

Mold No.: 295
Ref. No.: 047
Approx. Size: 7" diameter
Sculptor: G.Skrobek
2-D Original: Unknown
1995 Retail: $210

Bearing the *Surprise* motif, the **1995 Friends Forever Plate** completes this four-year series. It will be quite interesting to follow these editions on the secondary market in future years. Not particularly well received by collectors in the years of issue, these plates will prove to be in relatively short supply if demand later develops.

Trends in Selling TM7: $170-210

1995 MINI CHRISTMAS PLATE, FESTIVAL HARMONY W/FLUTE

Mold No.: 693
Ref. No.: 027
Approx. Size: 5.75" d.
2-D Original: H 459
1995 Retail: $125

This issue begins a new Christmas plate series and introduces a new technique into the M.I. Hummel line—one that involves the application of the relief design to the plate. The mini plate is designed to match the *1995 Christmas Bell*. Neither the issue price nor the planned duration of the series had been announced as this was being printed.

Trends in Selling TM7: $100-125

A BUDDING MAESTRO

Mold No.: 477
Ref. No. 292
Approx. Size: 4"
Copyright: 1987
Sculptor: G.Skrobek
2-D Original: H 489
1995 Retail: $100

A recent release, **A Budding Maestro** can be found only in TM6 and TM7.

Trends in Selling TM6-7: $80-100

A FREE FLIGHT

Mold No.: 569
Ref. No.: 160
Approx. Size: 4.75"
Copyright: 1989
Sculptor: G.Skrobek
2-D Original: Unknown
1995 Retail: $195

A Free Flight was introduced as a new figurine in 1993 and can be found only in TM7.

Trends in Selling: $155-195

A FAIR MEASURE

Mold No.: 345
Ref. No.: 773
Approx. Size: 5.5"
Copyright: 1956 & 1972
Sculptor: H.Wehlte
Restyled by: G.Skrobek
2-D Original: Unknown
1995 Retail: $285

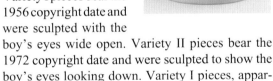

Variety I pieces bear the 1956 copyright date and were sculpted with the boy's eyes wide open. Variety II pieces bear the 1972 copyright date and were sculpted to show the boy's eyes looking down. Variety I pieces, apparently sparsely produced from original molds, are scarce and command a premium price.

Trends in Selling TM6-7: $230-285
  Var. I in TM5: $650-800
  Var. II in TM5: $240-285
   TM4: $825-975

A GENTLE GLOW CANDLEHOLDER

Mold No.: 439
Ref. No.: 445
Approx. Size: 5.25"
Copyright: 1983
Sculptor: G.Skrobek
2-D Original: H 420,
 F 817
1995 Retail: $200

Introduced in 1987, **A Gentle Glow** can be found only in TM6 and TM7.

Trends in Selling TM6-7: $160-200

A NAP

Mold No.: 534
Ref. No.: 213
Approx. Size: 2.25"
Copyright: 1988
Sculptor: G.Skrobek
2-D Original: Unknown
1995 Retail: $120

A Nap was introduced in 1991. It can be found in TM6 and 7, since production began in 1990 before trademark 7 took effect. The TM6 pieces may prove to be comparatively scarce.

Trends in Selling TM7: $95-120
   TM6: $125-150

NEW FOR 1991

The 1991 M.I. Hummel introductions included *Land in Sight* limited edition; *Honey Lover; Gift From a Friend; Two Hands, One Treat; We Wish You the Best; A Nap; Friend or Foe?; Art Critic; The Guardian; Angelic Guide* ornament; a small version of *Chicken-Licken!;* several pieces for the small nativity set; and the 1991 annuals.

A STORY FROM GRANDMA

Mold No.: 620
Ref. No.: 025
Approx. Size:
Copyright: 1993
Sculptor: team of artists
2-D Original: H 151
1995 Retail: n.a.

The pending release of **A Story from Grandma** was announced in mid-1994 with the introduction of its companion piece, *At Grandpa's*. However, **A Story from Grandma** would not be issued until June 1, 1995. The entire worldwide limited edition of 10,000 pieces is reserved for members of the M.I. Hummel Club. Those who purchased the *Grandpa* figurine get first option to purchase the **Grandma** piece in a matching number. Both will no doubt have a strong, continuing impact on the secondary market long after the editions sell out.

Trends in Selling TM7: n.a.

A SWEET OFFERING

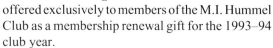

Mold No.: 549 3/0
Ref. No.: 144
Approx. Size: 3.5"
Copyright: 1992
Sculptor: H.Fischer
2-D Original: Unknown
1995 Retail: Closed
Edition

Available only in TM7, **A Sweet Offering** was offered exclusively to members of the M.I. Hummel Club as a membership renewal gift for the 1993–94 club year.

Trends in Selling TM7: $80-100

ACCOMPANIST (THE)

Mold No.: 453
Ref. No.: 295
Approx. Size: 3.25"
Copyright: 1984
Sculptor: G.Skrobek
2-D Original: H 387
1995 Retail: $100

Though bearing a 1984 copyright date, **The Accompanist** was not released until 1988. It is found only in TM6 and TM7.

Trends in Selling TM6-7: $80-100

ACCORDION BOY

Mold No.: 185
Ref. No.: 849
Approx. Size: 5"
Copyright: Unknown
Sculptor: R.Unger
2-D Original: Unknown
1995 Retail: Closed Edition

Accordion Boy was permanently retired by Goebel at the end of 1994, assuring a great increase in demand for the figurine in all trademarks. Originally modeled in 1947, the figurine is comparatively scarce in TM1. **Accordion Boy** became the seventh mold to be retired in annual succession

beginning with *Puppy Love* in 1988. Others, in chronological order, were *Strolling Along, Signs of Spring, Globe Trotter, Lost Sheep* and *Farewell.*

Trends in Selling TM6-7: $175-215
        TM5: $190-235
        TM4: $210-250
        TM3: $235-280
        TM2: $300-350
        TM1: $620-775

ADORATION
Mold No.: 23
2-D Original: H 368, F 214

Model 23/I
Ref. No.: 568
Approx. Size: 6.25"
Copyright: 1935, 1978
Sculptor: R.Unger
Restyled by: G.Skrobek
1995 Retail: $345

Model 23/III
Ref. No.: 567
Approx. Size: 9"
Copyright: 1935

Sculptor: R.Unger
1995 Retail: $535

This is one of the early pieces which has remained a favorite of serious collectors. Certain TM1 pieces of Model 23/III bear only the mold number *23* without suffix; these command a small premium.

Trends in Selling M 23/I in TM6-7: $275-345
        TM5: $295-345
        TM4: $330-400
        TM3: $380-450
        TM2: $480-565
        TM1: $900-1135

Trends in Selling M 23/III in TM6-7: $430-535
        TM5: $455-535
        TM4: $475-555
        TM3: $525-615
        TM2: $750-880
        TM1: $1400-1750

ADVENTURE BOUND'S STORY
An article in an old issue of *INSIGHTS*, publication of the M.I. Hummel Club, does a good job of relating the story of *Adventure Bound,* which is based on a fairy tale of the *Seven Swabians.* It's paraphrased here:

Hearing of a giant hare threatening the residents of Swabia, a guard enlists six other adventurers to hunt down the long-eared giant.

Lined up along a spear, they set out for the lair of the hare. As they approach, the object hops into view. But, being a mere bunny-sized rabbit, it runs in one direction while the "fierce" Swabians flee in another.

The hare only regains its monster dimensions as the group nears home and as the story is retold for years to come.

The leader of the Swabians is the toddler of the group; the largest were too afraid to go first. They ordered Hannemann, the shortest of the bunch, to the fore with the command: "Hannemann, you take the lead!"

Sister Hummel humorously portrays her little Swabians with eyes cast downward, the better to see the true size of the fearsome hare.

ADVENTURE BOUND
Mold No.: 347
Ref. No.: 771
Approx. Size: 7.5"
Copyright: 1957
Sculptor: T.Menzenbach
2-D Original: H 214
1995 Retail: $3600

With seven full figures on one base, **Adventure Bound** has, since its introduction, held the distinction of being the "most expensive" M.I. Hummel figurine. For its price, it has remained very popular and has found its way into many collections. It is relatively scarce in TM4. It is known, but very rare, in earlier marks.

Trends in Selling TM6-7: $2900-3600
        TM5: $3050-3600
        TM4: $4250-5000

AN APPLE A DAY
Mold No.: 403
Ref. No.: 272
Approx. Size: 6.5"
Copyright: 1974
Sculptor: G.Skrobek
2-D Original: H 117
1995 Retail: $275

Released for the first time in 1989, **An Apple a Day** bucks the recent trend toward downsized new pieces to fit more pocketbooks. It can only be found in TM6 and TM7.

Trends in Selling TM6-7: $220-275

ANGEL CLOUD FONT
Mold No.: 206
Ref. No.: 522
Approx Size: 4.75"
Copyright: 1949
Sculptor: R.Unger
2-D Original: Unknown
1995 Retail: $50

Scarce in the early trademarks, **Angel Cloud Font** has been in more or less steady production since 1978.

Trends in Selling TM6-7: $40-50
        TM5: $45-55
        TM4: $50-60
        TM3: $160-200
        TM2: $200-250
        TM1: $350-435

ANGEL DUET
Mold No.: 261
Ref. No.: 546
Approx. Size: 5"
Copyright: 1968
Sculptor: G.Skrobek
2-D Original: H 411
1995 Retail: $215

Scarce and somewhat pricey in TM4, **Angel Duet** is the later, figurine version of the Mold 193 candleholder.

Trends in Selling TM6-7: $175-215
        TM5: $185-215
        TM4: $480-580

ANGEL DUET ARS CHRISTMAS PLATE
(See 1988 ARS Christmas Plate)

68

ANGEL DUET CANDLEHOLDER

Mold No.: 193
Ref. No.: 536
Approx. Size: 5"
Copyright: 1948 & 1958
Sculptor: R.Unger
Restyled by:
  T.Menzenbach
2-D Original: H 411
1995 Retail: $215

First produced near the end of the TM1 era, **Angel Duet Candleholder** therefore is scarce with this mark and commands a large premium when found.

Trends in Selling TM6-7: $175-215
        TM5: $185-215
        TM4: $210-245
        TM3: $240-280
        TM2: $300-350
        TM1: $925-1150

ANGEL DUET FONT

Mold No.: 146
Ref. No.: 513
Approx. Size: 4.75"
Copyright: 1941
Sculptor: R.Unger
2-D Original: H 386
1995 Retail: $50

A number of mold changes have been made to **Angel Duet Font** through the years. None affect present values.

Trends in Selling TM6-7: $40-50
        TM5: $43-50
        TM4: $50-60
        TM3: $55-65
        TM2: $70-85
        TM1: $130-165

ANGEL FACING LEFT FONT

Mold No.: 91A
Ref. No.: 507
Approx. Size: 4.75"
Copyright: 1938
Sculptor: R.Unger
2-D Original: Unknown
1995 Retail: $40

This font is often sold as half of a pair that includes the following piece, *Angel Facing Right Font.*

ANGEL FACING RIGHT FONT

Mold No.: 91B
Ref. No.: 506
Approx. Size: 4.75"
Copyright: 1938
Sculptor: R.Unger
2-D Original: Unknown
1995 Retail: $40

This font is often sold as half of a pair that includes the preceding piece, *Angel Facing Left Font.*

The **Angel Facing Left** and **Angel Facing Right** fonts were originally sculpted without the halos. TM3 examples can be found with or without halos, with no bearing on value. Older pieces were created without halos and newer examples with halos. The pieces are relatively scarce in early trademarks.

Trends in Selling TM6-7: $32-40 each
        TM5: $35-40 each
        TM4: $40-46 each
        TM3: $45-52 each
        TM2: $90-110 each
        TM1: $180-225 each

ANGEL LIGHTS CANDLEHOLDER

Mold No.: 241/B
Ref. No: 548
Approx. Size: 10.25 x 8.25"
Copyright: 1976
Sculptor: G.Skrobek
2-D Original: H 444
1995 Retail: $235

Angel Lights, according to Goebel company records, bears the mold number 241/B *with plate* (the more common version), and it bears mold number 241 if offered without plate. It incorporates the *Heavenly Angel* figurine in its design. Given "temporarily withdrawn" status a few years ago, **Angel Lights with Plate** reappeared on official 1993 price lists.

Trends in Selling TM6-7: $190-235
     TM5: $200-235

ANGEL SERENADE WITH LAMB

Mold No.: 83
Ref. No.: 540
Approx. Size: 5.5"
Copyright: 1938
Sculptor: R.Unger
2-D Original: H 386
1995 Retail: $215

The name **Angel Serenade with Lamb** is used to distinguish this

figurine from the *Angel Serenade* figurine (mold 214/D or 260/E) used with nativity sets. Research indicates the figurine should be considered rare or nonexistent in TM3 and TM4. It was reinstated circa 1978.

Trends in Selling TM6-7: $175-215
     TM5: $185-215
     TM4: $300-355
     TM3: $300-355
     TM2: $300-355
     TM1: $550-685

ANGEL SHRINE FONT

Mold No.: 147
Ref. No.: 512
Approx. Size: 5"
Copyright: 1941
Sculptor: R.Unger
2-D Original: H 444
1995 Retail: $50

Angel Shrine Font can be found with variations in size and molding common to the older issues. It is somewhat difficult to find in TM1.

Trends in Selling TM6-7: $40-50
     TM5: $43-50
     TM4: $50-60
     TM3: $55-65
     TM2: $70-85
     TM1: $200-250

ANGEL SITTING FONT

Mold No.: 22
Ref. No.: 520
Approx. Size: 3.5"
Copyright: 1935
Sculptor: R.Unger
2-D Original: Unknown
1995 Retail: $40

Sometimes confused with the **Angel with Bird Font** (M 167), this piece can be found in all trademarks with the size designator 22/0. If found in TM1 bearing only the

22 mold number, it commands a small premium. If found in trademarks 1-3 with the mold number 22/I (slightly larger version), it commands a large premium.

Trends in Selling TM6-7: $32-40
       TM5: $35-40
       TM4: $40-50
       TM3: $45-55
       TM3 with /1: $180-225
       TM2: $90-115
       TM2 with /1: $240-300
       TM1: $180-225
       TM1 with /1: $360-450

(ANGELS WITH INSTRUMENTS TRIO)

ANGEL WITH ACCORDION
Mold No.: 238/B
Ref. No.: 551
Approx. Size: 2"
Copyright: 1967
Sculptor: G.Skrobek
2-D Original: Unknown
1995 Retail: $50

ANGEL W/ACCORDION CANDLEHOLDER
Mold No.: 39/0
Ref. No.: 532
Approx. Size: 2"
Copyright: 1935
Sculptor: R.Unger
2-D Original: Unknown
1995 Retail: $50

ANGEL WITH LUTE
Mold No.: 238/A
Ref. No.: 552
Approx. Size: 2"
Copyright: 1967
Sculptor: G.Skrobek
2-D Original: H 385
1995 Retail: $50

ANGEL W/LUTE CANDLEHOLDER
Mold No.: 38/0
Ref. No.: 534
Approx. Size: 2"
Copyright: 1935
Sculptor: R.Unger
2-D Original: H 385
1995 Retail: $50

ANGEL WITH TRUMPET
Mold No.: 238/C
Ref. No.: 550
Approx. Size: 2"
Copyright: 1967
Sculptor: G.Skrobek
2-D Original: H 435
1995 Retail: $50

ANGEL W/TRUMPET CANDLEHOLDER
Mold No.: 40/0
Ref. No.: 530
Approx. Size: 2"
Copyright: 1935
Sculptor: R.Unger
2-D Original: H 435
1995 Retail: $50

Due to price and popular appeal, these little musician angels and their candleholder counterparts are found in numerous collections. On the candleholders, in particular, markings may vary. A Roman numeral in front of the mold number—III/38/0, for example—refers to the size of candle. Other times, only the mold number *38* by itself is used. In trademarks 1-3, a slightly larger size 38/I, 39/I, and 40/I was issued in the candleholders. These command a large premium.

Mold 238 Figurines,
Trends in Selling TM6-7: $40-50 each
       TM5: $43-50 each
       TM4: $50-60 each

Mold 38, 39, 40 Candleholders,
Trends in Selling TM6: $40-50 each
       TM5: $43-50 each
       TM4: $50-60 each
       TM3: $55-65 each
       TM3 with /I: $200-250 each
       TM2: $70-85 each
       TM2 with /I: $225-280 each
       TM1: $135-175 each
       TM1 with /I: $255-320 each

ANGEL WITH BIRD FONT

Mold No.: 167
Ref. No.: 509
Approx. Size: 3.5"
Copyright: 1945
Sculptor: R.Unger
2-D Original: Unknown
1995 Retail: $50

Angel with Bird Font, sometimes called and confused with *Angel Sitting Font,* can be found with variations in size and molding common to the older issues. It is comparatively difficult to find in TM1 and TM2.

Trends in Selling TM6-7: $40-50
   TM5: $43-50
   TM4: $50-60
   TM3: $55-65
   TM2: $100-125
   TM1: $200-250

ANGEL W/CLOUD ORNAMENT (WHITE)
(See chapter *The Other Hummels)*

ANGEL WITH LUTE ORNAMENT (WHITE)
(See chapter *The Other Hummels)*

ANGEL W/TRUMPET ORNAMENT (WHITE)
(See chapter *The Other Hummels)*

ANGELIC GUIDE ANNUAL ORNAMENT
(See 1991 Annual Ornament)

ANGELIC SLEEP CANDLEHOLDER

Mold No.: 25
Ref. No.: 499
Approx. Size: 3.5 x 5"
Copyright: 1935
Sculptor: R.Unger and
 A.Moeller
2-D Original: H 423,
 F 211
1995 Retail: T.W.

Production of **Angelic Sleep Candleholder** was suspended effective Jan. 1, 1990, and it cannot be found in TM7.

Trends in Selling TM6: $140-175
   TM5: $150-175
   TM4: $170-200
   TM3: $190-225
   TM2: $245-290
   TM1: $450-560

ANGELIC SONG

Mold No.: 144
Ref. No.: 476
Approx. Size: 4"
Copyright: 1941
Sculptor: R.Unger
2-D Original: H 421,
 F 213
1995 Retail: $145

Angelic Song can be found in all trademarks without major varieties.

Trends in Selling TM6-7: $115-145
   TM5: $125-145
   TM4: $140-165
   TM3: $160-185
   TM2: $205-240
   TM1: $355-445

ANGLER (THE)

Mold No.: 566
Ref. No.: 052
Approx. Size: 5.88"
Copyright: 1989
Sculptor:
 G.Skrobek
2-D Original:
 Unknown
1995 Retail: $320

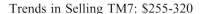

The Angler would be remarkable in its absence of the familiar Hummel base, except that it is one of three figurines introduced for 1995 that lack the usual bases. The others are *Just Dozing,* also sculpted by Skrobek, and *To Keep You Warm,* a Helmut Fischer creation.

Trends in Selling TM7: $255-320

APPLE TREE BOY

Mold No.: 142
Copyright: 1940
Sculptor: A.Moeller
Restyled by: G.Skrobek
2-D Original: H 297

Model No.: 142/I
Ref. No.: 878
Approx. Size: 6"
1995 Retail: $275

Model No.: 142 3/0
Ref. No.: 879
Approx. Size: 4"
1995 Retail: $140

Model No.: 142/V
Ref. No.: 877
Approx. Size: 10"
1995 Retail: $1200

Model No.: 142/X
Ref. No.: 876
Approx. Size: 33"
1995 Retail: Spec.Order

A perennial favorite, **Apple Tree Boy** appears with many slight variations. Smaller sizes lack the bird in the apple tree; early examples of M 142 3/0 and M 142/I have a tapered, tree-trunk base (Var. I). Early M 142/I pieces were marked only M 142 without suffix and command a slight premium. M 142/V was introduced in the early 1970s. M 142/X, one of the three so-called "jumbo" figurines, was introduced in the 1960s. It has not appeared on price lists since 1990, but can be specially ordered for about $21,000.

Trends in Selling M 142/I TM6-7: $220-275
    TM5: $235-275
    TM4: $270-315
    TM3: $310-355
  Var. I in TM2: $510-610
  Var. II in TM2: $385-450
    TM1: $700-875

Trends in Selling M 142 3/0 TM6-7: $115-140
    TM5: $120-140
    TM4: $135-160
    TM3: $150-180
  Var. I in TM2: $255-310
  Var. II in TM2: $195-230
    TM1: $360-450

Trends in Selling M 142/V TM6-7: $960-1200
    TM5: $1020-1200
    TM4: $1350-1650

Trends in Selling M 142/X TM6: $10,000-17,000
    TM5: $10,000-17,000
    TM4: $11,500-17,000
    TM3: $12,750-17,000

APPLE TREE BOY ANNUAL PLATE
(See 1977 Annual Plate)

APPLE TREE BOY & GIRL BOOKENDS

Mold No.: 252/A & B
Ref. No.: 705
Approx. Size: 5"
Copyright: 1962
Sculptor: n.a.
2-D Original: H 297, H 298
1995 Retail: T.W.

The **Apple Tree Boy & Girl Bookends** combine the popular figurines (molds 142 3/0 and 141 3/0) with wooden bases. The bookends were given "temporarily withdrawn" status at the end of 1989. They are not found in trademark 4.

Trends in Selling TM6: $275-345 pair
    TM5: $295-345 pair
    TM3: $385-450 pair

NEW FOR 1995

The 1995 M.I. Hummel introductions included *At Grandpa's; Strike Up the Band; Puppy Love Commemorative Plaque; Come Back Soon; Ooh, My Tooth; Just Dozing; The Angler; To Keep You Warm; Pixie;* a mini size of *Festival Harmony with Flute;* and the 1995 annuals.

APPLE TREE BOY & GIRL LAMPS
Mold No.: 230 & 229
Ref. No.: 642 & 643
Approx. Size: 7.5"
Copyright: 1953
Sculptor: A.Moeller
2-D Original: H 297, H 298
1995 Retail: T.W.

Designed to be paired and often found paired—even in older marks—these companion pieces were created together and semiretired together (given T.W. status) at the end of 1989. They are difficult to find in good condition in TM2.

Trends in Selling TM6: $280-350 each
    TM5: $295-350 each
    TM4: $345-405 each
    TM3: $385-455 each
    TM2: $675-825 each

APPLE TREE GIRL
Mold No.: 141
Copyright: 1940
Sculptor: A.Moeller
2-D Original: H 298

Model No.: 141/I	Model No.: 141 3/0
Ref. No.: 882	Ref. No.: 883
Approx. Size: 6"	Approx. Size: 6"
1995 Retail: $275	1995 Retail: $140
Model No.: 141/V	Model No.: 141/X
Ref. No.: 881	Ref. No.: 880
Approx. Size: 10"	Approx. Size: 33"
1995 Retail: $1200	1995 Retail: Spec.Order

Like the boy companion piece, **Apple Tree Girl** appears in many slightly different variations.

Smaller sizes lack the bird in the apple tree; early examples of M 141 3/0 and M 141/I have a tapered, tree-trunk base (Var. I). Some of the early M 141/I figurines were marked only M 141 without suffix; these command a slight premium. M 141/V was introduced in the 1970s and is not found with early trademarks. M 141/X, one of the three so-called "jumbo" figurines, was introduced in 1975. It has not appeared on price lists since 1990, but can be specially ordered for about $21,000.

Trends in Selling M 141/I TM6-7: $220-275
    TM5: $235-275
    TM4: $270-315
    TM3: $310-355
  Var. I in TM2: $510-610
  Var. II in TM2: $385-450
    TM1: $700-875

Trends in Selling M 141 3/0 TM6-7: $115-140
    TM5: $120-140
    TM4: $135-160
    TM3: $150-180
  Var. I in TM2: $255-310
  Var. II in TM2: $195-230
    TM1: $360-450

Trends in Selling M 141/V TM6-7: $960-1200
    TM5: $1020-1200
    TM4: $1350-1650

Trends in Selling M 141/X TM6: $10,000-17,000
    TM5: $10,000-17,000

APPLE TREE GIRL ANNUAL PLATE
(See 1976 Annual Plate)

APPLE TREE GIRL LAMP
(See Apple Tree Boy & Girl Lamps)

ART CRITIC

Mold No.: 318
Ref. No.: 798
Approx. Size: 5.5"
Copyright: 1955
Sculptor: H.Ashermann
2-D Original: H 252
1995 Retail: $285

Though modeled 36 years prior, **Art Critic** was not released until 1991. It can be found in TM6 and 7, since production began in 1990 before trademark 7 took effect. The TM6 pieces will no doubt prove to be comparatively scarce.

Trends in Selling TM7: $230-285
            TM6: $280-330

ARTIST

Mold No.: 304
Ref. No.: 811
Approx. Size: 5.5"
Copyright: 1955
Sculptor: K.Wagner
Restyled by: G.Skrobek
2-D Original: H 251
1995 Retail: $245

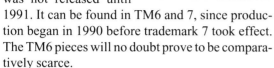

This figurine has been adopted as part of its logo by The Hummel Museum in New Braunfels, Texas, to symbolize Sister Hummel's artistic expression. Though modeled years before and bearing a 1955 copyright date, **Artist** was not released until 1971 after it had been remodeled by Skrobek. It is scarce in TM4 and commands a premium with this mark.

Trends in Selling TM6-7: $195-245
            TM5: $210-245
            TM4: $525-620

ARTIST FIGURINE PLAQUE
MUSEUM COMMEMORATIVE

Mold No.: 756
Ref. No.: 093
Approx. Size: 5" x 6.75"
Copyright: 1993
Sculptor: H.Fischer
2-D Original: H 251
1995 Retail: $260

This unusual creation features *Artist,* official symbol of The Hummel Museum, in full figure standing alongside a plaque as if he had just finished painting a sign. The first version (Var. I) includes the text, "Grand Opening 1993." This version was available only during the last quarter of 1993, and only 1500 of these pieces were produced. The second version deletes the grand opening text and was to be offered solely through The Hummel Museum. Issue price was $260.

Trends in Selling TM7 Var. I: $400-600
   Var. II in TM7: $260-300

THE U.S. ZONE MARK

M.I. Hummel figurines marked on bottom with the text *U.S. Zone Germany* are, for secondary market and pricing purposes, considered to be trademark 1 (or crown mark) pieces.

The U.S. Zone mark was used from 1946 to 1948 during what is considered the trademark 1 period. Some figurines show both the U.S. Zone mark and the crown mark.

AUF WIEDERSEHEN
Mold No.: 153
Copyright: 1943
Sculptor: A.Moeller
2-D Original: H 210

Model No.: 153/I
Ref. No.: 865
Approx. Size: 7"
1995 Retail: $295

Model No.: 153/0
Ref. No.: 866
Approx. Size: 5"
1995 Retail: $245

When the smaller, /0 size of **Auf Wiedersehen** was introduced after 1950, the boy in the figurine appeared briefly with a hat and without the handkerchief. Found in TM2 only, the "with hat" variety (Var. I) is now considered very rare. The piece commands a small premium if found with the 153 mold number without size suffix. The larger, /I size apparently was dropped from production soon after introduction of the smaller size and should be considered rare in TM3 and TM4. It was reinstated circa 1978 and is comparatively scarce in TM5.

In mid-1993, **Auf Wiedersehen** was used as part of a commemorative—the *Berlin Airlift Memorial*. In this version (Var. III), it was fitted onto a wooden base in company with a porcelain replica of the monument and a brass plaque. The *Memorial* as a set was limited to 25,000 pieces worldwide with an issue price of $330. The figurine in it differs from the norm only in the addition of a special backstamp. Price range given is for the complete *Memorial*.

Trends in Selling M 153/I TM6-7: $235-295
        TM5: $290-340
        TM4: $405-480
        TM3: $405-480
        TM2: $490-575
        TM1: $770-965

Trends in Selling M 153/0 TM6-7: $195-245
  Var. III in TM7: $280-330
        TM5: $210-245
        TM4: $240-285
        TM3: $265-315
  Var. I in TM2: $2750-3400
  Var. II in TM2: $345-405

AT GRANDPA'S
Mold No.: 621
Ref. No.: 051
Approx. Size:
Copyright: 1993
Sculptor: G.Skrobek
2-D Original: H 152
1995 Retail: $1300

Released in mid-1994, **At Grandpa's** continued the recent trend toward limitation in the spectacular new editions. In this case, the edition limit was only 10,000 pieces worldwide—the lowest edition limit ever for a Hummel figurine. Further, it was available at issue only with a redemption card issued to members of the M.I. Hummel Club. The combination of exclusivity and popular motif will give **At Grandpa's** an immediate impact on the secondary market. With the release of the figurine, plans for a 1995 companion piece, *A Story from Grandma*, were also announced. Purchasers of **At Grandpa's** will be given the opportunity to acquire the matching number of the *Grandma* figurine.

Trends in Selling TM7: $1300-1600

AUF WIEDERSEHEN ANNIVERSARY PLATE
(See 1985 Anniversary Plate)

AUTUMN HARVEST
Mold No.: 355
Ref. No.: 763
Approx. Size: 4.75"
Copyright: 1964
Sculptor: G.Skrobek
2-D Original: H 380
1995 Retail: $200

Not introduced until 1972 and accordingly very scarce in TM 4, **Autumn Harvest** can be more readily found with recent marks. Other than prototype examples, it probably does not exist in TM3.

Trends in Selling TM6-7: $160-200
        TM5: $170-200
        TM4: $950-1150

BA BEE RING-BOY PLAQUE
Mold No.: 30/A
Ref. No.: 691
Approx. Size: 4.75"
Copyright: 1935
Sculptor: R.Unger
2-D Original: H 101
1995 Retail: $95

Priced by the pair with the companion girl piece until recently, the **Ba Bee Ring-Boy** plaque now is bought and collected singly. Many examples are marked with a zero size designator, as in 30/0/A.

Trends in Selling M 30/A TM6-7: $75-95
        TM5: $80-95
        TM4: $95-110
        TM3: $105-120
        TM2: $130-155
        TM1: $230-285

BA BEE RING-GIRL PLAQUE
Mold No.: 30/B
Ref. No.: 692
Approx. Size: 4.75"
Copyright: 1935
Sculptor: R.Unger

2-D Original: H 101
1995 Retail: $95

Priced by the pair with the companion boy piece until recently, the **Ba Bee Ring-Girl** plaque now is bought and collected singly. Many examples are marked with a zero size designator, as in 30/0/B.

Trends in Selling TM6-7: $75-95
        TM5: $80-95
        TM4: $95-110
        TM3: $105-120
        TM2: $130-155
        TM1: $230-285

BAKER
Mold No.: 128
Ref. No.: 892
Approx. Size: 4.75"
Copyright: 1939
Sculptor: A.Moeller
2-D Original: H 243
1995 Retail: $195

Though no important variations are known for this long-running figurine, it has been restyled to give it the more modern texture. **Baker** seems to be rare—possibly nonexistent—in TM4.

Trends in Selling TM6-7: $155-195
        TM5: $165-195
        TM4: $270-320
        TM3: $215-355
        TM2: $270-320
        TM1: $500-630

BAKING DAY
Mold No.: 330
Ref. No.: 425
Approx. Size: 5.24"
Copyright: 1955
Sculptor: G.Skrobek
2-D Original: Unknown
1995 Retail: $275

An early Skrobek creation, **Baking Day** was shelved for 30 years before being introduced in 1985. Except for early prototypes, it is available only in TM6 and TM7.

Trends in Selling TM6-7: $220-275

BAND LEADER
Mold No.: 129
Copyright: 1939
Sculptor: A.Moeller
2-D Original: H 248,
  H 285

Model No.: 129
Ref. No.: 891
Approx. Size: 5"
1995 Retail: $200

Model No.: 129 4/0
Ref. No.: 398
Approx. Size: 3"
Copyright: 1985
1995 Retail: $100

This is the conductor of the Hummel orchestra which includes several of the musician figurines. The larger model incorporates a music stand. The mini version, released in 1987, is sans music stand.

Trends in Selling M 129 TM6-7: $160-200
        TM5: $170-200
        TM4: $205-240
        TM3: $225-265
        TM2: $290-340
        TM1: $550-690

Trends in Selling M 129 4/0 TM6-7: $80-100

BAND LEADER MINI PLATE
(See 1987 Mini Plate)

BARNYARD HERO
Mold No.: 195
Copyright: 1948
Sculptor: R.Unger
2-D Original: H 158

Model No.: 195/I
Ref. No.: 843
Approx. Size: 5.5"
1995 Retail: $300

Model No.: 195 2/0
Ref. No.: 844
Approx. Size: 4"
1995 Retail: $165

Both sizes of **Barnyard Hero** have been restyled to reflect the "modern" texturized finish. The smaller size was not introduced until circa 1955. Larger pieces produced before then lack the size designator and, due to a 1948 introduction, are scarce in TM1.

Trends in Selling M 195/I TM6-7: $240-300
        TM5: $255-300
        TM4: $290-345
        TM3: $325-385
        TM2: $420-495
        TM1: $900-1125

Trends in Selling M 195 2/0 TM6-7: $135-165
        TM5: $140-165
        TM4: $160-190
        TM3: $180-215
        TM2: $260-310

BASHFUL
Mold No.: 377
Ref. No.: 749
Approx. Size: 4.75"
Copyright: 1966 & 1971
Sculptor: G.Skrobek
2-D Original: H 350
1995 Retail: $195

Bashful is one of the TM4 semirarities due to its introduction in 1972 during the transition to TM5.

Trends in Selling TM6-7: $155-195
        TM5: $165-195
        TM4: $975-1150

BATH TIME
Mold No.: 412
Ref. No.: 258
Approx. Size: 6.125"
Copyright: 1978
Sculptor: G.Skrobek
2-D Original: H 457
1995 Retail: $375

Created 12 years before its 1990 introduction, **Bath Time** is available only in TM6 and TM7.

Trends in Selling TM6-7: $300-375

BE PATIENT
Mold No.: 197
Copyright: 1948
Sculptor: R.Unger
2-D Original: H 236

Model No.: 197/I
Ref. No.: 839
Approx. Size: 6.25"
1995 Retail: $295

Model No.: 197 2/0
Ref. No.: 840
Approx. Size: 4.25"
1995 Retail: $195

Be Patient was available in the larger size only until circa 1955, at which time the 197 2/0 model was introduced and the larger model was changed from 197 to 197/I. TM2 examples without size suffix command small premiums. All TM1 examples are comparatively scarce due to introduction shortly before the change from TM1 to TM2.

Trends in Selling M 197/I TM6-7: $235-295
           TM5: $250-295
           TM4: $290-340
           TM3: $325-380
           TM2: $405-480
           TM1: $850-1065

Trends in Selling M 197 2/0 TM6-7: $155-195
           TM5: $165-195
           TM4: $185-220
           TM3: $215-255
           TM2: $330-400

BEGGING HIS SHARE
Mold No.: 9
Ref. No.: 978
Approx. Size: 5.5"
Copyright: 1935
Sculptor: A.Moeller
2-D Original: H 355
1995 Retail: $250

The mold number and copyright date identify **Begging His Share** as one of the earliest M.I. Hummel figurines. It was originally a candleholder, with a hole in the cake serving as the holder. In the mid-1960s the hole was closed and it was marketed as a normal figurine. Both varieties can be found in TM3 without price differentiation.

Trends in Selling TM6-7: $200-250
           TM5: $210-250
           TM4: $245-290
           TM3: $275-325
           TM2: $355-420
           TM1: $650-820

BERLIN AIRLIFT MEMORIAL
(See Auf Wiedersehen)

BIG HOUSECLEANING
Mold No.: 363
Ref. No.: 759
Approx. Size: 4"
Copyright: 1960
Sculptor: G.Skrobek
2-D Original: H 173
1995 Retail: $285

Created in 1960, **Big Housecleaning** was first introduced in 1972 near the end of the TM4 era. It is scarce with this mark.

Trends in Selling TM6-7: $230-285
           TM5: $240-285
           TM4: $950-1125

BIRD DUET

Mold No.: 169
Ref. No.: 545
Approx. Size: 4"
Copyright: 1945
Sculptor: A.Moeller
Restyled by: G.Skrobek
2-D Original: H 833
1995 Retail: $140

Bird Duet can be found in a number of different colors, configurations and sizes.

Trends in Selling TM6-7: $110-140
                  TM5: $120-140
                  TM4: $135-160
                  TM3: $155-185
                  TM2: $195-230
                  TM1: $375-465

BIRD WATCHER

Mold No.: 300
Ref. No.: 814
Approx. Size: 5.25"
Copyright: 1956
Sculptor: G.Skrobek
2-D Original: Unknown
1995 Retail: $215

Shelved for almost 25 years before its 1979 release, **Bird Watcher** is reportedly the first M.I. Hummel figurine sculpted for Goebel by Skrobek.

Trends in Selling TM6-7: $175-215
                  TM5: $210-245

BIRTHDAY CAKE CANDLEHOLDER

Mold No.: 338
Ref. No.: 779
Approx. Size: 3.5"
Copyright: 1956
Sculptor: G.Skrobek
2-D Original: H 347
1995 Retail: $140

Sculpted in 1956, this piece was not introduced

until 1989—33 years later. Likely, it will not prove to be abundant in TM6.

Trends in Selling TM6-7: $115-140

BIRTHDAY CANDLE

Mold No.: 440
Ref. No.: 403
Approx. Size: 5.5"
Copyright: 1983
Sculptor:
  G.Skrobek
2-D Original: Un
  known
1995 Retail:
  Closed Edition

No. 10 in the prestigious annual series of M.I. Hummel Club exclusive redemption figurines, **Birthday Candle** was issued for the 1986–87 club year (June 1, 1986–May 31, 1987). It could originally be acquired only with a redemption certificate provided to each active club member. Issue price was $95.

Trends in Selling TM6: $180-215

BIRTHDAY PRESENT

Mold No.: 341 3/0
Ref. No.: 098
Approx. Size: 4"
Copyright: 1989
Sculptor: H.Fischer
2-D Original: H 347
1995 Retail: $140

Birthday Present was the special event piece for '94. Offered at $140, it bore a special *First Issue* and *Special Event* backstamp and would only be available at special sales promotions during 1994. Afterwards, the figurine could be reintroduced without the special backstamp. It is third in the line of special event pieces, following *Little Gardener* in 1992 and *One Plus One* in 1993.

Trends in Selling TM7: $125-155

BIRTHDAY SERENADE

Mold No.: 218
Copyright: 1952 & 1965
Sculptor: R.Unger
Restyled by: G.Skrobek
2-D Original: Unknown

Model No.: 218/0
Ref. No.: 825
Approx. Size: 5.5"
1995 Retail: $295

Model No.: 218 2/0
Ref. No.: 826
Approx. Size: 4.25"
1995 Retail: $170

Birthday Serenade can be found in two important varieties. In Variety I, the girl plays the accordion, and in Variety II, the boy plays the accordion. The instruments were reversed in Skrobek's restyling of 1964. In addition, TM2 examples showing mold number without suffix (larger size) command a slight premium. Research indicates the /0 size is scarce in TM3 and TM4 and relatively scarce in TM5. It had been out of production before being reinstated circa 1978.

Trends in Selling M 218/0 TM6-7: $235-295
    TM5: $290-315
  Var. I in TM4: $655-795
  Var. II in TM4: $355-430
  Var. I in TM3: $655-795
  Var. II in TM3: $355-430
    TM2: $690-840

Trends in Selling M 218 2/0 TM6-7: $135-170
    TM5: $145-170
  Var. I in TM4: $365-445
  Var. II in TM4: $165-195
  Var. I in TM3: $400-495
  Var. II in TM3: $185-220
    TM2: $430-535

NEW FOR 1986

 The 1986 M.I. Hummel introductions included *Chapel Time Clock, Birthday Candle, Valentine Gift plate, What Now?* mini pendant, a small version of *Soloist* and the 1986 annuals.

BIRTHDAY SERENADE LAMP

Mold No.: 231 & 234
Ref. No.: 641 & 639
Approx. Size: 9.75" & 7.75"
Copyright: 1954
Sculptor: R.Unger
Restyled by: R.Wittman
2-D Original: Unknown
1995 Retail: T.W.

For some reason, Goebel decided to use two different mold numbers to distinguish between the two sizes of this table lamp. Pre-TM4 examples in either size will have the girl playing the accordion (Var. I); TM5-6 examples will have the boy playing the accordion; and TM4 examples can be found either way. Both sizes of the lamp are scarce in all early marks. They were given T.W. status as of Jan. 1, 1990. The **Birthday Serenade Lamp** has traditionally been paired by Goebel with the *Happy Days Lamp*.

Trends in Selling M 231 TM6: $390-490
    TM5: $415-490
    TM2: $1150-1425

Trends in Selling M 234 TM6: $340-425
    TM5: $360-425
  Var. I in TM4: $500-615
  Var. II in TM4: $450-530
    TM3: $625-775
    TM2: $925-1125

BLESSED CHILD
Mold No.: 78
Copyright: 1937
Sculptor: E.Lautensack
Restyled by: G.Skrobek
2-D Original: Unknown

Known as the *Infant of Krumbad* before a 1984 name change, **Blessed Child** has been produced in eight different sizes/versions, but is currently available only in the latest, M 78/II 1/2. Made exclusively for sale in Germany, this version is similar in appearance to the pieces produced prior to the Skrobek restyling in 1965. Older examples command a premium if found in a finish other than the usual patina-stained bisque—about 100% for multicolored and about 200% for white glazed. Models 78/I, 78/II and 78/III last appeared on the Goebel price list of 1990. In 1992, the unexplained "83" was added to the suffix on these models.

Model No.: 78/III/83
Ref. No.: 489
Approx. Size: 5.25"
1995 Retail: T.W.

Model No.: 78/II/83
Ref. No.: 492
Approx. Size: 3.5"
1995 Retail: T.W.

Model No.: 78/I/83
Ref. No.: 495
Approx. Size: 2.5"
1995 Retail: T.W.

Model No.: 78/0
Ref. No.: n.a.
Approx. Size: 2.25"
1995 Retail: T.W.

Model No.: 78/V
Ref. No.: n.a.
Approx. Size: 7.5"
1995 Retail: T.W.

Model No.: 78/VI
Ref. No.: n.a.
Approx. Size: 10.5"
1995 Retail: T.W.

Model No: 78/VIII
Ref. No.: n.a.
Approx. Size: 13.5"
1995 Retail: T.W.

Model No.: 78/II 1/2
Ref. No.: n.a.
Approx. Size: 4.25"
1995 Retail: T.W.

Trends in Selling M 78/III/83 TM6: $52-65
        TM5: $56-65
        TM4: $65-75
        TM3: $70-85
        TM2: $180-225
        TM1: $250-315

Trends in Selling M 78/II/83 TM6: $40-50
        TM5: $43-50
        TM4: $50-60
        TM3: $55-65

Trends in Selling M 78/I/83 TM6: $36-45
        TM5: $39-45
        TM4: $45-52
        TM3: $48-60

Trends in Selling M 78/0 TM3: $130-195
        TM2: $175-220

Trends in Selling M 78/V TM6: $90-115
        TM5: $100-115
        TM4: $110-135
        TM3: $125-150

Trends in Selling M 78/VI TM6: $170-215
        TM5: $185-215
        TM4: $210-250
        TM3: $210-250
        TM2: $250-315
        TM1: $375-470

Trends in Selling M 78/VIII TM6: $260-325
        TM5: $280-325
        TM4: $315-375
        TM3: $315-375
        TM2: $450-540
        TM1: $675-845

Trends in Selling M 78/II 1/2 TM7: $40-60
        TM6: $60-100

BLESSED EVENT
Mold No.: 333
Ref. No.: 784
Approx. Size: 5.5"
Copyright: 1955–1957
Sculptor: A.Moeller
2-D Original: H 102
1995 Retail: $320

Found with varying copyright dates (1955, 1956, 1957), this popular figurine was introduced in 1964 during the transition to TM4. Production examples of **Blessed Event** bearing TM3 would be rare and quite valuable if located.

Trends in Selling TM6-7: $255-320
        TM5: $275-320
        TM4: $315-370

BOOK WORM

Mold No.: 3
Copyright: 1935 & 1972
Sculptor: A.Moeller
Restyled by: G.Skrobek
2-D Original: H 196

Model No.: 3/I
Ref. No.: 992
Approx. Size: 5.5"
1995 Retail: $295

Model No.: 3/II
Ref. No.: 991
Approx. Size: 8"
1995 Retail: T.W.

Model No.: 3/III
Ref. No.: 990
Approx. Size: 9"
1995 Retail: T.W.

Mold No.: 8
Ref. No.: 979
Approx. Size: 4"
Copyright: 1935
Sculptor: R.Unger
2-D Original: H 196
1995 Retail: $215

The M 3 **Book Worm** and the M 8 **Book Worm** are essentially size variations of the same figurine, though they do have different originating sculptors. With four different sizes produced for so many years, there are the normal minor variations in color and finish to be found. However, none affect the market values except earliest pieces marked FF 17 instead of the normal mold number; these are very rare. M 3/II and M 3/III are not in current production, having been given temporarily withdrawn status as of Jan. 1, 1990. Research indicates model 3/III is scarce in TM3 and rare in TM4. It was reinstated circa 1978 after being long out of production.

Trends in Selling M 3/I TM6-7: $235-295
        TM5: $245-295
        TM4: $280-330
        TM3: $320-375
        TM2: $405-475
        TM1: $760-960

Trends in Selling M 3/II TM6: $775-1175
        TM5: $835-1175
        TM4: $940-1175
        TM3: $1035-1295
        TM2: $1150-1425
        TM1: $1600-2000

Trends in Selling M 3/III TM6: $850-1290
        TM5: $925-1290
        TM4: $1040-1290
        TM3: $1150-1425
        TM2: $1265-1550
        TM1: $1925-2400

Trends in Selling M 8 TM6-7: $175-215
        TM5: $185-215
        TM4: $215-250
        TM3: $240-280
        TM2: $300-350
        TM1: $545-680

BOOK WORMS BOOKENDS

Mold No.: 14/A & B (Pair)
Ref. No.: 715
Approx. Size: 5.5"
Copyright: 1935
Sculptor: R.Unger
2-D Original: H 196
1995 Retail: T.W.

The girl in the bookends is distinguished from the 3/I *Book Worm* figurine only by the black-and-white pictures in the book (as opposed to color pictures in the figurine). Except for a relatively brief period, the boy has been available only as part of the set. Individual pieces from broken pairs command about half of the respective set price. This set was given temporarily withdrawn status as of Jan. 1, 1990.

Trends in Selling TM6: $325-410 pair
        TM5: $350-410 pair
        TM4: $400-470 pair
        TM3: $440-535 pair
        TM2: $500-625 pair
        TM1: $1000-1250 pair

BOOTS

Mold No.: 143
Copyright: 1940
Sculptor: A.Moeller
Restyled by: G.Skrobek
2-D Original: H 255

Model No.: 143/I
Ref. No.: 874
Approx. Size: 6.5"
1995 Retail: $330

Model No.: 143/0
Ref. No.: 875
Approx. Size: 5.5"
1995 Retail: $200

Both sizes of **Boots** are available in nearly all trademarks. Research indicates model 143/I may be scarce to nonexistent in TM4. It was reinstated circa 1978 after being out of production. Early pieces *without* size suffix—marked 143 only—command a slight premium.

Trends in Selling M 143/I TM6-7: $265-330
TM5: $325-380
TM4: $365-430
TM3: $365-430
TM2: $460-540
TM1: $720-900

Trends in Selling M 143/0 TM6-7: $160-200
TM5: $170-200
TM4: $200-235
TM3: $220-260
TM2: $280-330
TM1: $415-515

BOTANIST

Mold No.: 351
Ref. No.: 767
Approx. Size: 4.5"
Copyright: 1972
Sculptor: G.Skrobek
2-D Original: H 209
1995 Retail: $200

Botanist bears the 1972 copyright date on the bottom, but was not introduced until a decade later

in 1982. It has been a favorite ever since, witness its appearance on the cover of this book.

Trends in Selling: $160-200

BOY & GIRL WALL VASE

Mold No.: 360/A
Ref. No.: 662
Approx. Size: 4.5"
Copyright: 1958
Sculptor: G.Skrobek
2-D Original: Unknown
1995 Retail: T.W.

Originally available—but scarce—in the TM3 era, **Boy & Girl Wall Vase** was reintroduced in 1979. It was relatively common in TM6 before again being withdrawn from production at the end of 1989.

Trends in Selling TM6: $125-155
TM5: $135-155
TM3: $335-415

BOY WALL VASE
Mold No.: 360/B
Ref. No.: 661

GIRL WALL VASE
Mold No.: 360/C
Ref. No.: 660

The *Boy & Girl Wall Vase* shares a mold number with its two companion pieces, the **Boy Wall Vase** (M 360/B) and the **Girl Wall Vase** (M 360/C). From the beginning, they have been offered at the same time and under the same circumstances, and they are inspired by the same original.

Trends in Selling TM6: $105-130 each
TM5: $115-130 each
TM3: $300-375 each

BOY WITH ACCORDION

Mold No: 390
Ref. No: 734
Approx. Size: 2.25"
Copyright: 1968
Sculptor: G.Skrobek
2-D Original: Unknown
1995 Retail: $85

Boy with Accordion is often offered in company with the other two "Little Band" members, *Girl with Sheet Music* and *Girl with Trumpet*.

Trends in Selling TM6-7: $70-85
        TM5: $75-85
        TM4: $105-125

BOY WITH BIRD ASHTRAY

Mold No.: 166
Ref. No.: 671
Approx. Size: 3.5 x 6"
Copyright: 1946
Sculptor: A.Moeller
2-D Original: H 616
1995 Retail: T.W.

Production was suspended effective Jan. 1, 1990, and **Boy with Bird Ashtray** is not found in TM7.

Trends in Selling TM6: $105-155
        TM5: $115-155
        TM4: $135-175
        TM3: $150-190
        TM2: $200-245
        TM1: $320-400

BOY WITH HORSE	**GIRL WITH DOLL**
Mold No.: 239/C	Mold No.: 239/B
Ref. No.: 820	Ref. No.: 821
Approx. Size: 3.5"	Approx. Size: 3.5"

GIRL WITH NOSEGAY	Copyright: 1967
Mold No.: 239/A	Sculptor: G.Skrobek
Ref. No.: 822	2-D Original: Unknown
Approx. Size: 3.5"	1995 Retail: $50 ea.

These three figurines share the 239 mold number and were originally designed to be sold as a set.

Trends in Selling M 239 TM6-7: $45-55 each
        TM5: $47-55 each
        TM4: $55-65 each

BOY WITH HORSE CANDLEHOLDER	**GIRL WITH FIR TREE CANDLEHOLDER**
Mold No.: 117	Mold No.: 116
Ref. No.: 635	Ref. No.: 636
Approx. Size: 3.5"	Approx. Size: 3.5"

GIRL WITH NOSEGAY CANDLEHOLDER	Copyright: 1939
Mold No.: 115	Sculptor: R.Unger
Ref. No.: 637	2-D Original: Unknown
Approx. Size: 3.5"	1995 Retail: $55 ea.

These are the earlier, candleholder counterparts of the three preceding figurines. Like the figurines, they were designed to be sold together, and through the years they have been grouped together by Goebel.

Trends in Selling M 115, 116, 117
        TM6-7: $45-55 each
        TM5: $47-55 each
        TM4: $55-65 each
        TM3: $60-70 each
        TM2: $80-95 each
        TM1: $135-170 each

BOY WITH TOOTHACHE

Mold No.: 217
Ref. No.: 827
Approx. Size: 5.5"
Copyright: 1951
Sculptor: A.Moeller
2-D Original: H 257
1995 Retail: $210

Boy With Toothache
has been in steady pro-
duction since introduction and can be found in all
trademarks except TM1.

Trends in Selling TM6-7: $170-210
          TM5: $185-210
          TM4: $205-240
          TM3: $230-270
          TM2: $310-385

BUILDER

Mold No.: 305
Ref. No.: 810
Approx. Size: 5.5"
Copyright: 1955
Sculptor: G.Skrobek
2-D Original: Unknown
1995 Retail: $245

Though bearing a 1955
copyright date, **Builder**
was not introduced until
1963 just before Goebel's switch to TM4. It is very
scarce in TM3.

Trends in Selling TM6-7: $195-245
          TM5: $210-245
          TM4: $240-285
          TM3: $610-725

BROTHER

Mold No.: 95
Ref. No.: 911
Approx. Size: 5.5"
Copyright: 1938
Sculptor: n.a.
2-D Original: Unknown
1995 Retail: $200

Older examples of
Brother can be found
with the normal varia-
tions in size, molding
and color. However, none affect current values.

Trends in Selling TM6-7: $160-200
          TM5: $170-200
          TM4: $200-235
          TM3: $220-260
          TM2: $280-330
          TM1: $415-515

BUST OF SISTER HUMMEL

Mold No.: HU1, HU2, HU3
Ref. No.: n.a.
Approx. Size: 13" & 5.5"
Copyright: 1965, 1967 & 1978
Sculptor: G.Skrobek
2-D Original: n.a.
1995 Retail: Closed Edition

The **Bust of Sister Hummel** is *not* a true "Hummel."
That is, this figurine is not based on artwork
originally done by Sister Hummel. Rather, it is a
Gerhard Skrobek creation designed to honor and
promote Sister Hummel and her art. Perhaps for
this reason, the bust was slow to gain complete
acceptance when the colored version (HU3) was
issued in 1979 as the third annual club-exclusive

figurine available only to members of the M.I. Hummel Club. Throughout most of the 1980s, it was depressed in value compared to the other Club issues, frequently trading at close to its issue price of $75. In the 1990s, it has escalated in value and popularity and, deservedly, has gained a place alongside the other prestigious Club pieces. Both the HU1 and HU2 versions are white bisque and preceded the colored Club version on the market. The HU1 mold is about 13 inches tall. It was sparsely used as a special display piece to accent the M.I. Hummel line. The HU2 mold was a downsized version offered to the public in the late 1960s and again circa 1977.

Trends in Selling HU3 in TM5: $235-290
        HU2 in TM5: $70-90
        HU2 in TM4: $90-115
        HU1 in TM4: $1550-1900

CALL TO GLORY

Mold No.: 739/I
Ref. No.: 103
Approx. Size: 5.75"
Copyright: 1992
Sculptor: H.Fischer
2-D Original: n.a.
1995 Retail: $250

The little fellow in **Call to Glory** comes ready to be a patriot for a variety of countries. Goebel has equipped him with three authentic flags representing the United States, Germany and Europe, though only one at a time may be displayed. In its requirement for a "prop" for display, it is unusual among M.I. Hummel figurines. The figurine was one of the 1994 introductions.

Trends in Selling TM7: $200-250

BUSY STUDENT

Mold No.: 367
Ref. No.: 757
Approx. Size: 4.25"
Copyright: 1963
Sculptor: n.a.
2-D Original: H 193
1995 Retail: $160

Busy Student is somewhat scarce—and comparatively pricey—in TM3 due to being first produced just before the transition to TM4.

Trends in Selling: TM6-7: $130-160
        TM5: $135-160
        TM4: $155-185
        TM3: $565-665

BUSY STUDENT ANNUAL BELL

(See 1988 Annual Bell)

TERMS OF AVAILABILITY

The following terms are commonly used to describe the status of the various models of M.I. Hummel figurines:

Open Edition. The item is being produced in accordance with the real or perceived market demand.

Closed Edition. The item will no longer be produced. The term applies especially to limited edition or limited production pieces after the announced production limit has been achieved.

Retired. The item, otherwise not limited, has been permanently removed from production.

Temporarily Withdrawn. The item has been removed from production, but may again be produced at some future time, specified or unspecified.

Production Suspended. This means exactly the same thing as temporarily withdrawn.

Out of Production. This is synonymous with each of the four preceding terms. Additionally, it is sometimes used to refer to time lapses in the production of models which might otherwise have officially had *open edition* status.

CALL TO WORSHIP CLOCK
Mold No.: 441
Ref. No.: 300
Approx. Size: 13"
Copyright: 1983
Sculptor: G.Skrobek
2-D Original: H 477
1995 Retail: T.W.

After the success of *Chapel Time Clock* in 1986, Goebel probably couldn't wait to introduce **Call to Worship Clock** two years later as its third annual *Century Collection* issue. Though produced just for the one year in the twentieth century, the clock has enjoyed steady high demand in the secondary market and is traded on a day-to-day basis. A special bottom stamp reads, "M.I. Hummel Century Collection 1988 XX." The XX is found on each of the *Century Collection* issues to permanently distinguish these special issues. Issue price was $600 in 1988.

Trends in Selling TM6: $800-1000

CANDLELIGHT CANDLEHOLDER
Mold No.: 192
Ref. No.: 537
Approx. Size: 6.75"
Copyright: 1948
Sculptor: R.Unger
Restyled by:
    T.Menzenbach
2-D Original: H 412
1995 Retail: $230

Candlelight Candleholder, in the original model by Unger (Var. I), incorporates a ceramic candle as tall as the child. The restyled version deleted the portion of the candle which extended from the bottom of the angel's hands almost to the shoes (Var. II). Both varieties can be found in TM3. Earlier examples will be Var. I and more recent examples Var. II. TM1 examples are quite scarce.

Trends in Selling TM6-7: $185-230
            TM5: $195-230
            TM4: $220-260
    Var. I in TM3: $255-300
    Var. II in TM3: $355-430
            TM2: $515-610
            TM1: $975-1215

CARNIVAL
Mold No.: 328
Ref. No.: 789
Approx. Size: 6"
Copyright: 1955 & 1957
Sculptor: R.Unger &
    H.Wehlte
2-D Original: H 265
1995 Retail: $215

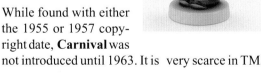

While found with either the 1955 or 1957 copyright date, **Carnival** was not introduced until 1963. It is very scarce in TM3.

Trends in Selling TM6-7: $175-215
            TM5: $185-215
            TM4: $210-245
            TM3: $1000-1175

CELESTIAL MUSICIAN

Mold No.: 188
Copyright: 1948
Sculptor: R.Unger
2-D Original: H 441

Model No.: 188/I
Ref. No.: 523
Approx. Size: 7"
1995 Retail: T.W

Model No.: 188/0
Ref. No.: 524
Approx. Size: 5.25"
Copyright: 1982
Sculptor: G.Skrobek & M. Mueller
1995 Retail: $215

Model No.: 188 4/0
Ref. No.: 154
Approx. Size: 3.125"
Copyright: 1991
Sculptor: G.Skrobek
1995 Retail: $90

Introduced at the end of the TM1 era, **Celestial Musician** was a popular 7-inch figurine marked mold 188 for 35 years. In 1983, the new, smaller 188/0 was introduced and the 7-inch size became 188/I. At the onset of 1993, model 188/I was withdrawn from production and the even smaller 188 4/0 was added to the market as part of the "holiday group" for that year. The large model is scarce in TM1, and it likely will prove to be a difficult find in TM7.

Trends in Selling M 188/I TM7: $240-285
TM6: $215-270
TM5: $230-270
TM4: $265-310
TM3: $295-350
TM2: $425-515
TM1: $750-940

Trends in Selling M 188/0 TM6-7: $175-215

Trends in Selling M 188 4/0 TM7: $70-90

CELESTIAL MUSICIAN ARS CHRISTMAS PLATE
(See 1987 ARS Christmas Plate)

CELESTIAL MUSICIAN CHRISTMAS BELL
(See 1993 Christmas Bell)

CELESTIAL MUSICIAN MINIATURE ORNAMENT

Mold No.: 646
Ref. No.: 152
Approx. Size: 2.785"
Copyright: 1991
Sculptor: H.Fischer
2-D Original: H 441
1995 Retail: $100

The *Celestial Musician* motif was used in 1993 to introduce the first of four annual "holiday groups." This one consisted of the *1993 Celestial Musician Christmas Bell*, the new M 188 4/0 *Celestial Musician* figurine, and **Celestial Musician Miniature Ornament**, the first of its kind. Unlike *Herald on High*, the *1993 Annual Ornament*, this and other miniature ornaments are not limited to year of issue.

Trends in Selling TM7: $80-100

CELESTIAL MUSICIAN ORNAMENT (WHITE)
(See chapter *The Other Hummels*)

CHAPEL TIME CLOCK
Mold No.: 442
Ref. No.: 420
Approx. Size: 11.5"
Copyright: 1983
Sculptor: G.Skrobek
2-D Original: H 377
1995 Retail: T.W.

Chapel Time Clock would certainly rank today as one of the five most avidly sought M.I. Hummel issues in the secondary market. It is also one of the most interesting. It's the first Hummel clock. It's a large piece with lots of appeal. It's the first issue in the highly successful *Century Collection*, in which Goebel, beginning in 1986, has annually issued a spectacular new creation "to be offered only this year in the Twentieth Century." Finally, it has been found in several varieties. The original variation (Variety I) is identified by closed, painted windows in the bell tower. Another variation (Variety II) is identified by open windows in *both* the bell tower and in the gable (small round hole above the clock face). The third and most common variation (Variety III) is identified by open windows in the bell tower and closed, painted windows in the gable (small round hole above the clock face). These changes probably occurred as Goebel experimented with the right combination to best permit the escape of kiln gases. Issue price was $500 in 1986.
Trends in Selling Var. I TM6: $2400-3000

Var. II: $2800-3500
Var. III: $1300-1600

CHEEKY FELLOW
Mold No.: 554
Ref. No.: 172
Approx. Size: 4"
Copyright: 1989
Sculptor: H.Fischer
2-D Original: H 352
1995 Retail: T.W.

Cheeky Fellow was issued in 1992 to introduce a new concept within the family of M.I. Hummel figurines. Pieces produced from mid-1992 through May 31, 1994, were offered at $120 and given a special stamp identifying each as a *Preview Edition*. These preview edition examples were made available only to active members of the M.I. Hummel Club. The figurine *could* be released for general sale again, but without the special *Preview Edition* stamp. As of this writing, there has been no indication that Goebel intends to reintroduce the figurine in the immediate future. The bet is that the special stamp and designation will elevate the demand of the preview edition figurines and give the line another built-in annual winner.

Trends in Selling TM7: $150-190

CHICK GIRL
Mold No.: 57
Copyright: 1936
Sculptor: R.Unger
Restyled by: G.Skrobek
2-D Original: H 371

Model No.: 57/I
Ref. No.: 942
Approx. Size: 4.25"
1995 Retail: $275

Model No.: 57/0
Ref. No.: 943
Approx. Size: 3.5"
1995 Retail: $165

Model No.: 57 2/0
Ref. No.: 417
Approx. Size: 3.25"
Copyright: 1984
1995 Retail: $145

Another of the all-time favorites, **Chick Girl** appears as a candy box, a music box, a bookend, an annual plate, and as a figurine in three sizes. The number of chicks in the basket will vary (two or three) depending upon the size of the figurine. No important varieties are known, but early pieces of model 57/I marked 57 (without size suffix) can command small premiums. It was created to be a companion piece to *Playmates* and is often found paired with this figurine. The small model 57 2/0 was one of the 1985 introductions.

Trends in Selling M 57/I TM6-7: $220-275
        TM5: $235-275
        TM4: $270-320
        TM3: $300-355
        TM2: $385-455
        TM1: $600-750

Trends in Selling M 57/0 TM6-7: $135-165
        TM5: $140-165
        TM4: $160-190
        TM3: $180-210
        TM2: $230-270
        TM1: $370-460

Trends in Selling M 57 2/0 TM6-7: $120-145

CHICK GIRL ANNUAL PLATE
(See 1985 Annual Plate)

CHICK GIRL BOOKEND
(See Playmates & Chick Girl Bookends)

CHICK GIRL CANDY BOX
Mold No.: III/57
Ref. No.: 667
Approx. Size: 6.25"
Copyright: 1936
Sculptor: n.a.
2-D Original: H 371
1995 Retail: T.W.

Originally given a bowl shape (Var. I), the container was redesigned to a box shape in 1964 at the onset of the TM4 era (Var. II). Some of the Variety II pieces bear the TM3 stamp. The box was withdrawn from production at the end of 1989.

Trends in Selling TM6: $145-180
        TM5: $155-180
        TM4: $175-210
    Var. I in TM3: $350-430
    Var. II in TM3: $250-315
        TM2: $425-530
        TM1: $525-650

GIFTS FOR NEW MEMBERS

The Hummel figurine *I Brought You a Gift* is given to each new member of the M.I. Hummel Club as a perk for joining the club. The figurine has been used for this purpose since club year 1989–90, which was also the year in which the club changed its name from Goebel Collectors' Club.

Prior to 1989—and dating to the founding of the club in 1977—the free gift for a new membership was a round white bisque plaque featuring the *Merry Wanderer* motif in bas-relief. Several variations were used.

CHICK GIRL MUSIC BOX
Mold No.: 324
Ref. No.: 6434
Approx. Size: 6.25" x 4.5"
Copyright: 1987
Sculptor: G.Skrobek
2-D Original: H 371
1995 Retail: Closed Edition

From 1987 through 1990, Goebel used the services of the famed Anri woodcarving firm in Italy and the famed Reuge music movement firm in Switzerland to produce a four-year, annual series of collector-quality music boxes. The theme was *Four Seasons*. The **Chick Girl Music Box** was the 1988, second issue in the series and represented spring of the four seasons. The bas-relief rendition of the *Chick Girl* motif was sculpted by Goebel master Gerhard Skrobek, and the painting was executed in accordance with the specifications of Goebel master painter Gunther Neubauer. However, actual execution of the production artwork in the form of a painted woodcarving was done by Anri artisans. The 36-note musical movement is a Romance movement by Reuge. The box was a worldwide limited edition of 10,000 pieces, and each music box is individually numbered. This number appears—along with the Goebel backstamp—on a special plaque attached to the underside of the lid. The box is now somewhat difficult to locate on the secondary market. Issue price was $400 in 1988.

Trends in Selling TM6: $400-500

CHICKEN LICKEN
Mold No.: 385
Copyright: 1971
Sculptor: G.Skrobek
2-D Original: H 376

Model No.: 385
Ref. No.: 741
Approx. Size: 4.75"
1995 Retail: $285

Model No.: 385 4/0
Ref. No.: 216
Copyright: 1987
Approx. Size: 3.125"
1995 Retail: $100

Chicken Licken was introduced in 1972 and, like the other introductions of that year, is scarce in TM4. The mini version, M 385 4/0, was added in 1987.

Trends in Selling M 385 TM6-7: $230-285
  TM5: $245-285
  TM4: $975-1150

Trends in Selling M 385 4/0 TM7: $80-100
  TM6: $100-120

CHICKEN LICKEN MINI PLATE
(See 1991 Mini Plate)

CHILD IN BED PLAQUE
Mold No.: 137
Ref. No.: 689
Approx. Size: 2.5 x 2.75"
Copyright: 1940
Sculptor: A.Moeller
2-D Original: H 104
1995 Retail: $65

Older examples of this plaque bear the mold number 137/B, but this has no bearing on value.

Trends in Selling TM6-7: $55-65
  TM5: $60-65
  TM4: $65-75
  TM3: $85-100
  TM2: $125-155
  TM1: $255-330

CHILD JESUS FONT

Mold No.: 26
Copyright: 1935
Sculptor: R.Unger
2-D Original: H 498

Model No.: 26/I
Ref. No.: n.a.
Approx. Size: 6"

Model No.: 26/0
Ref. No.: 519
Approx. Size: 5"
1995 Retail: $40

The larger-size model of **Child Jesus Font** has not been produced since the TM3 era.

Trends in Selling M 26/I TM3: $180-225
       TM2: $225-280
       TM1: $270-340

Trends in Selling M 26/0 TM6-7: $32-40
       TM5: $35-40
       TM4: $40-46
       TM3: $45-52
       TM2: $90-110
       TM1: $180-225

CHILD WITH FLOWERS FONT

Mold No.: 36
Copyright: 1935
Sculptor: R.Unger
2-D Original:
  Unknown

Model No.: 36/0
Ref. No.: 515
Approx. Size: 4"
1995 Retail: $40

Model No.: 36/I
Ref. No.: n.a.
Approx. Size: 5"

The larger size cannot be found after TM3; it can, however, be found with or without size suffix in TM1. Examples without suffix bring a small premium.

Trends in Selling M 36/0 TM6-7: $32-40
       TM5: $35-40

TM4: $40-46
TM3: $45-52
TM2: $90-110
TM1: $180-225

Trends in Selling M 36/I:
       TM3: $135-170
       TM2: $200-250
       TM1: $250-315

CHIMNEY SWEEP

Mold No.: 12
Copyright: 1935
Sculptor: A.Moeller
2-D Original: H 261

Model No.: 12/I
Ref. No.: 974
Approx. Size: 5.5"
1995 Retail: $215

Model No.: 12 2/0
Ref. No.: 975
Approx. Size: 4"
1995 Retail: $120

Due to its popularity, **Chimney Sweep** has traditionally been manufactured in quantity. Therefore, there are many minor variations in production which do not affect value. There is a small premium for early examples of model 12/I marked without size suffix.

Trends in Selling M 12/I TM6-7: $175-215
       TM5: $185-215
       TM4: $300-355
       TM3: $300-355
       TM2: $300-355
       TM1: $455-565

Trends in Selling M 12 2/0 TM6-7: $95-120
       TM5: $100-120
       TM4: $120-140
       TM3: $135-160
       TM2: $170-200

CHRIST CHILD

Mold No.: 18
Ref. No.: 502
Approx. Size: 6 x 2"
Copyright: 1935
Sculptor: R.Unger
2-D Original: Unknown
1995 Retail: T.W.

Christ Child was withdrawn from production as of Jan. 1, 1991.

Trends in Selling TM6: $100-130
        TM5: $110-130
        TM4: $125-150
        TM3: $140-170
        TM2: $180-215
        TM1: $295-365

CHRISTMAS ANGEL

Mold No.: 301
Ref. No.: 561
Approx. Size: 6.25"
Copyright: 1957
Sculptor:
   T.Menzenbach
Restyled by: G.Skrobek
2-D Original: H 442
1995 Retail: $250

Originally sculpted more than 30 years before, **Christmas Angel** was not released until 1989 after it had been restyled.

Trends in Selling TM6-7: $200-250

CHRISTMAS SONG

Mold No.: 343
Ref. No.: 547
Approx. Size: 6.5"
Copyright: 1957
Sculptor: G.Skrobek
2-D Original: H 453
1995 Retail: $215

Christmas Song was one of six new releases issued in 1981 after the onset of the TM6 era. Sculpted 25 years previously, it is rare if found in TM5 or earlier.

Trends in Selling TM6-7: $175-215

CINDERELLA

Mold No.: 337
Ref. No.: 780
Approx. Size: 4.5"
Copyright: 1958, 1960
  & 1972
Sculptor: A.Moeller
Restyled by: G.Skrobek
2-D Original: H 154
1995 Retail: $285

Bearing a 1958 or 1960 copyright date, Variety I pieces (Moeller) show **Cinderella** with eyes wide open. Shortly after its introduction in 1972, the figurine was restyled by Skrobek to the "modern" finish and eyes looking down. These Variety II pieces bear the 1972 copyright date. Both varieties can be found in TM5.

Trends in Selling TM6-7: $230-285
  Var. I in TM5: $850-1000
  Var. II in TM5: $240-285
      TM4: $1200-1500

NEW FOR 1984

The 1984 M.I. Hummel introductions consisted only of the club exclusive, *Coffee Break,* and the annual dated plate and bell.

CLOSE HARMONY

Mold No.: 336
Ref. No.: 781
Approx. Size: 5.5"
Copyright: 1955 & 1957
Sculptor: G.Skrobek
Restyled by: G.Skrobek
2-D Original: H 347
1995 Retail: $280

Introduced in 1963 just before the change to TM4, **Close Harmony** is very scarce in TM3.

Trends in Selling TM6-7: $230-285
       TM5: $240-285
       TM4: $280-330
       TM3: $785-925

CLUB MEMBER PLAQUE (WHITE)

Mold No.: n.a.
Ref. No.: n.a.
Approx. Size: 4" d.
2-D Original: H 228, F 202
1995 Retail: Closed Edition

This little M.I. Hummel collectible, featuring the *Merry Wanderer* motif in bas-relief, has been so unappreciated that it is not even mentioned in some of the major reference works. Actually, though, it holds a place of historical significance within the Hummel brand. From the initiation of the Goebel Collectors' Club in 1977 until the Goebel Collectors' Club became the M.I. Hummel Club on June 1, 1989, the **Club Member Plaque** was used continuously as a free gift for each *new* member joining the club. It was retired as of June 1, 1989. The production history of the plaque left three distinct varieties. Variety I, produced from 1977 to 1983, can be identified by a textured reverse side and the use of the stylized bee on the obverse side. Variety II, produced from 1983 to 1985, is conspicuous by the rays on the reverse side. Variety III has a half-circle rim on the reverse. All three varieties can be found in TM6. (Within Variety II, the plaque can be found in two different sizes caused by a change in production method from casting to pressing.)

Trends in Selling Var. I in TM5-6: $30-40
      Var. II in TM6: $25-35
      Var. III in TM6: $20-30

COFFEE BREAK

Mold No.: 409
Ref. No.: 470
Approx. Size: 4"
Copyright: 1976
Sculptor:
  G.Skrobek
2-D Original:
  H 270
1995 Retail:
  Closed Edition

Coffee Break was issued as the M.I. Hummel Club exclusive redemption figurine for the 1984–85 club year (June 1, 1984–May 31, 1985). It is number 8 in the club series and could originally be acquired only with a redemption certificate provided to each active club member. Issue price was $90.

Trends in Selling TM6: $190-225

COME BACK SOON

Mold No.: 545
Ref. No.: 054
Approx. Size: 4.25"
Copyright: 1989
Sculptor: H.Fischer
2-D Original: H 210
1995 Retail: $135

A Helmut Fischer design of 1989, **Come Back Soon** was released for 1995 as the figurine match to the historic *1995 Annual Plate*—historic as the 25th and final in what may be the most famous collector plate series of all time. Without doubt, the many who match figurine with plate in their collections welcomed this piece with the intended bit of nostalgia.

Trends in Selling TM7: $110-135

COME BACK SOON ANNUAL PLATE

(See 1995 Annual Plate)

CONFIDENTIALLY

Mold No.: 314
Ref. No.: 802
Approx. Size: 5.5"
Copyright: 1955 & 1972
Sculptor: H. Ashermann
Restyled by: G.Skrobek
2-D Original: H 254
1995 Retail: $285

Another from the large group introduced in 1972, **Confidentially** first appeared on the market in Ashermann's original version identified by the 1955 copyright date (Var. I). It was soon replaced with Skrobek's restyled version with a 1972 copyright date (Var. II). In the restyled version, the boy acquired a tie and the overall figurine was given the now-familiar textured finish. Prices reflect the scarcity of surviving examples of Variety I.

Trends in Selling TM6-7: $230-285
   Var. I. in TM5: $600-740
   Var. II in TM5: $240-285
     TM4: $950-1150

CONGRATULATIONS

Mold No.: 17
Copyright: 1935
Sculptor: R.Unger
Restyled by: G.Skrobek
2-D Original: H 454

Model No.: 17/0
Ref. No.: 964
Approx. Size: 6"
1995 Retail: $200

Model No.: 17/2
Ref. No.: n.a.
Approx. Size: 8.25"
1995 Retail: Closed
  Edition

The more common M 17/0 of **Congratulations** was given a major design change by Skrobek in 1971. Unger's original version lacked socks (Var. I). For Variety II, socks were added, the hairstyle was changed, and the finish was altered to the new, textured type. Due to the timing of Variety II, it is the scarce version in TM4 and TM3. The large size,

long retired, is rare and commands a high price when traded.

Trends in Selling M 17/0 in TM6-7: $160-200
     TM5: $170-200
  Var. I in TM4: $195-230
  Var. II in TM4: $280-330
  Var. I in TM3: $220-260
  Var. II in TM3: $280-330
     TM2: $280-330
     TM1: $510-635

Trends in Selling M 17/2:
     TM3: $2750-3450
     TM2: $3750-4700
     TM1: $4750-5950

COQUETTES

Mold No.: 179
Ref. No.: 852
Approx. Size: 5"
Copyright: 1948
Sculptor: A.Moeller
2-D Original: H 308
1995 Retail: $285

Coquettes can be found without major variation in all trademarks. However, it is comparatively scarce in TM1 due to its introduction shortly before the TM2 era.

Trends in Selling M 179/I TM6-7: $230-285
     TM5: $240-285
     TM4: $280-330
     TM3: $315-370
     TM2: $400-470
     TM1: $785-980

CROSSROADS

Mold No.: 331
Ref. No.: 786
Approx. Size: 6.75"
Copyright: 1955
Sculptor: A.Moeller
2-D Original: H 615
1995 Retail: $400

Crossroads has one of the most interesting histories of all the M.I. Hummel figurines. Originally modeled in 1955, it languished on the shelf for 17 years before becoming one of the 24 new introductions of 1972. Then it waited 18 more years before achieving great notoriety in 1990 by becoming the first *numbered limited edition* Hummel figurine—the Berlin Wall Commemorative with the halt sign down. Not only was the 20,000-piece limited edition an immediate sellout, it multiplied the demand for the regular version in all trademarks. Moreover, like the other 1972 releases, **Crossroads** is quite scarce and pricey in TM4.

In 1992, Goebel again used the figurine (regular version) as part of a three-piece vignette offered in limited edition form as the *Crossroads Military Commemorative*. In this version (Var. II), the figurine is fitted onto a wooden base alongside a casting representing a section of the Berlin Wall in miniature. A brass plaque is inscribed: "With esteem and grateful appreciation to the United States Military Forces for the preservation of peace and freedom." The *Military* Commemorative as a set was limited to 20,000 pieces worldwide and sold only at military base exchanges. The **Crossroads** figurine in it differs from the norm only in the addition of a special backstamp featuring the flags of the U.S. and Germany. Secondary market price range given is for the complete *Memorial*.

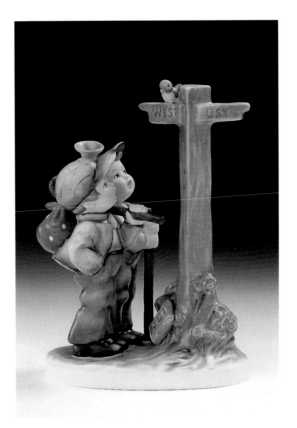

Trends in Selling TM6-7: $320-400
    Var. II in TM7: $600-750
      TM5: $340-400
      TM4: $900-1100

CROSSROADS BERLIN WALL COMMEMORATIVE
(Halt Sign Down Version)
Mold No.: 331
Ref. No.: 197
Approx. Size: 6.75
Copyright: 1955
Sculptor: A.Moeller
2-D Original: H 615
1995 Retail: Closed Edition

Despite sharing the 331 mold (Hum) number with the original *Crossroads* figurine, the **Crossroads Berlin Wall Commemorative** is treated here as a completely different figurine due to the limited edition status of the commemorative. When sold in 1990, it was the first-ever M.I. Hummel figurine

produced with an announced edition limit and an individual number. The edition limit, initially announced as 10,000 pieces, was changed to 20,000 prior to introduction. Even then, demand was such that the entire edition was an immediate sellout, and most retailers had to restrict customer purchase of the figurine in some fashion. Today, it remains one of the most popular Hummel figurines and is traded regularly on the secondary market. It commemorates the first anniversary of the tearing down of the wall dividing West and East Germany in 1989. The halt sign, nailed to a post in the original *Crossroads*, has been removed and is lying at the base of the post in the commemorative version. The figurine is also an example that scarcity is often a larger factor than age in building market value. As Goebel converted from TM6 to TM7 in 1990, it produced most of the **Crossroads Commemorative** pieces while the older trademark was still in use. Consequently, it is the more recent but less prevalent TM7 examples which command a premium. Issue price was $360.

Trends in Selling TM6: $900-1100
    TM7: $1150-1400

CULPRITS

Mold No.: 56/A
Ref. No.: 945
Approx. Size: 6.25"
Copyright: 1936
Sculptor: A.Moeller
2-D Original: H 330,
    F 223
1995 Retail: $290

Culprits pieces made before the early 1950s introduction of its companion figurine, *Out of Danger*, will not have the */A* designator in the mold number. In older examples, the eyes are open. In newer, restyled examples, the eyes are closed. This variation does not affect values.

Trends in Selling TM6-7: $235-290
            TM5: $245-290
            TM4: $285-335
            TM3: $320-375
            TM2: $405-480
            TM1: $730-910

CULPRITS LAMP BASE

Mold No.: 44/A
Ref. No.: 653
Approx. Size: 9.5"
Copyright: 1935
Sculptor: A.Moeller
2-D Original: H 330,
    F 223
1995 Retail: T.W.

OUT OF DANGER LAMP BASE

Mold No.: 44/B
Ref. No.: 652
Approx. Size: 9.5"
Copyright: 1936
Sculptor: A.Moeller
2-D Original: Unknown
1995 Retail: T.W.

As indicated by the mold number they share, these lamp bases have always been paired together by Goebel. Note by the copyright dates that **Culprits**

Lamp Base was apparently produced for about a year before the introduction of the **Out of Danger Lamp Base**. This explains the occasional **Culprits** base found without the */A* mold suffix. These command a premium of about 30% above the TM1 value. Both lamp bases were produced until Jan. 1, 1990, when Goebel withdrew all lamp base designs from production.

Trends in Selling TM6: $290-360 each
            TM5: $305-360 each
            TM4: $350-415 each
            TM3: $400-470 each
            TM2: $435-515 each
            TM1: $490-610 each

DADDY'S GIRLS

Mold No.: 371
Ref. No.: 753
Approx. Size: 4.75"
Copyright: 1964
Sculptor: G.Skrobek
2-D Original: H 219,
    F 208
1995 Retail: $225

Though bearing a 1964 copyright date, **Daddy's Girls** was not introduced until 1989. It may eventually prove to be comparatively hard to find in TM6.

Trends in Selling TM6-7: $180-225

DAISIES DON'T TELL

Mold No.: 380
Ref. No.: 746
Approx. Size: 4.5"
Copyright: 1972
Sculptor:
    G.Skrobek
2-D Original: Fink
    Card 651
1995 Retail:
    Closed Edition

Daisies Don't Tell was issued as the M.I. Hummel Club exclusive redemption figurine for the

1981–82 club year (June 1, 1981–May 31, 1982). It is number 5 in the club exclusive series and could originally be acquired only with a redemption certificate provided to each active club member. Issue price was $80.

Trends in Selling TM6: $235-285

DAISIES DON'T TELL PLATE
Mold No.: 736
Ref. No.: 302
Size: 6.25" d.
Copyright: 1985
Sculptor:
　G.Skrobek
2-D Orig.: Fink
　Card 651
1995 Retail:
　Closed Edition

Issued in 1988 exclusively for purchase by members of the M.I. Hummel Club (club year beginning June 1, 1988, and ending May 31, 1989), **Daisies Don't Tell Plate** was the third issue in the four-year *Celebration Plate Series*. Plates in the series are based on motifs previously used for club exclusive figurines, are executed in bas-relief, and were supplied with presentation boxes. Issue price was $115.

Trends in Selling TM6: $120-150

DEALER DISPLAY PLAQUES
Mold Nos.: 187 & 460
Copyright: 1947 & 1976
Sculptor: R.Unger
Restyled by: G.Skrobek

Model No.: 187
Ref. No.: 238
Approx. Size: 5.5" x 4"
2-D Original: H 228, F 202
1995 Retail: Retired

Model No.: 460
Ref. No.: 402
Approx. Size: 5" x 6"

Copyright: 1984
2-D Original: H 198
1995 Retail: $120

Model No.: 187/A
Ref. No.: 238
Approx. Size: 5.5" x 4"
1995 Retail: $100

Reintroduced at the beginning of 1995, the mold 460 plaque features what later became the figurine *One Plus One*. Known as *The Tally Plaque,* it was distributed in the last half of the 1980s before being shelved at the end of 1989. The mold 187 and mold 187/A plaques feature slightly different versions of *Merry Wanderer*. Used both prior to and after *The Tally*

Plaque—and now concurrently with—both can be found in trademarks 5 and 6, but only 187/A can be found in trademark 7. At times, the plaques have been inscribed for the collector (187/C). Plaques have been designed for sale in countries other than the U.S. (the mold 460 plaque for Germany is pictured here) and for special purposes. These scarcer examples have an avid following among advanced collectors and command premiums which are sometimes quite steep.

Trends in Selling M 187 and M 187/A:
　　　TM7: $80-100
　　　TM6: $85-130
　　　TM5: $120-150
　　　TM4: $320-400
　　　TM3: $355-475
　　　TM2: $535-665
　　　TM1: $650-800

Trends in Selling M 460 TM7: $95-120
　　　　　　　　TM6: $150-200

DOCTOR

Mold No.: 127
Ref. No.: 893
Approx. Size: 4.75"
Copyright: 1939
Sculptor: A.Moeller
2-D Original: H 256
1995 Retail: $155

This is another of the perennial favorites which has had a long, successful run in the marketplace. It can be found with a number of minor color and mold variations. None materially affect the values. However, **Doctor** is rare—possibly nonexistent—in TM4.

Trends in Selling TM6-7: $125-155
          TM5: $135-155
          TM4: $215-255
          TM3: $170-200
          TM2: $215-255
          TM1: $400-500

DOCTOR ANNUAL PLATE

(See 1994 Annual Plate)

DOLL BATH

Mold No.: 319
Ref. No.: 797
Approx. Size: 5"
Copyright: 1956
Sculptor: G.Skrobek
2-D Original: H 230,
  F 221
1995 Retail: $285

Doll Bath was introduced in 1962 shortly before the phase-in period to TM4. It is, therefore, quite scarce and pricey in TM3. It was restyled to the modern, textured finish in the early 1970s. A textured example bearing TM4 would be a rare find.

Trends in Selling TM6-7: $230-285
          TM5: $240-285
          TM4: $280-330
          TM3: $850-1025

DOLL BATH ANNUAL PLATE

(See 1993 Annual Plate)

DOLL MOTHER

Mold No.: 67
Ref. No.: 934
Approx. Size: 4.75"
Copyright: 1937
Sculptor: A.Moeller
2-D Original: H 164
1995 Retail: $210

Produced during all trademark periods, **Doll Mother** can be found with an assortment of minor color and mold variations which do not affect values.

Trends in Selling TM6-7: $170-210
          TM5: $180-210
          TM4: $205-240
          TM3: $235-275
          TM2: $295-345
          TM1: $545-680

DUET

Mold No.: 130
Ref. No.: 890
Approx. Size: 5"
Copyright: 1939
Sculptor:
  A.Moeller
2-D Original:
  H 284
1995 Retail: $280

Near the end of 1994, **Duet** was announced as the seventh in the annual series of ceremonial retirements of long-running M.I. Hummel figurines— all molds for the piece to be broken at the end of 1995. Examples sold during the year bear a special backstamp reading "Last Issue 1995." Two important mold variations have been found in **Duet,** which is composed of *Street Singer* (left) and *Soloist* (right). Within TM1, earliest pieces (Var. I) were made with incised musical notes on the sheet music and with a contoured base. Variety II pieces have only painted notes on the sheet music and a squared-off base. A very scarce Variety III exists in TM2 and TM3 in which *Street Singer* is without bow tie. (*Soloist* is without tie in all varieties.)

Trends in Selling TM6-7: $225-280
        TM5: $240-280
        TM4: $275-325
     Var. II in TM3: $305-360
     Var. III in TM3: $2000-2500
     Var. II in TM2: $390-460
     Var. III in TM2: $2000-2500
     Var. I in TM1: $1040-1300
     Var. II in TM1: $720-900

EASTER GREETINGS

Mold No.: 378
Ref. No.: 748
Approx. Size: 5.25"
Copyright: 1971
Sculptor: G.Skrobek
2-D Original: H 379
1995 Retail: $200

Easter Greetings, as one of the 1972 intro- ductory pieces, is very scarce in TM4.

Trends in Selling TM6-7: $160-200
        TM5: $170-200
        TM4: $850-1000

EASTER TIME

Mold No.: 384
Ref. No.: 742
Approx. Size: 4"
Copyright: 1971 ·
Sculptor: G.Skrobek
2-D Original: H 370, F 652
1995 Retail: $250

Easter Time is very scarce in TM4 due to its 1972 introduction at the onset of the TM5 era.

Trends in Selling TM6-7: $200-250
        TM5: $210-250
        TM4: $820-965

EVENING PRAYER

Mold No.: 495
Ref. No.: 191
Approx. Size: 4"
Copyright: 1988
Sculptor: H.Fischer
2-D Original: H 164
1995 Retail: $105

Evening Prayer was one of the new releases for 1992. It exemplifies Goebel's effort during this period to downscale the size—and thus the cost—of many M.I. Hummel figurines.

Trends in Selling TM7: $85-105

EVENTIDE

Mold No.: 99
Ref. No.: 906
Approx. Size: 4.75 x 7.25"
Copyright: 1938
Sculptor: n.a.
2-D Original: H 383
1995 Retail: $325

Despite its relatively high price, the serenity and complexity of **Even- tide** have given the figurine enduring popularity. It can be found with many slight color, mold, and size variations which do not affect the value, except for a pair of early molding varieties. One moves the lambs to the opposite side of the base, and the other omits the lambs altogether. These varieties, if found, command premiums of about 250% of the normal TM1 price.

Trends in Selling TM6-7: $260-325
        TM5: $275-325
        TM4: $320-375
        TM3: $360-425
        TM2: $455-535
        TM1: $840-1050

FAREWELL

Mold No.: 65
Ref. No.: 936
Approx. Size: 4.75"
Copyright: 1937
Sculptor: A.Moeller
Restyled by: G.Skrobek
2-D Original: H 310
1995 Retail: Retired

Continuing a tradition begun with *Puppy Love* (Hum 1) in 1988, molds were broken and **Farewell** was officially retired at the end of 1993. Through the years, **Farewell** was marked with and without the */I* suffix, and it can be found marked *65* and *65/ I* in most early trademarks. Size may vary from 4.5 to 5 inches. A smaller model, 65/0, was created in the mid-1950s, but was never put into production; the few surviving prototypes are extreme rarities. There are two varities of the figurine within TM6. Some pieces in the early 1980s were assembled so that the handle of the basket appears incomplete. This "missing handle" variation (Var. II) commands a modest premium.

Trends in Selling TM6-7: $235-285
    Var. II in TM6: $300-350
        TM5: $265-310
        TM4: $275-325
        TM3: $315-380
        TM2: $390-460
        TM1: $660-825

FAREWELL ANNUAL BELL

(See 1979 Annual Bell)

LOOK-ALIKE CONTESTS

If you have a fondness for Hummel figurines or cute little children, or both, you'll want to make a special effort to attend any of the M.I. Hummel *look-alike contests* you can possibly attend. Ask anyone who's been; they'll promise you a warm and memorable experience.

FARM BOY

Mold No.: 66
Ref. No.: 935
Approx. Size: 5"
Copyright: 1937
Sculptor:
  A.Moeller
2-D Original:
  Unknown
1995 Retail: $225

Farm Boy can be found in all trademarks with the normal minor variations characteristic of nearly all long-running M.I. Hummel figurines.

Trends in Selling TM6-7: $180-225
        TM5: $190-225
        TM4: $215-255
        TM3: $245-290
        TM2: $315-370
        TM1: $585-730

FARM BOY ANNUAL PLATE

(See 1989 Annual Plate)

FARM BOY BOOKEND

(See Goose Girl & Farm Boy Bookends)

FAVORITE PET

Mold No.: 361
Ref. No.: 761
Approx. Size: 4.25"
Copyright: 1960
Sculptor:
  T.Menzenbach
2-D Original: H 375
1995 Retail: $285

Introduced in 1964 during Goebel's transition from TM3 to TM4, **Favorite Pet** is accordingly difficult to find and expensive in TM3.

Trends in Selling TM6-7: $230-285
        TM5: $240-285
        TM4: $280-330
        TM3: $975-1175

FAVORITE PET ANNUAL BELL
(See 1991 Annual Bell)

FEATHERED FRIENDS
Mold No.: 344
Ref. No.: 774
Approx. Size: 4.75"
Copyright: 1956
Sculptor: G.Skrobek
2-D Original: H 157
1995 Retail: $275

Another of the 24 new releases of 1972, **Feathered Friends** is available but quite scarce and expensive in TM4.

Trends in Selling TM6-7: $220-275
TM5: $230-275
TM4: $940-1140

RECAP OF RETIRED HUMMELS

In 1988, Goebel began retiring on an annual basis an M.I. Hummel mold number which had long been in existence.

The retirements have been well received by collectors. They have helped create interest in the line, and they have served to provide a fanfare-type send-off to models which were beginning to get "lost in the shuffle," so to speak.

Beginning with *Signs of Spring* in 1990, each retiring figurine has been given a special backstamp in its last full year on the market. The stamp, placed inside an oval, reads: "Final Issue...Letzte Ausgabe..." plus year of retirement.

The retirements, in sequential order:

Name	Mold	Introd.	Ret'mt
Puppy Love	1	1935	1988
Strolling Along	5	1935	1989
Signs of Spring	203	1948	1990
Globe Trotter	79	1937	1991
Lost Sheep	68	1937	1992
Farewell	65	1937	1993
Accordion Boy	185	1947	1994
Duet	130	1939	1995

FEEDING TIME
Mold No.: 199
Copyright: 1948
Sculptor: A.Moeller
Restyled by: G.Skrobek
2-D Original: H 236

Model No.: 199/I
Ref. No.: 835
Approx. Size: 5.5"
1995 Retail: $275

Model No.: 199/0
Ref. No.: 836
Approx. Size: 4.25"
1995 Retail: $195

The size suffix was added to the larger model of **Feeding Time** when the smaller model was introduced in the mid-1950s. TM2 examples without the suffix command a small premium. TM1 examples are all without suffix, but are relatively scarce in any case due to introduction late in the TM1 era. Skrobek's redesign of the mid-1960s (Var. II) gave the girl her current look—smiling with head tilted—and altered her hair. In Moeller's original design (Var. I), the girl has blonde hair and is looking straight ahead with a neutral expression. Both varieties can be found in TM4.

Trends in Selling M 199/I TM6-7: $220-275
TM5: $230-275
Var. I in TM4: $300-350
Var. II in TM4: $270-315
TM3: $300-350
TM2: $380-445
TM1: $835-1040

Trends in Selling M 199/0 TM6-7: $155-195
TM5: $165-195
Var. I in TM4: $215-255
Var. II in TM4: $185-220
TM3: $215-255
TM2: $320-380

FEEDING TIME ANNUAL PLATE
(See 1987 Annual Plate)

FEEDING TIME BOOKEND
(See Little Goat Herder Bookend)

FESTIVAL HARMONY W/FLUTE

Mold No.: 173
Copyright: 1947
2-D Original: H 459

Model No.: 173/II
Ref. No.: 541
Approx. Size: 11"
Sculptor: R.Unger
1995 Retail: T.W.

Model No.: 173/0
Ref. No.: 542
Approx. Size: 8"
Sculptor:
   T.Menzenbach
1995 Retail: $310

Model No. 173 4/0
Ref. No.: 045
Approx. Size: 3.125"
Sculptor: G.Skrobek
Copyright: 1991
1995 Retail: $100

When first modeled, **Festival Harmony with Flute** was given a large bird and a large flower, which extended almost halfway up the gown (Var. I). In the early 1950s, it was simplified by downsizing both the bird and the flower, which then extended to just above the bottom of the gown (Var. II). Prior to 1970, it was given another design change to add a textured finish, and the flower no longer reached past the gown (Var. III). The large size was withdrawn from production at the end of 1984. All Variety I examples are rare, even though this is the only variety produced during the TM1 era. Due to its introduction in the early 1960s, the smaller M 173/0 is relatively scarce in TM3. Model 173 4/0 was introduced as part of the M.I. Hummel "holiday group" of 1995 and became the smallest offering of this design.

Trends in Selling M 173/II TM6: $340-425
            TM5: $360-425
            TM4: $415-490
        Var. II in TM3: $700-850
        Var. III in TM3: $460-550
        Var. I in TM2: $1900-2300
        Var. II in TM2: $950-1150
            TM1: $2275-2850

Trends in Selling M 173/0 TM6-7: $250-310
            TM5: $265-310
            TM4: $305-355
            TM3: $445-525

Trends in Selling M 173 4/0 TM7: $80-100

FESTIVAL HARMONY W/FLUTE CHRISTMAS BELL
(See 1995 Christmas Bell)

FESTIVAL HARMONY W/FLUTE MINIATURE ORNAMENT

Mold No.: 648
Ref. No.: 043
Approx. Size: 2.875"
Copyright: 1991
Sculptor: H.Fischer
2-D Original: H 459
1995 Retail: $100

With the new, mini size *Festival Harmony with Flute* figurine and the *Festival Harmony with Flute* Christmas bell, the 1995 **Festival Harmony with Flute Miniature Ornament** completed the third in a series of four annual holiday groupings planned by Goebel. The first, 1993 group was based on the *Celestial Musician* motif. The miniature ornament is not dated or limited.

Trends in Selling TM7: $80-100

FESTIVAL HARMONY W/FLUTE ORN. (WHITE)
(See chapter *The Other Hummels)*

FESTIVAL HARMONY W/MANDOLIN

Mold No.: 172
Copyright: 1947
2-D Original: H 458

Model No.: 172/II
Ref. No.: 543
Approx. Size: 10.75"
Sculptor: R.Unger
1995 Retail: T.W.

Model No.: 172/0
Ref. No.: 544
Approx. Size: 8"
Sculptor:
   T.Menzenbach
1995 Retail: $310

Model No. 172 4/0
Ref. No.: 107
Approx. Size: 3.125"
Sculptor: H.Fischer
Copyright: 1991
1995 Retail: $95

When first modeled, **Festival Harmony with Mandolin** was given a large flower with bird which extended almost halfway up the gown (Var. I). In the early 1950s, it was modified by placing the bird on the mandolin and downsizing the flower, which then extended to just above the bottom of the gown (Var. II). Prior to 1970, it was given another design change to add a textured finish, and the flower no longer reached past the gown (Var. III). The large size was withdrawn from production at the end of 1984. All Variety I examples are rare, even though this is the only variety produced during the TM1 era. Due to its introduction in the early 1960s, the smaller M 172/0 is relatively scarce in TM3. Model 172 4/0 was introduced as part of the M.I. Hummel "holiday group" of 1994 and became the smallest offering of this design.

Trends in Selling M 172/II TM6: $340-425
       TM5: $360-425
       TM4: $415-490
     Var. II in TM3: $700-850
     Var. III in TM3: $460-550
     Var. I in TM2: $1900-2300
     Var. II in TM2: $950-1150
       TM1: $2275-2850

Trends in Selling M 172/0 TM6-7: $250-310
       TM5: $265-310
       TM4: $305-355
       TM3: $445-525

Trends in Selling M 172 4/0 TM7: $75-95

FESTIVAL HARMONY W/MANDOLIN CHRISTMAS BELL
(See 1994 Christmas Bell)

FESTIVAL HARMONY W/MANDOLIN MINIATURE ORNAMENT

Mold No.: 647
Ref. No.: 106
Approx. Size: 2.875"
Copyright: 1991
Sculptor: H.Fischer
2-D Original: H 458
1995 Retail: $100

With the new, mini size *Festival Harmony with Mandolin* figurine and the *Festival Harmony with Mandolin* Christmas bell, the 1994 **Festival Harmony with Mandolin Miniature Ornament** completed the second in a series of four annual holiday groupings planned by Goebel. The first, 1993 group was based on the *Celestial Musician* motif. The miniature ornament is not dated or limited.

Trends in Selling TM7: $80-100

FESTIVAL HARMONY W/MANDOLIN ORN. (WHITE)
(See chapter *The Other Hummels*)

NEW FOR 1994

The 1994 M.I. Hummel introductions were *We Come in Peace, Rock-a-Bye, Little Visitor, Little Troubadour, Honey Lover mini pendant, The Poet, Morning Stroll, I'm Carefree, Heavenly Angel tree topper, Call to Glory, Birthday Present,* a mini size of *Festival Harmony with Mandolin* and the 1994 annuals.

FLITTING BUTTERFLY PLAQUE

Mold No.: 139
Ref. No.: 688
Approx. Size: 2.5 x 2.5"
Copyright: 1940
Sculptor: A.Moeller
2-D Original: Unknown
1995 Retail: $65

Research indicates **Flitting Butterfly Plaque** could be rare or nonexistent in TM3 and TM4. It was reinstated circa 1978.

Trends in Selling TM6-7: $55-65
        TM5: $60-65
        TM4: $90-110
        TM3: $90-110
        TM2: $90-110
        TM1: $155-195

FLOWER GIRL

Mold No.: 548
Ref. No.: 240
Approx. Size: 4.5"
Copyright: 1989
Sculptor: H.Fischer
2-D Original: H 351
1995 Retail: $135

Flower Girl was copyrighted in 1989 and was introduced in mid-1990 as a special figurine available only to members of the M.I. Hummel Club who had completed five successive years of membership in the club. To impatient collectors who did not

qualify, the piece assumed immediate importance in the secondary market. To obtain the figurine at issue price through primary market channels, a person must have a redemption certificate issued only to qualified individuals. Due to the timing of its release, **Flower Girl** may prove to be exceedingly scarce in TM6. Issue price was $105 in 1990, but by mid-1995 price increases had taken retail (with redemption certificate) to $135.

Trends in Selling TM7: $135-205
        TM6: $180-225

FLOWER MADONNA

Mold No.: 10
Copyright: 1935
Sculptor: R.Unger
Restyled by: T.Menzenbach
2-D Original: H 548, F 218

Mold No.: 10/III
Ref. No.: 591 & 590
Approx. Size: 11"
1995 Retail: T.W.

Mold No.: 10/I
Ref. No.: 593 & 592

Approx. Size: 8.25"
1995 Retail: $430 (multicolored)

Both sizes of **Flower Madonna** have traditionally been offered in either a multicolored or white (ivory) glaze finish, but the 1995 price list offers only the single multicolored piece. In a major restyling by Menzenbach in 1956, both models were downsized and the halo was simplified—likely to cut production costs. Both varieties can therefore be found in TM2; the original, larger variety with detailed halo (Var. I) will command a premium. Rarely found without size suffix, the larger mold (10/III) was given "T.W." status in early 1982 and may prove to be scarce in TM6, especially in the white version; it is also thought to be a difficult find in TM4. Finally, some major variations in color of the madonna's cloak—from the normal pastel blue or white—were made in the early years of production. These examples can command premiums of 300% or more.

Trends in Selling M 10/III

	Color	White
TM6:	$460-545	$460-545
TM5:	$460-495	$295-350
TM4:	$575-700	$385-460
TM3:	$575-700	$385-460
Var. I in TM2:	$800-1000	$550-695
Var. II in TM2:	$750-900	$475-585
TM1:	$880-1100	$590-735

Trends in Selling M 10/I

	Color	White
TM6-7:	$345-430	$145-180
TM5:	$365-430	$155-180
TM4:	$420-495	$175-205
TM3:	$465-550	$195-230
Var. I in TM2:	$730-895	$290-340
Var. II in TM2:	$575-700	$245-290
TM1:	$825-1030	$345-430

1982 WITHDRAWALS

Temporarily withdrawn from production as of spring 1982 were the following figurines: *Flower Madonna* model 10/III, *Hello* model 124/I, *Madonna w/Halo* model 45/III, *Madonna w/o Halo* model 46/III, *Lullaby Candleholder* model 24/III and *Spring Dance* model 353/I.

FLOWER VENDOR
Mold No.: 381
Ref. No.: 745
Approx. Size: 5.25"
Copyright: 1971
Sculptor: G.Skrobek
2-D Original: H 208
1995 Retail: $245

Flower Vendor is another in the group of 1972 new releases, and, like the others, is difficult to find in TM4.

Trends in Selling TM6-7: $195-245
                TM5: $210-245
                TM4: $1000-1200

FLYING ANGEL
(See Nativity Sets)

FLYING HIGH ANNUAL ORNAMENT
(See 1988 Annual Ornament)

FOLLOW THE LEADER
Mold No.: 369
Ref. No.: 755
Approx. Size: 7"
Copyright: 1964
Sculptor: G.Skrobek
2-D Original: H 351
1995 Retail: $1200

Follow the Leader was the "big piece" among the 24 introductions of 1972. Like the others, it is quite scarce and pricey in TM4 due to Goebel's changeover to TM5 at the time.

Trends in Selling TM6-7: $960-1200
                TM5: $1000-1200
                TM4: $1750-2100

FOR FATHER

Mold No.: 87
Ref. No.: 916
Approx. Size: 5.5"
Copyright: 1938
Sculptor: A.Moeller
2-D Original: H 302
1995 Retail: $210

A favorite of many, this figure is carrying two of the primary symbols of Bavaria—a Bavarian-shaped beer stein and a bunch of the large white radishes. Like most pieces with low mold numbers, it can be found with minor variations in size, color and mold. There is a very rare "orange carrots" variation. Add about $2000 to the listed values for it, but be aware that color can be altered.

Trends in Selling TM6-7: $170-210
    TM5: $180-210
    TM4: $205-240
    TM3: $235-275
    TM2: $295-345
    TM1: $530-660

FOR FATHER PLATE
(See 1993 Friends Forever Plate)

FOR KEEPS

Mold No.: 630
Ref. No.: 102
Approx. Size: 3.5"
Copyright: 1992
Sculptor: H.Fischer
2-D Original:
 H 235
1995 Retail: $80
 value

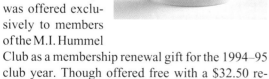

Available only in TM7, **For Keeps** was offered exclusively to members of the M.I. Hummel Club as a membership renewal gift for the 1994–95 club year. Though offered free with a $32.50 renewal membership in the club, Goebel valued the figurine at $80 retail.

Trends in Selling TM7: $60-80

FOR MOTHER

Mold No.: 257
Copyright: 1963
Sculptor: n.a.
2-D Original: H 381

Model No.: 257/0
Ref. No.: 816
Approx. Size: 5"
1995 Retail: $200

Model No.: 257 2/0
Ref. No.: 414
Approx. Size: 4"
1995 Retail: $120

For Mother was introduced in 1964 at the time TM4 was being phased in and is difficult to locate in TM3. The smaller size was introduced in 1985.

Trends in Selling M 257/0 TM6-7: $160-200
    TM5: $170-200
    TM4: $195-230
    TM3: $675-795

Trends in Selling M 257 2/0 TM6-7: $95-120

FOREST SHRINE

Mold No.: 183
Ref. No.: 564
Approx. Size: 9"
Copyright: 1946
Sculptor: R.Unger
2-D Orig.: H 273
1995 Retail: $530

Out of production during all of the TM4 era and for most of the TM3 and TM5 eras, **Forest Shrine** was at one time one of the most difficult Hummel finds. Bearing modernizing design changes, it is readily available in TM6 and TM7, but predictably scarce in all older marks.

Trends in Selling TM6-7: $425-530
    TM5: $500-590
    TM3: $680-800
    TM2: $900-1100
    TM1: $1200-1500

FRIEND OR FOE?

Mold No.: 434
Ref. No.: 461
Approx. Size: 3.875"
Copyright: 1982
Sculptor: G.Skrobek
2-D Original: H 109
1995 Retail: $215

A 1991 release which
came along just as TM7
was being phased in,
Friend or Foe should prove to be scarce in TM6.

Trends in Selling TM7: $175-215
          TM6: $215-255

FRIENDS

Mold No.: 136
Copyright: 1940
Sculptor: R.Unger
2-D Original: Unknown

Model No.: 136/V
Ref. No.: 884
Approx. Size: 10.75"
1995 Retail: $1200

Model No.: 136/I
Ref. No.: 885
Approx. Size: 5"
1995 Retail: $195

The smaller size, bearing a 1947 copyright, was
introduced in the latter part of the TM1 era and is
relatively scarce with the crown mark. Some early
examples of the larger size can be found without the
size suffix; these can demand small premiums.

Trends in Selling M 136/V TM6-7: $960-1200
          TM5: $1020-1200
          TM4: $1150-1370
          TM3: $1300-1540
          TM2: $1650-1940
          TM1: $2700-3350

Trends in Selling M 136/I TM6-7: $160-200
          TM5: $170-200
          TM4: $195-230
          TM3: $220-260
          TM2: $285-335
          TM1: $560-700

FRIENDS TOGETHER

Mold No.: 662
Copyright: 1990
Sculptor:
  H.Fischer
2-D Original:
  H 501

Model No.: 662/I
Ref. No.: 094
Approx. Size: 6"
1995 Retail: $500

Model No.: 662/0
Ref. No.: 104
Approx. Size: 4"
1995 Retail: $275

Introduced near the end of 1993 in a confused M.I.
Hummel marketplace, **Friends Together** is destined to become one of the historic figurines in the
series. It was issued in partnership with the U.S.
Committee for UNICEF, with a pledge from Goebel
to contribute $25 to the charitable children's orga-
nization for *each* figurine sold. In addition, the
larger, 662/I model became only the third sequentially numbered, limited edition Hummel figurine,
following the *Crossroads* commemorative of 1990
and the *Land in Sight* commemorative of 1991. The
edition limit of the larger **Friends Together** was set
at 25,000 pieces. The smaller 662/0 model is offered on an unlimited basis. The design is based on
one of the few pieces of original art in which Sister
Hummel incorporated a black child. At issue, it was
announced that **Friends Together** was to be the
first of three M.I. Hummel figurines in the UNICEF
series.

Trends in Selling M 662/I: $425-500

Trends in Selling M 662/0: $235-275

GAY ADVENTURE

Mold No.: 356
Ref. No.: 762
Approx. Size: 5"
Copyright: 1971
Sculptor: G.Skrobek
2-D Original: H 495
1995 Retail: $190

Gay Adventure, called *Joyful Adventure* when introduced in 1972, is scarce in TM4 due to the phase-in of TM5 at the time it was put on the market.

Trends in Selling TM6-7: $155-190
         TM5: $160-190
         TM4: $975-1150

GENTLE SONG ORNAMENT (WHITE)

(See chapter *The Other Hummels*)

GIFT FROM A FRIEND

Mold No.: 485
Ref. No.: 198
Approx. Size: 5"
Copyright: 1988
Sculptor:
  G.Skrobek
2-D Original:
  Unknown
1995 Retail:
  Closed Edition

Gift From a Friend was issued as the M.I. Hummel Club exclusive redemption figurine for the 1991–92 club year (June 1, 1991– May 31, 1992). It is number 15 in the club exclusive series and could originally be acquired only with a redemption certificate provided to each active club member. Issue price was $160.

Trends in Selling: $225-270

GIRL WALL VASE

(See Boy & Girl Wall Vase)

GIRL WITH DOLL

(See Boy w/Horse)

GIRL WITH FIR TREE CANDLEHOLDER

(See Boy w/Horse Candleholder)

GIRL WITH NOSEGAY

(See Boy w/Horse)

GIRL WITH NOSEGAY CANDLEHOLDER

(See Boy w/Horse Candleholder)

GIRL WITH SHEET MUSIC

Mold No.: 389
Ref. No.: 735
Approx. Size: 2.25"
Copyright: 1968
Sculptor: G.Skrobek
2-D Original: Unknown
1995 Retail: $85

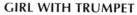

This piece is often offered in company with the other two "Little Band" members, **Boy with Accordion** and **Girl with Trumpet.**

Trends in Selling TM6-7: $70-85
         TM5: $75-85
         TM4: $105-125

GIRL WITH TRUMPET

Mold No.: 391
Ref. No.: 733
Approx. Size: 2.25"
Copyright: 1968
Sculptor: G.Skrobek
2-D Original: Unknown
1995 Retail: $85

This piece is often offered in company with the other two "Little Band" members, **Girl With Sheet Music** and **Boy With Accordion.**

Trends in Selling TM6-7: $70-85
         TM5: $75-85
         TM4: $105-125

GLOBE TROTTER

Mold No.: 79
Ref. No.: 926
Approx. Size: 5.25"
Copyright: 1937 &
  1955
Sculptor:
  A.Moeller
2-D Original: H 216
1995 Retail:
  Retired

Globe Trotter be-
came the fourth in
an annual series of ceremonial retirements of long-
running Hummel figurines. Introduced in 1937,
the figurine can be found in all trademarks. Due
perhaps to similarity to *Happy Traveller* and the
ever-popular *Merry Wanderer*, **Globe Trotter** enjoyed lackluster demand prior to retirement. However, all trademarks are now eagerly sought on the
secondary market. All TM7 examples should bear
the "Final Issue 1991" backstamp; a TM7 example
without the stamp would be a find.

Trends in Selling TM6-7: $185-230
              TM5: $200-250
              TM4: $225-265
              TM3: $245-295
              TM2: $320-375
              TM1: $560-695

GLOBE TROTTER ANNUAL PLATE

(See 1973 Annual Plate)

GOING HOME

Mold No.: 383
Ref. No.: 423
Approx. Size: 4.75"
Copyright: 1972
Sculptor: G.Skrobek
2-D Original: H 217
1995 Retail: $310

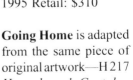

Going Home is adapted
from the same piece of
original artwork—H 217
Hansel and Gretel—
which is also responsible for *Grandma's Girl,*
Grandpa's Boy and *Mother's Darling.*

Trends in Selling TM6-7: $250-310

GOING TO GRANDMA'S

Mold No.: 52
Copyright: 1936
Sculptor: R.Unger
2-D Original: H 188

Model No.: 52/I
Ref. No.: 947
Approx. Size: 6.25"
1995 Retail: T.W.

Model No.: 52/0
Ref. No.: 948
Approx. Size: 4.75"
1995 Retail: $260

Due to the existence of older examples of the large
size without size suffix and the relative rarity of the
small size in TM1, it would appear that model 52/
0 was introduced substantially later than model 52/
I. Both sizes were originally given square bases
(Var. I). These were changed to oval bases (Var. II)
during restylings—on the small model in the early
1960s and on the large model in 1979. The large
model was out of production for an extended period
that included some of the 1950s and most of the
1960s and 1970s; it is, therefore, not available in
TM4 and is scarce to rare in TM3. In addition,
Variety II model 52/I is difficult to locate in TM5,
and, in TM1, this model commands a small premium if found without size suffix. It was again
withdrawn from production at the end of 1984.
Model 52/0 is available in both varieties within
TM3, with Variety II being scarcer. There were
extended periods when neither model of **Going to
Grandma's** was produced, and the figurine itself
may be rarer in certain trademarks than previously
thought.

Trends in Selling M 52/I TM6: $340-400
      Var. I in TM5: $400-475
      Var. II in TM5: $430-515
              TM3: $545-645
              TM2: $565-670
              TM1: $960-1200

Trends in Selling M 52/0 TM6-7: $210-260
              TM5: $220-260
              TM4: $255-300
      Var. I in TM3: $295-350
      Var. II in TM3: $320-380
              TM2: $365-430
              TM1: $580-725

GOOD FRIENDS

Mold No.: 182
Ref. No.: 851
Approx. Size: 5"
Copyright: 1946
Sculptor: A.Moeller
Restyled by: G.Skrobek
2-D Original: H 205
1995 Retail: $195

The Skrobek restyling was done in 1976 to add the modern texture to the piece.

Trends in Selling TM6-7: $155-195
      TM5: $165-295
      TM4: $185-220
      TM3: $215-255
      TM2: $265-320
      TM1: $425-530

GOOD FRIENDS & SHE LOVES ME, SHE LOVES ME NOT BOOKENDS

Mold No.: 251/A & B
Ref. No.: 708
Approx. Size: 5"
Copyright: n.a.
Sculptor: n.a.
2-D Original: H 205, H 126
1995 Retail: T.W.

With other pairs of bookends, this set was withdrawn from production as of Jan. 1, 1990. This set was assembled by affixing regular, factory-produced examples of the *Good Friends* and *She Loves Me, She Loves Me Not* figurines to wooden bases. Though the bookend set was first introduced in 1964, it is not found in TM4. It is likely that some surviving sets were either created with the use of

earlier trademark figurines or were "restored" with the use of earlier trademark figurines. The two figurines independently have a higher value in today's secondary marketplace than does the bookend set.

Trends in Selling TM6: $250-310 pair
      TM5: $265-310 pair
      TM3: $330-405 pair

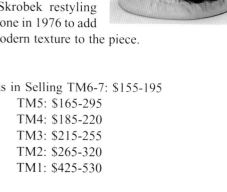

GOOD FRIENDS LAMP

Mold No.: 228
Ref. No.: 644
Approx. Size: 7.5"
Copyright: 1953
Sculptor: A.Moeller
2-D Original: H 205
1995 Retail: T.W.

SHE LOVES ME, SHE LOVES ME NOT LAMP

Mold No.: 227
Ref. No.: 645
Approx. Size: 7.5"
Copyright: 1953
Sculptor: A.Moeller
2-D Original: H 126
1995 Retail: T.W.

As indicated by the successive mold and reference numbers, these lamps have traditionally been offered paired together. They were given "T.W." status as of Jan. 1, 1990. Both have undergone mold modifications (*She Loves Me...* can be found with eyes open or eyes looking down) that thus far have had no affect on values.

Trends in Selling M 228 TM6: $275-345 each
      TM5: $290-345 each
      TM4: $335-395 each
      TM3: $380-450 each
      TM2: $750-900 each

Trends in Selling M 227 TM6: $275-345 each
      TM5: $290-345 each
      TM4: $335-395 each
      TM3: $380-450 each
      TM2: $750-900 each

GOOD HUNTING

Mold No.: 307
Ref. No.: 808
Approx. Size: 5"
Copyright: 1955
Sculptor: R.Unger and
  H.Wehlte
2-D Original: H 238
1995 Retail: $245

Modeled in 1955 but not
introduced until 1962,
Good Hunting is scarce in TM3.

Trends in Selling TM6-7: $195-245
        TM5: $210-245
        TM4: $265-315
        TM3: $565-665

GOOD NIGHT

(See Nativity Sets)

GOOD SHEPHERD

Mold No.: 42
Ref. No.: 477
Approx. Size: 6.25"
Copyright: 1935
Sculptor: R.Unger
2-D Original: H 499
1995 Retail: $220

Good Shepherd has al-
ways been produced in a
rust brown cloak with
green decorations. Variations to this color have
been reported and command high premiums. It
might be well to repeat that expensive varieties
based on color alone should have documented
histories; it is not difficult to alter color in a
professional-appearing manner. Until recently, the
figurine bore the mold number 42/0 because of a
larger model (42/I) which was rarely produced
during the TM1 and TM2 eras. Sized at about 7.5
inches and bearing the 42/I mold number, the
larger model, when offered, is priced at about 10
times the value of the smaller. Dropping of the /0
size suffix would indicate that Goebel considers the
large model permanently retired. The smaller model
can also be found without size suffix in TM1; these
examples command small premiums.

Trends in Selling TM6-7: $200-250
        TM5: $210-250
        TM4: $245-290
        TM3: $270-320
        TM2: $350-410
        TM1: $590-735

GOOD SHEPHERD FONT

Mold No.: 35
Copyright: 1935
Sculptor: R.Unger
2-D Original: Unknown

Mold No.: 35/I
Ref. No.: n.a.
Approx. Size: 5.75"
1995 Retail: Closed
  Edition

Model No.: 35/0
Ref. No.: 516
Approx. Size: 4.75"
1995 Retail: $40

Early TM1 examples of the larger size command a
small premium if found numbered only "35" without mold suffix.

Trends in Selling M 35/0 TM6-7: $32-40
        TM5: $35-40
        TM4: $40-46
        TM3: $45-52
        TM2: $90-110
        TM1: $180-225

Trends in Selling M 35/I: TM3: $135-170
        TM2: $200-250
        TM1: $250-315

THE FIRST HUMMEL FIGURINES

The first 46 M.I. Hummel figurine motifs
were produced by Goebel in 1935. The motifs
are represented by molds 1 through 46.

GOOSE GIRL

Mold No.: 47
Copyright: 1936
Sculptor: A.Moeller
2-D Original: H 155,
  F 220

Model No.: 47/II
Ref. No.: 959
Approx. Size: 7.5"
1995 Retail: T.W.

Model No.: 47/II (white)
Ref. No.: 165
Approx. Size: 7.5"
1995 Retail: $260

Model No.: 47/0
Ref. No.: 960
Approx. Size: 4.75"
1995 Retail: $225

Model No.: 47 3/0
Ref. No.: 961
Approx. Size: 4"
1995 Retail: $165

Goose Girl is one of the most recognizable and reproduced of the Hummel motifs. The 47/0 model was apparently the first produced; without size suffix it brings a premium over the normal TM1 price. Model 47/II in its multicolored form was withdrawn from production in 1992 concurrent with the introduction of this model as part of the white *Expressions of Youth* series; the multicolored version should prove to be scarce in TM7 if not reintroduced during the period. As is the case with most early mold numbers, there are minor variations within all models of size, color and mold which do not affect values.

Trends in Selling M 47/II in TM7: $370-460
    White Var. in TM7: $210-260
        TM6: $335-420
        TM5: $360-420
        TM4: $405-485
        TM3: $450-545
        TM2: $590-695
        TM1: $900-1125

Trends in Selling M 47/0 TM6-7: $180-225
        TM5: $190-225
        TM4: $215-255
        TM3: $245-290
        TM2: $315-370
        TM1: $580-730

Trends in Selling M 47 3/0 TM6-7: $135-165
        TM5: $140-165
        TM4: $160-190
        TM3: $180-210
        TM2: $230-270
        TM1: $370-460

GOOSE GIRL ANNUAL PLATE
(See 1974 Annual Plate)

GOOSE GIRL & FARM BOY BOOKENDS

Mold No.: 60 A & B
Ref. No.: 702
Approx. Size: 4.75"
Copyright: 1936
Sculptor: A.Moeller
2-D Original: H 155, Unknown
1995 Retail: T.W.

From the mold number and copyright sequence, it would appear that Moeller first modeled *Goose Girl* as a figurine, then shortly afterwards modified it slightly as half of this bookend set while creating *Farm Boy* as the other half, and, lastly, modified *Farm Boy* to sell as a stand-alone figurine. In any case, this bookend set—unlike some of the others—does not incorporate exact versions of the respective figurines. In nearly all cases, the bookends bear markings only on the wooden bases, not on the figures. This set was given "T.W." status as of Jan. 1, 1985.

Trends in Selling TM6: $310-390 pair
        TM5: $335-390 pair
        TM4: $375-450 pair
        TM3: $415-500 pair
        TM2: $550-645 pair
        TM1: $825-1025 pair

114

GRANDMA'S GIRL

Mold No.: 561
Ref. No.: 211
Approx. Size: 4"
Copyright: 1989
Sculptor: H.Fischer
2-D Original: H 217
1995 Retail: $145

Released in 1990, **Grandma's Girl** should eventually prove to be relatively scarce in TM6.

Trends in Selling TM6-7: $115-145

GRANDPA'S BOY

Mold No.: 562
Ref. No.: 210
Approx. Size: 4.125"
Copyright: 1989
Sculptor: H.Fischer
2-D Original: H 217
1995 Retail: $145

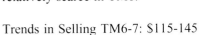

Released in 1990, **Grandpa's Boy** should eventually prove to be relatively scarce in TM6.

Trends in Selling TM6-7: $115-145

GUARDIAN (THE)

Mold No.: 455
Ref. No.: 214
Approx. Size: 2.75"
Copyright: 1985
Sculptor: G.Skrobek
2-D Original: H 389
1995 Retail: $165

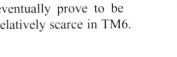

A Skrobek design from 1985, **The Guardian** was not released until 1991, though initial production occurred in 1990. It should be considered scarce in TM6.

Trends in Selling TM7: $135-165
            TM6: $165-195

GUARDIAN ANGEL FONT

Mold No.: 29/I & 29/0
Ref. No.: n.a.
Approx. Size: 6" & 6.375"
Copyright: 1935
Sculptor: R.Unger
2-D Original: Unknown
1995 Retail: Closed Edition

Mold No.: 248/0
Ref. No.: 511
Approx. Size: 5.5"
Copyright: 1959
Sculptor: G.Skrobek
2-D Original: Unknown
1995 Retail: $50

The Unger version is an early Hummel mold executed in two size versions which—presumably due to production problems—was rarely manufactured in either. In 1959, Skrobek completed a comprehensive redesign that was given a newer, mold number: 248. Examples of the Skrobek version are numbered 248/0, indicating the intent to produce a 248/I size which never reached the market. For some reason, the 248 model, though introduced at the onset of the TM3 era, is hard to find in that trademark.

Trends in Selling M 29/0 TM3: $740-925
                    TM2: $800-1000
                    TM1: $1040-1300

Trends in Selling M 29/I TM2: $1150-1440
                    TM1: $1300-1625

Trends in Selling M 248/0 TM6-7: $40-50
                    TM5: $45-55
                    TM4: $50-60
                    TM3: $160-200

THE FIRST ISSUE STAMP

Beginning with the introductions of 1991, Goebel began stamping each newly introduced figurine with a special year-of-issue backstamp. The stamp is in the form of an oval and reads: "First Issue...Erste Ausgabe..." plus year of issue. The stamp, of course, is omitted after production for the first year is completed.

GUIDING ANGEL

Mold No.: 357
Ref. No.: 528
Approx. Size: 2.75"
Copyright: 1960
Sculptor: R.Unger
2-D Original: Unknown
1995 Retail: $85

With its frequent companions, *Shining Light* and *Tuneful Angel*, **Guiding Angel** was one of the small items introduced in 1972. It is difficult to find in TM4.

Trends in Selling TM6-7: $70-85
      TM5: $75-85
      TM4: $170-200

GUIDING LIGHT ARS CHRISTMAS PLATE
(See 1989 ARS Christmas Plate)

HAPPINESS

Mold No.: 86
Ref. No.: 917
Approx. Size: 4.75"
Copyright: 1938
Sculptor: R.Unger
2-D Original: H 268
1995 Retail: $130

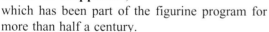

Minor varations in mold, size and color can be found in **Happiness**, which has been part of the figurine program for more than half a century.

Trends in Selling TM6-7: $105-130
      TM5: $110-130
      TM4: $125-150
      TM3: $140-165
      TM2: $180-215
      TM1: $290-360

HAPPY BIRTHDAY

Mold No.: 176
Copyright: 1945
Sculptor: A.Moeller
2-D Original: H 283

Model No.: 176/I
Ref. No.: 856
Approx. Size: 6"
1995 Retail: $295

Model No.: 176/0
Ref. No.: 857
Approx. Size: 5.5"
1995 Retail: $210

A restyling of the larger size in 1979 changed the base from a circular to an oval shape. Early pieces of the larger size command small premiums when located without size suffix in TM1 or TM2. There were extended periods when neither model of **Happy Birthday** was produced, and the figurine itself will likely prove difficult to locate in TM4. Additionally, model 176/I is scarce in TM3 and rare to nonexistent in TM4. It was reinstated circa 1978 after being long out of production.

Trends in Selling M 176/I TM6-7: $235-295
      TM5: $345-405
      TM4: $410-480
      TM3: $410-480
      TM2: $410-480
      TM1: $635-790

Trends in Selling M 176/0 TM6-7: $170-210
      TM5: $180-210
      TM4: $205-240
      TM3: $235-275
      TM2: $295-345

HAPPY DAYS

Mold No.: 150
Copyright: 1942
Sculptor: n.a.
2-D Original: H 338

Model No.: 150/I
Ref. No.: 871
Approx. Size: 6.25"
1995 Retail: $450

Model No.: 150/0	Model No.: 150 2/0	Copyright: 1954	Copyright: 1954
Ref. No.: 872	Ref. No.: 873	Sculptor: R.Unger	Sculptor: R. Unger
Approx. Size: 5.25"	Approx. Size: 4.25"	2-D Original: H 338	2-D Original: H 338
1995 Retail: $300	1995 Retail: $165	1995 Retail: T.W.	1995 Retail: T.W.

Happy Days is one of the few figurines to remain in production over an extended period of time in three or more size versions. Despite this, no major variations are recognized. Early examples of model 150/I without the */I* size suffix bring small premiums. Research indicates this model could be rare or nonexistent in TM3 and TM4. It was reinstated circa 1978 after being long out of production.

Trends in Selling M 150/I TM6-7: $360-450
     TM5: $425-500
     TM4: $625-735
     TM3: $625-735
     TM2: $625-735
     TM1: $930-1160

Trends in Selling M 150/0 TM6-7: $240-300
     TM5: $255-300
     TM4: $295-345
     TM3: $330-385
     TM2: $420-490

Trends in Selling M 150 2/0 TM6-7: $135-165
     TM5: $140-165
     TM4: $165-195
     TM3: $185-220
     TM2: $240-280

As with the companion *Birthday Serenade Lamp*, Goebel decided to use two different mold numbers to distinguish between the two sizes of the **Happy Days Lamp**. The 1954 copyright date was used until a mid-1970s restyling of both sizes. Both sizes of the lamp were given T.W. status as of Jan. 1, 1990.

Trends in Selling M 232 TM6: $390-490
     TM5: $415-490
     TM2: $825-970

Trends in Selling M 235 TM6: $365-455
     TM5: $385-455
     TM4: $440-515
     TM3: $550-675
     TM2: $700-870

HAPPY PASTIME

Mold No.: 69
Ref. No.: 931
Approx. Size: 3.5"
Copyright: 1937
Sculptor: A.Moeller
2-D Original: H 306
1995 Retail: $160

There have been no notable variations of **Happy Pastime** reported despite its long production tenure.

Trends in Selling TM6-7: $130-160
     TM5: $135-160
     TM4: $160-185
     TM3: $180-210
     TM2: $220-260
     TM1: $360-450

HAPPY DAYS LAMP
Mold No.: 232	Mold No.: 235
Ref. No.: 640	Ref. No.: 638
Approx. Size: 9.75"	Approx. Size: 7.75"

HAPPY PASTIME ANNUAL PLATE
(See 1978 Annual Plate)

HAPPY PASTIME ASHTRAY
Mold No.: 62
Ref. No.: 672
Approx. Size: 3.5 x 6.25"
Copyright: 1936
Sculptor: A.Moeller
2-D Original: H 306
1995 Retail: T.W.

The mold number and copyright date indicate that **Happy Pastime Ashtray** predates both the figurine and candy box. Like all Hummel ashtrays, this is not in current production, having been withdrawn as of Jan. 1, 1990.

Trends in Selling TM6: $105-155
            TM5: $115-155
            TM4: $135-175
            TM3: $150-190
            TM2: $200-245
            TM1: $320-400

HAPPY PASTIME CANDY BOX
Mold No.: III/69
Ref. No.: 664
Approx. Size: 6"

Copyright: 1937
Sculptor: Unknown
2-D Original: H 306
1995 Retail: T.W.

Originally given a bowl shape (Var. I), the container was redesigned to a box shape (Var. II) in 1964 at the onset of the TM4 era. Some of the Variety II pieces bear the TM3 stamp. The box was withdrawn from production at the end of 1989.

Trends in Selling TM6: $145-180
            TM5: $155-180
            TM4: $175-210
    Var. I in TM3: $350-430
    Var. II in TM3: $250-315
            TM2: $425-530
            TM1: $525-650

HAPPY TRAVELLER
Mold No.: 109
Copyright: 1938
Sculptor: A.Moeller
2-D Original: H 216

Model No.: 109/II
Ref. No.: 904
Approx. Size: 7.5"
1995 Retail: Closed
    Edition

Model No.: 109/0
Ref. No.: 905
Approx. Size: 5"
1995 Retail: $140

The smaller size was restyled to the modern, textured finish in 1980. Early TM6 examples without the textured finish (Var. I) are, therefore, likely to be quite scarce and should demand a premium. The larger size was permanently retired in early 1982 and is therefore scarce in TM6. Early examples of both sizes can be found without size suffix with no bearing on value.

Trends in Selling M 109/II TM6: $290-360
            TM5: $305-360
            TM4: $350-415
            TM3: $400-470
            TM2: $775-840
            TM1: $890-1115

Trends in Selling M 109/0 TM6-7: $115-140
   Var. I in TM6: $130-150
          TM5: $120-140
          TM4: $135-160
          TM3: $155-180
          TM2: $195-230
          TM1: $255-320

HARMONY IN FOUR PARTS
Mold No.: 471
Ref. No.: 286
Approx. Size: 9.75"
Copyright: 1987
Sculptor: G.Skrobek
2-D Original: H 284
1995 Retail: Closed Edition

Flushed with the success of *Chapel Time Clock* as its first "century release" in 1986, Goebel quickly put Skrobek to work on succeeding issues in the spectacular series. One was **Harmony in Four Parts**, which was released in 1989 as the fourth in the annual series. Produced just for the one year in the twentieth century, the piece has enjoyed a steady, strong demand in the secondary market and is somewhat difficult to locate. A special bottom stamp reads, "M.I. Hummel Century Collection 1989 XX." Issue price was $850 in 1989.

Trends in Selling TM6: $1500-1900

HARMONY IN FOUR PARTS CHRISTMAS BELL
(See 1992 Christmas Bell)

HEAR YE! HEAR YE!
Mold No.: 15
Copyright: 1935
Sculptor: A.Moeller
2-D Original: H 497

Model No.: 15/I
Ref. No.: 968
Approx. Size: 6"
1995 Retail: $250

Model No.: 15/II	Model No.: 15/II (white)
Ref. No.: 967	Ref. No.: 166
Approx. Size: 7"	Approx. Size: 7"
1995 Retail: T.W.	1995 Retail: $260
Model No.: 15/0	Model No.: 15 2/0
Ref. No.: 969	Ref. No.: 418
Approx. Size: 5"	Approx. Size: 4"
1995 Retail: $200	1995 Retail: $145

Model 15/II in multicolor was withdrawn from production in 1992 concurrent with the introduction of the white *Expressions of Youth* series; it may prove to be scarce in TM7. However, **Hear Ye, Hear Ye** is unusual in that four different sizes of the same figurine may be assembled bearing the same trademark (TM6 or TM7). The smallest, 15 2/0, was introduced in 1985 and bears a 1984 copyright.

Trends in Selling M 15/II TM6-7: $375-465
   White Var. in TM7: $210-260
          TM5: $395-465
          TM4: $450-530
          TM3: $510-600
          TM2: $645-760
          TM1: $980-1225

Trends in Selling M 15/I TM6-7: $200-250
          TM5: $215-250
          TM4: $245-290
          TM3: $275-325
          TM2: $345-405
          TM1: $585-730

Trends in Selling M 15/0 TM6-7: $160-200
          TM5: $170-200
          TM4: $200-235
          TM3: $220-260
          TM2: $280-330
          TM1: $415-515

Trends in Selling M 15 2/0 TM6-7: $120-145

HEAR YE, HEAR YE ANNUAL PLATE
(See 1972 Annual Plate)

HEAR YE, HEAR YE CHRISTMAS BELL
(See 1991 Christmas Bell)

HEAVENLY ANGEL
Mold No.: 21
Copyright: 1935
Sculptor: R.Unger
2-D Original: H 425,
  F 215

Model No.: 21/II
Ref. No.: 557
Approx. Size: 8.75"
1995 Retail: T.W.

Model No.: 21/II (white)
Ref. No.: 163
Approx. Size: 8.75"
1995 Retail: $260

Model No.: 21/I
Ref. No.: 558
Approx. Size: 6.75"
1995 Retail: $250

Model No.: 21/0 1/2   Model No.: 21/0
Ref. No.: 559   Ref. No.: 560
Approx. Size: 6"   Approx. Size: 4.75"
1995 Retail: $215   1995 Retail: $120

Model 21/II in multicolored form was withdrawn from production in 1992 concurrent with the introduction of this model as part of the white *Expressions of Youth* series; the multicolored version may prove to be relatively scarce in TM7. However, **Heavenly Angel** is unusual among Hummel figurines in that four different sizes of the same figurine are available in each of the seven trademarks. In other words, a collection of 28 pieces may currently be assembled without duplicating a size/trademark combination. The design is perhaps best known as the motif for the famous 1971 annual plate.

Trends in Selling M 21/II TM6-7: $350-440
    White Var. in TM7: $210-260
        TM5: $375-440
        TM4: $430-505
        TM3: $480-565
        TM2: $610-720
        TM1: $930-1160

Trends in Selling M 21/I TM6-7: $200-250
        TM5: $210-250
        TM4: $245-290
        TM3: $275-325
        TM2: $350-415
        TM1: $560-700

Trends in Selling M 21/0 1/2 TM6-7: $175-215
        TM5: $185-215
        TM4: $215-250
        TM3: $240-280
        TM2: $305-355
        TM1: $475-590

Trends in Selling M 21/0 TM6-7: $95-120
        TM5: $100-120
        TM4: $120-140
        TM3: $130-155
        TM2: $170-200
        TM1: $260-325

HEAVENLY ANGEL ANNUAL PLATE
(See 1971 Annual Plate)

HEAVENLY ANGEL FONT
Mold No.: 207
Ref. No.: 521
Approx. Size: 4.75"
Copyright: 1949
Sculptor: R.Unger
2-D Original: H 425,
  F 215
1995 Retail: $50

Copyrighted and produced in 1949 at the very end of the TM1 era, **Heavenly Angel Font** is predictably quite scarce with this mark.

Trends in Selling TM6-7: $40-50
        TM5: $45-55
        TM4: $50-60
        TM3: $160-200
        TM2: $200-250
        TM1: $350-435

HEAVENLY ANGEL ORNAMENT (WHITE)
(See chapter *The Other Hummels*)

HEAVENLY ANGEL TREE TOPPER
Mold No.: 755
Ref. No.: 099
Approx. Size: 7.5"
Copyright: 1992
Sculptor: H.Fischer
2-D Orig.: H 425, F 215
1995 Retail: $450

The ever-popular *Heavenly Angel* motif, used on the famous 1971, first-issue annual plate, also got the honor of becoming the first tree topper in the M.I. Hummel line. The tree topper, a 1994 introduction, comes supplied with a wooden stand for year-round display.

Trends in Selling TM7: $360-450

HEAVENLY LULLABY
Mold No.: 262
Ref. No.: 497
Approx. Size: 5" x 3.5"
Copyright: 1968
Sculptor: G.Skrobek
2-D Original: H 424,
  F 212
1995 Retail: $185

Modeled in 1968 but not introduced until later, **Heavenly Lullaby** is quite scarce in TM4. The piece itself is Skrobek's figurine version of the much older *Lullaby Candleholder*.

Trends in Selling TM6-7: $150-185
        TM5: $160-185
        TM4: $515-605

HEAVENLY PROTECTION
Mold No.: 88
Copyright: 1938 & 1961
Sculptor: R.Unger
2-D Original: Unknown

Model No.: 88/II
Ref. No.: 538
Approx. Size: 9"
1995 Retail: T.W.

Model No.: 88/I
Ref. No.: 539
Approx. Size:
  6.75"
1995 Retail: $425

The larger model of **Heavenly Protection** was created first and appeared marked *88* or *88.*; these early pieces command small premiums. The smaller size, created with a 1961 copyright date, was introduced shortly afterwards. In approximately the same time period, the larger size was given the */II* size suffix. The larger model was withdrawn from production at the end of 1992 and should prove to be relatively scarce in TM7.

Trends in Selling M 88/II TM6-7: $520-650
        TM5: $550-650
        TM4: $635-745
        TM3: $720-845
        TM2: $910-1070
        TM1: $1470-1835

Trends in Selling M 88/I TM6-7: $340-425
        TM5: $365-425
        TM4: $415-495
        TM3: $495-610

WHAT ARE THEY SINGING?

According to the notes on the sheet music, the quartet in the century release figurine *Harmony in Four Parts* is harmonizing to the well-known German children's song "Muss i denn?", the tune for which was adapted by Elvis Presley for his hit "Wooden Heart".

HEAVENLY SONG CANDLEHOLDER

Mold No.: 113
Ref. No.: n.a.
Approx. Size: 3.5" x
  4.75"
Copyright: 1938
Sculptor: A.Moeller
2-D Original: H 627
1995 Retail: Closed
  Edition

Probably due to its close
similarity to *Silent Night
Candleholder*, this piece
is extremely rare in any trademark despite not being
officially retired until 1980. Any example located
would likely bear TM1 or TM2, though TM3
examples are known to exist. There are no known
pieces bearing TM4, and there has been only a
single report of a piece bearing TM5. That example
is likely a prototype developed when **Heavenly
Song Candleholder** was being considered for reintroduction circa 1978.

Trends in Selling TM3: $2800-3500
      TM2: $3800-4750
      TM1: $4800-6000

HELLO

Mold No.: 124
Copyright: 1939
Sculptor: A.Moeller
2-D Original: H 239

Model No.: 124/I
Ref. No.: 894
Approx. Size: 7"
1995 Retail: T.W.

Model No.: 124/0
Ref. No.: 895
Approx. Size: 6.25"
1995 Retail: $215

Hello appears in various colors and sizes, and there
have been several minor mold design changes. The
larger size was withdrawn from production in early
1982 and may prove to be scarce in TM6. Early
examples of the larger size without size suffix
command small premiums. Research indicates this
model could also be scarce in TM3 and rare to
nonexistent in TM4. It was reinstated circa 1978

after being long out of production.There were extended periods when neither model of **Hello** was
produced, and the figurine itself will prove hard to
find in TM4.

Trends in Selling M 124/I TM6: $195-245
        TM5: $210-245
        TM4: $355-410
        TM3: $355-410
        TM2: $355-410
        TM1: $615-770

Trends in Selling M 124/0 TM6-7: $175-215
        TM5: $185-215
        TM4: $260-305
        TM3: $260-305
        TM2: $295-345

HELLO WORLD

Mold No.: 429
Ref. No.: 399
Approx. Size: 5.5"
Copyright: 1983
Sculptor:
  G.Skrobek
2-D Original:
  H 129
1995 Retail:
  Closed Edition

Hello World was
issued as the M.I.
Hummel Club re-
demption figurine for the 1989–90 club year (June
1, 1989–May 31, 1990). It is number 13 in the club
exclusive series and could originally be acquired
only with a redemption certificate. Issued during
the name change period, first examples were marked
Goebel Collectors' Club (Variety I) and subsequent examples were marked *M.I. Hummel Club*
(Variety II). It can be found in both TM6 and TM7,
though the latter trademark was not used until after
the redemption deadline for the figurine. This is
due to Goebel's long-standing practice of producing figurines to match redemption certificates for a
full year after the end of the club year in question.
The guess here is that the TM7 examples are
comparatively scarce. Issue price was $130.

Trends in Selling TM7: $205-240
  Var. I in TM6: $230-270
  Var. II in TM6: $185-215

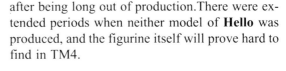

HERALD ANGELS CANDLEHOLDER

Mold No.: 37
Ref. No.: 553
Approx. Size: 4" x 2.25"
Copyright: 1935
Sculptor: R.Unger
2-D Original: H 385,
   H 435
1995 Retail: T.W.

This was among the pieces withdrawn from production at the end of 1989.

Trends in Selling TM6: $165-205
   TM5: $175-205
   TM4: $200-235
   TM3: $230-270
   TM2: $290-340
   TM1: $410-515

HERALD ON HIGH ANNUAL ORNAMENT

(See 1993 Annual Ornament)

HOLY CHILD

Mold No.: 70
Ref. No.: 472
Approx. Size:
   6.75"
Copyright: 1937
Sculptor: n.a.
2-D Original:
   Unknown
1995 Retail:
   T.W.

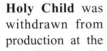

Holy Child was withdrawn from production at the end of 1990 and should not exist in TM7.

Trends in Selling TM6: $150-185
   TM5: $155-185
   TM4: $180-215
   TM3: $205-240
   TM2: $260-310
   TM1: $390-485

HOLY FAMILY FONT

Mold No.: 246
Ref. No.: 504
Approx. Size: 4.75"
Copyright: 1955
Sculptor:
   T.Menzenbach
2-D Original: H 546,
   F 210
1995 Retail: $50

Trends in Selling
   TM6-7: $40-50
   TM5: $45-55
   TM4: $50-60
   TM3: $75-100
   TM2: $200-250

HOME FROM MARKET

Mold No.: 198
Copyright: 1948
Sculptor: A.Moeller
2-D Original: H 227

Model No.: 198/I
Ref. No.: 837
Approx. Size: 5.5"
1995 Retail: $210

Model No.: 198 2/0
Ref. No.: 838
Approx. Size: 4.75"
1995 Retail: $145

When the smaller size was released in the mid-1950s, the larger size not only acquired the /I size suffix; it apparently was given a downsized remodeling. The out-sized (5.75–6") examples without size suffix demand small premiums within TM2.

Trends in Selling M 198/I TM6-7: $170-210
   TM5: $180-210
   TM4: $205-240
   TM3: $235-275
   TM2: $290-340
   TM1: $450-560

Trends in Selling M 198 2/0 TM6-7: $120-145
   TM5: $125-145
   TM4: $140-165
   TM3: $160-190
   TM2: $225-270

HOMEWARD BOUND

Mold No.: 334
Ref. No.: 783
Approx. Size: 5.25"
Copyright: 1955, 1956,
& 1975
Sculptor: A.Moeller
Restyled by: G.Skrobek
2-D Original: H 314
1995 Retail: $330

One of four new releases
of 1971, **Homeward
Bound** is scarce in TM4
and would be a rare find in TM3. Within TM5, it is
known for its "post variety." When Skrobek restyled the piece in 1974, he removed a support—or
post—under the goat that was part of Moeller's
original design. The Skrobek redesign (Var. II) is
also characterized by the modern, textured finish.

Trends in Selling TM6-7: $265-330
   Var. I in TM5: $325-385
   Var. II in TM5: $280-330
      TM4: $600-735

HONEY LOVER

Mold No.: 312
Ref. No.: 804
Approx. Size: 3.75"
Copyright: 1955
Sculptor: H.Wehlte
2-D Original: H 116
1995 Retail: $220

Honey Lover was first made available on June 1,
1991, as the M.I. Hummel Club's 15-year member-

ship figurine, and, as such, is highly desired and
difficult to obtain. To obtain the figurine at issue
prices through primary market channels, a person
must have a redemption certificate issued only to
individuals who have been members of the M.I.
Hummel Club for 15 consecutive years. The pres-
tige factor, combined with the inherent strong
appeal of the design itself, made the piece an
immediate favorite on the market. Many collectors,
unwilling to await eligibility, immediately began
paying premium prices to acquire the figurine on
the secondary market. It shares with its anniversary
companions, *The Little Pair* and *Flower Girl*, the
unusual circumstances of simultaneous strong primary and strong secondary market demand. Further, there seems to have been a preparatory production run of this figurine prior to Goebel's conversion from TM6 to TM7. The pieces marked with
trademark 6, made before actual introduction,
should command healthy premiums. **Honey Lover**
had been originally modeled by Wehlte in 1955 and
was shelved for more than 35 years before introduction. At least one TM2 prototype is known to exist;
it is in the Miller collection. Issue price of the
figurine was $190 in 1992, but in mid-1995 the
primary price (with redemption certificate) had
been increased to $220.

Trends in Selling TM7: $220-445
      TM6: $435-510

HONEY LOVER PENDANT

Mold No.: n.a.
Ref. No.: 826022
Approx. Size: .875"
Sculptor: n.a.
2-D Original: H 116
1995 Retail: $165

Offered as a M.I.
Hummel Club Special
Edition for 1994–95,
Honey Lover Pendant
represents the fourth
club exclusive in the
form of a hand-painted bronze miniature. Available beginning June 1, 1994, the pendant retires
after the club year ends on May 31, 1995. Redemption certificates acquired prior to May 31, 1995,
must be used by May 31, 1996.

Trends in Selling: $165-195

HORSE TRAINER

Mold No.: 423
Ref. No.: 256
Approx. Size: 4.5"
Copyright: 1981
Sculptor: G.Skrobek
2-D Original: H 626
1995 Retail: $215

Though bearing a 1981 copyright date, **Horse Trainer** was not introduced until 1990. It should prove to be relatively scarce in TM6.

Trends in Selling TM6-7: $175-215

HOSANNA

Mold No.: 480
Ref. No.: 265
Approx. Size: 3.875"
Copyright: 1987
Sculptor: G.Skrobek
2-D Original: H 452
1995 Retail: $100

A 1989 release, **Hosanna** is typical of Goebel's effort at the time to downsize its offerings to appeal in price to new collectors. The piece may prove to be somewhat scarce in TM6.

Trends in Selling TM6-7: $80-100

I BROUGHT YOU A GIFT

Mold No.: 479
Ref. No.: n.a.
Approx. Size: 4"
Copyright: 1987
Sculptor:
   G.Skrobek
2-D Original:
   H 489
1995 Retail: See
   below

The little figurine **I Brought You a Gift** has a relatively short but interest-ing history in the M.I. Hummel line. **I Brought You a Gift** was introduced at the same time as the former Goebel Collectors' Club was renamed the M.I. Hummel Club on June 1, 1989. It simultaneously became 1) the first M.I. Hummel figurine given free with a *new* membership in the club, and 2) the first free membership *renewal figurine* offered by the club. The renewal offer was only for the club year beginning June 1, 1989, and ending May 31, 1990. The figurine is still currently being used as a new membership gift, replacing the long-running white bisque membership plaque. Original retail value in 1989 was $55. Today, it would be about $95 in comparison to similar figurines; however, it can be acquired free by persons newly joining the M.I. Hummel Club for a $40 membership fee. The earliest production pieces of this figurine were stamped *Goebel Collectors' Club* (Var. I); subsequent production is labeled *M.I. Hummel Club* (Var. II).

Trends in Selling TM7: $40-60
   Var. I in TM6: $160-200
   Var. II in TM6: $80-100

I DIDN'T DO IT

Mold No.: 626
Ref. No.: 142
Approx. Size: 5.5"
Copyright: 1992
Sculptor:
   H.Fischer
2-D Original:
   Unknown
1995 Retail:
   Closed Edition

I Didn't Do It was issued as the M.I. Hummel Club exclusive redemption figurine for the 1993–94 club year (June 1, 1993–May 31, 1994). It is number 17 in the club exclusive series and could originally be acquired only with a redemption certificate provided to each active club member. Issue price was $175.

Trends in Selling TM7: $185-225

I WONDER
Mold No.: 486
Ref. No.: 241
Approx. Size: 5.25"
Copyright: 1988
Sculptor: H.Fischer
2-D Original: H 653
1995 Retail: Closed Edition

I Wonder was issued as the M.I. Hummel Club exclusive redemption figurine for the 1990–91 club year (June 1, 1990–May 31, 1991). It is number 14 in the club exclusive series and could originally be acquired only with a redemption certificate provided to each active club member. It can be found in both TM6 and TM7. Issue price was $140.

Trends in Selling TM7: $165-205
TM6: $190-230

I'M CAREFREE
Mold No.: 633
Ref. No.: 112
Approx. Size: 4.75"
Copyright: 1990
Sculptor: H.Fischer
2-D Original: H 150
1995 Retail: $375

A 1994 introduction, **I'm Carefree** will likely go down as one of the early premier achievements of Helmut Fischer, who was groomed in the late 1980s to succeed Gerhard Skrobek as Goebel's principal designer. With its wooden wagon, the figurine reminds one of *Pleasant Journey*. Truly unusual among M.I. Hummel figurines, however, is the absence of the customary base.

Trends in Selling TM7: $300-375

I'LL PROTECT HIM
Mold No.: 483
Ref. No.: 266
Approx. Size: 3.25"
Copyright: 1987
Sculptor: G.Skrobek
2-D Original:
  H Fleissbildchen
1995 Retail: $85

Created in 1987 and issued as a new release for 1989, **I'll Protect Him** may eventually prove to be somewhat scarce in TM6.

Trends in Selling TM6-7: $70-85

I'M HERE
Mold No.: 478
Ref. No.: 285
Approx. Size: 3.125"
Copyright: 1987
Sculptor: G.Skrobek
2-D Original: H 489
1995 Retail: $100

Created in 1987 and issued as a new release for 1989, **I'm Here** may eventually prove to be somewhat scarce in TM6.

Trends in Selling TM6-7: $80-100

IN D MAJOR

Mold No.: 430
Ref. No.: 287
Approx. Size: 4.25"
Copyright: 1981
Sculptor: G.Skrobek
2-D Original: H 141
1995 Retail: $200

Copyrighted in 1981 but not released until 1989, **In D Major** may eventually prove to be somewhat scarce in TM6.

Trends in Selling TM6-7: $160-200

IN THE MEADOW

Mold No.: 459
Ref. No.: 408
Approx. Size: 4"
Copyright: 1985
Sculptor: G.Skrobek
2-D Original: H 128
1995 Retail: $200

In the Meadow was one of the new releases of 1987.

Trends in Selling TM6-7: $160-200

IN TUNE

Mold No.: 414
Ref. No.: 724
Approx. Size: 4"
Copyright: 1979
Sculptor: G.Skrobek
2-D Original: H 144
1995 Retail: $280

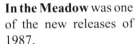

The introduction of **In Tune** in 1981 was unusual in that the motif was also used on the annual bell of that year. Previously, the motifs for the annual bell and plate designs had been borrowed from long-established favorites in the figurine category.

Trends in Selling TM6-7: $225-280

IN TUNE ANNUAL BELL

(See 1981 Annual Bell)

IN TUNE MUSIC BOX

Mold No.: 66202
Ref. No.: 6935
Approx. Size: 6.25" x 4.5"
Copyright: 1987
Sculptor: G.Skrobek
2-D Original: H 144
1995 Retail: Closed Edition

From 1987 through 1990, Goebel used the services of the famed Anri woodcarving firm in Italy and the famed Reuge music movement firm in Switzerland to produce a four-year, annual series of collector-quality music boxes. The theme was *Four Seasons.* The **In Tune Music Box** was the 1989, third issue in the series and represented summer of the four seasons. The bas-relief rendition of the *In Tune* motif was sculpted by Goebel master Gerhard Skrobek, and the painting was executed in accordance with the specifications of Goebel master painter Gunther Neubauer. However, actual execution of the production artwork in the form of a painted woodcarving was done by Anri artisans. The 36-note musical movement is a Romance movement by Reuge. The box was a worldwide limited edition of 10,000 pieces, and each music box is individually numbered. This number appears—along with the Goebel backstamp—on a special plaque attached to the underside of the lid. The box is now somewhat difficult to locate on the secondary market. Issue price was $425 in 1989.

Trends in Selling TM6: $425-525

INFANT OF KRUMBAD

(See Blessed Child)

IS IT RAINING?

Mold No.: 420
Ref. No.: 268
Approx. Size:
 6.125"
Copyright: 1981
Sculptor:
 G.Skrobek
2-D Original:
 H 224, F 690
1995 Retail: $255

Copyrighted in 1981 but not released until 1989, **Is It Raining?** may eventually prove to be somewhat scarce in TM6.

Trends in Selling TM6-7: $205-255

IT'S COLD

Mold No.: 421
Ref. No.: 722
Approx. Size: 5"
Copyright: 1981
Sculptor: G.Skrobek
2-D Original: H 626
1995 Retail: Closed Edition

It's Cold was issued as the M.I. Hummel Club redemption figurine for the 1982–83 club year (June 1, 1982–May 31, 1983). It is number 6 in the club exclusive series and could originally be acquired only with a redemption certificate provided to each active club member. Issue price was $80.

Trends in Selling TM6: $245-305

IT'S COLD PLATE

Mold No.: 735
Ref. No.: 281
Approx. Size:
 6.25" d.
Copyright: 1985
Sculptor:
 G.Skrobek
2-D Original:
 H 626
1995 Retail:
 Closed Edition

Issued in 1989 exclusively for purchase by members of the M.I. Hummel Club (club year beginning June 1, 1989, and ending May 31, 1990), **It's Cold Plate** was the fourth and final issue in the four-year *Celebration Plate Series*. The series' name derives from the club's 10th anniversary year when the series was begun. Plates in the series are based on motifs previously used for club exclusive figurines, are executed in bas-relief, and were supplied with presentation boxes. Issue price of this plate was $120.

Trends in Selling: $120-150

JOYFUL

Mold No.: 53
Ref. No.: 946
Approx. Size: 4"
Copyright: 1936
Sculptor: R.Unger
2-D Original: H 385
1995 Retail: $120

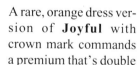

A rare, orange dress version of **Joyful** with crown mark commands a premium that's double the normal TM1 value. (However, again the reminder that colors can be altered with skill!) Greatly oversized pieces are also available in early trademarks and can command small premiums.

Trends in Selling TM6-7: $100-120
 TM5: $105-120
 TM4: $115-135
 TM3: $130-155
 TM2: $165-195
 TM1: $275-345

JOYFUL ASHTRAY
Mold No.: 33
Ref. No.: 674
Approx. Size: 3.5" x 6"
Copyright: 1935
Sculptor: R.Unger
2-D Original: H 385
1995 Retail: T.W.

The **Joyful Ashtray**, which preceded the figurine in both copyright date and mold number, was given "T.W." status as of Jan. 1, 1985. No important variations have been found.

Trends in Selling TM6: $105-155
           TM5: $115-155
           TM4: $135-175
           TM3: $150-190
           TM2: $200-245
           TM1: $300-375

JOYFUL CANDY BOX
Mold No.: III/53
Ref. No.: 668
Approx. Size: 6.25"
Copyright: 1936

Sculptor: R.Unger
2-D Original: H 385
1995 Retail: T.W.

Originally given a bowl shape (Var. I), this piece was redesigned to a box shape in 1964 at the onset of the TM4 era (Var. II). Some of the Variety II pieces bear the TM3 stamp. The box was withdrawn at the end of 1989.

Trends in Selling TM6: $145-180
           TM5: $155-180
           TM4: $175-210
     Var. I in TM3: $350-430
    Var. II in TM3: $250-315
           TM2: $425-530
           TM1: $525-650

JOYFUL NEWS
(See *Angel with ... Candleholders*)

JOYOUS NEWS
Mold No.: 27/III
Ref. No.: 555
Approx. Size: 4.25" x
  4.75"
Copyright: 1935
Sculptor: R.Unger
2-D Original: H 435
1995 Retail: $215

When it was restyled with the modern, textured finish in 1979, the size designator of **Joyous News** was changed from an Arabic */3* (Var. I) to a Roman */III* (Var. II). Both varieties can be found with some difficulty in TM5. Before the late 1970s, the figurine was rarely produced. It is not known in TM4, is rare to nonexistent in TM3, and is pricey in the earlier marks.

Trends in Selling TM6-7: $175-215
   Var. I in TM5: $200-235
  Var. II in TM5: $235-275
           TM3: $635-780
           TM2: $800-1000
           TM1: $1200-1500

JOYOUS NEWS CANDLEHOLDER

Mold No.: 27/I
Ref. No.: n.a.
Approx. Size: 2.75"
Copyright: 1935
Sculptor: R.Unger
2-D Original: H 435
1995 Retail: Closed
 Edition

Photo not available. This piece looks similar to *Joyous News* figurine (page 129) and to *Angel with Trumpet* candleholder (page 71). As is shown on the latter piece, the small candleholder is added as an extension of the base.

Except for the mold number, this piece is almost identical to the 40/I model of *Angel With Trumpet Candleholder*. This likely explains why **Joyous News Candleholder** is seldom found and why it is listed by Goebel as a closed edition. Roman numerals in *front* of the mold number pertain to candle size in millimeters and do not affect values.

Trends in Selling TM2: $265-330
 TM1: $370-460

JUBILEE

Mold No.: 416
Ref. No.: 421
Approx. Size: 6.25"
Copyright: 1980
Sculptor: G.Skrobek
2-D Original: H 348 & H 349
1995 Retail: Closed Edition

Jubilee was packaged in a special presentation box and offered only in 1985 in celebration of "50 Years M.I. Hummel Figurines 1935–1985," as it says on the bottom of the figurine. Production was limited to year of issue. Only recently, however, has the figurine earned respect on the secondary market. Apparently, stockpiles held by speculators have dwindled, and available pieces are now quickly purchased by eager collectors. Issue price was $200 in 1985.

Trends in Selling TM6: $340-425

JUST DOZING

Mold No.: 451
Ref. No.: 056
Approx. Size: n.a.
Copyright: 1984
Sculptor: G.Skrobek
2-D Original: H 114
1995 Retail: $220

A Skrobek design originally modeled 11 years previously, **Just Dozing** would be remarkable in its absence of the familiar Hummel base, except that it is one of three figurines introduced for 1995 that lack the usual bases. The others are *The Angler*, also sculpted by Skrobek, and *To Keep You Warm,* a Helmut Fischer creation. It will be interesting to see if this is a trend which continues.

Trends in Selling TM7: $175-220

JUST FISHING

Mold No.: 373
Ref. No.: 424
Approx. Size: 4.25"
Copyright: 1965
Sculptor: G.Skrobek
2-D Original: H 237
1995 Retail: $225

Just Fishing was issued as a new release in 1985—20 years after its 1965 copyright date.

Trends in Selling TM6-7: $180-225

JUST RESTING

Mold No.: 112
Copyright: 1938
Sculptor: R.Unger
2-D Original: H 290

Model No.: 112/I
Ref. No.: 898
Approx. Size: 5"
1995 Retail: $280

Model No.: 112 3/0
Ref. No.: 899
Approx. Size: 4"
1995 Retail: $145

Approx. Size: 9.5"	Approx. Size: 9.5"
1995 Retail: T.W.	1995 Retail: T.W.
Model No.: 225/I	Model No.: 224/I
Ref. No.: 647	Ref. No.: 649
Approx. Size: 7.5"	Approx. Size: 7.5"
1995 Retail: T.W.	1995 Retail: T.W.

Just Resting was designed as a companion piece to *Wayside Harmony*. The larger size preceded the smaller. Early, slightly oversized examples without the /I suffix command small premiums.

Trends in Selling M 112/I TM6-7: $225-280
            TM5: $240-280
            TM4: $275-325
            TM3: $315-370
            TM2: $395-460
            TM1: $470-710

Trends in Selling M 112 3/0 TM6-7: $120-140
            TM5: $125-145
            TM4: $140-165
            TM3: $160-185
            TM2: $205-240
            TM1: $300-375

Designed together and meant to be paired, these companion lamps originally incorporated the respective /I figurines on the 7.5-inch lamp bases (models 112 & 111). In the 1950s, Unger redesigned the 7.5-inch models with smaller figures and modeled the 9.5-inch versions, both of which were assigned the new 225 and 224 mold numbers by Goebel. All versions can be found in TM2 and TM3. The larger models, 225/II and 224/II, measure about 6.25 inches in base diameter. These command premiums if found numbered without the size suffix. Production of the lamps in both sizes was withdrawn as of Jan. 1, 1990.

JUST RESTING ANNUAL PLATE

(See 1991 Annual Plate)

JUST RESTING LAMP	WAYSIDE HARMONY LAMP
Mold No.: 225	Mold No.: 224
Copyright: 1938	Copyright: 1938
Sculptor: R.Unger	Sculptor: R.Unger
2-D Original: H 290	2-D Original: H 289
Model No.: II/112	Model No.: II/111
Ref. No.: n.a.	Ref. No.: n.a.
Approx. Size: 7.5"	Approx. Size: 7.5"
1995 Retail: Closed Edition	1995 Retail: Closed Edition
Model No.: 225/II	Model No.: 224/II
Ref. No.: 646	Ref. No.: 648

Trends in Selling M ¹I/112 & M II/111
            TM3: $460-575 each
            TM2: $570-710 each
            TM1: $675-840 each

Trends in Selling M 225/II & M 224/II
            TM6: $350-435 each
            TM5: $370-435 each
            TM4: $425-400 each
            TM3: $475-565 each
            TM2: $600-750 each

Trends in Selling M 225/I & M 224/I
            TM6: $295-370 each
            TM5: $315-370 each
            TM4: $360-425 each
            TM3: $410-485 each
            TM2: $515-645 each

KINDERGARTNER

Mold No.: 467
Ref. No.: 409
Approx. Size: 5.25"
Copyright: 1985
Sculptor: G.Skrobek
2-D Original: H 701
1995 Retail: $200

Kindergartner was copyrighted in 1985 and first released in 1987.

Trends in Selling TM6-7: $160-200

KISS ME

Mold No.: 311
Ref. No.: 805
Approx. Size: 6"
Copyright: 1955
Sculptor: R.Unger
Restyled by:
   G.Skrobek
2-D Original:
   H 231
1995 Retail: $285

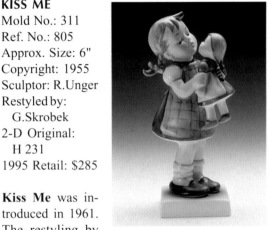

Kiss Me was introduced in 1961.
The restyling by Skrobek came two years later during the transition from TM3 to TM4. Both Variety I (large doll with socks) and Variety II (smaller doll without socks) can be found in these trademarks.

Trends in Selling TM6-7: $230-285
         TM5: $245-285
   Var. I in TM4: $520-620
   Var. II in TM4: $280-330
   Var. I in TM3: $520-620
   Var. II in TM3: $555-680

KNIT ONE, PURL ONE

Mold No.: 432
Ref. No.: 720
Approx. Size: 3"
Copyright: 1982
Sculptor: G.Skrobek
2-D Original: H 195
1995 Retail: $115

The 1983 release of **Knit One, Purl One** was timed to coincide with the annual bell of that year, which also featured the motif. Many collectors like to pair their bells and plates with the matching figurines in a display.

Trends in Selling
   TM6-7: $95-115

KNIT ONE, PURL ONE ANNUAL BELL
(See 1983 Annual Bell)

KNITTING LESSON

Mold No.: 256
Ref. No.: 817
Approx. Size: 7.5"
Copyright: 1963
Sculptor: n.a.
2-D Original: H 197
1995 Retail: $500

Knitting Lesson was introduced in 1964 during the transition from TM3 to TM4. It is, therefore, scarce in TM3.

Trends in Selling TM6-7: $400-500
         TM5: $425-500
         TM4: $485-570
         TM3: $880-1075

LAND IN SIGHT

Mold No.: 530
Ref. No.: 190
Approx. Size: 9" x 9.5"
Copyright: 1988
Sculptor: G.Skrobek
2-D Original: H 460
1995 Retail: $1600

One can say about **Land in Sight** (facing page) that 1) it is a magnificent figurine that perhaps more

(Continued overleaf)

than any other crowns Gerhard Skrobek's long tenure as Goebel master sculptor; 2) it is perhaps the most spectacular creation commemorating the 500th anniversary of Columbus' discovery of America; and 3) it is certainly one of the most detailed and difficult M.I. Hummel figurines ever created, requiring more than 24 separate molds and a production process incorporating more than 325 separate steps. What can also be said is that—from a secondary market perspective—there were mistakes in the release and introduction of the figurine in mid-1991. While **Land in Sight** carried a $1600 issue price, Goebel expected the edition of 30,000 pieces to be a complete sell-out by the end of the year—meaning all available examples would be in the hands of collectors or retailers. It didn't happen. Conversely, numerous retailers over-ordered on the figurine, and, in order to quickly rid themselves of expensive inventory, began discounting the piece drastically on the market. For brief periods, the piece has commanded unbelievably low prices. Too expensive to be held long by speculators, however, the figurine has begun to make a price recovery. It stands as the second *sequentially numbered limited edition* M.I. Hummel figurine ever produced, following in the footsteps of the *Crossroads Berlin Wall Commemorative* of a year earlier.

Trends in Selling TM7: $1280-1600

LATEST NEWS
Mold No.: 184/0
Ref. No.: 850
Approx. Size: 5"
Copyright: 1946
Sculptor: A.Moeller
2-D Original: H 245
1995 Retail: $290

Latest News was redesigned in the mid-1960s. Moeller's original mold (Var. I) depicts the boy standing on a square base with his eyes wide open. The restyled mold (Var. II) gives him a round base, and his eyes look down at the paper. In this figurine, one can encounter expensive variations in the name of the newspaper. The factory normally titled the paper *Latest News, Das Allerneueste* or *Munchener Presse.* These titles are common. However, it was simple to customize the title of the paper for a customer.

These substituted titles usually demand premiums of 50 to 100% above normal values.

Trends in Selling TM6-7: $235-290
    TM5: $245-290
  Var. I in TM4: $355-415
  Var. II in TM4: $285-335
    TM3: $355-415
    TM2: $405-475
    TM1: $610-755

LATEST NEWS BELL
(See 1989 Annual Bell)

LET'S SING
Mold No.: 110
Copyright: 1938
Sculptor: R.Unger
2-D Original: H 167, H 179

Model No.: 110/I
Ref. No.: 902
Approx. Size: 4"
1995 Retail: $165

Model No.: 110/0
Ref. No.: 903
Approx. Size: 3"
1995 Retail: $125

Early examples of the larger size of **Let's Sing** lack the */I* size suffix. These pieces demand small premiums when found.

Trends in Selling M 110/I TM6-7: $135-165
    TM5: $140-165
    TM4: $160-190
    TM3: $180-210
    TM2: $230-270
    TM1: $355-440

Trends in Selling M 110/0 TM6-7: $100-125
    TM5: $105-125
    TM4: $125-145
    TM3: $135-160
    TM2: $175-205
    TM1: $270-335

LET'S SING ANNUAL BELL
(See 1978 Annual Bell)

LET'S SING ASHTRAY
Mold No.: 114
Ref. No.: 675
Approx. Size: 3.5" x 6.25"
Copyright: 1938
Sculptor: R.Unger
Restyled by: T.Menzenbach
2-D Original: H 167, H 179
1995 Retail: T.W.

Menzenbach's restyling came in 1959 and moved the ashtray from the boy's right side to the boy's left side. All examples are rare in TM1 and scarce in TM2. The piece was withdrawn from production at the end of 1989.

Trends in Selling TM6: $105-155
                TM5: $115-155
                TM4: $135-175
                TM3: $150-190
                TM2: $250-315
                TM1: $500-625

LET'S SING CANDY BOX
Mold No.: III/110
Ref. No.: 669
Approx. Size: 6"
Copyright: 1938
Sculptor: n.a.
2-D Original: H 167, H 179
1995 Retail: T.W.

Originally given a bowl shape (Var. I), the container was redesigned to a box shape in 1964 at the onset of the TM4 era (Var. II). Some of the Varitey II pieces bear the TM3 stamp. The box was withdrawn from production at the end of 1989.

Trends in Selling TM6: $145-180
                TM5: $155-180
                TM4: $175-210
           Var. I in TM3: $350-430
          Var. II in TM3: $250-315
                TM2: $425-530
                TM1: $525-650

MOLD NUMBERS AND HUM NUMBERS

Veteran Hummel chasers using this book will wonder what happened to the *HUM numbers*. This book, for instance, will tell you that the figurine *Botanist* is *mold 351*, while most previous works refer to it as *HUM 351*.

I hope you'll bear with me in this regard. A HUM number is a mold number; it is simply part of Goebel's unusual numbering system whereby a portion of the artist's name is incorporated into the mold number for record-keeping purposes.

The Goebel system has a certain charm, but it does tend to confuse most beginners.

MEASURING HUMMELS

When sizing a Hummel figurine, measure from the bottom of the base to the topmost point. This distance in inches should approximately equal listed sizes.

The word approximately is used because sizes, particularly in older figurines, do fluctuate quite a bit. Normally, this fluctuation is due to expansion of plaster working molds created by usage. This is called "mold growth" in the trade. Many other factors may also cause minor variations in size.

LETTER TO SANTA CLAUS

Mold No.: 340
Ref. No.: 777
Approx. Size: 7.25"
Copyright: 1957
Sculptor: H. Wehlte
Restyled by: G.Skrobek
2-D Original: H 318
1995 Retail: $330

One of the spectacular new offerings of 1971— the year also produced *Adventure Bound, Homeward Bound and Artist*—**Letter to Santa Claus** had already been given a modern restyling by Skrobek prior to introduction. With its release just before the transition to TM5, this item is very scarce in TM4 and would be very rare in any earlier trademark.

Trends in Selling TM6-7: $265-330
            TM5: $280-330
            TM4: $600-740

LETTER TO SANTA CLAUS CHRISTMAS BELL
(See 1990 Christmas Bell)

LIGHT UP THE NIGHT ORNAMENT
(See 1992 Annual Ornament)

LITTLE ARCHITECT

Mold No.: 410/I
Ref. No.: 162
Approx. Size: 6"
Copyright: 1978
Sculptor: G.Skrobek
2-D Original: H 262
1995 Retail: $300

Though copyrighted in 1978, **Little Architect** was not released until 1993 and can be found only in TM7. Upon introduction, it was renamed from *Truant*, which was also the name Sister Hummel had given to her original.

Trends in Selling TM7: $240-300

LET'S TELL THE WORLD

Mold No.: 487
Ref. No.: 254
Approx. Size: 10.5" x 7"
Copyright: 1987
Sculptor: G.Skrobek
2-D Original: H 478
1995 Retail: Closed Edition

Flushed with the success of *Chapel Time Clock* as its first "century release" in 1986, Goebel quickly put Gerhard Skrobek to work on succeeding issues in the spectacular series. Among these was **Let's Tell the World**, which was released in 1990 as the fifth in the annual series. Produced just for the one year in the twentieth century, the piece has enjoyed a steady demand in the secondary market, but has not escalated in value as rapidly as the issues preceding it. A special bottom stamp reads, "M.I. Hummel Century Collection 1990 XX." The XX is found on each of the *Century Collection* issues to permanently distinguish these special issues. Issue price was $875 in 1990.

Trends in Selling TM6: $925-1150

LITTLE BAND

Mold No.: 392
Ref. No.: 732
Approx. Size: 3" x 4.75"
Copyright: 1968
Sculptor: G.Skrobek
2-D Original: Unknown
1995 Retail: T.W.

When Skrobek designed the popular **Little Band** threesome of *Boy with Accordion, Girl with Sheet Music* and *Girl with Trumpet* as candleholders in late 1967, Goebel obviously sought additional ways to offer the creations. This item puts the three figurines together on a circular base without the candleholder itself. It was withdrawn from production as of Jan. 1, 1985.

Trends in Selling TM6: $200-250
        TM5: $215-250
        TM4: $245-290

LITTLE BAND CANDLEHOLDER

Mold No.: 388
Ref. No.: 738
Approx. Size: 4.75" x 3"
Copyright: 1968
Sculptor: G.Skrobek
2-D Original: Unknown
1995 Retail: T.W.

This piece is almost identical to *Little Band* figurine, but incorporates the candleholder. It was withdrawn from production at the end of 1990, appeared on 1992 and 1993 price lists, and was withdrawn again before 1994.

Trends in Selling TM6-7: $175-220
        TM5: $190-220
        TM4: $215-255

NEW FOR 1993

The 1993 M.I. Hummel introductions included *I Didn't Do It, A Sweet Offering, Sweet As Can Be, Parade of Lights, A Free Flight, Little Architect, Welcome Spring, One Plus One,* a new small size of *Celestial Musician, Celestial Musician mini ornament,* and the various 1993 annuals.

LITTLE BAND W/CANDLE MUSIC BOX

Mold No.: 388/M
Ref. No.: 737
Approx. Size: 4.75" x 5"
Copyright: 1968
Sculptor: G.Skrobek
2-D Original: Unknown
1995 Retail: T.W.

This is simply the *Little Band Candleholder* mounted on a wooden, Swiss-made musical base, as per photo. Tunes vary. This item was withdrawn from production at the end of 1990.

Trends in Selling TM6: $270-340
        TM5: $290-340
        TM4: $330-390

LITTLE BAND W/O CANDLE MUSIC BOX

Mold No.: 392/M
Ref. No.: 731
Approx. Size: 4.75" x 5"
Copyright: 1968
Sculptor: G.Skrobek
2-D Original: Unknown
1995 Retail: T.W.

This is simply the *Little Band* figurine mounted on a wooden, Swiss-made musical base. It lacks the candleholder. Tunes vary. This item was withdrawn from production at the end of 1990.

Trends in Selling TM6: $270-340
        TM5: $290-340
        TM4: $330-390

LITTLE BOOKKEEPER

Mold No.: 306
Ref. No.: 809
Approx. Size: 4.75"
Copyright: 1955
Sculptor: A.Moeller
2-D Original: H 202
1995 Retail: $285

Not introduced until 1962, **Little Book-keeper** was available in only the last portion of the TM3 era and is thus scarce in that trademark.

Trends in Selling TM6-7: $230-285
        TM5: $240-285
        TM4: $2l80-330
        TM3: $820-1000

examples of the larger size numbered without size suffix can command slight premiums.

Trends in Selling M 89/II TM6-7: $330-415
   White Var. in TM7: $210-260
        TM5: $350-415
        TM4: $410-480
        TM3: $460-540
        TM2: $585-690
        TM1: $875-1090

Trends in Selling M 89/I TM6-7: $170-210
        TM5: $180-210
        TM4: $205-240
   Var. I in TM3: $295-345
   Var. II in TM3: $270-320
        TM2: $285-335
        TM1: $495-615

LITTLE CELLIST

Mold No.: 89
Copyright: 1938
Sculptor: A.Moeller
2-D Original: H 250

Model No.: 89/II
Ref. No.: 914
Approx. Size: 7.5"
1995 Retail: T.W.

Model No.: 89/II (white)
Ref. No.: 164
Approx. Size: 7.5"
1995 Retail: $260

Model No.: 89/I
Ref. No.: 915
Approx. Size: 6"
1995 Retail: $210

Until the smaller size was redesigned in the early 1960s, it depicted **Little Cellist** with eyes wide open (Var. I), while on the larger counterpart the eyes were looking down as on both current models (Var. II). Both varieties of the smaller piece can be found in TM3, with one not noticeably harder to find than the other. Model 89/II in its multicolored form was withdrawn from production in 1992 concurrent with the introduction of this model as part of the white *Expressions of Youth* series. Early

LITTLE DRUMMER

Mold No.: 240
Ref. No.: 819
Approx. Size: 4.25"
Copyright: 1955
Sculptor: R.Unger
2-D Original: H 655
1995 Retail: $145

Little Drummer was introduced not too long after design. No important varieties have been discovered.

Trends in Selling TM6-7: $120-145
        TM5: $125-145
        TM4: $140-165
        TM3: $205-240
        TM2: $245-300

LITTLE FIDDLER

Mold No.: 2 & 4
Copyright: 1935
Sculptor: A.Moeller
2-D Original: H 229, F 203

Model No.: 2/III	Model No.: 2/II
Ref. No.: 993	Ref. No.: 994
Approx. Size: 12.25"	Approx. Size: 10.75"
1995 Retail: T.W.	1995 Retail: T.W.

Model No.: 2/I
Ref. No.: 995
Approx. Size: 7.5"
1995 Retail: T.W.

Model No.: 2/I (white)
Ref. No.: 169
Approx. Size: 6"
1995 Retail: $260

Model No.: 2/0
Ref. No.: 996
Approx. Size: 6"
1995 Retail: $215

Model No.: 2 4/0
Ref. No.: 426
Approx. Size: 3"
1995 Retail: $100

Model No.: 4
Ref. No.: 989
Approx. Size: 4.75"
1995 Retail: $200

The mold numbers and copyright date identify this as one of the very first M.I. Hummel figurines. The mold 4 examples can be treated as just another size of **Little Fiddler**; otherwise, these differ only in the color of the hat—black versus the normal brown. The large models 2/III and 2/II were withdrawn from production at the end of 1989, and model 2/I in its multicolored form was withdrawn in 1992 concurrent with the introduction of this model as part of the white *Expressions of Youth* series. When model 2 4/0 was introduced in 1984, all six sizes of **Little Fiddler** were listed as being in current production! Research indicates model 2/III could be rare or nonexistent in TM3 and TM4. It was reinstated circa 1978 after being long out of production. Despite the long runs of the many different sizes, this figurine displays only the normal variations in size, color and mold construction except earliest pieces marked FF 16 instead of the normal mold number. These are very rare.

Trends in Selling M 2/III TM6: $1075-1340
        TM5: $1140-1340
        TM4: $1870-2200
        TM3: $1870-2200
        TM2: $1870-2200
        TM1: $2700-3350

Trends in Selling M 2/II TM6: $990-1235
        TM5: $1050-1235
        TM4: $1200-1420
        TM3: $1360-1600
        TM2: $1735-2040
        TM1: $2450-3040

Trends in Selling M 2/I TM6-7: $325-405
    White Var. TM7: $210-260
        TM5: $345-405
        TM4: $400-470
        TM3: $450-530
        TM2: $570-670
        TM1: $930-1160

Trends in Selling M 2/0 TM6-7: $175-215
        TM5: $185-215
        TM4: $210-245
        TM3: $240-280
        TM2: $300-355
        TM1: $575-700

Trends in Selling M 4 TM6-7: $160-200
        TM5: $170-200
        TM4: $195-230
        TM3: $2220-260
        TM2: $275-325
        TM1: $455-565

Trends in Selling M 2 4/0 TM6-7: $80-100

LITTLE FIDDLER MINI PLATE
(See 1984 Mini Plate)

LITTLE FIDDLER PLAQUE
Mold No.: 93
Ref. No.: 676
Approx. Size: 5" x 5.5"
Copyright: 1938
Sculptor: A.Moeller
2-D Original: H 229,
    F 203
1995 Retail: T.W.

This item was withdrawn from production as of Jan. 1, 1990. In TM1, the original version (Var. I) was made with fewer buildings in the background. It is quite rare.

Trends in Selling TM6: $110-140
        TM5: $120-140
        TM4: $135-160
        TM3: $150-180
        TM2: $195-230
     Var. I in TM1: $2000-2500
     Var. II in TM1: $310-390

LITTLE GABRIEL

Mold No.: 32
Copyright: 1935
Sculptor: R.Unger
2-D Original: H 435

Model No.: 32/I
Ref. No.: n.a.
Approx. Size: 6"
1995 Retail: Closed
    Edition

Model No.: 32 or 32/0
Ref. No.: 554
Approx. Size: 5"
1995 Retail: $140

The larger size of **Little Gabriel** was seldom produced and is considered rare in any trademark; when found, it may be numbered with or without the /I size designator. Newest examples of the smaller size are also found without size designator.

Trends in Selling M 32/I:
        TM3: $1000-1250
        TM2: $1300-1625
        TM1: $1600-2000

Trends in Selling M 32/0 TM6-7: $115-140
        TM5: $120-140
        TM4: $140-165
        TM3: $155-185
        TM2: $195-230
        TM1: $310-385

LITTLE GARDENER

Mold No.: 74
Ref. No.: 927
Approx. Size: 4"
Copyright: 1937
Sculptor: R.Unger
2-D Original: FB 207
1995 Retail: $120

Little Gardener is one of the figurines with minor color and mold variations which do not affect values. An exception might be the special bottom stamp given to examples made available in 1992 only during in-store Hummel promotions (Var. II). Only time will determine how much these

pieces will be sought in the secondary market as special varieties.

Trends in Selling TM6-7: $100-120
    Var. II in TM7: $115-135
        TM5: $105-120
        TM4: $115-135
        TM3: $130-155
        TM2: $165-195
        TM1: $275-345

LITTLE GOAT HERDER

Mold No.: 200
Copyright: 1948
Sculptor: A.Moeller
2-D Original: H 235

Model No.: 200/I
Ref. No.: 833
Approx. Size: 5.5"
1995 Retail: $235

Model No.: 200/0
Ref. No.: 834
Approx. Size: 4.75"
1995 Retail: $195

Little Goat Herder is relatively difficult to find in TM1. If found with the crown mark, it will lack the size designator which was added with the introduction of the smaller size in the mid-1950s. Early TM2 examples also lack the size designator and command small premiums when found.

Trends in Selling M 200/I TM6-7: $190-235
        TM5: $200-235
        TM4: $230-270
        TM3: $260-305
        TM2: $330-385
        TM1: $560-700

Trends in Selling M 200/0 TM6-7: $155-195
        TM5: $165-195
        TM4: $185-220
        TM3: $215-255
        TM2: $270-320

LITTLE GOAT HERDER ANNUAL PLATE
(See 1988 Annual Plate)

LITTLE GOAT HERDER
& FEEDING TIME BOOKENDS
Mold No.: 250/A & B
Ref. No.: 711
Approx. Size: 5.5"
Copyright: 1960
Sculptor: n.a.
2-D Original: H 235, H 236
1995 Retail: T.W.

The bookend set consists of the respective figurines mounted on wooden bases. The bookends were withdrawn from production Dec. 31, 1989. The values of the individual figurines exceed the set.

Trends in Selling TM6: $255-315 pair
TM5: $270-315 pair
TM3: $335-410 pair

LITTLE GUARDIAN
Mold No.: 145
Ref. No.: 475
Approx. Size: 4"
Copyright: 1941
Sculptor: R.Unger
2-D Original: Unknown
1995 Retail: $145

Though more or less in continuous production for more than 50 years, no important variations have been found in **Little Guardian**.

Trends in Selling TM6-7: $120-145
TM5: $125-145
TM4: $140-165
TM3: $160-185
TM2: $205-240
TM1: $355-445

LITTLE HELPER
Mold No.: 73
Ref. No.: 928
Approx. Size: 4.25"
Copyright: 1937
Sculptor: R.Unger
2-D Original: H 340
1995 Retail: $120

Though more or less in continuous production for more than 55 years, no important variations have been found in **Little Helper**.

Trends in Selling TM6-7: $100-120
TM5: $105-120
TM4: $115-135
TM3: $130-155
TM2: $165-195
TM1: $275-345

LITTLE HELPER ANNUAL PLATE
(See 1984 Annual Plate)

THE FF HUMMELS

At the onset of Goebel's production of figurines based on the artwork of Sister Hummel, some of the earliest prototypes were made before the *Hum number* mold numbering system was adopted.

An interim marking system was used on these prototypes, and today rare examples exist of *Puppy Love* marked FF 15 rather than (mold or Hum) 1; *Little Fiddler* marked FF 16 rather than 2; and *Book Worm* marked FF 17 rather than 3.

LITTLE HIKER

Mold No.: 16
Copyright: 1935
Sculptor: A.Moeller
2-D Original: H 307

Model No.: 16/I
Ref. No.: 965
Approx. Size: 6"
1995 Retail: $215

Model No.: 16 2/0
Ref. No.: 966
Approx. Size: 4.5"
1995 Retail: $120

Examples of the larger size **Little Hiker** can be found in TM1 and TM2 without size suffix. These command small premiums. Otherwise, this is one of the more unchanged of the original figurines, and both sizes can be found in all trademarks.

Trends in Selling M 16/I TM6-7: $175-215
        TM5: $185-215
        TM4: $210-245
        TM3: $240-280
        TM2: $300-350
        TM1: $480-600

Trends in Selling M 16 2/0 TM6-7: $100-120
        TM5: $105-120
        TM4: $115-135
        TM3: $130-155
        TM2: $165-195
        TM1: $275-345

LITTLE NURSE

Mold No.: 376
Ref. No.: 750
Approx. Size: 4"
Copyright: 1972
Sculptor: G.Skrobek
2-D Original: H 660
1995 Retail: $245

Copyrighted in 1972, **Little Nurse** was not released until 1982. It can only be found in TM6 and TM7.

Trends in Selling TM6-7: $195-245

LITTLE PAIR (THE)

Mold No.: 449
Ref. No.: 239
Approx. Size: 4.5"
Copyright: 1985
Sculptor: G.Skrobek
2-D Original: Unknown
1995 Retail: $210

A Skrobek design which was copyrighted in 1985, **The Little Pair** sat on the samples shelf for five years before being chosen as a special edition offered only to M.I. Hummel Club members who had completed 10 successive years of membership in the club. To obtain the figurine at issue prices through primary market channels, a person needs a redemption certificate which is issued only to individuals who have been members of the Club for the required time. Destined, therefore, to always be a prize possession—and of immediate importance in the secondary market—*The Little Pair* with its mid-1990 introduction should prove to be exceedingly scarce in TM6. Issue price was $170 in 1990, but in mid-1995 price increases had taken retail (with redemption certificate) to $210.

Trends in Selling TM7: $210-310
        TM6: $310-385

LITTLE SCHOLAR'S PACKAGE
The item being carried by *Little Scholar* is a traditional German item called a *Schultüte* or *Zuckertüte*, a paper cone of school supplies and goodies sent with children for the first day of school.

LITTLE PHARMACIST

Mold No.: 322
Ref. No.: 793
Approx. Size: 6"
Copyright: 1955
Sculptor: K.Wagner
2-D Original: H 241
1995 Retail: $240

Copyrighted in 1955, **Little Pharmacist** was not released until 1962 and is difficult to find in TM3. It was given a major restyling in 1987, with older examples (Var. I) easily identified by the square corners of the base and a straightened bowtie. The word "Vitamins" is most commonly found on the bottle. Examples with the word "Rizinusol" were made for the German market and command a small premium. Examples with the word "Castor bil" were made for the Spanish market and are considered very rare. Both words mean castor oil.

Trends in Selling TM6-7: $195-240
   Var. I in TM6: $205-240
        TM5: $205-240
        TM4: $235-275
        TM3: $725-875

LITTLE SHOPPER

Mold No.: 96
Ref. No.: 910
Approx. Size: 5"
Copyright: 1938
Sculptor: n.a.
2-D Original: Unknown
1995 Retail: $135

Though more or less in continuous production for more than 55 years, no important variations have been found in **Little Shopper**.

Trends in Selling TM6-7: $115-135
        TM5: $120-135
        TM4: $135-160
        TM3: $155-180
        TM2: $195-230
        TM1: $300-370

LITTLE SCHOLAR

Mold No.: 80
Ref. No.: 925
Approx. Size: 5.5"
Copyright:1937
Sculptor: A.Moeller
2-D Original: H 192
1995 Retail: $210

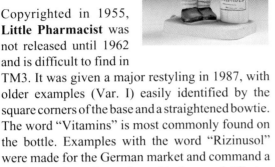

Except for normal variations in size and color— early examples had brown shoes versus the current black or gray— **Little Scholar** has undergone little change. The parcel the boy is carrying is a *Schultute* (school cone) holding his supplies for school.

Trends in Selling TM6-7: $170-210
        TM5: $180-210
        TM4: $205-240
        TM3: $235-275
        TM2: $2890349
        TM1: $495-615

1984 WITHDRAWALS

A large group of M.I. Hummel figurines was given "T.W." status—temporarily withdrawn from production—at the end of 1984. These included *Festival Harmony w/Mandolin* model 172/II, *Festival Harmony w/Flute* model 173/II, *Volunteers* model 50/I, *Spring Cheer, Madonna w/Halo* model 45/0, *Madonna w/oHalo* model 46/0, *Sensitive Hunter* model 6/II, *Meditation* model 13/II, *Joyful Ashtray, To Market* model 49/I, *Village Boy* model 51/I, *Going to Grandma's* model 52/I, *Telling Her Secret* model 196/I, *Little Band, Madonna Plaque* model 48/II, *Farm Boy/ Goose Girl Bookends, Playmates/Chick Girl Bookends* and the German-language version (only) of *Little Pharmacist*.

LITTLE SWEEPER

Mold No.: 171
Copyright: 1944, 1986
Sculptor: R.Unger
Restyled by: G.Skrobek
2-D Original: H 234

Model No.: 171/0
Ref. No.: 860
Approx. Size: 4.25"
1995 Retail: $135

Model No.: 171 4/0
Ref. No.: 305
Approx. Size: 3"
1995 Retail: $100

Little Sweeper—along with *Wash Day, Stitch in Time* and *Chicken Licken*—is now perhaps best known as part of the "Little Homemakers" group due to the four-year mini plate series of 1988–1991. **Little Sweeper** was used to introduce the series, and the smaller, 4/0 size was first issued in 1988 as a companion piece to the mini plate. At the same time, the larger size was given a /0 size designator. Earlier examples are simply numbered 171. The larger size was restyled by Skrobek with the modern, textured finish in 1981. Coming when it did, this restyling makes the original version (Var. I) comparatively scarce in TM6.

Trends in Selling M 171/0 TM6-7: $110-135
  Var. I in TM6: $125-150
      TM5: $125-150
      TM4: $130-155
      TM3: $150-175
      TM2: $185-220
      TM1: $300-375

Trends in Selling M 171 4/0 TM6-7: $80-100

LITTLE SWEEPER MINI PLATE

(See 1988 Mini Plate)

LITTLE TAILOR

Mold No.: 308
Ref. No.: 807
Approx. Size: 5.5"
Copyright: 1955 & 1972
Sculptor: H.Ashermann
Restyled by: G.Skrobek
2-D Original: H 258
1995 Retail: $245

Originally modeled in 1955, **Little Tailor** is another of the pieces given a modernizing redesign by Skrobek as it was being released in 1972. With the introduction and design change coming during the phase-in of TM5, Ashermann's original design is very scarce in both TM5 and TM4. The varieties are easily distinguished by the incised copyright date—1955 for Variety I and 1972 for Variety II.

Trends in Selling TM6-7: $195-245
  Var. I in TM5: $535-680
    Var. II in TM5: $210-245
      TM4: $880-1095

LITTLE THRIFTY

Mold No.: 118
Ref. No.: 663
Approx. Size: 5"
Copyright: 1939
Sculptor: A.Moeller
Restyled by: R.Wittman
2-D Original: H 163
1995 Retail: $145

The only M.I. Hummel coin bank, **Little Thrifty** is supplied with a key and metal lock plug on the base. There is usually a small price deduction if either of these is missing. The item has not been found and should be considered rare in TM4. A 1973 catalog lists the item as "not available and not in current production." Price lists dated 1971 and 1978 simply do not list the item; however, it does appear on a 1979 price list. This suggests that **Little Thrifty** might also be a difficult find within TM5.

Trends in Selling TM6-7: $115-145
      TM5: $165-195
      TM3: $190-225
      TM2: $325-385
      TM1: $425-525

LITTLE TOOTER
(See Nativity Sets)

LITTLE TROUBADOUR
Mold No.: 558
Ref. No.: 101
Approx. Size: 4"
Copyright: 1989
Sculptor: H.Fischer
2-D Original: H 338
1995 Retail: $130

Little Troubadour was introduced in mid-1994 as the special M.I. Hummel Club Preview Edition for club year 1994–95. The third annual in this series, the preview edition required a redemption certificate and was marked with the standard Club Exclusive backstamp. The figurine may be released as part of the regular M.I. Hummel line as an open edition after May 31, 1996, but without the special Preview Edition backstamp.

Trends in Selling: $130-150

LITTLE VISITOR
Mold No.: 563/0
Ref. No.: 100
Approx. Size: 5"
Copyright: 1991
Sculptor:
   H.Fischer
2-D Original:
   H 219
1995 Retail: $180

In the spring of 1994, **Little Visitor** became No. 18 in the distinguished series of Members' Exclusive Editions for the M.I. Hummel Club. With the required redemption card, it was to be available at issue price through May 31, 1995. After that time, it will be a retired edition though still deliverable through May 31, 1996, to holders of redemption certificates. Issue price was $180.

Trends in Selling: $180-210

LOST SHEEP
Mold No.: 68
Copyright: 1937
Sculptor:
   A.Moeller
Restyled by:
   Various
2-D Original:
   H 293

Model No.: 68/0
Ref. No.: 932
Approx. Size: 5.5"
1995 Retail:
   Retired

Model No.: 68 2/0
Ref. No.: 933
Approx. Size: 4.5"
1995 Retail: Retired

Continuing a tradition begun with *Puppy Love* (Hum 1) in 1988, molds were broken and both models of **Lost Sheep** were officially retired at the end of 1992. The larger model was marked without the size suffix until the smaller model was introduced sometime after 1955. This model commands a small premium when found in TM2 or TM3 without the size suffix. Otherwise, the figurine can be found with the normal varations in size and color which do not affect values. Examples sold during its farewell year bear a special backstamp reading "Last Issue 1992."

Trends in Selling M 68/0 TM6-7: $190-235
         TM5: $215-250
         TM4: $230-270
         TM3: $260-305
         TM2: $330-385
         TM1: $530-660

Trends in Selling M 68 2/0 TM6-7: $135-165
         TM5: $150-175
         TM4: $160-190
         TM3: $185-215
         TM2: $230-270

LOST STOCKING

Mold No.: 374
Ref. No.: 752
Approx. Size: 4.25"
Copyright: 1965
Sculptor: G.Skrobek
2-D Original: H 119
1995 Retail: $140

Another from the large group introduced in 1972, **Lost Stocking** is very difficult to find in TM4 and would be rare in TM3.

Trends in Selling TM6-7: $115-140
          TM5: $120-140
          TM4: $775-975

LOVE FROM ABOVE ANNUAL ORNAMENT
(See 1989 Annual Ornament)

LUCKY FELLOW

Mold No.: 560
Ref. No.: 174
Approx. Size: 3.5"
Copyright: 1989
Sculptor:
  H.Fischer
2-D Original:
  Unknown
1995 Retail:
  Closed Edition

Lucky Fellow was included in the kit received by each renewing member of the M.I. Hummel Club for the club year beginning June 1, 1992, and ending May 31, 1993. With a value of $75, it could originally be acquired for a $35 club renewal fee.

Trends in Selling TM7: $75-90

LULLABY CANDLEHOLDER

Mold No.: 24
Copyright: 1935
Sculptor: Moeller & Unger
2-D Original: H 424, F 212

Model No.: 24/III
Ref. No.: 500
Approx. Size: 6.25" x 8.75"
1995 Retail: T.W.

Model No.: 24/I
Ref. No.: 501
Approx. Size: 3.5" x 5.5"
1995 Retail: T.W.

Both sizes of **Lullaby Candleholder** have been withdrawn from production—the larger size in 1982 and the smaller size at the end of 1989. The larger size is difficult to find in almost all trademarks. Research indicates it may be nonexistent in TM4. It was reinstated circa 1978 after being long out of production.

Trends in Selling M 24/III TM6: $410-510
            TM5: $435-510
            TM4: $495-585
            TM3: $560-665
            TM2: $725-900
            TM1: $1130-1415

Trends in Selling M 24/I TM6: $145-180
            TM5: $155-180
            TM4: $175-205
            TM3: $195-230
            TM2: $255-300
            TM1: $460-575

MADONNA & CHILD FONT

Mold No.: 243
Ref. No.: 514
Approx. Size: 4"
Copyright: 1955
Sculptor: R.Unger
2-D Original: H 533
1995 Retail: $50

This item is one of those with an unclear history. It is rare, if existent, in TM2, apparently not having been released until the TM3 era.

Trends in Selling TM6-7: $40-50
    TM5: $45-55
    TM4: $50-60
    TM3: $75-100
    TM2: $200-250

MADONNA HOLDING CHILD

Mold No.: 151
Copyright: 1942
Sculptor: R.Unger
2-D Original: H 682

Model No.: 151/II	Model No.: 151/W
Ref. No.: 572	Ref. No.: 571
Approx. Size: 12"	Approx. Size: 12"
1995 Retail: T.W.	1995 Retail: T.W.

Out of production for an extended early period, **Madonna Holding Child** was produced again from 1977 until it was given "T.W." status at the end of 1989. Research indicates this piece is probably nonexistent in TM3 and TM4. The multicolored madonna is supplied with a pastel blue cloak. Within TM1, other colors have been reported, but are considered rare and command premiums of 400% or more. This piece was shown on price lists of 1992 and 1993, but apparently was produced sparsely if at all with a TM7 mark.

Trends in Selling M 151

	Color	White
TM6:	$850-1000	$340-400
TM5:	$925-1100	$375-445
TM2:	$2250-2750	$950-1150
TM1:	$2750-3250	$1200-1450

ONE SHOE OFF, ONE SHOE ON

Four different M.I. Hummel figurines depict children shoeless and sockless on one foot. Why?

Glad you asked.

In the corresponding original drawings, Sister Hummel no doubt was paying homage to the German children's fable about a stocking knitter who lost a sock at (the town of) Lauterbach.

The word Lauterbach appears on one of the four figurines, *Weary Wanderer*. The other sockless figurines are *Lost Stocking, Signs of Spring* and *Out of Danger*.

A number of Sister Hummel's motifs can be associated with children's songs and fables.

MADONNA PLAQUE

Mold No.: 48
Copyright: 1936
Sculptor: R.Unger
2-D Original: H 545, F 209

Model No.: 48/II
Ref. No.: 574
Approx. Size: 4.75" x 5.75"
1995 Retail: T.W.

Model No.: 48/0
Ref. No.: 575
Approx. Size: 3" x 4"
1995 Retail: T.W.

Model No.: 48/V
Ref. No.: n.a.
Approx. Size: 8.75 x 10.75"
1995 Retail: Closed Edition

All sizes of **Madonna Plaque** are out of production. Early TM1 examples of the model 48/II can be found without size suffix, marked 48 only, and these command small premiums.

Trends in Selling M 48/II TM6: $120-150
    TM5: $130-150
    TM4: $145-175
    TM3: $160-195
    TM2: $230-290
    TM1: $450-560

Trends in Selling M 48/0 TM6: $75-95
    TM5: $85-95
    TM4: $95-110
    TM3: $100-125
    TM2: $135-155
    TM1: $260-325

Trends in Selling M 48/V:
    TM3: $900-1125
    TM2: $1125-1400
    TM1: $1350-1700

MADONNA W/HALO

Mold No.: 45
Copyright: 1935
Sculptor: R.Unger
2-D Original: H 667

Model No.: 45/III
Ref. No.: 584
Aprox. Size: 15.5"
1995 Retail: T.W.

Model No.: 45/III/W
Ref. No.: 583
Approx. Size: 15.5"
1995 Retail: T.W.

Model No.: 45/I
Ref. No.: 586
Approx. Size: 12"
1995 Retail: $125

Model No.: 45/I/W
Ref. No. 585
Approx. Size: 12"
1995 Retail: T.W.

Model No.: 45/0
Ref. No.: 589
Approx. Size: 10.5"
1995 Retail: T.W.

Model No.: 45/0/W
Ref. No.: 588
Approx. Size: 10.5"
1995 Retail: T.W.

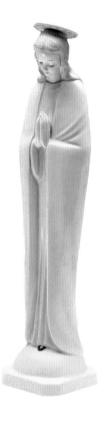

Before the withdrawal of the white model 45/I at the end of 1994, all sizes traditionally had been offered in both a multicolored and white glaze finish. By the end of 1989, two of the sizes had been withdrawn from production—the 45/III model in 1982 and the 45/0 model in 1984. Research indicates model 45/III could be rare or nonexistent in TM3 and TM4. It was reinstated circa 1978 after being long out of production. Some variety in colors can be found in early examples of all sizes.

Trends in Selling M 45/III

	Color	White
TM6:	$130-165	$85-105
TM5:	$140-165	$90-105
TM4:	$230-275	$145-175
TM3:	$230-275	$145-175

TM2: $230-275 $145-175

TM1: $325-405 $210-265

Model No.: 45/0/W
Ref. No.: 581
Approx. Size: 10.25"
1995 Retail: T.W.

Trends in Selling M 45/I

	Color	White
TM6-7:	$100-125	$60-75
TM5:	$105-125	$65-75
TM4:	$125-145	$75-85
TM3:	$135-160	$80-95
TM2:	$175-205	$105-120
TM1:	$280-345	$155-195

All sizes traditionally have been offered in both a multicolored and white glaze finish. By the end of 1989, all three sizes had been withdrawn from production—the 46/III model in 1982, the 46/0 model in 1984, and the 46/I model in 1989. Some variety in colors can be found in early examples.

Trends in Selling M 45/0

	Color	White
TM6:	$52-65	$32-40
TM5:	$56-65	$35-40
TM4:	$65-75	$40-46
TM3:	$70-85	$43-52
TM2:	$90-110	$55-65
TM1:	$175-220	$100-125

Trends in Selling M 46/III

	Color	White
TM6:	$130-165	$85-105
TM5:	$140-165	$90-105
TM4:	$160-190	$100-120
TM3:	$175-215	$115-135
TM2:	$230-275	$145-175
TM1:	$325-405	$210-265

Trends in Selling M 46/I

	Color	White
TM6-7:	$100-125	$60-75
TM5:	$105-125	$65-75
TM4:	$125-145	$75-85
TM3:	$135-160	$80-95
TM2:	$175-205	$105-120
TM1:	$280-345	$155-195

MADONNA W/O HALO

Mold No.: 46
Copyright: 1935
Sculptor: R.Unger
2-D Original: H 667

Model No.: 46/III
Ref. No.: 577
Approx. Size: 15.25"
1995 Retail: T.W.

Model No.: 46/III/W
Ref. No.: 576
Approx. Size: 15.25"
1995 Retail: T.W.

Model No.: 46/I
Ref. No.: 579
Approx. Size: 11.25"
1995 Retail: T.W.

Model No.: 46/I/W
Ref. No.: 578
Approx. Size: 11.25"
1995 Retail: T.W.

Model No.: 46/0
Ref. No.: 582
Approx. Size: 10.25"
1995 Retail: T.W.

Trends in Selling M 46/0

	Color	White
TM6:	$52-65	$32-40
TM5:	$56-65	$35-40
TM4:	$65-75	$40-46
TM3:	$70-85	$43-52
TM2:	$90-110	$55-65
TM1:	$175-220	$100-125

MAIL IS HERE (THE)
Mold No.: 226
Ref. No.: 823
Approx. Size: 6" x 4.5"
Copyright: 1952
Sculptor: A.Moeller
2-D Original: H 617
1995 Retail: $530

During the 1970s, **The Mail Is Here** was irregularly produced by Goebel and was one of the many desirable figurines available to retailers only on a "quota" basis. In recent years, it has been regularly available.

Trends in Selling TM6-7: $425-530
        TM5: $450-530
        TM4: $575-605
        TM3: $640-750
        TM2: $735-915

MAIL IS HERE PLAQUE
Mold No.: 140
Ref. No.: 687
Approx. Size: 4.25" x 6.25"
Copyright: 1940
Sculptor: A.Moeller
2-D Original: H 617
1995 Retail: T.W.

This piece, withdrawn from production at the end of 1989, predates the much more famous figurine of the same name.

Trends in Selling TM6: $190-240
        TM5: $205-240
        TM4: $235-275
        TM3: $255-310
        TM2: $335-395
        TM1: $500-625

MAKE A WISH
Mold No.: 475
Ref. No.: 267
Approx. Size: 4.5"
Copyright: 1987
Sculptor: G.Skrobek
2-D Original: H 132
1995 Retail: $200

Make a Wish was introduced in 1989 and may prove to be slightly scarce in TM6.

Trends in Selling TM6-7: $160-200

MARCH WINDS
Mold No.: 43
Ref. No.: 962
Approx. Size: 5"
Copyright: 1935
Sculptor: R.Unger
2-D Original: H 317
1995 Retail: $155

Though more or less in continuous production since the first year of M.I. Hummel figurines, no important variations have been found in **March Winds**.

Trends in Selling TM6-7: $125-155
        TM5: $130-155
        TM4: $150-175
        TM3: $170-200
        TM2: $215-255
        TM1: $350-435

MAX & MORITZ
Mold No.: 123
Ref. No.: 896
Approx. Size: 5"
Copyright: 1939
Sculptor: A.Moeller
2-D Original: H 352
1995 Retail: $215

A relatively early piece, **Max and Moritz** was restyled to the modern, textured finish (like photo, Var. II) in the early 1970s. Examples in the original finish (Var. II) will, therefore, be comparatively hard to find within TM5.

Trends in Selling TM6-7: $175-215
  Var. I in TM5: $210-245
  Var. II in TM5: $185-215
      TM4: $210-245
      TM3: $235-275
      TM2: $300-355
      TM1: $445-555

MEDITATION
Mold No.: 13
Copyright: 1935 & 1962
Sculptor: R.Unger
Restyled by: G.Skrobek
2-D Original: H 345,
  F 201

Model No.: 13/II
Ref. No.: 971
Approx. Size: 7.25"
1995 Retail: T.W.

Model No.: 13/0
Ref. No.: 972
Approx. Size: 5.5"
1995 Retail: $205

Model No.: 13/V
Ref. No.: 970
Approx. Size: 13.75"
1995 Retail: T.W.

Model No.: 13/V (white)
Ref. No.: 167
Sculptor: T.Menzenbach
Approx. Size: 13.75"
1995 Retail: $800

Model No.: 13 2/0
Ref. No.: 973
Sculptor: G.Skrobek
Approx. Size: 4.5"
1995 Retail: $130

As one of the earliest of the M.I. Hummel figurines, **Meditation** was originally offered in two sizes—models 13/0 and 13/II. The 13/II size, also found marked 13/2 or simply 13, is not found in TM4 and is rare in earlier trademarks. After a 1978 restyling by Skrobek, it was made available during the late TM5 and early TM6 eras before again being given withdrawn status at the end of 1984. The large, 13/V size was added in the TM2 era, but is scarce in that trademark and is scarce to nonexistent in TM3 and TM4; it was given "T.W." status as of Jan. 1, 1990. Model 13/V, however, was brought back as part of the white *Expressions of Youth* series first introduced in 1992. The small, 13 2/0 size was introduced in 1962. It is also relatively scarce in TM2, but is readily available in recent trademarks.

Trends in Selling M 13/II TM6: $290-360
      TM5: $335-395
      TM3: $2000-2500
      TM2: $2500-3125
      TM1: $3000-3750

Trends in Selling M 13/0 TM6-7: $175-215
      TM5: $85-215
      TM4: $210-245
      TM3: $235-275
      TM2: $300-355
      TM1: $445-555

Trends in Selling M 13/V TM6: $1070-1340
  White Var. in TM7: $640-800
      TM5: $1140-1340
      TM4: $1850-2200
      TM3: $1850-2200
      TM2: $1850-2200

Trends in Selling M 13 2/0 TM6-7: $115-140
      TM5: $120-140
      TM4: $135-160
      TM3: $150-180
      TM2: $195-230

MEDITATION PLATE
(See 1992 Friends Forever Plate)

MERRY CHRISTMAS PLAQUE
Mold No.: 323
Ref. No.: 556
Approx. Size: 5.25"
Copyright: 1955
Sculptor: G.Skrobek
2-D Original: H 437
1995 Retail: $125

Merry Christmas Plaque was introduced in 1979 at the end of the TM5 era. Though market prices may not adequately reflect it, this piece should be comparatively scarce in this trademark. Created almost 25 years before its introduction, the item has been reported—rarely—in earlier trademarks.

Trends in Selling TM6-7: $100-125
      TM5: $135-160

MERRY WANDERER

Mold No.: 7 & 11
Copyright: 1935,
1972
Sculptor:
A.Moeller
Restyled by:
G.Skrobek
2-D Original:
H 228, F 202

Model No.: 7/III
Ref. No.: 981
Approx. Size:
11.25"
1995 Retail: T.W.

Model No.: 7/II
Ref. No.: 982
Approx. Size: 9.5"
1995 Retail: T.W.

Model No.: 7/I
Ref. No.:983
Approx. Size: 7"
1995 Retail: T.W.

Model No.: 7/I (white)
Ref. No.: 168
Approx. Size: 6.25"
1995 Retail: $260

Model No.: 7/0
Ref. No.: 984
Approx. Size: 6.25"
1995 Retail: $275

Model No.: 7/X
Ref. No.: 980
Approx. Size: 33"
1995 Retail: Spec.Order

Model No.: 11/0
Ref. No.: 976
Approx. Size: 4.75"
1995 Retail: $195

Model No.: 11 2/0
Ref. No.: 977
Approx. Size: 4.25"
1995 Retail: $135

Out of all the figurines available, **Merry Wanderer** was chosen by Goebel as the "trademark" figurine to represent the M.I. Hummel brand. Further attesting to its lasting popularity is the fact that it has more size versions than any other Hummel figurine—and all seven sizes were produced concurrently and can be found in TM5 and TM6! It shares with *Little Fiddler* and *Book Worm* the distinction of having more than one mold number. Several of the models have been restyled. The most important variation involves model 7/I. Within TM3, this model may be found with either the original tiered, "double" base (Var. I) or with the normal, squared base (Var. II). Model 11 2/0 is

sometimes found with six or seven buttons on the vest (versus the normal five); these command small premiums. So does model 11/0 without size suffix. Currently, only the three smallest sizes are in regular production. Model 7/III was withdrawn at the end of 1989 and models 7/II and 7/I at the end of 1992. The latter two may eventually prove to be scarce in TM7 unless put back into production. Model 7/I in its multicolored form was withdrawn from production in 1992 concurrent with the introduction of this model as part of the white *Expressions of Youth* series. Research indicates model 7/III could be rare or nonexistent in TM3 and TM4. It was reinstated circa 1978 after being long out of production. Model 7/X last appeared on price lists in 1990. It can be special ordered (est. $21,000).

Trends in Selling M 7/III TM6: $1075-1340
    TM5: $1140-1340
    TM4: $1870-2200
    TM3: $1870-2200
    TM2: $1870-2200
    TM1: $2680-3350

Trends in Selling M 7/II TM6-7: $990-1235
    TM5: $1050-1235
    TM4: $1200-1420
    TM3: $1350-1595
    TM2: $1700-2000
    TM1: $2480-3100

Trends in Selling M 7/I TM6-7: $315-390
    White Var. in TM7: $210-260
    TM5: $330-390
    TM4: $385-455
    Var. I in TM3: $750-930
    Var. II in TM3: $425-510
    TM2: $825-1030
    TMI: $1115-1390

Trends in Selling M 7/0 TM6-7: $220-275
    TM5: $235-275
    TM4: $270-315
    TM3: $300-355
    TM2: $390-455
    TM1: $665-830

Trends in Selling M 11/0 TM6-7: $155-195
    TM5: $165-195
    TM4: $185-220
    TM3: $215-255
    TM2: $270-315
    TM1: $420-525

Trends in Selling M 7/X TM6: $10,000-17,000
TM5: $10,000-17,000

Trends in Selling M 11 2/0 TM6-7: $110-135
TM5: $115-135
TM4: $130-155
TM3: $150-175
TM2: $185-220
TM1: $295-365

MERRY WANDERER PENDANT
Mold No.: n.a.
Ref. No.: n.a.
Approx. Size: .875"
Sculptor: n.a.
2-D Original: H 228, F 202
1995 Retail: Closed Edition

(Not pictured) With a place as one of the most obscure M.I. Hummel releases of the M.I. Hummel Club, **Merry Wanderer Pendant** was the last non-figurine offered as the renewal gift to club members. As opposed to the hand-painted bronze pendants designed by Robert Olszewski, this was an unpainted creation of sterling silver. It is executed in bas-relief (three-dimensional on the obverse half only). It was offered for the 1990–91 club year (June 1, 1990, through May 31, 1991) and could originally be acquired free with membership renewal. Original retail value was listed by Goebel at $50. It was normally supplied with a 20-inch sterling silver chain to use as a necklace. However, some pieces were supplied with short chains to be used as men's tie chains.

Trends in Selling: $40-55

THE JUMBOS

The so-called "jumbos" are the largest regular production M.I. Hummel figurines ever made. The *Merry Wanderer* and the *Apple Tree Girl* jumbos are listed at 32 inches each, the *Apple Tree Boy* jumbo at 30 inches. These are the only three designs available in this size class. These pieces have not been regularly offered since 1990, but can be specially ordered for about $21,000 each.

MERRY WANDERER PLAQUE
Mold No.: 92
Ref. No.: 677
Approx. Size: 5" x 5.5"
Copyright: 1938
Sculptor: A.Moeller
2-D Original: H 228, F 202
1995 Retail: T.W.

Subject to several restylings, **Merry Wanderer Plaque** can be found in a variety of sizes and markings. None of these affect values. The item was given "T.W." status at the end of 1989.

Trends in Selling TM6: $110-140
TM5: $120-140
TM4: $135-160
TM3: $150-180
TM2: $195-230
TM1: $310-390

MINIATURE FIGURINES
(See chapter *The Other Hummels*)

MISCHIEF MAKER
Mold No.: 342
Ref. No.: 775
Approx. Size: 5"
Copyright: 1958 & 1960
Sculptor: A.Moeller
2-D Original: H 300
1995 Retail: $275

Another of the 24 new releases of 1972, **Mischief Maker** is scarce in TM4 and would be rare with an earlier mark.

Trends in Selling TM6-7: $220-275
TM5: $235-275
TM4: $850-1000

MORNING CONCERT

Mold No.: 447
Ref. No.: 427
Approx. Size: 5.25"
Copyright: 1984
Sculptor: G.Skrobek
2-D Original: H 247
1995 Retail: Closed Edition

The M.I. Hummel Club exclusive redemption figurine for club year 1987–88 (June 1, 1987–May 31, 1988), **Morning Concert** is number 11 in the club exclusive series and could originally be acquired only with a redemption certificate provided to active club members. Issue price was $98.

Trends in Selling TM6: $175-215

MORNING CONCERT MINI W/DISPLAY

Mold No.: n.a.
Ref. No.: 030
Approx. Size: .875"
Copyright: 1990
2-D Original: H 247
1995 Retail: Closed
   Edition

Packaged with a hand-painted cold-cast bandstand and a tiny glass dome, **Morning Concert** reappeared as a M.I. Hummel Club special exclusive for 1991–92 in the form of a bronze miniature. Issue price was $175.

Trends in Selling: $190-240

MORNING STROLL

Mold No.: 375 3/0
Ref. No.: 114
Approx. Size: 3.75"
Copyright: 1991
Sculptor: H.Fischer
2-D Original: H 215
1995 Retail: $175

In the tradition of *Doll Mother* and *Doll Bath*, Goebel in 1994 gave us **Morning Stroll**, a rendering of a little girl with her wooden doll carriage. This is another of the releases of that year which promises to become a favorite.

Trends in Selling TM7: $140-175

MOTHER'S DARLING

Mold No.: 175
Ref. No.: 858
Approx. Size: 5.5"
Copyright: 1945
Sculptor: A.Moeller
2-D Original: H 217
1995 Retail: $210

Known for its color variations, **Mother's Darling** has undergone several minor restylings. Early examples are likely to have pink and green bags and solid head scarves; later examples have blue and red bags and polka-dot scarves. Values are not affected.

Trends in Selling TM6-7: $170-210
                  TM5: $180-210
                  TM4: $205-240
                  TM3: $235-275
                  TM2: $290-340
                  TM1: $495-615

MOTHER'S HELPER

Mold No.: 133
Ref. No.: 887
Approx. Size: 5"
Copyright: 1939
Sculptor: A.Moeller
2-D Original: H 201
1995 Retail: $195

Mother's Helper, an early figurine, has been restyled to the modern, textured finish and can be found with the usual variations in sizes, coloration and mold placement. However, none of these affect values.

Trends in Selling TM6-7: $155-195
        TM5: $165-195
        TM4: $185-220
        TM3: $215-255
        TM2: $270-320
        TM1: $420-525

MOUNTAINEER

Mold No.: 315
Ref. No.: 801
Approx. Size: 5"
Copyright: 1955
Sculptor: G.Skrobek
2-D Original: H 203
1995 Retail: $195

Copyrighted in 1955 but not introduced until 1964, **Mountaineer** is quite scarce in TM3. The figurine has enjoyed great popularity.

Trends in Selling TM6-7: $170-210
        TM5: $180-210
        TM4: $205-240
        TM3: $1050-1300

MOUNTAINEER ANNUAL BELL
(See 1984 Annual Bell)

MY WISH IS SMALL

Mold No.: 463/0
Ref. No.: 176
Approx. Size: 5.5"
Copyright: 1985
Sculptor: G.Skrobek
2-D Original: H 133
1995 Retail: Closed Edition

No. 16 in the prestigious annual series of M.I. Hummel Club exclusive redemption figurines, **My Wish Is Small** was issued for the 1992–93 club year (June 1, 1992–May 31, 1993). It could originally be acquired only with a redemption certificate provided to each active club member. Issue price was $170.

Trends in Selling TM7: $190-235

NEW FOR 1987

The 1987 M.I. Hummel introductions included *Pleasant Journey, Morning Concert, Valentine Joy plate, A Gentle Glow, In the Meadow, Sing Along, Kindergartner,* a small version of *Band Leader* and the 1987 annuals.

NATIVITY SET 214

Mold No.: 214
Copyright: 1951
Sculptor: R.Unger
2-D Original: Various

Model No.: 214/I
Ref. No.: 619
Approx. Size: 7.5" (tallest figures)
1995 Retail: $1990 (16 pieces; stable extra)

Model No. 214/I
Ref. No.: 618
Approx. Size: 7.5" (tallest figures)
1995 Retail: $1525 (12 pieces, stable extra)

For more than 35 years, the **mold (Hum) 214 Nativity Set** (without size suffix) was simply considered *the* M.I. Hummel nativity set, not easily confused with the *mold 260 Nativity Set*, which came along later and has always been referred to as the *large* or *jumbo* Hummel nativity set. That all changed beginning in 1988 with the phased-in introduction of a slightly downsized model 214/0 set. Confusion—among dealers, as well as collectors—has reigned since. It is fostered by the similar size of the sets and the common mold number. In any case, all components for a 214 nativity set produced between 1952 and 1988 will be marked without size suffix. Components produced from 1988 to present *should* be marked with either the /I (original size) or /0 (new size) suffix.

Even with its brief history, the model 214/0 set can be a challenge to collectors. In 1988, Goebel introduced the set in the form of the holy family components—the *Madonna* (214/A/M/0), *Infant Jesus* (214/A/K/0) and *Joseph* (214/B/0). In 1989, it added *Flying Angel* (366/0), a *Donkey* (214/J/0), an *Ox* (214/K/0) and a *Lamb* (214/O/0). In 1990, it added *King standing* (214/L/0), *King on one knee* (214/M/0) and *King on both knees* (214/N/0). In 1991, it added *Shepherd standing with sheep* (214/F/0), *Shepherd Boy kneeling* (214/G/0) and *Little Tooter* (214/H/0). We think! Actually, Goebel's official M.I. Hummel price list of Jan. 1, 1990, prices the set complete with all the foregoing pieces *except Little Tooter,* which makes its first appearance on the 1991 price list. What makes this interesting is Goebel's conversion from TM6 to TM7 at the beginning of 1991. Can a complete 214/ 0 set be assembled in TM6? If available at all, how scarce are the shepherds in this trademark? How

many of the kings exist in TM6? Does the 214/H/0 *Little Tooter* exist as a TM6 rarity? With most Hummel figurines, these questions might already have answers. However, the nativities are not as frequently traded, and there is comparatively little secondary market information on them. In comparison to the 214/I set, the 214/0 set is currently missing only three pieces—downsized versions of angel mold 214/C, angel mold 214/D and the figurine, *We Congratulate,* mold 214/E. Also provided optionally since 1992 are three Goebel camels—camel standing, camel kneeling and camel lying—in the sizes of 6.5, 4 and 3.25 inches, respectively. These are *not* M.I. Hummel items but are well received as accessories to the Hummel nativity sets, nevertheless. Current suggested retail for the camels is $200 each.

The 214/I set also has an interesting history. When originally modeled by Unger and introduced in 1952, it temporarily assumed a position as the most elaborate and expensive offering in the M.I. Hummel line. Earliest examples were produced with the *Madonna* (Mary) and the *Infant Jesus* molded together in a one-piece sculpture given mold number 214/A. This sculpture is considered a rarity today. Probably due to production reasons, the *Madonna* and *Infant Jesus* were soon made into separate sculptures, but continued to be offered together and shared the 214/A mold number until sometime later. Currently, the *Madonna* is numbered 214/A/M and the *Infant Jesus* is numbered 214/A/K. Then, there are the white glazed sets. Sparsely produced during the 1950s and 1960s, these sets are very scarce and bring a premium of 50 to 100% above the normal, multicolored sets. The Holy Family pieces (*Madonna, Infant Jesus, Joseph*) are more readily found in white overglaze than are the companion pieces; also, they are the only pieces which can be found in white in TM5 and TM6. This is because the three-piece Holy Family sets have traditionally been offered as an alternative to the full nativity.

The original basic 11-piece 214 or 214/I set included the following: *Madonna* 214/A/M/I, *Infant Jesus* 214/A/K/I, *Joseph* 214/B/I, *Shepherd w/ Sheep* 214/F/I, *Shepherd Boy* 214/G/I, *Donkey* 214/J/I, *Ox* 214/K/I, *Moorish King* 214/L/I, *King on one knee* 214/M/I, *King on both knees* 214/N/I and *Lamb* 214/O/I. Early sets had four optional components—*Good Night* angel 214/C/I, *Angel Serenade* 214/D/I, *We Congratulate* 214/E/I and

Little Tooter 214/H/I. (Note: The presence of *We Congratulate* and *Little Tooter* has been the subject of some controversy due to "costuming" not consistent with the times.) In 1963, Gerhard Skrobek modeled *Flying Angel* 366/I as an addition to the set. Since then, it has been part of the basic set, now 12 pieces, and the expanded set, now 16 pieces. Neither includes the wooden stable; new, it currently has a suggested retail price of $100. The three original Goebel camels—a 11.5-inch standing camel, a 9-inch kneeling camel and a 8-inch lying camel—have also been offered as optional accessories since 1991. Current suggested retail for the camels is $250 each.

Comparative approximate sizes in the two sets:

Basic Mold No.	Model 214/I	Model 214/0
214/A/M	6.5"	5.25"

214/A/K	3.5"	2.875"
214/B	7.5"	6.125"
214/C	3.5"	n.a.
214/D	3"	n.a.
214/E	3.5"	n.a.
214/F	7"	5.5"
214/G	4.75"	4"
214/H	4"	3.125"
214/J	5"	4"
214/K	6.25"	5"
214/L	8.25"	6.375"
214/M	5.5"	4.25"
214/N	5.5"	4.25"
214/O	2"	1.5"
366	3.5"	3.125"

(Note: Sizes on older pieces will vary.)

(Continued on next page)

Trends in Selling 12-pc. Set 214/I w/o Stable
    TM6-7: $1220-1525
    TM5: $1295-1525
    TM4: $1465-1725
    TM3: $1550-1825 (11 pieces)
    TM2: $1925-2275 (11 pieces)

Trends in Selling 16-pc.Set 214/I w/o Stable
    TM6-7: $1595-1990
    TM5: $1690-1990
    TM4: $1950-2300
    TM3: $2050-2400 (15 pieces)
    TM2: $2500-3000 (15 pieces)

Trends in Selling Madonna 214/A/M/I
    TM6-7: $140-175
    TM5: $150-175
    TM4: $170-200
    TM3: $195-230
    TM2: $240-285

Trends in Selling Infant Jesus 214/A/K/I
    TM6-7: $52-65
    TM5: $55-65
    TM4: $65-75
    TM3: $70-85
    TM2: $90-105

Trends in Selling Joseph 214/B/I
    TM6-7: $140-175
    TM5: $150-175
    TM4: $170-200
    TM3: $195-230
    TM2: $240-285

Trends in Selling Good Night 214/C/I
    TM6-7: $75-90
    TM5: $80-90
    TM4: $90-105
    TM3: $100-115
    TM2: $125-145

Trends in Selling Angel Serenade 214/D/I
    TM6-7: $75-90
    TM5: $80-90
    TM4: $90-105
    TM3: $100-115
    TM2: $125-145

Trends in Selling We Congratulate 214/E/I
    TM6-7: $130-160
    TM5: $135-160
    TM4: $155-185
    TM3: $175-210
    TM2: $225-265

Trends in Selling Shepherd w/Sheep 214/F/I
    TM6-7: $140-175
    TM5: $145-175
    TM4: $170-200
    TM3: $190-230
    TM2: $245-290

Trends in Selling Shepherd Boy 214/G/I
    TM6-7: $105-130
    TM5: $110-130
    TM4: $125-150
    TM3: $145-170
    TM2: $180-215

Trends in Selling Little Tooter 214/H/I
    TM6-7: $100-125
    TM5: $105-125
    TM4: $120-140
    TM3: $140-165
    TM2: $170-200

Trends in Selling Donkey 214/J/I
    TM6-7: $55-70
    TM5: $60-70
    TM4: $70-80
    TM3: $75-90
    TM2: $95-115

Trends in Selling Ox 214/K/I
    TM6-7: $55-70
    TM5: $60-70
    TM4: $70-80
    TM3: $75-90
    TM2: $95-115

Trends in Selling Moorish King 214/L/I
    TM6-7: $150-185
    TM5: $160-185
    TM4: $180-210
    TM3: $205-240
    TM2: $255-300

Trends in Selling King on One Knee 214/M/I
TM6-7: $140-175
TM5: $150-175
TM4: $170-200
TM3: $195-230
TM2: $240-285

Trends in Selling King on Both Knees 214/N/I
TM6-7: $130-160
TM5: $135-160
TM4: $155-185
TM3: $175-210
TM2: $225-265

Trends in Selling Lamb 214/O/I
TM6-7: $15-20
TM5: $17-20
TM4: $20-25
TM3: $22-28
TM2: $30-35

Trends in Selling Flying Angel 366/I
TM6-7: $100-125
TM5: $105-125
TM4: $170-200

Trends in Selling 13-pc. Set 214/0 w/o Stable
TM6-7: $1045-1310

Trends in Selling Madonna 214/A/M/0
TM6-7: $105-130

Trends in Selling Infant Jesus 214/A/K/0
TM6-7: $32-40

Trends in Selling Joseph 214/B/0
TM6-7: $105-130

Trends in Selling Shepherd w/Sheep 214/F/0
TM7: $120-150
TM6: $155-180

Trends in Selling Shepherd Boy 214/G/0
TM7: $95-120
TM6: $125-145

Trends in Selling Little Tooter 214/H/0
TM7: $80-100
TM6: $110-130

Trends in Selling Donkey 214/J/0
TM6-7: $40-50

Trends in Selling Ox 214/K/0
TM6-7: $40-50

Trends in Selling Moorish King 214/L/0
TM7: $120-150
TM6: $125-160

Trends in Selling King on One Knee 214/M/0
TM7: $120-140
TM6: $135-155

Trends in Selling King on Both Knees 214/N/0
TM7: $110-135
TM6: $130-150

Trends in Selling Lamb 214/O/0
TM6-7: $15-20

Trends in Selling Flying Angel 366/0
TM6-7: $75-95

FORMAL APPRAISALS

Formal appraisals of M.I. Hummel figurines are often needed when one is a) wanting to insure a collection or b) wanting to donate a collection that would result in tax benefit.

Expect to pay for a formal appraisal on a fee basis, but be leery of an appraiser who quotes a cost based on percentage. Don't expect a good no-charge appraisal.

Don't ask for an appraisal by someone you are planning to sell or offer the collection to.

If you are donating to a museum or other charitable institution, or if you are selling your collection in a reputable consignment situation, you can normally expect help with the appraisal process.

From a practical standpoint, many persons who ask a dealer for an appraisal are actually wanting a purchase offer from the dealer. Most want to dispose of a collection intact and are uncertain how to go about it. Selling to a dealer can be one of the quickest and easiest—but least compensated—means of doing this. This book covers the subject, disposing of your collection, in more detail elsewhere.

NATIVITY SET 260

Mold No.: 260
Ref. No.: 595
Approx. Size: 11.75" (tallest figures)
Copyright: 1968
Sculptor: G.Skrobek
2-D Original: Various
1995 Retail: T.W.

Though officially withdrawn from production at the end of 1989, the so-called **Large Nativity** (Mold or Hum 260) last appeared on Goebel's 1990 price list. The last suggested retail—for the standard 16 figures plus large wooden stable—was $4540. Standard pieces provided with the set include *Madonna* 260/A, *Joseph* 260/B, *Infant Jesus* 260/C, *Good Night* angel 260/D, *Angel Serenade* 260/E, *We Congratulate* children 260/F, *Shepherd standing* 260/G, *Sheep w/Lamb* 260/H, *Shepherd Boy kneeling* 260/J, *Little Tooter* shepherd boy 260/K, *Donkey* 260/L, *Ox lying* 260/M, *Moorish King* 260/N, *King standing* 260/O, *King kneeling* 260/P and *Sheep lying* 260/R. The *wooden stable*, as the 17th piece of the official set, was priced at $400 alone on the 1990 list. The *We Congratulate* figurine which is part of the nativity differs from the mold 220 *We Congratulate* figurine in size and in

the absence of a base. It should also be mentioned that Skrobek's **Large Nativity**, a spectacular creation not likely forgotten once seen fully set up, is regularly found with one or more of three large *camels* (camel lying, camel standing, camel kneeling) which were sculpted by Skrobek as optional additions to the set. The camels add to the value of the set but are *not* M.I. Hummel items; that is, they are not based on any artwork done by Sister Hummel.

Trends in Selling 16-pc. Set w/Stable
     TM6: $4400-5500
     TM5: $4675-5500
     TM4: $5500-6500

Trends in Selling Madonna 260/A
     TM6: $590-610
     TM5: $520-610
     TM4: $595-700

Trends in Selling Joseph 260/B
     TM6: $490-610
     TM5: $520-610
     TM4: $595-700

Trends in Selling Infant Jesus 260/C
     TM6: $100-125

TM5: $105-125
TM4: $125-145

Trends in Selling Good Night 260/D
TM6: $125-155
TM5: $130-155
TM4: $155-180

Trends in Selling Angel Serenade 260/E
TM6: $120-150
TM5: $125-150
TM4: $145-170

Trends in Selling We Congratulate 260/F
TM6: $340-425
TM5: $360-425
TM4: $415-490

Trends in Selling Shepherd 260/G
TM6: $495-620
TM5: $525-620
TM4: $600-710

Trends in Selling Sheep w/Lamb 260/H
TM6: $80-100
TM5: $85-100
TM4: $95-115

Trends in Selling Shepherd Boy 260/J
TM6: $280-350
TM5: $295-350
TM4: $340-400

Trends in Selling Little Tooter 260/K
TM6: $150-185
TM5: $155-185
TM4: $175-210

Trends in Selling Donkey 260/L
TM6: $115-145
TM5: $125-145
TM4: $140-165

Trends in Selling Ox 260/M
TM6: $130-165
TM5: $140-165
TM4: $160-190

Trends in Selling Moorish King 260/N
TM6: $470-585
TM5: $495-585
TM4: $575-675

Trends in Selling King 260/O
TM6: $470-585
TM5: $495-585
TM4: $575-675

Trends in Selling King 260/P
TM6: $450-560
TM5: $475-560
TM4: $550-645

Trends in Selling Sheep 260/R
TM6: $40-50
TM5: $45-50
TM4: $50-60

NOT FOR YOU!

Mold No.: 317
Ref. No.: 799
Approx. Size: 6"
Copyright: 1955
Sculptor: A.Moeller
2-D Original: H 292
1995 Retail: $240

Copyrighted in 1955 but not introduced until 1961, **Not for You!** is difficult to find in TM3.

Trends in Selling TM6-7: $195-240
TM5: $205-240
TM4: $235-275
TM3: $725-875

ON HOLIDAY

Mold No.: 350
Ref. No.: 768
Approx. Size: 4.25"
Copyright:1965
Sculptor: G.Skrobek
2-D Original: H 357,
 H 367
1995 Retail: $170

On Holiday was not introduced until 1981, 16 years after its copyright date.

Trends in Selling TM6-7: $135-170

ON SECRET PATH
Mold No.: 386
Ref. No.: 740
Approx. Size: 5.25"
Copyright: 1971
Sculptor: G.Skrobek
2-D Original: H 225,
 F 697
1995 Retail: $245

On Secret Path was another of the 1972 introductions and, like the others, is quite scare in TM4.

Trends in Selling TM6-7: $195-245
                TM5: $210-245
                TM4: $995-1170

ON OUR WAY
Mold No.: 472
Ref. No.: 175
Approx. Size: 8"
Copyright: 1987
Sculptor: G.Skrobek
2-D Original: H 399, H 400
1995 Retail: T.W.

Flushed with the success of *Chapel Time Clock* as its first "century release" in 1986, Goebel quickly put Gerhard Skrobek to work on succeeding issues in the spectacular series. Among these was **On Our Way**, sculpted in 1987 but not released until 1992 as the seventh in the annual series. Produced just for the one year in the twentieth century, the piece has already found a niche in the secondary market. A special bottom stamp reads, "M.I. Hummel Century Collection 1992 XX." The XX is found on each of the *Century Collection* issues to permanently distinguish these special issues. Issue price was $950 in 1992.

Trends in Selling TM7: $1000-1250

ONE FOR YOU, ONE FOR ME
Mold No.: 482
Ref. No.: 282
Approx. Size: 3.125"
Copyright:1987
Sculptor: G.Skrobek
2-D Orig.:
 H Fleissbildchen
1995 Retail: $100

A 1989 release, **One for You, One for Me** is typical of Goebel's effort at the time to downsize its offerings to appeal in price to new collectors.

Trends in Selling TM6-7: $80-100

NEW FOR 1992

The 1992 M.I. Hummel introductions included *My Wish Is Small, Lucky Fellow, The Professor, Story Time, On Our Way, Evening Prayer, Scamp, Whistler's Duet, Light Up the Night ornament* and the various 1992 annuals.

ONE PLUS ONE

Mold No.: 556
Ref. No.: 129
Approx. Size: 4"
Copyright: 1989
Sculptor: H.Fischer
2-D Original: H 198
1995 Retail: $130

One Plus One was introduced in 1993 as the *special event piece* for the year. By being available only during special in-store promotions in the U.S. and at artist promotions in Canada, it was used to help build attendance at these events. It was temporarily withdrawn from production at the end of 1993 but was reintroduced as part of the normal M.I. Hummel program effective Jan. 1, 1995. Pieces sold in 1993 bear a "special event" backstamp; they sold for $115 retail. **One Plus One** is the second in an ongoing annual series of special event pieces. *Little Gardener* was the first in 1992. However, the *Little Gardener* figurine was already in existence; it was simply taken off the normal market in 1992 and given the special event backstamp. On the other hand, **One Plus One** and the succeeding special event pieces, *Birthday Present* and *Ooh, My Tooth,* are new figurines never previously offered, greatly enhancing the appeal of the program.

Trends in Selling: $115-145

OOH, MY TOOTH

Mold No.: 533
Ref. No.: 053
Approx. Size: 3"
Copyright: 1988
Sculptor: G.Skrobek
2-D Original: Unknown
1995 Retail: $110

One of the new releases for 1995, **Ooh, My Tooth** was designated as the *special event piece* for the year, available for collectors to purchase only at special in-store promotions. Pieces produced in 1995 bear the "special event" backstamp. Later pieces will lack this backstamp.

Trends in Selling TM7: $100-120

OUT OF DANGER

Mold No.: 56/B
Ref. No.: 944
Approx. Size: 6.25"
Copyright: 1952
Sculptor: A.Moeller
2-D Original: Unknown
1995 Retail: $290

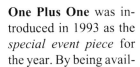

Out of Danger shares the *56* mold number and is nearly always paired with its older companion piece, *Culprits.* In older examples, the eyes are open. In newer, restyled examples, the eyes are closed. This variation does not affect values.

Trends in Selling TM6-7: $235-290
TM5: $245-290
TM4: $285-335
TM3: $325-375
TM2: $405-580

OUT OF DANGER LAMP

(See Culprits Lamp)

PARADE OF LIGHTS

Mold No.: 616
Ref. No.: 159
Approx. Size: 6"
Copyright: 1990
Sculptor: H.Fischer
2-D Original: H 265
1995 Retail: $250

Parade of Lights was introduced in 1993 and can only be found in TM7.

Trends in Selling TM7: $200-250

PEACE ON EARTH ANNUAL ORNAMENT

(See 1990 Annual Ornament)

PHOTOGRAPHER

Mold No.: 178
Ref. No.: 853
Approx. Size: 5"
Copyright: 1948
Sculptor: R.Unger
2-D Original: H 260
1995 Retail: $285

Introduced near the end of the TM1 era, **Photographer** is relatively scarce with this mark. It can be found with the normal minor variations in size, color and molding.

Trends in Selling M 197/I TM6-7: $230-285
        TM5: $245-285
        TM4: $280-330
        TM3: $315-370
        TM2: $400-470
        TM1: $795-990

PIXIE

Mold No.: 768
Ref. No.: 029
Approx. Size: 3.5"
Copyright: 1994
Sculptor: H.Fischer
2-D Original: H 353
1995 Retail: $105

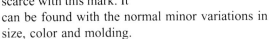

One of the new releases for 1995, **Pixie** is the only current M.I. Hummel figurine bearing a 1994 copyright date, and it has the distinction of having the highest mold number of *any figurine* now in production.

Trends in Selling TM7: $85-105

PLAYMATES

Mold No.: 58
Copyright: 1936, 1964, 1984
Sculptor: R.Unger
Restyled by: G.Skrobek
2-D Original: H 372

Model No.: 58/I
Ref. No.: 940
Approx. Size: 4.25"
1995 Retail: $275

Model No.: 58/0
Ref. No.: 941
Approx. Size: 4"
1995 Retail: $165

Model No.: 58 2/0
Ref. No.: 416
Approx. Size: 3.25"
1995 Retail: $135

Created to be a companion piece to *Chick Girl*, **Playmates** appears as a candy box, a bookend, an annual plate, and a figurine in three sizes. Older models of the figurine have been restyled, but no important varieties are known. Early pieces of model 58/I marked 58 (without size designator) may command a small premium. The small, 58 2/0 size was introduced in 1986.

Trends in Selling M 58/I TM6-7: $220-275
        TM5: $235-275
        TM4: $270-320
        TM3: $300-355
        TM2: $385-455
        TM1: $600-750

Trends in Selling M 58/0 TM6-7: $135-165
        TM5: $140-165
        TM4: $160-190
        TM3: $180-210
        TM2: $230-270
        TM1: $370-460

Trends in Selling M 58 2/0: $115-145

PLAYMATES ANNUAL PLATE

(See 1986 Annual Plate)

HASENVATER   KÜCKENMÜTTERCHEN

PLAYMATES & CHICK GIRL BOOKENDS
Mold No.: 61/A & B
Ref. No.: 699
Approx. Size: 4"
Copyright: 1936
Sculptor: n.a.
2-D Original: H 372, H 371
1995 Retail: T.W.

The bookend set consists of the respective figurines mounted on wooden bookend bases. The bookends were withdrawn from production as of Jan. 1, 1985. The values of the individual figurines exceed those of the set.

Trends in Selling TM6: $310-390 pair
          TM5: $335-390 pair
          TM4: $375-450 pair
          TM3: $415-500 pair
          TM2: $550-645 pair
          TM1: $825-1025 pair

PLAYMATES CANDY BOX
Mold No.: III/58
Ref. No.: 666
Approx. Size: 6.25"
Copyright: 1936
Sculptor: n.a.
2-D Original: H 372
1995 Retail: T.W.

Originally given a bowl shape (Var. I), the container was redesigned to a box shape in 1964 at the onset of the TM4 era (Var. II). Some of the Variety II pieces bear the TM3 stamp. The box was withdrawn from production at the end of 1989.

Trends in Selling TM6: $145-180
          TM5: $155-180
          TM4: $175-210
    Var. I in TM3: $350-430
    Var. II in TM3: $250-315
          TM2: $425-530
          TM1: $525-650

MOLD NUMBERS AND HUM NUMBERS

Veteran Hummel chasers using this book will wonder what happened to the *HUM numbers*. This book, for instance, will tell you that the figurine *Botanist* is *mold 351*, while most previous works refer to *it* as *HUM 351*.

I hope you'll bear with me in this regard. A HUM number is a mold number; it is simply part of Goebel's unusual numbering system whereby a portion of the artist's name is incorporated into the mold number for record-keeping purposes.

This mold number nomenclature is being used to assist the new collector.

PLEASANT JOURNEY
Mold No.: 406
Ref. No.: 448
Approx. Size: 7.125" x 6.5"
Copyright: 1976
Sculptor: G.Skrobek
2-D Original: H 353
1995 Retail: Closed Edition

What's currently the most-sought-but-difficult-to-find figurine in the entire M.I. Hummel line? Arguably, it's **Pleasant Journey**, which was released in 1987 as the second in the annual "century release" series. At the time of its release, it followed on the heels of the highly successful *Chapel Time Clock* (1986) and—being the second rather than first in a series—was put on the market with relatively little fanfare. Sales, accordingly, must have been somewhat light because the figurine is now exceedingly difficult to locate. And, many of those found are being shipped back to Europe from the U.S.! The current high secondary market value may be but a prelude of prices to come. Produced just for the one year in the twentieth century, the piece bears a special bottom stamp which reads, "M.I. Hummel Century Collection 1987 XX." The XX is found on each of the *Century Collection* issues to permanently distinguish these special issues. Issue price was $500 in 1987.

Trends in Selling TM6: $1900-2400

POET (THE)
Mold No.: 397/I
Ref. No.: 113
Approx. Size: 6"
Copyright: 1974
Sculptor: G.Skrobek
2-D Original: H 253
1995 Retail: $225

The Poet had waited in the wings for 20 years before his 1994 debut.

Trends in Selling TM7: $180-225

POSTMAN
Mold No.: 119
Copyright: 1939 & 1985
Sculptor: A.Moeller
Restyled by: G.Skrobek
2-D Original: H 246

Model No.: 119
Ref. No.: 897
Approx. Size: 5"
1995 Retail: $200

Model No.: 119 2/0
Ref. No.: 269
Approx. Size: 4.5"
Sculptor: G.Skrobek
1995 Retail: $135

Skrobek's restyling of **Postman** in the modern, textured finish was done in 1970 near the end of the TM4 era. Though it isn't reflected in current market prices, the piece seems to be relatively scarce in TM4 with either the old or new finish. The small size was released in 1989.

Trends in Selling M 119 TM6-7: $160-200
　　　TM5: $170-200
　　　TM4: $220-260
　　　TM3: $220-260
　　　TM2: $280-330
　　　TM1: $415-515

Trends in Selling M 119 2/0 TM6-7: $110-135

POSTMAN ANNUAL PLATE
(See 1983 Annual Plate)

PRAYER BEFORE BATTLE

Mold No.: 20
Ref. No.: 963
Approx. Size: 4.25"
Copyright: 1935
Sculptor: A.Moeller
2-D Original: H 165
1995 Retail: $165

Prayer Before Battle is another of the very first M.I. Hummel figurines (1935) which has been in the line for some 60 years. Despite this, there are only the normal minor variations in size, color and molding. The figurine is rare—possibly nonexistent—in TM4.

Trends in Selling TM6-7: $135-165
             TM5: $140-165
             TM4: $355-420
             TM3: $225-265
             TM2: $250-295
             TM1: $375-470

PRAYER OF THANKS ORNAMENT (WHITE)

(See chapter, *The Other Hummels)*

PROFESSOR (THE)

Mold No.: 320/0
Ref. No.: 195
Approx. Size: 4.875"
Copyright: 1989
Sculptor: G.Skrobek
2-D Original: H 240
1995 Retail: $200

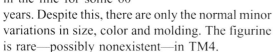

One of the new introductions for 1992, **The Professor** can be found only in TM7.

Trends in Selling TM7: $160-200

PUPPY LOVE

Mold No.: 1
Ref. No.: 997
Approx. Size: 5.25"
Copyright: 1935
Sculptor: A.Moeller
2-D Original: H 229
1995 Retail: Closed Edition

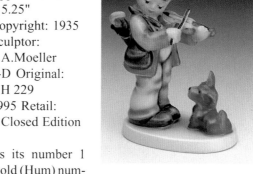

As its number 1 mold (Hum) number would suggest, **Puppy Love**, originally called *Little Violinist,* dates to the very beginning of M.I. Hummel figurines in 1935. However, today it is perhaps best known—and most widely sought—for being first in an annual series of "retirements" conducted by Goebel. At the beginning of 1988, it was announced that **Puppy Love** would be permanently retired at the end of the year. This one-year fanfare "selling tour" set the precedent for the 1989 ceremonial retirement of *Strolling Along* and other successors in the program. During this farewell year, more recent figurines in the program are given a special bottom stamp and medallion. In any case, each has enjoyed increased demand and higher secondary market values after retirement. With exceptions, **Puppy Love** was produced for more than 50 years without important variations. The exceptions came during the earliest years. A black hat, no tie variety is known to exist (TM1 only), as are pieces marked FF 15 instead of with the normal mold number. Both of these are very rare.

Trends in Selling TM6: $220-270
             TM5: $240-285
             TM4: $265-310
             TM3: $325-395
             TM2: $370-440
             TM1: $660-825

PUPPY LOVE FIGURINE PLAQUE
Mold No.: 767
Ref. No.: 042
Approx. Size: 4.75"
Copyright: 1993
Sculptor: H.Fischer
2-D Original: H 229
1995 Retail: $240

To commemorate its 60th year of producing M.I. Hummel figurines, Goebel used the design from the very first mold, *Hum 1—Puppy Love,* to fashion the **Puppy Love Figurine Plaque** as a special offering for 1995. The plaque will be retired at the end of 1995 and will likely become an important item in the secondary market afterwards.

Trends in Selling TM7: $200-240

QUARTET PLAQUE
Mold No.: 134
Ref. No.: 690
Approx. Size: 6" x 6"
Copyright: 1939
Sculptor: A.Moeller
2-D Original: H 284
1995 Retail: T.W.

This item was withdrawn from production as of Jan. 1, 1991.

Trends in Selling TM6: $200-250
TM5: $215-250
TM4: $240-290
TM3: $265-325
TM2: $350-415
.TM1: $550-690

RETREAT TO SAFETY
Mold No.: 201
Copyright: 1948
Sculptor: R.Unger
2-D Original: H 158

Model No.: 201/I
Ref. No.: 831
Approx. Size: 5.5"
1995 Retail: $300

Model No.: 201 2/0
Ref. No.: 832
Approx. Size: 4"
1995 Retail: $160

Retreat to Safety is relatively difficult to find in TM1. If found with the crown mark, it will lack the size designator which was added with the introduction of the smaller size in the mid-1950s. Early TM2 examples also lack the size designator and command small premiums when found.

Trends in Selling M 201/I TM6-7: $240-300
TM5: $255-300
TM4: $295-345
TM3: $330-390
TM2: $420-495
TM1: $800-1000

Trends in Selling M 201 2/0 TM6-7: $130-160
TM5: $135-160
TM4: $155-185
TM3: $175-210
TM2: $295-360

RETREAT TO SAFETY PLAQUE
Mold No.: 126
Ref. No.: 694
Approx. Size: 4.75" x
  4.75"
Copyright: 1939
Sculptor: A.Moeller
2-D Original: H 158
1995 Retail: T.W.

Retreat to Safety Plaque preceded the popular figurine by almost a decade. It was withdrawn from production at the end of 1989.

Trends in Selling TM6: $150-190
      TM5: $160-190
      TM4: $185-220
      TM3: $200-250
      TM2: $265-315
      TM1: $425-530

RIDE INTO CHRISTMAS

Mold No.: 396
Copyright: 1971 &
   1981
Sculptor:
   G.Skrobek
2-D Original:
   H 316

Model No.: 396/I
Ref. No.: 726
Approx. Size:
   5.75"
1995 Retail: $425

Model No.: 396 2/0
Ref. No.: 727
Approx. Size: 4.25"
1995 Retail: $235

Of the superb large group of introductions of 1972, **Ride Into Christmas** has to rank as the most significant. Arguably, it has—at times—been the most popular of all the M.I. Hummel figurines. The larger size is very scarce in TM4. The smaller size was introduced in 1982, and at that time model 396/I acquired its size suffix. Examples of the larger size in TM6 but without size suffix may demand small premiums.

Trends in Selling M 396/I TM6-7: $340-425
      TM5: $365-425
      TM4: $1375-1700

Trends in Selling M 396 2/0 TM6-7: $190-235

RIDE INTO CHRISTMAS ANNUAL PLATE
(See 1975 Annual Plate)

RIDE INTO CHRISTMAS CHRISTMAS BELL
(See 1989 Christmas Bell)

RIDE INTO CHRISTMAS MUSIC BOX
Mold No.: 396
Ref. No.: 6433
Approx. Size: 6.25" x 4.5"
Copyright: 1987
Sculptor: G.Skrobek
2-D Original: H 316
1995 Retail: Closed Edition

From 1987 through 1990, Goebel used the services of the famed Anri woodcarving firm in Italy and the famed Reuge music movement firm in Switzerland to produce a four-year, annual series of collector-quality music boxes. The theme was *Four Seasons*. The **Ride Into Christmas Music Box** was the 1987, first issue in the series and represented winter of the four seasons. The bas-relief rendition of the *Ride Into Christmas* motif was sculpted by Goebel master Gerhard Skrobek, and the painting was executed in accordance with the specifications of Goebel master painter Gunther Neubauer. However, actual execution of the production artwork in the form of a painted woodcarving was done by Anri artisans. The 36-note musical movement is a Romance movement by Reuge. The box was a worldwide limited edition of 10,000 pieces, and each music box was individually numbered. This number appears—along with the Goebel backstamp—on a special plaque attached to the underside of the lid. This music box is thought to be the first individually numbered, limited edition M.I. Hummel item issued by Goebel. The box is now somewhat difficult to locate on the secondary market. Issue price was $390 in 1987.

Trends in Selling TM6: $525-650

RING AROUND THE ROSIE
Mold No.: 348
Ref. No.: 770
Approx. Size: 6.75"
Copyright: 1957
Sculptor: G.Skrobek
2-D Original: H 204
1995 Retail: $2600

One of Skrobek's early large pieces, **Ring Around the Rosie**, like *Adventure Bound* of the same era, has overcome the obstacle of a very large price to remain surprisingly popular through the years. Since its introduction in 1960, no significant varieties have been reported.

Trends in Selling TM6-7: $2080-2600
         TM5: $2200-2600
         TM4: $2500-2990
         TM3: $2950-3695

RING AROUND THE ROSIE
ANNIVERSARY PLATE
(See 1980 Anniversary Plate)

NEW FOR 1982

The 1982 M.I. Hummel introductions included the club exclusive, *It's Cold*; three perennial favorites, *Botanist*, *Little Nurse* and the smaller size of *Ride Into Christmas*; and the 1982 annuals.

ROCK-A-BYE
Mold No.: 574
Ref. No.: 111
Approx. Size: 7.5"
Copyright: 1991
Sculptor: H.Fischer
2-D Original: H 102
1995 Retail: Closed Edition

Since Goebel initiated its *Century Release* program in 1986—each year introducing a spectacular new Hummel offering with the promise that it would not be produced again in this century—collectors have awaited each new century piece with dual anticipation. The anticipation concerns both the intricacy and beauty of the issues—and the correspondingly

hefty prices! With its baby cradle, baby, five full figures and a large doll, **Rock-a-Bye**, the 1994 addition to the series, certainly did its bit to add to this heritage. It is the ninth in the century series and bore an issue price of $1150.

Trends in Selling TM7: $1150-1450

RUN-A-WAY (THE)
Mold No.: 327
Ref. No.: 790
Approx. Size: 5.25"
Copyright: 1955 & 1972
Sculptor: H.Wehlte
Restyled by: G.Skrobek
2-D Original: H 218
1995 Retail: $250

Not only was **The Run-a-way** among the 1972

introductions—and, therefore, quite scarce in TM4—it received a major restyling by Skrobek at about the same time. All of the TM4 and some of the earliest TM5 examples were produced from the original molds with the 1955 copyright (Var. I). Restyled examples have the incised 1972 copyright date (Var. II).

Trends in Selling TM6-7: $200-250
    Var. I in TM5: $775-950
    Var. II in TM5: $215-250
        TM4: $935-1165

SAINT GEORGE

Mold No.: 55
Ref. No.: 474
Approx. Size: 6.75"
Copyright: 1936
Sculptor: R.Unger
2-D Original:
    Found in 1st Ed.
    Das Hummel
    Buch by Fink
1995 Retail: $320

Unusual among M.I. Hummel figurines due to its motif, **Saint George** has remained in production for almost 60 years. Early TM1 examples were sometimes painted with red saddles on the horse; these are considered rare and command premiums of 200 to 300% over normal TM1 price. Older examples of the normal version sometimes prove to be suprisingly difficult to find.

Trends in Selling TM6-7: $255-320
        TM5: $270-320
        TM4: $315-370
        TM3: $350-415
        TM2: $450-530
        TM1: $850-1065

HOW MANY LASHES TO AN EYE?

M.I. Hummel figurines are known for being painted with three eyelashes. Be advised, however, that there are many exceptions, ranging from no eyelashes to as many as five on *School Boy* model 82/II.

SCAMP

Mold No.: 553
Ref. No.: 189
Approx. Size: 3.5"
Copyright: 1989
Sculptor: H.Fischer
2-D Original: H 352
1995 Retail: $110

One of Fischer's earliest creations as a Goebel master sculptor, **Scamp** was issued in 1992 and can be found only in TM7. The figure is the *Max* half of the *Max and Moritz* figurine.

Trends in Selling TM7: $90-110

SCHOOL BOY

Mold No.: 82
Copyright: 1938
Sculptor: A.Moeller
2-D Original: H 194

Model No.: 82/II
Ref. No.: 920
Approx. Size: 7.5"
1995 Retail: $450

Model No.: 82/0
Ref. No.: 921
Approx. Size: 5"
1995 Retail: $195

Model No.: 82 2/0
Ref. No.: 922
Approx. Size: 4"
1995 Retail: $140

School Boy and its companion piece, *School Girl*, have had significant roles in the enduring popularity of Hummel figurines by serving as relatively inexpensive collection starters. One or both is found in nearly every collection. Perhaps because of this, the two smaller sizes have always been much more popular and, indeed, have sometimes determined the size of subsequent purchases for a collection. The large model 82/II is not available in TM4, rare to nonexistent in TM3, and scarce in early trademarks. Model 82/0 commands a small premium if found without size suffix in TM1 or TM2. All models are in current production.

Trends in Selling M 82/II TM6-7: $360-450
    TM5: $380-450
    TM3: $560-660
    TM2: $620-730
    TM1: $930-1160

Trends in Selling M 82/0 TM6-7: $155-195
    TM5: $165-195
    TM4: $185-220
    TM3: $215-255
    TM2: $270-320
    TM1: $420-525

Trends in Selling M 82 2/0 TM6-7: $115-140
    TM5: $120-140
    TM4: $135-160
    TM3: $150-180
    TM2: $1850239
    TM1: $295-370

SCHOOL BOYS
Mold No.: 170
Copyright: 1943, 1961 & 1972
Sculptor: R.Unger
Restyled by: G.Skrobek
2-D Original: H 198

Model No.: 170/I   Model No.: 170/III
Ref. No.: 862   Ref. No.: 861
Approx. Size: 7.5"   Approx. Size: 10.25"
1995 Retail: $1200   1995 Retail: Retired

The large size of **School Boys** was the original model and was produced until 1982, when it became one of the first M.I. Hummel figurines given "permanently retired" status by Goebel. It was restyled by Skrobek both in 1961 and 1972. The large size was numbered without a size suffix until the introduction of the smaller size circa 1961.

Trends in Selling M 170/III TM6: $1575-1975
    TM5: $1650-1975
    TM4: $1725-2150
    TM3: $1800-270
    TM2: $2725-3400
    TM1: $3700-4600

Trends in Selling M 170/I TM6-7: $960-1200
    TM5: $1000-1200
    TM4: $1150-1365
    TM3: $1220-1525

SCHOOL GIRL
Mold No.: 81
Copyright: 1937
Sculptor: A.Moeller
2-D Original: H 191

Model No.: 81/0
Ref. No.: 923
Approx. Size: 5"
1995 Retail: $195

Model No.: 81 2/0
Ref. No.: 924
Approx. Size: 4.25"
1995 Retail: $140

Like its *School Boy* companion piece, **School Girl** has served as a relatively inexpensive collection starter. One or both is found in nearly every collection. Model 81/0 commands a premium if found without size suffix in TM1 or TM2. The size equivalent to *School Boy* model 82/II was never produced.

Trends in Selling M 81/0 TM6-7: $155-195
    TM5: $165-195
    TM4: $185-220
    TM3: $215-255
    TM2: $270-320
    TM1: $420-525

Trends in Selling M 81 2/0 TM6-7: $115-140
    TM5: $120-140
    TM4: $135-160
    TM3: $150-180
    TM2: $1850239
    TM1: $295-370

SCHOOL GIRL ANNUAL PLATE
(See 1980 Annual Plate)

SCHOOL GIRLS
Mold No.: 177
Copyright: 1946, 1961 & 1972
Sculptor: R.Unger
Restyled by: T.Menzenbach
2-D Original: H 197

Model No.: 177/I	Model No.: 177/III
Ref. No.: 855	Ref. No.: 854
Approx. Size: 7.5"	Approx. Size: 9.5"
1995 Retail: $1200	1995 Retail: Retired

The large size of **School Girls** was the original model and was produced until 1982, when it became one of the first M.I. Hummel figurines given "permanently retired" status by Goebel. It was restyled by Skrobek both in 1961 and 1972. The large size was numbered without a size suffix until the introduction of the smaller size circa 1961.

Trends in Selling M 177/III TM6: $1575-1975
          TM5: $1650-1975
          TM4: $1725-2150
          TM3: $1800-270
          TM2: $2725-3400
          TM1: $3700-4600

Trends in Selling M 177/I TM6-7: $960-1200
          TM5: $1000-1200
          TM4: $1150-1365
          TM3: $1220-1525

SEARCHING ANGEL PLAQUE
Mold No.: 310
Ref. No.: 535
Approx. Size: 4.125" x
    3.375"
Copyright: 1955
Sculptor: G.Skrobek
2-D Original: H 451
1995 Retail: $120

An early Skrobek creation, **Searching Angel Plaque** was not introduced until 1979. It is relatively scarce in TM5, but enjoys limited demand.

Trends in Selling TM6-7: $95-120
          TM5: $120-155

SENSITIVE HUNTER
Mold No.: 6
Copyright: 1935 & 1984
Sculptor: A.Moeller
2-D Original: H 222, F 217

Model No.: 6/II
Ref. No.: 985
Approx. Size: 7.5"
1995 Retail: T.W.

Model No.: 6/I
Ref. No.: 986
Approx. Size: 5.5"
1995 Retail: $250

Model No.: 6/0
Ref. No.: 987
Approx. Size: 4.75"
1995 Retail: $195

Model No.: 6 2/0
Ref. No.: 419
Approx. Size: 4"
1995 Retail: $145

The large, 6/II model of **Sensitive Hunter** was withdrawn from production at the end of 1984, and the smallest, 6 2/0 size was added the next year. The 6/0 size has been in more or less continuous production since the beginning of M.I. Hummel figurines. Earliest examples lack the size suffix and demand small premiums. More importantly, until restyled in the TM2 era, model 6/0 wore lederhosen suspenders which had an "H" shape in the back (Var. I); the redesign gave him crossed or X-shaped suspenders in the back (Var. II). Other models have X-shaped suspenders in all trademarks. In 1981, the rabbit in model 6/0 was changed from its traditional orange color (Var. III) to a more natural brown color. Within TM6, the orange rabbit variety should prove to be relatively scarce.

Trends in Selling M 6/II TM6: $295-365
        TM5: $310-365
        TM4: $360-425
        TM3: $400-475
        TM2: $575-710
        TM1: $775-970

Trends in Selling M 6/I TM6-7: $200-250
        TM5: $210-250
        TM4: $245-290
        TM3: $275-325
        TM2: $350-415
        TM1: $560-700

Trends in Selling M 6/0 TM6-7: $155-195
    Var. III in TM6: $190-225
        TM5: $165-195
        TM4: $200-235
        TM3: $215-255
    Var. I in TM2: $430-530
    Var. II in TM2: $275-325
        TM1: $510-640

Trends in Selling M 6 2/0 TM6-7: $115-145

NEW FOR 1985

The 1985 M.I. Hummel introductions included *Jubilee; Smiling Through; Sing With Me; Baking Day; Going Home; Just Fishing; Stormy Weather* model 71/II*; For Mother* model 257/II*; Hear Ye, Hear Ye* model 15 2/0*; Sensitive Hunter* model 6/II*; Chick Girl* model 57/II*;* a miniature version of *Serenade;* the *1985 Anniversary Plate;* and the '85 annuals.

SERENADE
Mold No.: 85
Copyright: 1938, 1984
Sculptor: A.Moeller
2-D Original: H 342

Model No.: 85/II
Ref. No.: 918
Approx. Size: 7.5"
1995 Retail: $425

Model No.: 85/0
Ref. No.: 919
Approx. Size: 4.75"
1995 Retail: $130

Model No.: 85 4/0
Ref. No.: 413
Approx. Size: 3"
1995 Retail: $100

Another of the pieces which make up the Hummel orchestra, **Serenade** can be found in a variety of sizes, colors and mold variations. Early, TM1 or TM2 examples of model 85/II command premiums when found without size suffix. The 4/0 mini size bears a 1984 copyright date and was introduced in 1985 to match the mini plate of that year.

Trends in Selling M 85/II TM6-7: $360-450
        TM5: $380-450
        TM4: $470-510
        TM3: $495-580
        TM2: $620-730
        TM1: $975-1085

Trends in Selling M 85/0 TM6-7: $105-130
        TM5: $110-130
        TM4: $125-150
        TM3: $140-165
        TM2: $175-215
        TM1: $290-360

Trends in Selling M 85 4/0 TM6-7: $80-100

SERENADE MINI PLATE
(See 1985 Mini Plate)

SHE LOVES ME, SHE LOVES ME NOT

Mold No.: 174
Ref. No.: 859
Approx. Size: 4.5"
Copyright: 1945 & 1955
Sculptor: A.Moeller
2-D Original: H 126
1995 Retail: $190

There have been a number of design changes in **She Loves Me...** through the years. At different times, a flower has adorned the fence post opposite the bird; current pieces omit the flower. Older examples depict the boy with eyes open looking forward (Var. I), and newer examples depict him with eyes cast distinctly downward (Var. II). Both examples can be found in some marks.

Trends in Selling TM6-7: $155-190
TM5: $160-190
Var. I in TM4: $255-300
Var. II in TM4: $180-215
Var. I in TM3: $255-300
Var. II in TM3: $205-245
TM2: $295-350
TM1: $440-550

SHE LOVES ME... ANNUAL BELL
(See 1982 Annual Bell)

SHE LOVES ME... BOOKEND
(See Good Friends Bookend)

SHE LOVES ME... LAMP
(See Good Friends Lamp)

SHEPHERD'S BOY

Mold No.: 64
Ref. No.: 937
Approx. Size: 5.5"
Copyright: 1937
Sculptor: A.Moeller
Restyled by: G.Skrobek
2-D Original: H 293,
F 204
1995 Retail: $225

Shepherd's Boy was given the modern, textured finish by Skrobek in the late 1970s, shortly before the onset of the TM6 era. It should prove to be comparatively scarce in the textured finish (Var. II) in TM5.

Trends in Selling TM6-7: $180-225
Var. I in TM5: $190-225
Var. II in TM5: $235-280
TM4: $220-260
TM3: $245-290
TM2: $315-370
TM1: $465-580

SHEPHERD'S BOY ANNUAL PLATE
(See 1990 Annual Plate)

SHINING LIGHT

Mold No.: 358
Ref. No.: 527
Approx. Size: 2.75"
Copyright: 1960
Sculptor: R.Unger
2-D Original: H 444
1995 Retail: $85

With its frequent companions, *Guiding Angel* and *Tuneful Angel*, **Shining Light** was one of the small introductions of 1972. It is difficult to find in TM4.

Trends in Selling TM6-7: $70-85
TM5: $75-85
TM4: $160-200

SIGNS OF SPRING

Mold No.: 203
Copyright: 1948
Sculptor:
    A.Moeller
2-D Original: H 228

Model No.: 203/I
Ref. No.: 829
Approx. Size: 5.5"
1995 Retail:
    Closed Edition

Model No.: 203 2/0
Ref. No.: 830
Approx. Size: 4"
1995 Retail:
    Closed Edition

The molds for both models of **Signs of Spring** were broken at the end of 1990, and the figurine became the third in an annual series of ceremonial retirements of long-running M.I. Hummel figurines. First introduced in 1948 in the larger size only, this model is marked 203 without size suffix in TM1 and early TM2 examples and is overall comparatively scarce in TM1. The smaller model was introduced circa 1955 and, when first produced during the TM2 period, the girl was modeled with both feet on the ground and wearing shoes (Var. I). Later, it was changed to depict one bare foot off the ground. Like the other retired pieces, **Signs of Spring** is now eagerly sought in all trademarks on the secondary market.

Trends in Selling M 203/I in TM6: $190-235
        TM5: $210-245
        TM4: $230-270
        TM3: $260-305
        TM2: $330-380
        TM1: $480-595

Trends in Selling M 203 2/0 in TM6: $160-195
        TM5: $180-210
        TM4: $195-230
        TM3: $255-310
    Var. I in TM2: $635-790
    Var. II in TM2: $325-400

SILENT NIGHT CANDLEHOLDER

Mold No.: 54
Ref. No.: 498
Approx. Size: 3.5" x 4.75"
Copyright: 1936
Sculptor: R.Unger
2-D Original: H 627
1995 Retail: T.W.

Silent Night Candleholder is perhaps best known for a black child version (mold 31) sculpted a year earlier by Arthur Moeller. The standing child is black and barefoot in the Moeller version; this extremely rare figurine can be seen at The Hummel Museum thanks to a donation from Mr. and Mrs. James Pierce. The more common, mold 54 version was withdrawn from production in the 1980s.

Trends in Selling TM6: $235-295
        TM5: $250-295
        TM4: $285-335
        TM3: $320-385
        TM2: $410-480
        TM1: $630-785

SING ALONG

Mold No.: 433
Ref. No.: 447
Approx. Size: 4.375"
Copyright: 1982
Sculptor: G.Skrobek
2-D Original: H 146,
    H 178
1995 Retail: $275

Though bearing a 1982 copyright date, **Sing Along** was not released until 1987—probably due to collector demand for the figurine to match the *1986 Annual Bell* which had been issued the previous year with the *Sing Along* motif.

Trends in Selling TM6-7: $2220-275

SING ALONG ANNUAL BELL
(See 1986 Annual Bell)

SING WITH ME
Mold No.: 405
Ref. No.: 422
Approx. Size: 4.75"
Copyright: 1974
Sculptor: G.Skrobek
2-D Original: H 131
1995 Retail: $310

Copyrighted in 1974, **Sing With Me** was not introduced until 1985. It can be found only in TM6 and TM7.

Trends in Selling TM6-7: $250-310

SINGING LESSON
Mold No.: 63
Ref. No.: 938
Approx. Size: 2.75"
Copyright: 1937
Sculptor: A.Moeller
2-D Original: H 146,
    H 178, H 305
1995 Retail: $120

An early release available in all trademarks, **Singing Lesson** can be found with the normal minor variations in mold, size and color, but none affect values.

Trends in Selling TM6-7: $95-120
    TM5: $100-120
    TM4: $120-135
    TM3: $130-155
    TM2: $165-195
    TM1: $280-345

SINGING LESSON ANNUAL PLATE
(See 1979 Annual Plate)

SINGING LESSON ASHTRAY
Mold No.: 34
Ref. No.: 673
Approx. Size: 3.5" x 6.25"
Copyright: 1935
Sculptor: A.Moeller
2-D Original: H 305
1995 Retail: T.W.

The mold number and copyright date indicate that **Singing Lesson Ashtray** predates both the figurine and candy box. Like all Hummel ashtrays, this is not in current production, having been given "T.W." status as of Jan. 1, 1990.

Trends in Selling TM6: $105-155
    TM5: $115-155
    TM4: $135-175
    TM3: $150-190
    TM2: $200-245
    TM1: $320-400

RARE SIGHTINGS

Want to see the rare figurine *Silent Night With Black Child* (mold 31)? Or the same figurine with white child, thought to be even more rare?

Both can be seen side by side at the M.I. Hummel Museum in New Braunfels, Texas, along with numerous other rarities.

SINGING LESSON CANDY BOX
Mold No.: III/63
Ref. No.: 665
Approx. Size: 6"
Copyright: 1937
Sculptor: n.a.
2-D Original: H 146, H 305
1995 Retail: T.W.

Originally given a bowl shape (Var. I), the piece was redesigned to a box shape at the onset of the TM4 era (Var. II). Some of the Variety II pieces bear the TM3 stamp. The box was given "T.W." status at the end of 1989.

Trends in Selling TM6: $145-180
       TM5: $155-180
       TM4: $175-210
   Var. I in TM3: $350-430
   Var. II in TM3: $250-315
       TM2: $425-530
       TM1: $525-650

SISTER
Mold No.: 98
Copyright: 1938 & 1962
Sculptor: A.Moeller
2-D Original: H 219,
  F 208

Model No.: 98/0
Ref. No.: 907
Approx. Size: 5.5"
1995 Retail: $200

Model No.: 98 2/0
Ref. No.: 908
Approx. Size: 4.75"
1995 Retail: $135

Sister was produced in the larger size only until circa 1962. Pieces produced before this time were numbered without size suffix, and in TM3 these will command small premiums.

Trends in Selling M 98/0 TM6-7: $160-200
       TM5: $170-200
       TM4: $200-235
       TM3: $220-260
       TM2: $280-330
       TM1: $415-515

Trends in Selling M 98 2/0 TM6-7: $110-135
       TM5: $115-135
       TM4: $130-155
       TM3: $145-185

SITTING ANGEL FONT
(See *Angel Sitting Font*)

SKIER
Mold No.: 59
Ref. No.: 939
Approx. Size: 5"
Copyright: 1936
Sculptor: R.Unger
2-D Original: H 264
1995 Retail: $200

One of the perennial favorites, **Skier** enjoys extra demand in the earlier trademarks due to the wooden ski poles used during the TM1-4 periods. Metal poles have been used since circa 1970. A small number of transitional pieces were equipped with plastic poles.

Trends in Selling TM6-7: $160-200
       TM5: $170-200
       TM4: $205-240
       TM3: $230-270
       TM2: $315-385
       TM1: $435-545

SLEEP TIGHT

Mold No.: 424
Ref. No.: 255
Approx. Size: 4.5"
Copyright: 1981
Sculptor: G.Skrobek
2-D Original: H 624
1995 Retail: $215

Copyrighted in 1981 but not introduced until 1990, **Sleep Tight** could prove to be somewhat scarce in TM6.

Trends in Selling TM6-7: $175-215

SMART LITTLE SISTER

Mold No.: 346
Ref. No.: 772
Approx. Size: 4.75"
Copyright: 1956
Sculptor: G.Skrobek
2-D Original: H 193
1995 Retail: $250

Copyrighted in 1956 but not introduced until 1962 near the onset of the TM4 era, **Smart Little Sister** is scarce and pricey in TM3.

Trends in Selling TM6-7: $200-250
    TM5: $215-250
    TM4: $245-290
    TM3: $1200-1500

SMILING THROUGH

Mold No.: 408/0
Ref. No.: 459
Approx. Size: 4.75"
Copyright: 1983
Sculptor: G.Skrobek
2-D Original: H 354
1995 Retail: Closed Edition

Smiling Through was issued as the M.I. Hummel Club exclusive redemption figurine for the 1985–86 club year (June 1, 1985–May 31, 1986). It is number 9 in the club exclusive series and could originally be acquired only with a redemption certificate provided to each active club member. Issue price was $125.

Trends in Selling TM6: $250-310

SMILING THROUGH PLAQUE

Mold No.: 690
Ref. No.: n.a.
Approx. Size: 5.75" Ø
Copyright: 1978
Sculptor: G.Skrobek
2-D Original: H 354
1995 Retail: Closed Edition

Smiling Through Plaque was issued as the M.I. Hummel Club exclusive redemption figurine for the 1978–79 club year (June 1, 1978–May 31, 1979). It is number 2 in the club exclusive series and could originally be acquired only with a redemption certificate provided to each active club member. Almost since introduction—and probably due to the fact it is not a figurine—this piece has enjoyed little demand in comparison to the other annual club exclusives. Noteworthy is the fact that, though offered during the transition period from TM5 to TM6, only TM5 examples are known. This would indicate that early factory production satisfied all resulting demand. Issue price was $50.

Trends in Selling TM5: $105-130

SOLDIER BOY
Mold No.: 332
Ref. No.: 785
Approx. Size: 6"
Copyright: 1955 & 1957
Sculptor: G.Skrobek
2-D Original: H 233
1995 Retail: $210

Soldier Boy was introduced in 1963 and con-
sequently is scarce in
TM3. Older examples usually have red hat ornaments (Var. I); newer models have blue ornaments
(Var. II). Both colors can be found in TM4.

Trends in Selling TM6-7: $170-210
            TM5: $180-210
    Var. I in TM4: $335-395
    Var. II in TM4: $205-240
            TM3: $835-1035

SOLOIST
Mold No.: 135
Copyright: 1940 & 1985
Sculptor: A.Moeller
2-D Original: H 284

Model No.: 135/0
Ref. No.: 886
Approx. Size: 4.75"
1995 Retail: $130

Model No.: 135 4/0
Ref. No.: 407
Approx. Size: 3"
1995 Retail: $100

Soloist was introduced in miniature size in 1986 as
the figurine match to the *Little Music Makers* mini
plate issue of that year. At the same time, the larger
size was first given its */0* size suffix. Combined with
Street Singer, **Soloist** also forms the *Duet* figurine.

Trends in Selling M 135/0 TM6-7: $105-130
            TM5: $110-130
            TM4: $130-150
            TM3: $140-165
            TM2: $185-215
            TM1: $290-360

Trends in Selling M 135 4/0 TM6-7: $80-100

SOLOIST MINI PLATE
(See 1986 Mini Plate)

SONG OF PRAISE
Mold No.: 454
Ref. No.: 294
Approx. Size: 3"
Copyright: 1984
Sculptor: G.Skrobek
2-D Original: H 448,
  H 520
1995 Retail: $100

A 1988 introduction,
Song of Praise can be
found only in TM6 and
TM7.

Trends in Selling TM6-7: $80-100

SONG OF PRAISE ORNAMENT (WHITE)
(See chapter, *The Other Hummels*)

SOUND THE TRUMPET
Mold No.: 457
Ref. No.: 303
Approx. Size: 3"
Copyright: 1984
Sculptor: G.Skrobek
2-D Original: H 346
1995 Retail: $100

A 1988 introduction,
Sound the Trumpet can
be found only in TM6
and TM7.

Trends in Selling TM6-7: $80-100

SOUNDS OF THE MANDOLIN
Mold No.: 438
Ref. No.: 304
Approx. Size: 3.75"
Copyright: 1984
Sculptor: G.Skrobek
2-D Original: H 420, H 520
1995 Retail: $120

A 1988 introduction, **Sounds of the Mandolin** can be found only in TM6 and TM7. Most introductions of the year were small and relatively inexpensive in an effort to appeal to beginning collectors.

Trends in Selling
TM6-7: $95-120

SPRING CHEER
Mold No.: 72
Ref. No.: 929
Approx. Size: 5.5"
Copyright: 1937
& 1965
Sculptor: R.Unger
Restyled by:
G.Skrobek
2-D Original:
H 271
1995 Retail:
T.W.

At the end of 1984—before Goebel began permanently retiring some of the older mold numbers—**Spring Cheer** was given temporarily withdrawn status and taken off the market. Announced in advance, the withdrawal created special interest—and sales—in the figurine, possibly leading to the "permanent retirements" of later years. There are two distinct varieties of the figurine. In Unger's original version, the girl holds no flowers in her right hand and she wears a yellow dress (Var. I). In Skrobek's restyled version of 1965, she holds flowers in both hands and wears a green dress (Var. II). Both varieties can be found in TM3. Coming at the end of TM3, the Skrobek variety is no doubt much scarcer than reflected in current values. Also within TM3, some of the Variety I pieces were painted with green dresses; these examples (green dress, no flowers in right hand) command premiums of more than $1000 above normal TM3 price.

Trends in Selling TM6: $155-190
TM5: $160-190
TM4: $175-205

Var. I in TM3: $205-240
Var. II in TM3: $260-305
TM2: $260-305
TM1: $400-500

SPRING DANCE
Mold No.: 353
Copyright: 1963
Sculptor: n.a.
2-D Original:
H 204

Model No.: 353/I
Ref. No.: 764
Approx. Size:
6.75"
1995 Retail: T.W.

Model No.: 353/0
Ref. No.: 765
Approx. Size: 5.25"
1995 Retail: $310

Comprised of half of the foursome in *Ring Around the Rosie*, **Spring Dance** bears a 1963 copyright date on both sizes. However, only the larger size is known in TM3. The smaller size not only is unknown in TM3, but is rare in TM4. Shortly after its introduction, production was suspended until reinstatement circa 1978. The larger size was withdrawn from production in 1982.

Trends in Selling M 353/I TM6: $445-555
TM5: $470-555
TM4: $540-635
TM3: $695-860

Trends in Selling M 353/0 TM6-7: $250-310
TM5: $2300-355
TM4: $2575-3200

WHAT IS SOLOIST SINGING?
Regular readers of *INSIGHTS*, publication of the M.I. Hummel Club, may already know that the music shown as part of *Soloist* figurine represents an actual song—this a German folk song titled *Wenn Ich ein Vöglein War* (If I Were a Little Bird) in G-Major for two voices, in thirds and fifths.

STANDING BOY PLAQUE
Mold No.: 168
Ref. No.: 678
Approx. Size: 5.75" x
    5.75"
Copyright: 1948
Sculptor: A.Moeller
2-D Original: H 335
1995 Retail: T.W.

Early production runs of
Standing Boy Plaque
were not only sporadic,
but apparently executed
for the European market. In any case, it is scarce to
nonexistent in early trademarks and was relatively
unknown in the U.S. until after 1970. It was withdrawn from production at the end of 1989. It is
unknown in TM4.

Trends in Selling TM6: $130-160
        TM5: $140-160
        TM3: $225-280
        TM2: $350-440
        TM1: $525-655

STAR GAZER
Mold No.: 132
Ref. No.: 888
Approx. Size: 4.75"
Copyright: 1939
Sculptor: A.Moeller
Restyled by: G.Skrobek
2-D Original: H 242
1995 Retail: $205

Pre-1980 examples of
Star Gazer exhibit the
normal variations in
color and molding. Skrobek redesigned the piece
with the modern, textured finish in 1980. The
original Moeller design (Var. I) is no doubt somewhat scare in TM6.

Trends in Selling TM6-7: $165-205
    Var. I in TM6: $200-235
        TM5: $175-205
        TM4: $200-235
        TM3: $225-265
        TM2: $285-335
        TM1: $480-600

STITCH IN TIME
Mold No.: 255
Copyright: 1963
Sculptor: n.a.
2-D Original: H 197

Model No.: 255/I
Ref. No.: 818
Approx. Size: 6.75"
1995 Retail: $285

Model No.: 255 4/0
Ref. No.: 259
Approx. Size: 3.25"
1995 Retail: $95

The larger size of **Stitch in Time** was introduced in
1964, the smaller size in 1990 in the last year of
TM6. Accordingly, these pieces will likely be difficult to find in TM3 and TM6, respectively. The
mini size was introduced as the figurine match to
the *1990 Little Homemakers Mini Plate*. At its
introduction, the larger size was given its */I* size
suffix; examples with suffix may prove to be scarce
in TM6 and should command small premiums.

Trends in Selling M 255/I TM6-7: $230-285
        TM5: $245-285
        TM4: $280-330
        TM3: $655-785

Trends in Selling M 255 4/0 TM6-7: $75-95

STITCH IN TIME MINI PLATE
(See 1990 Mini Plate)

STORMY WEATHER
Mold No.: 71
Copyright: 1937
Sculptor: R.Unger
2-D Original: H 288

Model No.: 71/I
Ref. No.: 930
Approx. Size: 6.25"
1995 Retail: $450

Model No.: 71 2/0
Ref. No.: 415
Approx. Size: 4.75"
1995 Retail: $300

Another old favorite with universal appeal, **Stormy Weather** has the normal variations in size, color and molding found in the long-running figurines. These do not affect values. When the smaller size was introduced in 1985, the large size first acquired the /I size suffix. TM6 examples without the suffix command small premiums.

Trends in Selling M 71/I TM6-7: $360-450
        TM5: $380-450
        TM4: $435-515
        TM3: $550-650
        TM2: $610-725
        TM1: $920-1150

Trends in Selling M 71 2/0 TM6-7: $240-300

STORMY WEATHER ANNIVERSARY PLATE
(See 1975 Anniversary Plate)

STORYBOOK TIME
Mold No.: 458
Ref. No.: 193
Approx. Size: 5.125"
Copyright: 1985
Sculptor: G.Skrobek
2-D Original: H 151
1995 Retail: $380

Copyrighted in 1985, **Storybook Time** was introduced in 1992 and can only be found in TM7.

Trends in Selling TM7: $305-380

STREET SINGER
Mold No.: 131
Ref. No.: 889
Approx. Size: 5"
Copyright: 1939
Sculptor: A.Moeller
2-D Original: H 284
1995 Retail: $190

Combined with *Soloist*, **Street Singer** also forms the *Duet* figurine. In more or less continuous pro-

duction for more than 50 years, it can be found with the normal minor variations in size, color and molding.

Trends in Selling TM6-7: $155-190
        TM5: $160-190
        TM4: $185-220
        TM3: $205-245
        TM2: $295-350
        TM1: $440-550

STRIKE UP THE BAND
Mold No.: 668
Ref. No.: 050
Approx. Size: 7.375"
Copyright: 1993
Sculptor: H.Fischer
2-D Original: H 346
1995 Retail: $1200

Strike Up the Band was released for 1995 as the 10th in Goebel's famous *Century Release* series of M.I. Hummel figurines. Produced just for the one year in the twentieth century, the complex figurine will join a group begun with the introduction of *Chapel Time Clock* in 1986. A special bottom stamp reads, "M.I. Hummel Century Collection 1995 XX." The XX is found on each of the *Century Collection* issues to permanently distinguish these special issues.

Trends in Selling TM7: $1000-1200

STROLLING ALONG

Mold No.: 5
Ref. No.: 988
Approx. Size: 5"
Copyright: 1935
Sculptor:
  A.Moeller
Restyled by:
  G.Skrobek
2-D Original:
  Unknown
1995 Retail:
  Retired

Strolling Along has
had strong demand
in all trademarks since being designated the second
in the current annual series of permanent retirements in 1989. The figurine will never again be
produced by Goebel. Moeller's original design
(Var. I) displays two rings under the base and
depicts the boy with eyes cast down over left shoul-
der. Skrobek's redesign of 1962 (Var. II) displays
only a single ring and depicts the boy with eyes cast
upward. Both can be found in TM3, with the newer
version scarcer. Color variations, especially in the
dog, can be found.

Trends in Selling TM6: $185-230
          TM5: $205-240
          TM4: $215-255
     Var. I in TM3: $245-295
     Var. II in TM3: $270-320
          TM2: $310-365
          TM1: $530-660

SUPREME PROTECTION

Mold No.: 364
Ref. No.: 570
Approx. Size: 9.25"
Copyright: 1964
Sculptor: G.Skrobek
2-D Original: H 549
1995 Retail: Closed Edition

Supreme Protection, originally modeled by
Skrobek 20 years beforehand, was packaged in a
special presentation box and offered only in 1985 to
commemorate what would have been Sister
Hummel's 75th birthday year. Production was limited to year of issue. Despite the short production
life, three recognized varieties were produced—all

due to the fact that
a capital *I* In Ger-
man is printed like
our capital *J*. The
first pieces were
produced with a
signature reading
M.J. Hummel (Var.
I). Subsequent
pieces were pro-
duced using the
M.J. Hummel de-
cal with the hook
of the J manually
removed (Var. II,
the so-called *altered J variety)*. Finally, the decal
was reprinted with the more familiar M.I. Hummel
signature (Var. III). Recently, the figurine has
gained impetus on the secondary market. Apparently, stockpiles held by speculators have dwindled,
and available pieces are now quickly purchased by
eager collectors. Issue price was $150 in 1984.

Trends in Selling:
  Var. I in TM6: $400-500
  Var. II in TM6: $500-600
  Var. III in TM6: $300-375

SURPRISE

Mold No.: 94
Copyright: 1938
Sculptor: n.a.
2-D Original: Unknown

Model No.: 94/I
Ref. No.: 912
Approx. Size: 5.5"
1995 Retail: $285

Model No.: 94 3/0
Ref. No.: 913
Approx. Size: 4"
1995 Retail: $150

Slight variations in molding can be found in older
examples of **Surprise**, but these do not affect values. Older examples of the large size, when found
without size suffix, command small premiums.

Trends in Selling M 94/I TM6-7: $230-285
          TM5: $245-285
          TM4: $280-330

TM3: $3150369
TM2: $400-470
TM1: $645-805

Trends in Selling M 94 3/0 TM6-7: $120-150
TM5: $125-250
TM4: $145-170
TM3: $160-190
TM2: $210-245
TM1: $345-430

SURPRISE (THE)

Mold No.: 431
Ref. No.: 307
Approx. Size:
  4.25"
Copyright: 1981
Sculptor:
  G.Skrobek
2-D Original:
  Unknown
1995 Retail:
  Closed Edition

No. 12 in the annual series of M.I. Hummel Club exclusive redemption figurines, **The Surprise** was issued for the 1988–89 club year (June 1, 1988–May 31, 1989). It could originally be acquired only with a redemption certificate provided to each active club member. Issue price was $125.

Trends in Selling TM6: $165-205

SURPRISE PLATE

(See 1995 Friends Forever Plate)

NEW FOR 1988

The 1988 M.I. Hummel introductions included *Call to Worship clock, The Surprise, Daisies Don't Tell plate, Song of Praise, The Accompanist, Sounds of the Mandolin, A Budding Maestro, Sound the Trumpet, Winter Song, Flying High ornament, Chick Girl music box,* a small version of *Little Sweeper,* the holy family for the small nativity set and the 1988 annuals.

SWAYING LULLABY PLAQUE

Mold No.: 165
Ref. No.: 686
Approx. Size: 5.25" x
  5.25"
Copyright: 1946 & 1979
Sculptor: A.Moeller
2-D Original: H 120
1995 Retail: T.W.

Early production runs of **Swaying Lullaby Plaque** were apparently executed for the European market. In any case, it is rare to nonexistent in early trademarks and was relatively unknown in the U.S. until after 1970. It was regularly produced from 1978 until withdrawn from production at the end of 1989. It is unknown in TM4.

Trends in Selling TM6: $130-160
TM5: $140-160
TM3: $225-280
TM2: $350-440
TM1: $525-655

SWEET AS CAN BE

Mold No.: 541
Ref. No.: 143
Approx. Size: 4"
Copyright: 1988
Sculptor: H.Fischer
2-D Original: H 283
1995 Retail: T.W.

Sweet as Can Be was introduced in mid-1993 as the special M.I. Hummel Club Preview Edition for club year 1993–94. The second annual in this series, the preview edition required a redemption certificate and was marked with the standard Club Exclusive backstamp. The figurine may be released as part of the regular M.I. Hummel line as an open edition after May 31, 1995, but without the special Preview Edition backstamp. Issue price of the Preview Edition was $125.

Trends in Selling: $145-180

SWEET GREETINGS

Mold No.: 352
Ref. No.: 766
Approx. Size: 4.25"
Copyright: 1964
Sculptor: G.Skrobek
2-D Original: H 357
1995 Retail: $200

Copyrighted in 1964 but not introduced until 1981, **Sweet Greetings** can be found only in TM6 and TM7.

Trends in Selling TM6-7: $260-200

SWEET GREETINGS PLATE
(See 1994 Friends Forever Plate)

SWEET MUSIC

Mold No.: 186
Ref. No.: 848
Approx. Size: 5"
Copyright: 1947
Sculptor: R.Unger
2-D Original: Unknown
1995 Retail: $180

Sweet Music can be found with the normal variations in size, color and molding. None affect values except for the "striped slippers" color variety in TM1— striped slippers versus the normal brownish, monotone slippers. The striped variety is rare and commands a premium of $800-1000 above the normal TM1 value. However, buyers should be cautious as color alterations are not difficult to execute.

Trends in Selling TM6-7: $160-200
TM5: $170-200
TM4: $220-260
TM3: $220-260
TM2: $280-330
TM1: $435-545

SWEET SONG ANNUAL BELL
(See 1985 Annual Bell)

TELLING HER SECRET

Mold No.: 196
Copyright: 1948
Sculptor: R.Unger
2-D Original: H 291

Model No.: 196/I
Ref. No.: 841
Approx. Size: 6.75"
1995 Retail: T.W.

Model No.: 196/0
Ref. No.: 842
Approx. Size: 5"
1995 Retail: $295

Telling Her Secret was available in the larger size only until circa 1955, at which time the 196/0 model was introduced and the larger model was changed from 196 to 196/I. At the end of 1984, the larger model was withdrawn from production. TM2 examples without size suffix command small premiums. All TM1 examples are comparatively scarce.

Trends in Selling M 196/I TM6: $315-390
TM5: $330-390
TM4: $380-450
TM3: $425-510
TM2: $550-645
TM1: $1030-1290

Trends in Selling M 196/0 TM6-7: $235-295
TM5: $250-295
TM4: $290-340
TM3: $335-410
TM2: $460-570

TENDER WATCH ARS CHRISTMAS PLATE
(See 1990 ARS Christmas Plate)

THE...
(See following word for alphabetical listing)

NEW FOR 1981

The 1981 M.I. Hummel introductions, put on the market in midyear, included *Daisies Don't Tell, Thoughtful, On Holiday, Sweet Greetings, In Tune, Christmas Song, Timid Little Sister* and the 1981 annuals.

THOUGHTFUL

Mold No.: 415
Ref. No.: 723
Approx. Size: 4.25"
Copyright: 1980
Sculptor: G.Skrobek
2-D Original: H 196
1995 Retail: $215

Introduced in 1981, **Thoughtful** was issued as the figurine companion for the *1980 Annual Bell*. It is available only in TM6 and TM7.

Trends in Selling TM6-7: $175-215

THOUGHTFUL ANNUAL BELL

(See 1980 Annual Bell)

TIMID LITTLE SISTER

Mold No.: 394
Ref. No.: 729
Approx. Size: 6.75"
Copyright: 1972
Sculptor: G.Skrobek
2-D Original: H 223,
  F 206
1995 Retail: $390

Copyrighted in 1972 but not introduced until 1981, **Timid Little Sister** is available only in TM6 and TM7.

Trends in Selling TM6-7: $340-425

TO KEEP YOU WARM

Mold No.: 759
Ref. No.: 049
Approx. Size: 5"
Copyright: 1993
Sculptor: H.Fischer
2-D Original: H 199
1995 Retail: $195

To Keep You Warm would be remarkable in its absence of the familiar Hummel base, except that it is one of three figurines introduced for 1995 that lack the usual bases. The others are *The Angler* and *Just Dozing*.

Trends in Selling TM7: $155-195

TO MARKET

Mold No.: 49
Copyright: 1936
Sculptor: A.Moeller
2-D Original: H 219,
  H 220, F 207, F 208

Model No.: 49/I
Ref. No.: 956
Approx. Size: 6.5"
1995 Retail: T.W.

Model No.: 49/0	Model No.: 49 3/0
Ref. No.: 957	Ref. No.: 958
Approx. Size: 5.5"	Approx. Size: 4"
1995 Retail: $285	1995 Retail: $160

Research indicates **To Market** model 49/I could be rare or nonexistent in TM3 and TM4. When re-issued circa 1978 after being long out of production, some early examples were shipped without the size suffix; these will be found in TM5 marked *49* and command a premium of about $100 above normal TM5 price. Model 49/I was again taken out of production at the end of 1984. It also commands a premium without size suffix in TM1 and TM2.

Trends in Selling M 49/I TM6: $370-460
    TM5: $435-515
    TM4: $550-670
    TM3: $550-670
    TM2: $645-760
    TM1: $990-1240

Trends in Selling M 49/0 TM6-7: $230-285
    TM5: $245-285
    TM4: $280-330
    TM3: $310-365
    TM2: $395-465
    TM1: $610-770

Trends in Selling M 49 3/0 TM6-7: $130-160
    TM5: $135-160
    TM4: $160-185
    TM3: $175-205
    TM2: $225-265
    TM1: $355-440

TRUMPET BOY
Mold No.: 97
Ref. No.: 909
Approx. Size: 4.75"
Copyright: 1938
Sculptor: A.Moeller
2-D Original: Unknown
1995 Retail: $130

Within TM1, **Trumpet Boy** may be found—rarely—with the crown mark in combination with an English-language bottom inscription, "Design Patent No. 116.404" (Var. I). More commonly within the TM1 period, it will bear the post-war U.S. Zone mark, in which case it may sometimes be found with a blue coat versus the normal green.

Trends in Selling TM6-7: $105-130
       TM5: $125-145
       TM4: $130-150
       TM3: $140-165
       TM2: $180-215
       TM1: $305-360
    Var. I in TM1: $730-915

TO MARKET LAMP
Copyright: 1937 & 1952
Sculptor: A.Moeller
2-D Original: H 219, H 220, F 207, F 208

Mold No.: 101	Mold No.: 223
Ref. No.: n.a.	Ref. No.: 650
Approx. Size: 7.5"	Approx. Size: 9.5"
1995 Retail: Retired	1995 Retail: T.W.

When Moeller originally modeled this lamp (mold 101) in 1937, he gave it a plain white post. Due to now unknown reasons, only a few examples were made before the lamp was retired. These crown-marked "plain post" lamps (Var. I) are now considered very rare and valuable. Moeller later redesigned the mold 101 lamp with the customary "tree trunk" post (Var. II); the redesigned version is also available but scarce in TM1. In 1952, Moeller modeled the larger, mold 223 lamp, and this became the standard offering until it, too, was withdrawn from production as of Jan. 1, 1990. Both sizes can be found in TM2 and TM3. Contrary to some of the other lamps, **To Market Lamp** apparently has no identifiable companion piece with which to be paired.

Trends in Selling M 101:
       TM3: $500-625
       TM2: $675-850
    Var. I in TM1: $5000-6250
    Var. II in TM1: $1200-1500

Trends in Selling M 223 TM6: $340-425
       TM5: $360-425
       TM4: $415-490
       TM3: $460-550
       TM2: $590-695

TUBA PLAYER
Mold No.: 437
Ref. No.: 271
Approx. Size: 6.125"
Copyright: 1983
Sculptor: G.Skrobek
2-D Original: H 171
1995 Retail: $260

Copyrighted in 1983, **Tuba Player** was one of the figurines featured on the cover of the *M.I. Hummel Golden Anniversary Album* several years before its 1989 release. It can only be found in TM6 and TM7.

Trends in Selling TM6-7: $210-260

TUNEFUL ANGEL

Mold No.: 359
Ref. No.: 526
Approx. Size: 2.75"
Copyright: 1960
Sculptor: R.Unger
2-D Original: H 834
1995 Retail: $80

With its frequent companions, *Guiding Angel* and *Shining Light*, **Tuneful Angel** was one of the smaller figurine introductions of 1972. It is difficult to find in TM4.

Trends in Selling TM6-7: $70-85
        TM5: $75-85
        TM4: $170-200

TUNEFUL GOOD NIGHT PLAQUE

Mold No.: 180
Ref. No.: 696
Approx. Size: 5" x 5.75"
Copyright: 1946 & 1981
Sculptor: A.Moeller
Restyled by: R.Wittman
2-D Original: H 331
1995 Retail: T.W.

Early production runs of **Tuneful Good Night Plaque** were not only sporadic, but apparently executed for the European market. In any case, it is scarce to rare in early marks and is not abundant in TM4. The plaque is readily available in TM5 and TM6. However, it was restyled in 1981 to change the girl's hairstyle and facial expression. In the original Variety I, her horn is attached to the heart background; in Variety II, it is separated from the background. The piece was given "T.W." status at the end of 1989.

Trends in Selling TM7: $130-165
   Var. I in TM6: $175-215
   Var. II in TM6: $130-165
       TM5: $140-165
       TM4: $175-215
       TM3: $200-250
       TM2: $280-350
       TM1: $450-565

TWO HANDS, ONE TREAT

Mold No.: 493
Ref. No.: 192
Approx. Size: 4"
Copyright: 1988
Sculptor: H.Fischer
2-D Original: H 197
1995 Retail: Closed Edition

Two Hands, One Treat was the second *figurine* to be offered as a M.I. Hummel Club renewal gift. It was included in the kit for all renewing members beginning on June 1, 1991, and ending on May 31, 1992. With an announced value of $65, it could originally be acquired for the price of a $32.50 membership renewal.

Trends in Selling TM7: $80-90

NEW FOR 1989

The 1989 M.I. Hummel introductions included *Harmony in Four Parts; Hello World; I Brought You a Gift; It's Cold* plate; *Tuba Player; In D Major; Birthday Cake; I'm Here; One for You, One for Me; An Apple a Day; Christmas Angel; Love From Above* ornament; *In Tune* music box; a small version of *Wash Day;* several pieces for the small nativity set; and the 1989 annuals.

UMBRELLA BOY
Mold No.: 152/A
Copyright: 1942,
 1951, 1956 &
 1957
Sculptor:
 A.Moeller
2-D Original:
 H 294

Model No.:
 152/A/II
Ref. No.: 870
Approx. Size: 8"
1995 Retail: $1450

Model No.: 152/A/0
Ref. No.: 868
Approx. Size: 4.75"
1995 Retail: $575

UMBRELLA GIRL
Mold No.: 152/B
Copyright: 1949,
 1951
Sculptor:
 A.Moeller
2-D Original:
 H 296

Model No.:
 152/B/II
Ref. No.: 869
Approx. Size: 8"
1995 Retail: $1450

Model No.: 152/B/0
Ref. No.: 867
Approx. Size: 4.75"
1995 Retail: $575

Though copyrighted as early as 1942, the larger size of **Umbrella Boy** apparently was not put into full production until much later, as it is rare in TM1. Known examples are marked only 152, lacking the size suffix. The larger size was restyled to the new, textured finish in 1972. In the original version (Var. I), the umbrella handle touches the boy's right shoe. In the current version (Var. II), it touches his left shoe. Both varieties can be found bearing TM4, with the newer version being scarcer. The smaller size was first introduced in 1954 and has remained relatively unchanged.

Trends in Selling M 152/A/II TM6-7: $1160-1450
 TM5: $1250-1450
 Var. I in TM4: $1450-1775
 Var. II in TM4: $1550-1880
 TM3: $1550-1880
 TM2: $1975-2425
 TM1: $3800-4900

Trends in Selling M 152/A/0 TM6-7: $460-575
 TM5: $490-575
 TM4: $565-660
 TM3: $640-750
 TM2: $800-1000

Copyrighted in 1949 as TM2 was being phased in, the larger size of **Umbrella Girl** is very rare to nonexistent in TM1. The larger size was restyled to the new, textured finish in 1972. In the original version (Var. I), the umbrella is more massive, and examples are usually marked 152/B. In the current version (Var. II), the umbrella is thinner, and the mark usually includes the Roman numeral *II* size suffix. Both varieties can be found bearing TM4, with the newer version being scarcer. The smaller size was first introduced in 1954 and has remained relatively unchanged.

Trends in Selling M 152/B/II TM6-7: $1160-1450
 TM5: $1250-1450
 Var. I in TM4: $1450-1775
 Var. II in TM4: $1550-1880
 TM3: $1550-1880
 TM2: $1975-2425
 TM1: $4350-5400

Trends in Selling M 152/B/0 TM6-7: $460-575
 TM5: $490-575
 TM4: $565-660
 TM3: $640-750
 TM2: $800-1000

UMBRELLA BOY ANNUAL PLATE
(See 1981 Annual Plate)

UMBRELLA GIRL ANNUAL PLATE
(See 1982 Annual Plate)

UMBRELLA GIRL MUSIC BOX

Mold No.: 203
Ref. No.: 6936
Approx. Size: 6.25" x 4.5"
Copyright: 1987
Sculptor: G.Skrobek
2-D Original: H 296
1995 Retail: Closed Edition

From 1987 through 1990, Goebel used the services of the famed Anri woodcarving firm in Italy and the famed Reuge music movement firm in Switzerland to produce a four-year, annual series of collector-quality music boxes. The theme was *Four Seasons*. The **Umbrella Girl Music Box** was the 1990, fourth and final issue in the series and represented fall of the four seasons. The bas-relief rendition of the *Umbrella Girl* motif was sculpted by Goebel master Gerhard Skrobek, and the painting was executed in accordance with the specifications of Goebel master painter Gunther Neubauer. However, actual execution of the production artwork in the form of a painted woodcarving was done by Anri artisans. The 36-note musical movement is a Romance movement by Reuge. The box was a worldwide limited edition of 10,000 pieces, and each music box was individually numbered. This number appears—along with the Goebel backstamp—on a special plaque attached to the underside of the lid. The box is now somewhat difficult to locate on the secondary market. Issue price was $500 in 1990.

Trends in Selling TM6: $600-750

VACATION TIME PLAQUE

Mold No.: 125
Ref. No.: 695
Approx. Size: 4" x 4.75"
Copyright: 1939 & 1960
Sculptor: A.Moeller
Restyled by:
    T.Menzenbach
2-D Original: H 206
1995 Retail: T.W.

In the 1960 redesign by Menzenbach, **Vacation Time Plaque** "lost" one of the support posts in the planter box.The original design (Var. I) had six posts; the newer design (Var. II) has five. Both varieties can be found within TM3. The plaque was withdrawn from production at the end of 1989.

Trends in Selling TM6: $150-185
    TM5: $160-185
    TM4: $180-215
    Var. I in TM3: $265-330
    Var. II in TM3: $220-275
        TM2: $305-360
        TM1: $475-595

NEW FOR 1990

The 1990 M.I. Hummel introductions included the limited edition version of *Crossroads, Flower Girl, Little Pair, I Wonder, Merry Wanderer* sterling silver pendant, *Let's Tell the World, What's New?, Bath Time, Sleep Tight, Horse Trainer, Grandma's Girl, Grandpa's Boy,* a small version of *Stitch in Time, Umbrella Girl Music Box,* several pieces for the small nativity set and the 1990 annuals.

VALENTINE GIFT
PENDANT
Mold No.: n.a.
Ref. No.: n.a.
Approx. Size: .875"
Sculptor: R.Olszewski
2-D Original: H 336
1995 Retail: Closed
Edition

Produced in the lost-wax
method common to the
Hummel miniatures, the
Valentine Gift Pendant was well received as the
first of Olszewski's creations offered as a M.I.
Hummel Club special edition exclusive for the club
year beginning June 1, 1983, and ending May 31,
1984. It could originally be acquired only with a
redemption certificate provided to each active club
member. Issue price was $85.

Trends in Selling: $220-275

VALENTINE GIFT
Mold No.: 387
Ref. No.: 739
Approx. Size: 5.75"
Copyright: 1972
Sculptor: G.Skrobek
2-D Original: H 336
1995 Retail: Closed Edition

First figurine in the prestigious annual series of
M.I. Hummel Club exclusive redemption figurines,
Valentine Gift was issued for the first club year
(June 1, 1977–May 31, 1978). It could originally be
acquired only with a redemption certificate provided to each active club member. This figurine,
combining wide appeal and status as the first in a
popular and well-received series, has always enjoyed great demand on the secondary market. As
Valentine Gift and several other collector club
issues were offered and sold primarily in the U.S.,
there has been special demand for these in Germany
and Europe in recent years. Many of these figurines
are being shipped back to their country of origin—
only one of the reasons secondary market values
have recently escalated. Issue price was $45.

Trends in Selling TM5: $530-660

VALENTINE GIFT PLATE
Mold No.: 738
Ref. No.: 406
Approx. Size:
   6.25" d.
Copyright: 1985
Sculptor:
   G.Skrobek
2-D Original:
   H 336
1995 Retail:
   Closed Edition

Issued in 1986 ex-
clusively for pur-
chase by members
of   the   M.I.
Hummel Club (club year beginning June 1, 1986,
and ending May 31, 1987), **Valentine Gift Plate**
was the first issue in the four-year *Celebration
Plate Series*. The series name derives from the
club's 10th anniversary year, and the motif of the
plate was borrowed from that of the club's first
exclusive figurine. It is executed in bas-relief and
was supplied with a presentation box. Issue price
was $90.

Trends in Selling TM6: $120-150

VALENTINE JOY

Mold No.: 399
Ref. No.: 725
Approx. Size: 5.75"
Copyright: 1979
Sculptor: G.Skrobek
2-D Original: H 335
1995 Retail: Closed Edition

Valentine Joy was issued as the M.I. Hummel Club exclusive redemption figurine for the 1980–81 club year (June 1, 1980–May 31, 1981). It is number 4 in the club exclusive series and could originally be acquired only with a redemption certificate provided to each active club member. At the time of issue, it was obviously offered as a companion piece for the immensely popular *Valentine Gift* figurine and, as such, was very well received. Issue price was $95.

Trends in Selling TM6: $255-320

CELEBRATION PLATE SERIES

Purpose of the Celebration Plate Series tends to be somewhat obscure for many collectors. The series was initiated in 1986 to celebrate the 10th anniversary of the M.I. Hummel Club (then called Goebel Collectors' Club). The four-year series of plates featured motifs previously used with club-exclusive figurines. First was *Valentine Gift*, followed sequentially by *Valentine Joy, Daisies Don't Tell* and *It's Cold*. The series ended in 1989.

VALENTINE JOY PLATE

Mold No.: 737
Ref. No.: 449
Approx. Size:
 6.25" d.
Copyright: 1985
Sculptor:
 G.Skrobek
2-D Original:
 H 335
1995 Retail:
 Closed Edition

Issued in 1987 for purchase by members of the M.I. Hummel Club (club year beginning June 1, 1987, and ending May 31, 1988), **Valentine Joy Plate** was the second issue in the *Celebration Plate Series*. The series name derives from the club's 10th anniversary year when the series was begun. Plates in the series are based on motifs previously used for club exclusive figurines, are executed in bas-relief, and were supplied with presentation boxes. Issue price of this plate was $98.

Trends in Selling: $120-150

VILLAGE BOY

Mold No.: 51
Copyright: 1936 & 1961
Sculptor: A.Moeller
Restyled by: T.Menzenbach
2-D Original: H 220,
 F 207

Model No.: 51/I
Ref. No.: 949
Approx. Size: 8"
1995 Retail: T.W.

Model No.: 51/0
Ref. No.: 950
Approx. Size: 6"
1995 Retail: $250

Model No.: 51 2/0
Ref. No.: 951
Approx. Size: 5"
1995 Retail: $140

Model No.: 51 3/0
Ref. No.: 952
Approx. Size: 4"
1995 Retail: $120

One of the early designs, **Village Boy** was apparently first released in the large, /I size. Early TM1 examples of this size lack the size suffix and command a small premium when found. The large size cannot be found in TM7, as it was withdrawn from production at the end of 1984. Moreover, this size apparently was out of production for an extended period that may have encompassed much of the 1950s and 1960s. It may be much scarcer in TM2 and TM3 than is reflected in market values. Within the TM1 period, a color variety has been reported in model 51 3/0; if found with a blue coat and yellow tie, the piece commands a premium of about 250%. Otherwise, the figurine can be found with the normal variations in size, color and molding with no affect on values.

Trends in Selling M 51/I TM6: $215-265
        TM5: $225-265
        TM4: $260-305
        TM3: $290-340
        TM2: $370-435
        TM1: $575-715

Trends in Selling M 51/0 TM6-7: $200-250
        TM5: $215-250
        TM4: $245-290
        TM3: $270-320
        TM2: $345-410
        TM1: $515-645

Trends in Selling M 51 2/0 TM6-7: $115-140
        TM5: $120-140
        TM4: $135-160
        TM3: $160-185
        TM2: $190-225
        TM1: $305-380

Trends in Selling M 51 3/0 TM6-7: $95-120
        TM5: $100-120
        TM4: $115-135
        TM3: $140-165
        TM2: $170-200
        TM1: $280-350

VISITING AN INVALID

Mold No.: 382
Ref. No.: 744
Approx. Size: 5"
Copyright: 1971
Sculptor: G.Skrobek
2-D Original: H 226, F 810
1995 Retail: $200

Visiting an Invalid is scarce in TM4 due to its 1972 introduction just before the TM5 era.

Trends in Selling TM6-7: $160-200
        TM5: $170-200
        TM4: $1000-1230

VOLUNTEERS

Mold No.: 50
Copyright: 1936, 1943
Sculptor: R.Unger
2-D Original: H 655

Model No.: 50/I
Ref. No.: 953
Approx. Size: 7"
1995 Retail: T.W.

Model No.: 50/0
Ref. No.: 954
Approx. Size: 5.5"
1995 Retail: $295

Model No.: 50 2/0
Ref. No.: 955
Approx. Size: 5"
1995 Retail: $215

Volunteers was apparently initially released in the large, /I size. Early TM1 examples of this size lack the size suffix and command a small premium when found. The large size cannot be found in TM7, as it was withdrawn from production at the end of 1984. It is also rare in TM4 and relatively scarce in TM3 and TM2. It had been out of production for an extended period before being reintroduced circa 1978. Model 50/0 was re-introduced at the same time and is also hard to locate in older marks. The smaller model 50 2/0, on the other hand, has been in comparatively steady production since introduction in the TM2 era. In combination with a special bottom stamp (Var. II), this model was used in 1991 to commemorate the Desert Storm/Desert Shield military operation in Iraq.

Trends in Selling M 50/I TM6: $360-450
        TM5: $380-450
        TM4: $630-780
        TM3: $630-780
        TM2: $680-845
        TM1: $1150-1450

Trends in Selling M 50/0 TM6-7: $235-295
        TM5: $250-295
        TM4: $290-340
        TM3: $320-380
        TM2: $410-480
        TM1: $705-880

Trends in Selling M 50 2/0 TM6-7: $175-215
    Var. II in TM7: $425-525
        TM5: $185-215
        TM4: $2210-245
        TM3: $240-280
        TM2: $300-355

WAITER

Mold No.: 154
Copyright: 1943
Sculptor: A.Moeller
2-D Original: H 244

Model No.: 154/I
Ref. No.: 863
Approx. Size: 7"
1995 Retail: $285

Model No.: 154/0
Ref. No.: 864
Approx. Size: 6"
1995 Retail: $210

Initially produced in the large, /I size, early examples of **Waiter** may lack the size suffix. These examples command a small premium when found. On model 154/0, the bottle has been found (rarely) with a "Whisky" label instead of the normal "Rhein Wine"; the whiskey examples, reported in combination with the TM2 mark, command a premium in the $1500 to $2000 range. Both sizes of the figurine were at some point restyled to the modern, textured finish.

Trends in Selling M 154/I TM6-7: $230-285
        TM5: $245-285
        TM4: $280-330
        TM3: $215-370
        TM2: $400-470
        TM1: $790-990

Trends in Selling M 154/0 TM6-7: $170-210
        TM5: $180-210
        TM4: $205-240
        TM3: $235-275
        TM2: $290-340
        TM1: $490-615

WASH DAY

Mold No.: 321
Copyright: 1957 & 1987
Sculptor: R.Unger &
  H.Wehlte
2-D Original: H 232

Model No.: 321/0
Ref. No.: 795
Approx. Size: 6"
1995 Retail: $285

Model No.: 321 4/0
Ref. No.: 288
Approx. Size: 3"
1995 Retail: $100

Copyrighted in 1957, **Wash Day** was not introduced until 1963 and is consequently quite scarce in TM3. The mini version, M 321 4/0, was added in 1989 to match the mini "Little Homemakers" plate of that year. It bears a 1987 copyright date. With the introduction of the mini size, the six-inch model first acquired its /0 size designator; previously, it had been numbered *321* only.

Trends in Selling M 321/0 TM6-7: $230-285
        TM5: $245-285
        TM4: $280-330
        TM3: $800-1000

Trends in Selling M 321 4/0 TM6-7: $80-100

WASH DAY MINI PLATE
(See 1989 Mini Plate)

WAYSIDE DEVOTION
Mold No.: 28
Copyright: 1935
Sculptor: R.Unger
Restyled by: G.Skrobek
2-D Original:
H 383

Model No.: 28/III
Ref. No.: 565
Approx. Size:
8.75"
1995 Retail: $540

Model No.: 28/II
Ref. No.: 566
Approx. Size: 7.5"
1995 Retail: $410

One of the original, 1935 group of M.I. Hummel figurine introductions, **Wayside Devotion** is still being produced and offered in both sizes. In view of its relatively large size and corresponding price tag, this is a strong testimonial to its enduring appeal. Old price lists indicate that both models—particularly the larger /III—have been out of production at times, but these periods of unavailability appear to have been relatively brief. Early examples of the larger model can be found without the /III size suffix; these command small premiums in TM1.

Trends in Selling M 28/III TM6-7: $435-540
        TM5: $460-540
        TM4: $530-620
        TM3: $580-700
        TM2: $765-930
        TM1: $1200-1500

Trends in Selling M 28/II TM6-7: $330-410
        TM5: $350-410
        TM4: $400-470
        TM3: $450-530
        TM2: $605-705
        TM1: $855-1075

WATCHFUL ANGEL
Mold No.: 194/I
Ref. No.: 478
Approx. Size: 6.75"
Copyright: 1948
Sculptor: R.Unger
Restyled by: G.Skrobek
2-D Original: H 436
1995 Retail: $310

Watchful Angel was given its /I size designator for the first time in 1993; previously, it had been numbered 194 only. Skrobek's restyling in 1959 provided only minor changes to the piece.

Trends in Selling TM6-7: $250-310
        TM5: $265-310
        TM4: $300-355
        TM3: $340-400
        TM2: $430-505
        TM1: $955-1190

WAYSIDE HARMONY

Mold No.: 111
Copyright: 1938
Sculptor: R.Unger
2-D Original: H 289

Model No.: 111/I
Ref. No.: 900
Approx. Size: 5"
1995 Retail: $270

Model No.: 111 3/0
Ref. No.: 901
Approx. Size: 4"
1995 Retail: $145

Copyrighted and introduced circa 1938, **Wayside Harmony** can be found in either model in all trademarks. Early examples of the larger model can be found without size suffix; these examples command small premiums when located.

Trends in Selling M 111/I TM6-7: $215-270
        TM5: $230-270
        TM4: $270-320
        TM3: $310-365
        TM2: $385-455
        TM1: $580-715

Trends in Selling M 111 3/0 TM6-7: $115-145
        TM5: $120-145
        TM4: $140-165
        TM3: $155-185
        TM2: $200-245
        TM1: $300-375

WAYSIDE HARMONY ANNUAL PLATE

(See 1992 Annual Plate)

WAYSIDE HARMONY LAMP

(See Just Resting Lamp)

WE COME IN PEACE

Mold No.: 754
Ref. No.: 044
Approx. Size: 3.5"
Copyright: 1993
Sculptor: H.Fischer
2-D Original: H 627
1995 Retail: $350

We Come in Peace was introduced in 1994 as the second of three figurines in the UNICEF series.

Working in partnership with the U.S. Committee for UNICEF, Goebel contributes $25 to the charitable children's organization for *each* figurine sold. Like the smaller model of the *Friends Together* figurine which preceded it in the series, **We Come in Peace** is unlimited and offered only in the U.S. The motif is the same as that previously used in *Silent Night Candleholder* (molds 54 and 31) and in *Heavenly Song Candleholder* (mold 113). It was restyled and resculpted into figurine form by Helmut Fischer. It bears a special UNICEF Commemorative Edition backstamp.

Trends in Selling TM7: $280-350

WE CONGRATULATE

Mold No.: 220
Ref. No.: 824
Approx. Size: 4"
Copyright: 1952
Sculptor: A.Moeller
2-D Original: Unknown
1995 Retail: $150

When introduced in the TM2 era, early examples of **We Congratulate** were numbered *220 2/0* and lacked the copyright date information (Var. I). Soon thereafter, the size suffix was dropped, and the 1952 copyright date was added (Var. II). This figurine, bearing the mold number 214/E or 260/F, is part of the respective M.I. Hummel nativity sets. However, the nativity pieces have no bases, and a garland of flowers was added for the girl's hair.

Trends in Selling TM6-7: $120-150
        TM5: $125-150
        TM4: $145-175
        TM3: $165-195
   Var. I in TM2: $280-330
   Var. II in TM2: $200-250

WEARY WANDERER
Mold No.: 204
Ref. No.: 828
Approx. Size: 6"
Copyright: 1949
Sculptor: R.Unger
2-D Original: Unknown
1995 Retail: $250

Copyrighted in 1949 near the end of the TM1 era, **Weary Wanderer** is relatively scarce with that mark. It was restyled to the modern, textured finish circa 1970s. A very rare color variation—the girl has *blue* eyes—has been reported. With only a couple of known examples, it would command a premium of about 300% if offered for sale.

Trends in Selling TM6-7: $200-250
             TM5: $210-250
             TM4: $245-290
             TM3: $275-325
             TM2: $345-410
             TM1: $670-835

WE WISH YOU THE BEST
Mold No.: 600
Ref. No.: 209
Approx. Size: 8.25" x 9.5"
Copyright: 1989
Sculptor: H.Fischer
2-D Original: H 283
1995 Retail: Closed Edition

We Wish You the Best, one of the "century release" pieces, was one of the first M.I. Hummel triumphs for Goebel master Helmut Fischer as heir apparent to Gerhard Skrobek. The spectacular figurine was released in 1991 as the sixth in the series. Produced just for the one year in the twentieth century, the piece has enjoyed steady demand in the secondary market, but has not escalated in value as rapidly some early issues. Introduced as it was in the transition period between TM6 and TM7, it can be found in both trademarks. A special bottom stamp reads, "M.I. Hummel Century Collection 1991 XX." The XX is found on *Century Collection* issues to permanently distinguish these special issues. Issue price was $1300.

Trends in Selling TM7: $1250-1550
             TM6: $1450-1800

WELCOME SPRING
Mold No.: 635
Ref. No.: 158
Approx. Size: 12.25"
Copyright: 1990
Sculptor: H.Fischer
2-D Original: H 282
1995 Retail: Closed Edition

Welcome Spring, another spectacular large figurine, was released in 1993 as the eighth in the annual "century release" series. Produced just for the one year in the twentieth century, the piece has already found a niche in the secondary market. A special bottom stamp reads, "M.I. Hummel Century Collection 1993 XX." The XX is found on each of the *Century Collection* issues to permanently distinguish these special issues. Issue price was $1085.

Trends in Selling TM7: $1125-1400

WHAT NOW?

Mold No.: 422
Ref. No.: 721
Approx. Size: 5.25"
Copyright: 1981
Sculptor: G.Skrobek
2-D Original: H 624
1995 Retail: Closed Edition

What Now? was issued as the M.I. Hummel Club exclusive redemption figurine for the 1983–84 club year (June 1, 1983–May 31, 1984). It is number 7 in the club exclusive series and could originally be acquired only with a redemption certificate provided to each active club member. Issue price was $80.

Trends in Selling: $270-335

WHAT NOW? PENDANT

Mold No.: n.a.
Ref. No.: n.a.
Approx. Size: .875"
Sculptor: R.Olszewski
2-D Original: H 624
1995 Retail: Closed Edition

What Now? Pendant was the second of Olszewski's hand-painted bronze miniature creations to be offered as a M.I. Hummel Club special edition exclusive. It was offered for the 1986–87 club year (June 1, 1986, through May 31, 1987) and could originally be acquired with a redemption certificate provided to each active club member. Issue price was $125.

Trends in Selling: $180-225

WHAT'S NEW?

Mold No.: 418
Ref. No.: 257
Approx. Size: 5.25"
Copyright: 1980
Sculptor: G.Skrobek
2-D Original: H 199
1995 Retail: $275

Copyrighted in 1980, **What's New?** was not introduced until 1990. Available only in TM6 and TM7, it could prove to be relatively scarce in the former mark.

Trends in Selling TM6-7: $220-275

WHAT'S NEW? ANNUAL BELL
(See 1990 Annual Bell)

WHICH HAND?

Mold No.: 258
Ref. No.: 815
Approx. Size: 5.5"
Copyright: 1963
Sculptor: n.a.
2-D Original: H 291
1995 Retail: $195

Which Hand? bears a 1963 copyright date and was introduced in 1964 near the onset of the TM4 era. It should, therefore, be comparatively scarce in TM3.

Trends in Selling TM6-7: $155-195
       TM5: $165-195
       TM4: $190-225
       TM3: $535-665

WHISTLER'S DUET

Mold No.: 413
Ref. No.: 194
Approx. Size: 4.25"
Copyright: 1979
Sculptor: G.Skrobek
2-D Original: H 145
1995 Retail: $280

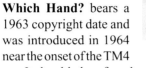

One of the new introductions for 1992, **Whistler's Duet** can be found only in TM7, though—with a 1979 copyright date—some earlier-marked prototypes could exist.

Trends in Selling TM7: $225-280

WHISTLER'S DUET ANNUAL BELL
(See 1992 Annual Bell)

WHITE ANGEL FONT

Mold No.: 75
Ref. No.: 508
Approx. Size: 3.5"
Copyright: 1937
Sculptor: R.Unger
2-D Original: Unknown
1995 Retail: $40

Though in current production, **White Angel Font** is missing from many of the older price lists and may be scarcer in certain marks than indicated by current values. There are two varieties. The original mold provided a hanging devise on the rear; the newer has the pictured hole for hanging. However, the transition date to the newer variety has not yet been documented.

Trends in Selling M 35/0 TM6-7: $32-40
       TM5: $35-40
       TM4: $40-46
       TM3: $45-52
       TM2: $90-110
       TM1: $180-225

THE GRAY MARKET

Along with other currently popular collectibles, the M.I. Hummel brand has been bothered in recent years by an infusion of illicit figurines through the so-called "gray market".

In its most common form, the gray market works this way: An import house is set up in a third country—for example, a Brazil in South America or a Belgium in Europe—to purchase the figurines directly from the Goebel factory. The figurines are then transshipped to an unauthorized distributor or retailer in the United States.

By circumventing normal, authorized distribution channels, these businesses are able to avoid restrictive controls otherwise designed to protect the line from exploitation.

A hint: Be suspicious that you *may* be dealing with a gray marketer if the firm is a major, discount-oriented retailer of Hummel figurines, but is not affiliated with the M.I. Hummel Club.

WINTER SONG
Mold No.: 476
Ref. No.: 293
Approx. Size: 4.25"
Copyright: 1987
Sculptor: G.Skrobek
2-D Original: H 478
1995 Retail: $110

Winter Song was introduced in 1988 and can be found only in TM6 and TM7.

Trends in Selling TM6-7: $90-110

WITH LOVING GREETINGS
Mold No.: 309
Ref. No.: 806
Approx. Size: 3.5"
Copyright: 1955
Sculptor: K.Wagner
2-D Original: H 623
1995 Retail: $190

Copyrighted in 1955, **With Loving Greetings** was shelved for 28 years before being introduced in 1983. For several years after introduction, the figurine was painted with a *blue* ink bottle (Var. I). Circa 1987 to present, it has been executed with a *brown* ink bottle.

Trends in Selling TM6-7: $155-190
    Var. I in TM6: $205-240

WITH LOVING GREETINGS ANNUAL BELL
(See 1987 Annual Bell)

WHITSUNTIDE
Mold No.: 163
Ref. No.: 473
Approx. Size: 7"
Copyright: 1946
Sculptor: A.Moeller
2-D Original: H 477
1995 Retail: $300

The reintroduction of **Whitsuntide** in 1978 created a stir among advanced collectors at the time. The piece apparently had not been produced by Goebel for almost 20 years and was very difficult to find in any of the older trademarks. It can be called nonexistent in TM4, relatively scarce in TM5, and scarce in earlier marks.

Trends in Selling TM6-7: $240-300
            TM5: $285-335
            TM3: $540-645
            TM2: $680-845
            TM1: $1050-1295

NEW FOR 1983

The 1983 M.I. Hummel introductions, put on the market in midyear, included *What Now?; Valentine Gift mini pendant; Knit One, Purl One; With Loving Greetings; Celestial Musician model 188/0;* and the 1983 annuals.

WORSHIP

Mold No.: 84
Copyright: 1938
Sculptor: R.Unger
2-D Original:
   H 267

Model No.: 84/0
Ref. No.: 563
Approx. Size: 5"
1995 Retail: $160

Model No.: 84/V
Ref. No.: 562
Approx. Size:
   12.75"
1995 Retail: T.W.

In the smaller model 84/0, **Worship** has been consistently produced and is available in all trademarks. A white overglaze color variety has been found in TM1 and commands a premium of about 250%. Early examples of this model can be found without the /0 size suffix and command small premiums. The larger model 84/V, on the other hand, was out of production for extended periods and may not exist in TM4. It is also unavailable in TM7, having been returned to "T.W." status at the end of 1989.

Trends in Selling M 84/0 TM6-7: $130-160
        TM5: $135-160
        TM4: $160-185
        TM3: $180-210
        TM2: $220-260
        TM1: $360-450

Trends in Selling M 84/V TM6: $950-1185
        TM5: $1000-1185
        TM4: $1150-1440
        TM3: $1150-1440
        TM2: $1400-1750
        TM1: $1950-2575

WORSHIP FONT

Mold No.: 164
Ref. No.: 510
Approx. Size: 3.25 x 5"
Copyright: 1946
Sculptor: R.Unger
2-D Original: H 267
1995 Retail: $50

The fact that it can be found in all trademarks attests to the lingering popularity of **Worship Font**. It can be found with color and molding variations, but none affect values.

Trends in Selling TM6-7: $40-50
        TM5: $43-50
        TM4: $50-60
        TM3: $55-65
        TM2: $100-125
        TM1: $165-210

MULTIPLE TRADEMARKS

Some figurines bear two Goebel trademarks. This is particularly true within the TM1 (trademark 1 or crown trademark) period.

Figurines bearing "double crown" marks (usually an incised crown mark in combination with a stamped crown mark) are considered quite desirable and can command a small premium in the secondary market.

Commonly, one will find an old figurine bearing both the TM1 (crown) mark and the TM2 (full bee) mark. These pieces, obviously produced during the transition period from TM1 to TM2, usually trade at TM1 values.

Double trademarks in later periods are seldom encountered and would probably enhance the value of a given figurine as a curiosity.

CHAPTER NINE

The Scarce, The Rare, The Nonexistent

Once a person acquires a Hummel figurine from any source other than a retailer's shelf, he or she typically and quickly comes to the question:

Is it possible that I have a find? Is this figurine just possibly a rarity worth much more than I thought it was?

Hey, don't be ashamed to admit this! Nearly all of us participate in a lottery of some sort. And, my guess is that there's not one among us who wouldn't scour the ground for that pot of gold should he actually happen upon one end of a rainbow!

Accordingly, this handbook is much concerned with the words *scarce* and *rare* and *nonexistent*. Because chances are you will be using it in no small part for the purpose of searching for the *scarce* and the *rare*.

There needs to be, therefore, some type of short treatise on *scarce* and *rare* and *nonexistent* so that we're all more or less on the same wavelength as to how these terms apply to the M.I. Hummel figurines.

I thought to look up these terms in *Webster's Dictionary* to confirm what I thought I already knew. Wrong!

Oh, I can agree with Webster on *nonexistent*; the thing doesn't exist. And I can agree on the word *unique*; this means the *one and only*, and you will not find this word otherwise used in this book.

But, of *scarce*, Webster says, "not plentiful or abundant; being in small supply in proportion to the demand; uncommon."

And, of *rare*, Webster says, "uncommon; not frequently found; unusual; scarce."

In other words, to Webster the terms *scarce* and *rare* seem to be synonymous.

With all due apologies to Mr. Webster and his infernal correctness, I have opted to go with what I think is common usage. Namely, *rare* means scarcer than *scarce.*

If I identify an item as *scarce*, I intend this to mean that the item is not common. I intend it to mean that the item cannot usually be readily located, but that it probably can be acquired with time, a diligent search and a little luck.

If I identify an item as *rare*, I intend this to mean that the item is not likely to be found. It probably cannot be acquired even with time and a diligent search.

Nonexistent speaks for itself. The term is repeatedly used because there's always the chance you will find an example of an item only *thought* to be nonexistent. The item then, naturally, would become a *rarity.*

In reading through the sections on figurines, be sure to watch for and understand my use of the words *relatively* or *comparatively* when used in conjunction with *scarce*. You should understand that *relatively or comparatively scarce* does not necessarily mean *scarce.*

For instance, in writing of the figurine *Coquettes*, I say, "*Coquettes* can be found without major variation in all trademarks. However, it is comparatively scarce in TM1 due to its introduction shortly before the TM2 era."

In this example, I am utilizing a simple deduction based on common sense. Since *Coquettes* was not created and put on the market until circa 1948 and since general usage of TM1 ended circa 1949, it stands to reason that there are far fewer *Coquettes* figurines bearing TM1 than if the figurine had first been introduced in, say, 1936.

When I can identify a case like this, I like to point it out. *Coquettes* probably does not qualify as *scarce* in TM1. On the other hand, it is *comparatively* or *relatively* much more difficult to find in TM1 than if it had been in production and marked TM1 a full decade earlier.

In attempting to identify *scarcities* and *rarities* and the *relative scarcities*, I have often resorted to the deductive reasoning such as that just referred to. I have also drawn on almost two decades of experience as a retailer of the figurines.

Additionally, I have analyzed availability data included in a number of old M.I. Hummel catalogs and price lists. I have certainly taken advantage of the wealth of information in books authored by Robert Miller, Carl Luckey and others.

And, I have drawn on personal resources both domestic and abroad. Rue Dee Marker and John Hobe, veteran secondary market specialists in Hummels, have been especially generous and patient in providing loads of trivial details on numerous occasions. In the area of Hummel miniatures, the assistance of Dick Hunt has been invaluable.

After taking advantage of what I know, adding all of the reference data, and consulting specialists in person, what do I think?

I think, collectively, existing information on *relative rarity* of Hummel figurines only scratches the surface of the true situation and is saturated with errors and misconceptions. I think this very work has lots of honest misinformation which hopefully can be corrected in the future.

Not enough research has yet been done to definitively answer questions surrounding availability of the figurines during specific trademark periods. Sometimes, what is known is ignored.

For instance, I had a lot of trouble reconciling the values of the candy boxes—those which incorporate the figurines *Chick Girl, Happy Pastime, Joyful, Let's Sing, Playmates* and *Singing Lesson.*

It is documented that a major design change was made in the shape of all these boxes in 1964. The year 1964 also marked, according to Goebel, the switch from TM3 to the three-line trademark 4.

The design change gave a "box" shape to the boxes instead of the previous "bowl" shape. Some portion of these new, box-shaped boxes were marked TM3 instead of the more usual TM4.

Reasoning says a box-shaped candy box marked TM3 should be much *scarcer* than a bowl-shaped candy box marked TM3. Unless the boxes had been out of production for most of the preceding TM3 era—admittedly an undocumented possibility.

In any case, the existing market—perhaps influenced by price guides—says, in TM3, the bowl-shaped candy box has a value about 250% greater than the box-shaped candy box!

I called one of my advisers: "How can this be, if reason dictates that the newer shape is scarcer in this particular trademark?"

The answer was somewhat surprising. "The older version is always more valuable than the newer," he said, "regardless of the relative scarcity."

I'm reluctantly accepting this answer at this time, but, based on my experience in secondary market collectibles, I don't really think it's true. What do I really think? I think that:

1. It has not yet been established whether one of the varieties of these candy boxes is quite scarce or even rare in TM3.

2. Should one variety be established as quite scarce or rare and *should the buying public be made aware of this,* the supply-and-demand situation—and thus the values—

would favor the scarcer variety, even if was the newer one.

This is but one of the complex riddles yet to be solved in determining the *relative* scarcity and rarity within the M.I. Hummel figurine line. In many ways, the figurines have been wonderfully documented. Only when one arrives at seemingly minute details is one thwarted. However, it is such details for which the dedicated collector yearns. What he yearns, he buys. What he buys affects values.

PROTOTYPES AS RARITIES

Now that we've established some of the ground rules for understanding terms as used in this book, let's explore the field of *rarities* as it pertains to Hummel figurines so that we can all understand how they occur, why some are important in the marketplace and others aren't, and why, in comparison to previous works, this book *almost* totally ignores many of the documented rarities. (*Almost,* because at the end of this chapter many of these are acknowledged in the form of a mold number index.)

Specifically, there needs to be a discussion here of *prototypes* and the role prototypes play in creating Hummel figurine rarities.

Repeatedly, one can find references in this book to long periods between the *creation* or *copyrighting* of a particular figurine and its actual *introduction* in the marketplace.

Let's consider the figurine *Bird Watcher* as one of numerous possible examples. Elsewhere in this book, I say of this figurine:

"Shelved for almost 25 years before its 1979 release, **Bird Watcher** is reportedly the first M.I. Hummel figurine sculpted for Goebel by Skrobek."

Values are given to the figurine *only* bearing trademarks 5, 6 or 7. Other books have attempted to value the figurine in trademarks 2, 3 and 4, as well.

The difference is in the existence, or potential existence, of prototypes—or samples, if you prefer the word.

Bird Watcher was first sculpted in 1954; we can assume, therefore, that at least one example—presumably several—would have been finished as *prototypes* at this time. In fact, Robert Miller reports one of these in his collection. Predictably, it bears the full bee trademark (TM2) used in 1954.

As the mold for *Bird Watcher* languished on some Goebel factory shelf during the remainder of the trademark 2 period and for all of the trademark

3 and 4 periods (to circa 1972), there is also the *possibility* that further prototypes could have been produced from this mold at any time in these intervening years.

A prototype produced during the early 1960s would likely bear TM3, if it exists. One produced during the late 1960s would likely bear TM4, if it exists.

As it was very, very late in the trademark 5 era before the figurine was actually *put into production* for sale in the marketplace, any example bearing an earlier trademark would almost surely first, be a prototype, and second, be a *rarity* unlikely to be encountered by even a very avid, knowledgeable collector.

In determining common values for the Hummel figurines, I choose to ignore the existence of such prototypes. Only *production* pieces—or what are perceived to be production pieces—are normally considered in the value tables which are part of this book. Therefore, I do not attempt to assign values for trademarks which prevailed before a figurine was actually produced for sale.

Yes, such pieces exist in the form of prototypes or samples. Yes, it is possible in a factory setting that a figurine of today might mistakenly be marked with a trademark of yesteryear. Yes, such pieces would demand large premium prices on the secondary market.

So, in short, I address this complex matter thusly:

If, in my value tables, I assign values to *Mischief Maker* only in trademarks 4, 5, 6 and 7, I do so because a full *production* set of this figurine can be assembled with those marks.

As *Mischief Maker* was originally modeled in 1956, it is possible that there are surviving examples bearing trademark 2 or even trademark 3. Predating actual introduction of the figurine (meaning an initial *production run from working molds*), these early examples beg to be considered separately.

If you have or find a Hummel figurine with a trademark older than those listed in the value tables in this book, then you have either a) *found a very valuable rarity,* or b) *uncovered one of the author's errors*! You will, of course, want to find which alternative it is, and, in the event it is the latter, the author and publisher would appreciate being advised.

This prototype *of the* 1980 Anniversary Plate, Ring Around the Rosie, *is a rarity because of the two stars in the field. These stars were removed before production pieces were made.*

THE BIRTH OF A PROTOTYPE

Before leaving the subject of prototypes, it is probably a good idea to briefly explain how prototypes come to be and to hypothesize on what might become of them after they are created.

Much of this can only be conjecture. However, I have long operated a business which has had a hand in producing and having produced for it figurines and other collectibles in which the creation—and, yes, disposal—of prototypes is no small matter. So, the conjecture will at least be tempered with personal experience.

The creation:

WHAT IS THE SECONDARY MARKET?

Those of us who work in it on a day-to-day basis have the habit of overlooking the fact that many persons are initially confused by the term *secondary market* as it relates to M.I. Hummel figurines and other collectibles. The label is, however, quite descriptive.

When an item is sold out, discontinued or in any other fashion reaches a point where it can no longer be supplied through normal manufacturer-to-wholesaler-to-retailer-to-consumer channels, the lone remaining source for the item is through persons who previously acquired it and who are now willing to resell it through the secondary market.

Modeler creates a new sculpture (in *disposable, nonpermanent* material such as clay) which gets preliminary approval. A master or mother mold is made from the sculpture in some permanent or semipermanent material. It is from this master mold that, later, the *working models*, which are used to create the actual *working models,* will be made.

As the making of working models is a major undertaking within itself, there are nearly always a small number of prototypes or samples created directly or indirectly from the master mold. Typically, these prototypes are used to gauge aesthetic and production qualities of the piece and for painter's samples. Occasionally, a certain amount of test marketing in the form of sales samples might be done using prototypes rather than production pieces.

In the case of prototypes of Hummel figurines, we can assume that Goebel, as a large and established company, would normally have multiple prototypes produced of a new sculpture.

Common sense dictates more than one painter's sample, plus examples for technical mold evaluation, and at least one finished piece with which to obtain final approval from Convent Siessen, whose approval is needed before *actual production* of any M.I. Hummel figurine.

Prototypes are to figurines what rough drafts are to a printer. Some are finished and some are unfinished, but all are created to serve as steps toward creation of a final, produceable product.

In the Fall 1993 issue of *INSIGHTS*, the offical publication of the M.I. Hummel Club, an Alabama collector reported acquiring at an estate auction a piece which, as it developed, was the girl portion of *Happy Pastime Ashtray* without the customary ashtray attached. The figurine bore the ashtray mold number (62) and was postured like the ashtray version of *Happy Pastime*, rather than the figurine version.

Another prototype had been uncovered!

As the mold for the ashtray portion of the final product would have already been developed (it is identical to earlier models), there would have been no need to duplicate this portion to serve as, say, a painter's sample.

So, the prototype of the little girl was assembled, painted, and kiln-fired for pre-production approval, and, more importantly today, somehow left the factory. How?

Well, based on experiences at my business, I can at least offer some suppositions.

Book Worm. The ultimate Hummel prototype rarity may be this piece from the first mother mold in 1934. It was sample painted by Sister Hummel herself using watercolors on what appears to be procelain!

Certain of the prototypes would have been incomplete. Some would have also been unacceptable. Some, such as the "ashtray" cited above, might have been incomplete, but acceptable.

While some of these incomplete examples might have been relatively worthless at the time and consequently thrown away or destroyed, others no doubt were spared. In 1936 or 1954 or 1965, little thought would have been given to the potential future value of these prototypes.

You can almost hear some supervisor at the factory telling one of his painters: "No, we have no further use for that sample. Take it home for one of the children."

It's still what we might do today.

You might prefer to think of it in terms of housecleaning. At different points, Goebel no doubt would have accumulated such an assortment of prototype figurines—finished and unfinished, painted and unpainted, marked and unmarked—that it became imperative to dispose of some.

What would you do at home with items you no longer have the space to keep? Chances are, at spring-cleaning time you'll throw some away, assign some to the garage or attic, and attempt to give some away.

Chances are, this is precisely what Goebel has done at different times. And that's why the occasional Hummel rarity, previously unknown, is still found.

VALUING PROTOTYPE RARITIES

The task of adequately appraising or valuing rarities ranges from difficult to nearly impossible. Secondary market values are determined by supply and demand, plus—in the case of Hummel figurines—by relationships to prevailing prices of newly produced figurines.

In the case of a rarity, there is not enough supply to adequately measure the demand at any given price. Therefore, values, in most cases, can only be assigned through the use of relationships.

Bird Watcher, cited earlier, was recently offered by secondary market specialist Rue Dee Marker for $6500 in trademark 2. Translated, this means somewhere close to 2500% (i.e., 25 times the price) of the same figurine *had it been produced* during the TM2 era!

Using relationships, can we therefore assume a similar value for a trademark 2 example of *Kiss Me*, which also should not exist except for a rare prototype?

The answer is maybe. As I said, we who establish values must resort to relationships when there is not enough actual experience on which we can rely. However, this is a very inexact science.

Did Marker sell his TM2 *Bird Watcher* for his $6500 asking price? If he didn't, is it really worth less than $6500? If he did, was the piece undervalued and actually worth more?

See the problem with valuing rarities?

Of the writers, Miller is the acknowledged specialist on rare Hummel figurines. For years, he has sought them out and collected them. Persons deeply interested in this aspect of the hobby certainly should seek out a current copy of his book.

However, it would be a simple matter to discredit his evaluation of rarities by citing the actual results of sales and non-sales. Unfortunately, I have no hope that any effort of mine would turn out any better.

Instead, I will offer a few generalities. First, a prototype rarity should be worth at least 500% (five-fold) the value of an equivalent production piece. Second, a prototype with a signficant mold deviation from the eventual production piece is worth substantially more than that. Third, a prototype of a mold number *never put into production* is worth the most of all.

Any one of these in your possession is worth an independent appraisal, in my opinion.

ACCIDENTS AND ERRORS

Now that we've beaten the subject of prototypes to exhaustion with a lash made of question marks, let's turn our attention to other sources of rarities. We'll start with accidents and errors.

It's a tribute to the long-lasting quality control practiced by Goebel and a source of some amaze-

ment to me that there aren't far more of these rarities than there are.

Consider that a typical Hummel figurine consists of several different molds attached together in the clay form prior to firing in a kiln. Add the thousands upon thousands of figurines produced in 60 years of almost continuous production.

Yet, we can get excited and declare a rarity when one of the elements is positioned a little differently on the base (i.e., the lambs in *Eventide*). The same goes for using the wrong or different shade of color on an apron or dress or hat.

The valuing of such molding and color variations within the secondary marketplace does not, in my opinion, seem to be at all consistent. A variation which in one figurine might command a large premium might, in another, be noted without a premium. Again, much needs to be learned and documented before any type of precise guide on Hummel rarities can be put together.

And here a word of caution: At different places within this book, I have advised care in the purchase or identification of color varieties. With today's materials and techniques, it is no difficult matter to alter colors quite expertly.

To a much lesser extent, the same can be said of mold varieties. It would be no simple task to "remove" the lambs from *Eventide* and to finish and color the base so that the alteration could not be easily detected. But I'm sure it could be done. And, given a monetary incentive high enough, I'm real sure it would be tried!

EXPERIMENTAL RARITIES

There's another source of Hummel figurine rarities which we'll simply call experimentation.

Goebel has always been a very diverse company, creating products in several mediums. In the earliest, mid-1930's days of M.I.Hummel figurines, Goebel experimented with other materials before deciding upon the general usage of fine ceramic (earthenware) for the figurines.

Results of that experimentation, however, are still around in the form of *terra cotta* rarities and *hard-paste porcelain* rarities. Any nice surviving example in one of these materials deserves and gets a very healthy premium when offered for sale.

INSIGHTS addresses this matter in one of its 1988 issues:

"Prior to 1935, Goebel figurines were created in porcelain and decorated with strikingly brilliant and bold colors applied in many layers." This finish

__Terra cotta__ is one of the materials with which Goebel experimented, witness these pieces from the Nativity Set 214. *Any surviving terra cotta piece would be desirable rarity today.*

and the bold colors were not, however, compatible with Sister Hummel's matte-colored originals.

"The material...chosen was a fine earthenware. Porcelain, although highly admired, was not chosen for two reasons. First, it...made the faces, bodies and clothes too finely featured for these figurines. The other is...the unique whiteness of the material wouldn't allow for the rosy-cheeked charm of the children.

"Terra-cotta figurines were also considered, but after the Leipzig fair (German trade fair of 1935), the idea was abandoned. Everyone agreed that earthenware was the perfect medium."

The Spring 1992 issue of *INSIGHTS* pictures a group of early Hummel figurine prototypes made from faience. Faience is a soft earthenware material coated with a white tin glaze which was originally developed to emulate porcelain.

There were also marketing experimentations. At one time and for some unrecorded reason, figurines were created for the Belgian market in a white overglaze finish rather than the normal multicolored finish. These are likewise pricey rarities today.

And, perhaps you are already ahead of me on an interesting parallel to which I am heading. Since 1990, Goebel has conducted no less than three marketing tests with Hummel figurines which could be called experimental.

In 1991, the company introduced a dozen M.I. Hummel motifs produced from frosted 24% lead crystal. Figurines produced included *Apple Tree Girl, Visiting an Invalid, Meditation, Merry Wanderer, Postman, Soloist, Little Sweeper, Village Boy, For Mother, Sister, March Winds* and *Botanist.*

The idea, no doubt, was to channel some of the Hummel production to Goebel's crystal manufacturing facility, while at the same time introducing some less-expensive, collection-starter figurines into the market place.

Nice idea, but the buying public wasn't quick to adopt it, and by the end of 1992 there was talk that the crystal Hummels might be phased out. In 1995, they were still considered *open editions*, with their fate dependent upon finding a niche in the market.

In mid-1992, two new "experiments" were initiated, both encompassing the old idea of a white overglaze finish.

The first series, marketed under the name "Expressions of Youth," consists of *Meditation* in the 13.5-inch size plus six other seven-inch figurines—*Goose Girl; Hear Ye, Hear Ye; Heavenly Angel; Little Cellist; Little Fiddler;* and *Merry Wanderer.* Other than lustrous white, the only color on the figurines is in delicate touches to the mouth, eyes and nostrils.

In the fall of 1992, the company began shipping a series of similarly finished Chistmas angel ornaments. There are 10 in the group, and color highlights include gold tips to the wings.

What sets the angel ornaments apart more than color, however, is the molding. By compressing—*flattening,* if you will—the figurines, Goebel greatly simplified the mold making and handling process. This, combined with the simpler painting techniques, produced a figurine which could be sold for under $30 retail.

As this was written, it appeared the experiment with the glass Hummels and the experiments with the larger "white Hummels" were iffy, and the jury was still out on the white Christmas angels.

If one or more of these experiments does not succeed, count on the fact that it will *eventually be a force* in the secondary market. Too many will have been made to qualify them as experimental rarities, but chances are excellent that sooner or later they will assume a place as desired Hummels.

UNPAINTED HUMMELS

Aside from the Belgian white Hummels and the current "Expressions of Youth" pieces, there are other all-white—or nearly all-white—Hummel figurines offered on the secondary market with some regularity. These are figurines which were prepared for painting, but were never painted.

The original sources for these rarities are at least two-fold. Some escaped from the factory after molding, after glazing and after first firing, but before painting and final firing.

Others escaped at artist showings and events in America. As most know, Goebel sculptors and painters make regular appearances at favored retailers to demonstrate the art of making and painting the figurines and to build interest in the line.

The sample, *white* figurines used in these artist demonstrations are routinely destroyed after the events. That is, they are *usually* destroyed. Enough have escaped this fate that they are a minor factor in the market.

Figure a white Hummel of this type will bring two to ten times what an equivalent, normally colored example should command. Rule of thumb here: the more expensive the "normal" piece is, the lower the percentage of premium for a white example, and vice versa.

LISTING SOME OF THE RARE ONES

Any of the following would be considered a "rare" find worth independent appraisal. In most cases, no market value has been established due to lack of activity. In any case, no evaluation will be offered here.

Because many of these items are so little known and so seldom listed, their names, if known, are not documented well enough for use. Therefore, they will be listed here in sequential mold number order.

Remember, rare by definition implies these items are not likely to be encountered in the normal course of collecting.

Mold 1—Earliest, circa 1935 examples of *Puppy Love* were known to be marked FF 15 versus the normal mold number. Also during earliest production, a variety was made which can be identified by a black hat and absence of the usual tie. These are exceedingly rare.

Mold 2—Earliest, circa 1935 examples of *Little Fiddler* were known to be marked FF 16 versus the normal mold number. These are exceedingly rare.

Mold 3—Earliest, circa 1935 examples of *Book Worm* were known to be marked FF 17 versus the normal mold number. These are exceedingly rare.

Mold 19—*Prayer Before Battle Ashtray* apparently exists as prototype only, if that.

Mold 30/I—*Ba Bee Ring Plaque* in the large size is seldom encountered. It is also very rare in either size with red rings, instead of the normal tan.

Mold 31—This *Silent Night Candleholder* is famous for its rare and valuable black child version. The white child version may be even more rare!

Mold 41—No surviving prototype of *Singing Lesson without base* has been reported.

Mold 42/I—The large size of *Good Shepherd* is seldom encountered.

Mold 65/0—This smallest size of *Farewell* apparently exists only in the form of a few prototypes.

Mold 76—There is only one known surviving example, and it is only the *Doll Mother* side of a pair of bookends which also included *Prayer Before Battle*.

Mold 77—This is *Cross with Doves Font*, and there are apparently few surviving prototypes or samples.

Mold 90—This is another set of bookends—*Eventide* and *Adoration without Shrine*—which was never put into production. Only prototypes exist.

Mold 100—This number belongs to *Shrine Lamp*, of which only a few examples are thought to exist.

Mold 102—There are only a few examples of *Volunteers Lamp* thought to exist.

Mold 103—There are only a few examples of *Farewell Lamp* thought to exist.

Mold 104—There are only a few examples of *Eventide Lamp* thought to exist.

Mold 105—There are only a few examples of this figurine, *Adoration with Bird*, thought to exist.

Mold 106—There are only a few examples of this *Merry Wanderer Plaque with wooden frame* thought to exist.

Mold 107—There are only a few examples of this *Little Fiddler Plaque with wooden frame* thought to exist.

Mold 108—This number was never produced, and an existing prototype has not yet been found. Records indicate it is a wall decoration of an angel overlooking two children.

Mold 120—No surviving prototype of this bookend set—*Joyful* and *Let's Sing*—has been reported.

Mold 121—There is only one known surviving example, and it is only the *Wayside Harmony* side of a pair of bookends which also included *Just Resting*.

Mold 122—There is only one known surviving prototype of *Puppy Love* and *Serenade with Dog* bookends.

The Town Children pieces were never produced. These prototypes of Town Girl with Dog *(mold 158), left, and* Town Boy with Flower Basket *(mold 157) are thought to be unique. They were sculpted by Arthur Moeller in 1943.*

Mold 137/A—There are only a few examples of this plaque thought to exist. It was originally designed to be paired with *Child in Bed Plaque*.

Mold 138—This *Baby in Crib Plaque* was never produced, and only a few prototypes are thought to exist.

Mold 148—No surviving prototype of *Farm Boy without base* has been reported.

Mold 149—No surviving prototype of *Goose Girl without base* has been reported.

Mold 155—No surviving prototype of this *Madonna with Child* has been reported.

Mold 156—No surviving prototype of this *Sitting Woman and Child Plaque* has been reported.

Mold 157—Only one surviving prototype of *Town Boy with Flower Basket* is thought to exist.

Mold 158—Only one surviving prototype of *Town Girl with Dog* is thought to exist.

Mold 159—Only one surviving prototype of *Town Girl with Flowers* is thought to exist.

Mold 160—Only one surviving prototype of *Town Girl in Evening Dress* is thought to exist.

Mold 161—Only one surviving prototype of *Town Girl with Hands in Pockets* is thought to exist.

Mold 162—No surviving prototype of *Town Girl with Handbag* has been reported.

Mold 181—A few surviving prototypes of *Old Man Reading Newspaper* have been reported.

Mold 189—A few surviving prototypes of *Old Woman Knitting* have been reported.

Mold 190—A few surviving prototypes of *Old Woman Walking to Market* have been reported.

Mold 191—A few surviving prototypes of *Old Man Walking to Market* have been reported.

Mold 202—Only one surviving prototype of *Old Man Reading Newspaper Lamp* is thought to exist.

Mold 203—There is known to exist a very rare four-fence-post variation of the smaller (203 2/0) size of *Signs of Spring*. It is quite possibly an early prototype.

Mold 205—This is an early *Store Display Plaque* in the German language. It was sparsely produced.

Molds 208 through 213—These are early *Store Display Plaques* which were sparsely produced.

Mold 215—No surviving prototype of *Child Jesus with Lamb* has been reported.

Mold 216—No surviving prototype of this *Joyful Ashtray* has been reported.

Mold 219—There are only a few examples of this figurine of a girl, dubbed *Little Velma*, thought to exist.

Mold 221—Only one surviving prototype of *Happy Pastime Candy Box* is thought to exist.

Mold 222—This is a *Madonna Plaque with metal frame* which was sparsely produced with older marks.

Mold 233—No surviving prototype of this *Boy Feeding Birds* has been reported.

Mold 236/A—Only one surviving prototype of this figurine of *Angels in Tree* is thought to exist.

Mold 236/B—Only one surviving prototype of this figurine of *Angels in Tree* is thought to exist.

Mold 237—Only one surviving prototype of *Star Gazer Plaque* is thought to exist.

Mold 241—Only one surviving prototype of *Joyous News with Lute Font* is thought to exist.

Mold 242—Only one surviving prototype of *Joyous News with Trumpet Font* is thought to exist.

Mold 247—Only one surviving prototype of this *Standing Madonna with Child* is thought to exist.

Mold 249—Only one surviving prototype of this *Madonna and Child* wall decoration is thought to exist.

Mold 253—No surviving prototype of this *Girl with Basket* has been reported.

Mold 254—No surviving prototype of this *Girl with Mandolin* has been reported.

Mold 259—Only one surviving prototype of this figurine—*Girl with Accordion*—is thought to exist.

Mold 263—Only one surviving prototype of this *Merry Wanderer Plaque* is thought to exist.

Mold 309—An early, rejected version of the figurine, *With Loving Greetings,* exists only in the form of prototypes. In the rare version, the boy holds a paintbrush under his arm.

Mold 340—An early, rejected version of the figurine *Letter to Santa Claus* exists only in the form of prototypes. In the rare version, the mailbox is attached to a tree trunk.

Mold 354/A—Only one surviving prototype of *Angel with Lantern Font* is thought to exist.

Mold 354/B—Only one surviving prototype of *Angel with Trumpet Font* is thought to exist.

Mold 354/C—Only one surviving prototype of this *Angel with Bird Font* is thought to exist.

Mold 387—The ever-popular *Valentine Gift,* offered in 1977 as the first redemption figurine of the then Goebel Collectors' Club, was originally modeled by Skrobek in 1967. Predictably, a few early prototypes have surfaced. These show a 1968 copyight date and are marked TM4.

Mold 730—The *1985 Anniversary Bell, Just Resting,* is a modern rarity. It exists only in the form of prototypes, as it was never issued.

Molds in the 800 Series—
Molds in the 900 Series—

These numbers were apparently reserved for the so-called *International Figurines,* typical M.I. Hummel children dressed in the traditional costumes of other European countries. All are rare and valuable. While there seems to be no record of how many different international figurines were produced, Robert Miller identifies more than 20 in his book.

POSSIBLE FUTURE EDITIONS

In addition to the rare mold numbers detailed above, there is another category of *potential* rarities in the form of existing prototypes of M.I. Hummel items which have not yet been released for production. Goebel calls each of these a *possible future edition.*

Here, we'll concern ourselves only with those pieces sculpted *before* 1991, or—in other words—

before the current, trademark 7 era. On these prototypes, the trademark, if there is one, will pre-date the TM7 mark, thus creating the *rarity* which this section deals with. (Bear in mind that any of these could be released at any time after publication of this book. *With trademark 7,* the piece would *not* be the type of rarity we are dealing with here.)

Mold 302, originally modeled in 1955 and tenatively named *Concentration.*

Mold 313, originally modeled in 1955 and tentatively named *Sunny Morning.*

Mold 316, originally modeled in 1955 and tenatively named *Relaxation.*

Mold 324, originally modeled in 1955 and tentatively named *At the Fence.*

Mold 325, originally modeled in 1955 and tentatively named *Helping Mother.* (A prototype bearing TM2 has been discovered.)

Mold 326, copyrighted 1955 and tentatively named *Being Punished Plaque.* (A prototype bearing TM2 has been discovered.)

Mold 329, originally modeled in 1955 and tentatively named *Off to School.*

Mold 335, originally modeled in 1956 and tentatively named *Lucky Boy.*

Mold 339, originally modeled in 1956 and tentatively named *Behave!* (A painter's sample bearing TM3 has been discovered.)

Mold 349, originally modeled in 1957 and tentatively named *Florist.*

Mold 362, originally modeled in 1959 and tentatively named *I Forgot.*

Mold 365, originally modeled in 1963 and tentatively named *Littlest Angel.*

Mold 368, originally modeled in 1964 and tentatively named *Lute Song.*

Mold 370, originally modeled in 1964 and tentatively named *Companions.*

Mold 379, originally modeled in 1966 and tentatively named *Don't Be Shy.*

Mold 395, originally modeled in 1971 and tentatively named *Shepherd Boy.*

Mold 398, originally modeled in 1973 and tentatively named *Spring Bouquet.*

Mold 400, originally modeled in 1973 and tentatively named *Well Done.*

Mold 401, originally modeled in 1973 and tentatively named *Forty Winks.*

Mold 402, originally modeled in 1973 and tentatively named *True Friendship.*

Mold 404, originally modeled in 1973 and tentatively named *Sad Song.*

Mold 407, originally modeled in 1974 and tentatively named *Flute Song.*

Mold 411, originally modeled in 1978 and tentatively named *Do I Dare?*

Mold 417, copyrighted 1982 and tentatively named *Where Did You Get That?*

Mold 419, originally modeled in 1981 and tentatively named *Good Luck!*

Mold 425, copyrighted 1981 and tentatively named *Pleasant Moment.*

Mold 426, copyrighted 1981 and tentatively named *Pay Attention.*

Mold 427, copyrighted 1981 and tentatively named *Where Are You?*

Mold 428, copyrighted 1981 and tentatively named *I Won't Hurt You.*

Mold 435, copyrighted 1982 and tentatively named *Delicious.*

Mold 436, copyrighted 1983 and tentatively named *An Emergency.*

Mold 443, copyrighted 1983 and tentatively named *Country Song Clock.*

Mold 448, copyrighted 1984 and tentatively named *Children's Prayer.*

Mold 450, originally modeled in 1984 and tentatively named *Will It Sting?*

Mold 456, originally modeled in 1984 and tentatively named *Sleep, Little One, Sleep.*

Mold 461, originally modeled in 1984 and tentatively named *In the Orchard.*

Mold 462, originally modeled in 1984 and tentatively named *Tit for Tat.*

Mold 464, originally modeled in 1985 and tentatively named *Young Scholar.*

Mold 465, originally modeled in 1985 and tentatively named *Where Shall I Go?*

Mold 466, originally modeled in 1985 and tentatively named *Do Re Mi.*

Mold 468, originally modeled in 1986 and tenatively named *Come On.*

Mold 469, originally modeled in 1986 and tentatively named *Starting Young.*

Mold 470, originally modeled in 1986 and tentatively named *Time Out.*

Mold 473, originally modeled in 1986 and tentatively named *Father Christmas.*

Mold 474, originally modeled in 1986 and tentatively named *Gentle Care.*

Footnote: There are numerous other rarities within the M.I. Hummel figurine line. The list above is devoted primarily to mold rarities not treated elsewhere in this handbook. Persons with serious interest in the rare, museum-quality figurines are referred to Miller's excellent book *M.I. Hummel.*

CHAPTER TEN

The Other Hummels

One of the problems any writer will face when writing about the M.I. Hummel brand is where to stop. Aside from the earthenware figurines produced by Goebel, there have been and are *lots and lots* of products produced based on the artwork of Sister Hummel.

In two-dimensional (printed) form, here's some of the products which can be found today:

Plates
Miniature tea services
Porcelain eggs
Hand-colored etchings
Greeting cards
Prints
Tapestries
Calendars
Postcards
Watches & clocks
Jewelry
Books
First day covers
Music boxes
Decorative tins
Wooden boxes
Ornaments
Lithographs
Canisters & cookie jars
Wall plaques
Spice jars
Salt & pepper shakers
Thimbles
Puzzles
Paperweights
Personal checks & checkbook covers
Diaries
Bells
Candles
Stationery
Stained glass...and so on

Many of these items are assuming ever-increasing importance in both the M.I. Hummel primary market and the secondary market.

They deserve full treatment in this and other books relating to Hummel. Unfortunately, it hasn't come, and I don't feel qualified to offer it here.

Of the reference books on M.I. Hummel, Carl Luckey's new edition of *Hummel Figurines & Plates* seems to give the most comprehensive coverage to these *other Hummels*. However, Luckey would probably be the first to agree that monumental research is needed to do these items justice in print.

A comprehensive price guide on 2-D Hummels? I don't see it on the horizon.

There are, however, certain of the *other Hummels* which simply cannot be ignored. They have in common the facts that they are three-dimensional (3-D) and that they have been made by or produced for Goebel. Because in the marketplace they are often entwined with the better-known earthenware figurines, they beg for consideration.

HUMMEL FAKES

Yes, there are fake Hummels. No, they will not be treated in this work except for—or perhaps because of—the following:

1. Unlike fakes in some other specialties, fake Hummels are easily detected by all but the most inexperienced eyes.

2. Fakes are not really abundant, and they do not tend to confuse the M.I. Hummel marketplace.

3. Most are quite old, and they are fascinating collectibles in their own right.

4. Those interested in fake Hummels for whatever reason should attempt to acquire a copy of Lawrence L. Wonsch's excellent book, *Hummel Copycats with Values.*

Crystal Hummels, from left: *Meditation, For Father, Apple Tree Girl, Apple Tree Boy, Postman*

THE CRYSTAL HUMMELS

When the crystal M.I. Hummel figurines were released in 1992, they represented a dozen familiar motifs in sizes ranging from 2 7/8 to 3 5/8 inches.

Produced from 24% lead crystal in a silky matte finish were *Apple Tree Girl, Visiting an Invalid, Meditation, Merry Wanderer, Postman, Soloist, Little Sweeper, Village Boy, For Mother, Sister, March Winds* and *Botanist.*

Though all of the pieces continue to maintain a current production status, it's unclear whether there have been actual production runs of the crystal figurines since 1991. Sales were below expectations, and the future of the crystal figurines would seem to depend upon whether they find a niche in the marketplace.

CRYSTAL HUMMEL, APPLE TREE GIRL
Mold No.: n.a.
Ref. No.: 85010
Approx. Size: 3.75"
Copyright: 1990
2-D Original: H 298
1995 Retail: $59

Trends in Selling: $46-59

CRYSTAL HUMMEL, BOTANIST
Mold No.: n.a.
Ref. No.: 85020
Approx. Size: 3.125"
Copyright: 1990
2-D Original: H 209
1995 Retail: $59

Trends in Selling: $46-59

CRYSTAL HUMMEL, FOR MOTHER
Mold No.: n.a.
Ref. No.: 165104
Approx. Size: 2.875"
Copyright: 1990
2-D Original: H 381
1995 Retail: $40

Trends in Selling: $32-40

CRYSTAL HUMMEL, LITTLE SWEEPER
Mold No.: n.a.
Ref. No.: 84980
Approx. Size: 2.875"
Copyright: 1990
2-D Original: H 234
1995 Retail: $39

Trends in Selling: $30-39

CRYSTAL HUMMEL, MARCH WINDS
Mold No.: n.a.
Ref. No.: 84960
Approx. Size: 2.875"
Copyright: 1990
2-D Original: H 317
1995 Retail: $39

Trends in Selling: $30-39

Crystal Hummels, from left: *March Winds, For Mother, Soloist, Little Sweeper, Village Boy, Sister*

CRYSTAL HUMMEL, MEDITATION
Mold No.: n.a.
Ref. No.: 85120
Approx. Size: 3.5"
Copyright: 1990
2-D Original: H 345, F 201
1995 Retail: $59

Trends in Selling: $46-59

CRYSTAL HUMMEL, MERRY WANDERER
Mold No.: n.a.
Ref. No.: 85110
Approx. Size: 3.5"
Copyright: 1990
2-D Original: H 228, F 202
1995 Retail: $59

Trends in Selling: $46-59

CRYSTAL HUMMEL, POSTMAN
Mold No.: n.a.
Ref. No.: 85130
Approx. Size: 3.875"
Copyright: 1990
2-D Original: H 246
1995 Retail: $59

Trends in Selling: $46-59

CRYSTAL HUMMEL, SISTER
Mold No.: n.a.
Ref. No.: 85340
Approx. Size: 2.875"
Copyright: 1990

2-D Original: H 219, F 208
1995 Retail: $39

Trends in Selling: $30-39

CRYSTAL HUMMEL, SOLOIST
Mold No.: n.a.
Ref. No.: 85100
Approx. Size: 3"
Copyright: 1990
2-D Original: H 284
1995 Retail: $40

Trends in Selling: $32-40

CRYSTAL HUMMEL, VILLAGE BOY
Mold No.: n.a.
Ref. No.: 84970
Approx. Size: 3"
Copyright: 1990
2-D Original: H 220, F 207
1995 Retail: $39

Trends in Selling: $30-39

CRYSTAL HUMMEL, VISITING AN INVALID
Mold No.: n.a.
Ref. No.: 85030
Approx. Size: 3.75"
Copyright: 1990
2-D Original: H 226, F 810
1995 Retail: $59

Trends in Selling: $46-59

THE DOLLS

Goebel is located in the doll-making center of Germany. The rather small town of Roedental in northern Bavaria houses not just the Goebel factory, but doll-producing firms such as Engel, Goetz and Lissi, which are well known in the U.S. as well as Europe.

It shouldn't be surprising, then, that dolls have been a part of Goebel production off and on throughout this century. More surprising, in retrospect, is that the M.I. Hummel doll designs have never achieved a semblance of the popularity or longevity of the figurines.

(I have often felt this was due to the practice of creating multiple designs from one mold. For example, the eight porcelain dolls introduced in the 1980s were based on two molds—one for the boys and one for the girls. Otherwise, the dolls are distinguishable from each other only by the costuming. Figurines have independent molds.)

Most of the many dolls produced in Roedental are vinyl. In the past, dolls were sometimes produced of rubber and occasionally of porcelain or other materials. More often than not, only the head and limbs are molded from the material; the bodies are filled cloth.

In the briefest manner possible, this also sums up Goebel's production of M.I. Hummel dolls.

For 30 years—from the early 1950s to the early 1980s—the company sporadically produced several series of rubber or vinyl dolls based on Hummel designs but not given Hummel names. These dolls are best chronicled today in Wolfgang Schwatlo's *M.I. Hummel Handbook Part I.*

It could be they are more important on the European secondary market than on the U.S. market, where they are relatively unknown and ignored. In any case, values depend drastically upon condition as many of the older pieces were not constructed for longevity.

The so-called porcelain dolls (so-called because heads and limbs are from Goebel's special blend of earthenware, not true procelain) are detailed here.

They are treated individually, but for cataloging purposes could easily be assigned to three distinct groups—the four boy dolls of the mid-1980s, the four girl dolls of the mid-1980s, and the seven dolls made especially for The Danbury Mint beginning in 1988.

The first of the porcelain dolls were released in late 1983 and were titled *Birthday Serenade* (boy), *Birthday Serenade* (girl), *On Holiday* and *Post-*

man. About a year later, four more dolls were released under the names of *Carnival, Easter Greetings, Lost Sheep* and *Signs of Spring.* All were removed from the market at the end of 1988.

The creations marketed by Danbury Mint were *Friend or Foe?, Goose Girl, Little Fiddler, Merry Wanderer, Ride Into Christmas, Umbrella Boy* and *Umbrella Girl.*

The Danbury dolls, now available only on the secondary market, differ from the previous, Goebel-marketed dolls in two very important ways. They are smaller (about 13 inches versus 15.75 inches) and each has its own individual mold.

DOLL, BIRTHDAY SERENADE—BOY
Mold No.: n.a.
Ref. No.: 718
Approx. Size: 15.75"
2-D Original: n.a.
1995 Retail: Closed Edition

Trends in Selling: $280-350

DOLL, BIRTHDAY SERENADE—GIRL
Mold No.: n.a.
Ref. No.: 717
Approx. Size: 15.75"
2-D Original: n.a.
1995 Retail: Closed Edition

Trends in Selling: $280-350

DOLL, CARNIVAL
Mold No.: n.a.
Ref. No.: 465
Approx. Size: 15.75"
2-D Original: n.a.
1995 Retail: Closed Edition

Trends in Selling: $280-350

DOLL, EASTER GREETINGS
Mold No.: n.a.
Ref. No.: 444
Approx. Size: 15.75"
2-D Original: n.a.
1995 Retail: Closed Edition

Trends in Selling: $280-350

Three of the most recent M.I. Hummel dolls *are shown above, from left:* Little Fiddler, Ride Into Christmas, Goose Girl. *These were made by Goebel exclusively for the Danbury Mint.*

DOLL, FRIEND OR FOE?
Mold No.: 514
Ref. No.: n.a.
Approx. Size: 13"
2-D Original: H 109
1995 Retail: Closed Edition

Trends in Selling: $280-350

DOLL, GOOSE GIRL
Mold No.: 517
Ref. No.: n.a.
Approx. Size: 13"
2-D Original: H 155, F 220
1995 Retail: Closed Edition

Trends in Selling: $280-350

DOLL, LITTLE FIDDLER
Mold No.: 513
Ref. No.: n.a.
Approx. Size: 13"

2-D Original: H 229, F 203
1995 Retail: Closed Edition

Trends in Selling: $280-350

DOLL, LOST SHEEP
Mold No.: n.a.
Ref. No.: 443
Approx. Size: 15.75"
2-D Original: n.a.
1995 Retail: Closed Edition

Trends in Selling: $280-350

DOLL, MERRY WANDERER
Mold No.: 516
Ref. No.: n.a.
Approx. Size: 13"
2-Ð Original: H 228, F 202
1995 Retail: Closed Edition

Trends in Selling: $280-350

DOLL, ON HOLIDAY

Mold No.: n.a.
Ref. No.: 716
Approx. Size: 15.75"
2-D Original: n.a.
1995 Retail: Closed Edition

Trends in Selling: $280-350

DOLL, POSTMAN

Mold No.: n.a.
Ref. No.: 719
Approx. Size: 15.75"
2-D Original: n.a.
1995 Retail: Closed Edition

Trends in Selling: $280-350

DOLL, RIDE INTO CHRISTMAS

Mold No.: 519
Ref. No.: n.a.
Approx. Size: 13"
2-D Original: H 316
1995 Retail: Closed Edition

Trends in Selling: $280-350

DOLL, SIGNS OF SPRING

Mold No.: n.a.
Ref. No.: 446
Approx. Size: 15.75"
2-D Original: n.a.
1995 Retail: Closed Edition

Trends in Selling: $280-350

DOLL, UMBRELLA BOY

Mold No.: 518
Ref. No.: n.a.
Approx. Size: 13"
2-D Original: H 294
1995 Retail: Closed Edition

Trends in Selling: $280-350

DOLL, UMBRELLA GIRL

Mold No.: 512
Ref. No.: n.a.

Approx. Size: 13"
2-D Original: H 296
1995 Retail: Closed Edition

Trends in Selling: $280-350

THE MINIATURE HUMMELS

California artist Robert Olszewski, creator of the original miniature Hummels, became associated with Goebel in 1978, sculpting wax miniature representations of M.I. Hummel and Disney figurines, among others.

The wax originals are converted to hand-painted bronze miniatures such as are used on *Valentine Gift* and *What Now?* pendants. Great talent is needed to preserve sculpturing detail in this miniaturized form.

However, it's not Olszewski's talent which initially attracted Goebel's attention. It was possible copyright infringement.

Olszewski had sculpted, produced and sold several bronze miniature versions of popular M.I. Hummel motifs—*Barnyard Hero, Kiss Me, Ride Into Christmas, Ring Around the Rose* and *Stormy Weather*—before deciding to address a letter to Wilhelm Goebel regarding this activity.

A top Goebel executive was dispatched to California to assess this unauthorized "factory" of M.I. Hummel figurines. Today, the pre-Goebel, unauthorized Hummel figurines, though not authentic M.I. Hummel items, are considered prized collector pieces.

Olszewski's "factory" turned out to be a small work area in his home, and the factory staff consisted of Olszewski alone.

Goebel was enchanted with Olszewski's work and his personality, signed him to a contract, and gave him the job of producing legitimate M.I. Hummel bronze miniatures.

The first of these were the pendants, *Valentine Gift and What Now?,* which were created as exclusive offerings of the M.I. Hummel Club (then Goebel Collectors' Club).

The miniature collector club exclusives, which also included a *Morning Concert* vignette, are treated in the chapter with Goebel-made figurines due to their higher degree of relative importance in the secondary market.

The regular production of miniature Hummels spanned a comparatively short period—1988 through 1992.

Production of all miniatures was suspended as of January 1, 1993. As of 1994, Olszewski no longer worked for Goebel, but the Goebel Miniatures facility in Camarillo, California, was still actively producing non-Hummel motifs.

Similar to the larger earthenware figurines, secondary market values of the miniatures are greatly influenced in many cases by the trademark they bear.

There is an authoritative book, *The Goebel Miniatures of Robert Olszewski* by Dick Hunt, which goes into great detail on the miniatures and their trademarks. Here, we'll attempt to simplify matters.

When the very first Hummel miniatures were released in 1988, they were given a circular, backstamp trademark which incorporated the mold number of the piece, the year, the name *Olszewski* and the name *Goebel USA.*

The miniatures bearing this mark are scarce and highly sought today. In the pricing trends which follow, this mark is identified as the *Goebel/ Olszewski Trademark.*

Soon afterwards—and again affecting only the 1988 releases—the trademark was changed to drop Olszewski's name and to add the word *Miniatures.* This *Miniatures Trademark* identifies pieces actually produced in 1988.

After the introductory year, the trademark was changed again. Beginning with the 1989 releases, the word *miniatures* was dropped. The trademark henceforth would incorporate the text *USA,* the year, © *Goebel,* the mold number of the figurine, and a line designating whether production was part of 1) the *1st Edition* or 2) a *2nd Release.*

From a collector's viewpoint, the first-edition designation is more desirable. Figurines with this trademark command premiums.

The three new miniature releases of 1992— *Goose Girl, School Boy* and *Wayside Harmony*— had scarcely reached the market before the decision was made to abandon the Hummel miniatures program at the end of the year. These pieces are probably much harder to find than current values would indicate.

ACCORDION BOY MINIATURE

Mold No.: 266-P
Ref. No.: 37225
Approx. Size: 1"
Introduced: 1991
Sculptor: R.Olszewski
2-D Original: Unknown
1995 Retail: T.W.

The **Accordion Boy Miniature** was one of four mini figurines released in 1991. Issue price was $105.

Trends in Selling: $100-125

APPLE TREE BOY MINIATURE

Mold No.: 257-P
Ref. No.: 37219
Approx. Size: 1"
Introduced: 1989
Sculptor: R.Olszewski
2-D Original: H 297
1995 Retail: T.W.

The **Apple Tree Boy Miniature** was one of three miniature designs released in 1989. Issue price was $115.

Trends in Selling: $125-150
    1st Edition Trademark: $200-250

BAKER MINIATURE

Mold No.: 262-P
Ref. No.: 37222
Approx. Size: 1"
Introduced: 1990
Sculptor: R.Olszewski
2-D Original: H 243
1995 Retail: T.W.

The **Baker Miniature** was one of three miniature designs released in 1990. Issue price was $100.

Trends in Selling: $100-125
    1st Edition Trademark: $125-160

BUSY STUDENT MINIATURE

Mold No.: 268-P
Ref. No.: 37226
Approx. Size: .75"
Introduced: 1991
Sculptor: R.Olszewski
2-D Original: H 193
1995 Retail: T.W.

The **Busy Student Miniature** was one of four mini figurines released in 1991. Issue price was $105.

Trends in Selling: $100-125

CINDERELLA MINIATURE

Mold No.: 264-P
Ref. No.: 37223
Approx. Size: .75"
Introduced: 1990
Sculptor: R.Olszewski
2-D Original: H 154
1995 Retail: T.W.

The **Cinderella Miniature** was one of three miniature designs released in 1990. Issue price was $105.

Trends in Selling: $110-140
    1st Edition Trademark: $160-200

DEALER DISPLAY PLAQUE MINIATURE

Mold No.: 280-P
Ref. No.: 37229
Approx. Size: 1.125"
Introduced: 1991
Sculptor: R.Olszewski
2-D Original: H 228, F 202
1995 Retail: T.W.

The **Dealer Display Plaque Miniature**, released in 1991, features the *Merry Wanderer* figurine. Available in a German language version as well, the piece is quite scarce due to a short exposure to the marketplace. It measures 3.25" wide and slightly more than an inch in height. Issue price was $130.

Trends in Selling: $125-160

DOLL BATH MINIATURE

Mold No.: 252-P
Ref. No.: 37214
Approx. Size: .875"
Introduced: 1988
Sculptor: R.Olszewski
2-D Original: H 230, F 221
1995 Retail: T.W.

The **Doll Bath Miniature** was one of five designs with which Goebel introduced Robert Olszewski's work to M.I. Hummel collectors in 1988. Issue price was $95.

Trends in Selling: $100-125
    Miniatures Trademark: $140-175
    Goebel/Olszewski Trademark: $150-190

CREATION OF A MINIATURE

Persons unfamiliar with manufacturing processes are often surprised by the prices of the bronze miniatures, which are relatively high compared to the much larger earthenware figurines. The prices, however, relate to the complexity of creating the tiny Hummels.

First, the sculptor, working with minute modeling tools, carves a new creation in wax, a process that may require 200 or more hours.

The wax sculpture is converted into a sterling silver master mold. Then, plaster working molds are created. Molten bronze is poured into the plaster molds and, after hardening, is separated from the molds.

Final steps involve finishing, painting and packaging each figurine.

GOOSE GIRL MINIATURE
Mold No.: 283-P
Ref. No.: 37238
Approx. Size: .875"
Introduced: 1992
Sculptor: R.Olszewski
2-D Original: H 155, F 220
1995 Retail: T.W.

(Not pictured) The **Goose Girl Miniature** was one of three mini figurines released and sparsely produced in 1992. Issue price was $130.

Trends in Selling: $170-215

LITTLE FIDDLER MINIATURE
Mold No.: 250-P
Ref. No.: 37211
Approx. Size: .875"
Introduced: 1988
Sculptor: R.Olszewski
2-D Original: H 229, F 203
1995 Retail: T.W.

The **Little Fiddler Miniature** was one of five designs with which Goebel introduced Robert Olszewski's work to M.I. Hummel collectors in 1988. Issue price was $90.

Trends in Selling: $100-125
    Miniatures Trademark: $140-175
    Goebel/Olszewski Trademark: $170-215

LITTLE SWEEPER MINIATURE
Mold No.: 253-P
Ref. No.: 37212
Approx. Size: .875"
Introduced: 1988
Sculptor: R.Olszewski
2-D Original: H 234
1995 Retail: T.W.

The **Little Sweeper Miniature** was one of five designs with which Goebel introduced Robert Olszewski's work to Hummel collectors in 1988. Issue price was $90.

Trends in Selling: $100-125
    1st Edition Trademark: $140-175
    Goebel/Olszewski Trademark: $350-440

MERRY WANDERER MINIATURE
Mold No.: 254-P
Ref. No.: 37213
Approx. Size: .875"
Introduced: 1988
Sculptor: R.Olszewski
2-D Original: H 228, F 202
1995 Retail: T.W.

The **Merry Wanderer Miniature** was one of five designs with which Goebel introduced Robert Olszewski's work to Hummel collectors in 1988. Issue price was $95.

Trends in Selling: $100-125
    1st Edition Trademark: $145-180
    Goebel/Olszewski Trademark: $160-200

POSTMAN MINIATURE
Mold No.: 255-P
Ref. No.: 37217
Approx. Size: .875"
Introduced: 1989
Sculptor: R.Olszewski
2-D Original: H 246
1995 Retail: T.W.

The **Postman Miniature** was one of three miniature designs released in 1989. Issue price was $95.

Trends in Selling: $100-125
    1st Edition Trademark: $130-160

SCHOOL BOY MINIATURE
Mold No.: 281-P
Ref. No.: 37236
Approx. Size: .875"
Introduced: 1992
Sculptor: R.Olszewski
2-D Original: H 194
1995 Retail: T.W.

(Not pictured) The **School Boy Miniature** was one of three mini figurines released and sparsely produced in 1992. Issue price was $120.

Trends in Selling: $160-200

SERENADE MINIATURE
Mold No. 265-P:
Ref. No.: 37228
Approx. Size: 1"
Introduced: 1991
Sculptor: R.Olszewski
2-D Original: H 342
1995 Retail: T.W.

The **Serenade Miniature** was one of four mini figurines released in 1991. The figurines, created from hand-painted bronze, were produced in Olszewski's California studio. Issue price was $105.

Trends in Selling: $100-125

STORMY WEATHER MINIATURE
Mold No.: 251-P
Ref. No.: 37215
Approx. Size: 1"
Introduced: 1988
Sculptor: R.Olszewski
2-D Original: H 288
1995 Retail: T.W.

The **Stormy Weather Miniature** was one of five designs with which Goebel introduced Robert Olszewski's work to M.I. Hummel collectors in 1988. Issue price was $115.

Trends in Selling: $130-160
   1st Edition Trademark: $160-200
    Goebel/Olszewski Trademark: $180-225

VISITING AN INVALID MINIATURE
Mold No.: 256-P
Ref. No.: 37218
Approx. Size: .875"
Introduced: 1989
Sculptor: R.Olszewski
2-D Original: H 226, F 810
1995 Retail: T.W.

The **Visiting an Invalid Miniature** was one of three miniature designs released in 1989. Issue price was $105.

Trends in Selling: $110-140
   1st Edtion Trademark: $125-160

WAITER MINIATURE
Mold No.: 263-P
Ref. No.: 37221
Approx. Size: 1"
Introduced: 1990
Sculptor: R.Olszewski
2-D Original: H 244
1995 Retail: T.W.

The **Waiter Miniature** was one of three miniature designs released in 1990. Issue price was $100.

Trends in Selling: $110-140
   1st Edition Trademark: $130-160

WAYSIDE HARMONY MINIATURE
Mold No.: 282-P
Ref. No.: 37237
Approx. Size: .875"
Introduced: 1992
Sculptor: R.Olszewski
2-D Original: H 289
1995 Retail: T.W.

(Not pictured) The **Wayside Harmony Miniature** was one of three mini figurines released and sparsely produced in 1992. Issue price was $140.

Trends in Selling: $180-225

WE CONGRATULATE MINIATURE
Mold No.: 267-P
Ref. No.: 37227
Approx. Size: 1"
Introduced: 1991
Sculptor: R.Olszewski
2-D Original: Unknown
1995 Retail: T.W.

The **We Congratulate Miniature** was one of four mini figurines released in 1991. Issue price was $130.

Trends in Selling: $120-150

WHITE ANGEL ORNAMENTS

In late 1992, Goebel simultaneously introduced 10 new angels to the M.I. Hummel line. However, these differ from usual Hummel figurines both in color and execution.

The color is white except for mouth, eyes and gold wing tips.

Execution is simplified to create a new, lower price point. The bas-relief decoration is quite shallow, especially on the reverse side of the figurine. The angels will not stand alone; instead, they are designed to be hung.

Multicolored versions of these ornaments were previously sold exclusively by Danbury Mint, a direct-mail marketer, beginning in 1990.

ANGEL WITH CLOUD ORNAMENT
Mold No.: 585
Ref. No.: 131
Approx. Size: 2.5"
Copyright: 1988
Sculptor: H.Fischer
2-D Original: H 415
1995 Retail: $30

Trends in Selling TM7: $25-30

ANGEL WITH LUTE ORNAMENT
Mold No.: 580
Ref. No.: 134
Approx. Size: 2.5"
Copyright: 1988
Sculptor: H.Fischer
2-D Original: H 449
1995 Retail: $30

Trends in Selling TM7: $25-30

ANGEL W/TRUMPET ORNAMENT
Mold No.: 586
Ref. No.: 130
Approx. Size: 2.5"
Copyright: 1988
Sculptor: H.Fischer
2-D Original: H 415
1995 Retail: $30

Trends in Selling TM7: $25-30

CELESTIAL MUSICIAN ORNAMENT
Mold No.: 578
Ref. No.: 136
Approx. Size: 3"
Copyright: 1988
Sculptor: H.Fischer
2-D Original: H 441
1995 Retail: $30

Trends in Selling TM7: $25-30

FESTIVAL HARMONY W/FLUTE ORNAMENT
Mold No.: 577
Ref. No.: 137
Approx. Size: 3"
Copyright: 1988
Sculptor: H.Fischer
2-D Original: H 459
1995 Retail: $30

Trends in Selling TM7: $25-30

FESTIVAL HARMONY W/MANDOLIN ORNAMENT
Mold No.: 576
Ref. No.: 138
Approx. Size: 3"
Copyright: 1988
Sculptor: H.Fischer
2-D Original: H 458
1995 Retail: $30

Trends in Selling TM7: $25-30

GENTLE SONG ORNAMENT
Mold No.: 582
Ref. No.: 132
Approx. Size: 3"
Copyright: 1988
Sculptor: H.Fischer
2-D Original: H 459
1995 Retail: $30

Trends in Selling TM7: $25-30

The White Angel Ornaments. *Top three pieces, from left:* Angel w/Trumpet *(M 586)*, Heavenly Angel *(M 575)*, Angel w/Lute *(M 580)*. *Middle four pieces, from left:* Prayer of Thanks *(M 581)*, Celestial Musician *(M 578)*, Angel in Cloud *(M 585)*, Festival Harmony w/Mandolin *(M 576)*. *Bottom three pieces, from left:* Song of Praise *(M 579)*, Festival Harmony w/Flute *(M 577)*, Gentle Song *(M 582)*.

HEAVENLY ANGEL ORNAMENT
Mold No.: 575
Ref. No.: 139
Approx. Size: 3"
Copyright: 1988
Sculptor: H.Fischer
2-D Original: H 425
1995 Retail: $30

Trends in Selling TM7: $25-30

PRAYER OF THANKS ORNAMENT
Mold No.: 581
Ref. No.: 133
Approx. Size: 3"
Copyright: 1988
Sculptor: H.Fischer
2-D Original: Unknown
1995 Retail: $30

Trends in Selling TM7: $25-30

SONG OF PRAISE ORNAMENT
Mold No.: 579
Ref. No.: 135
Approx. Size: 2.5"
Copyright: 1988
Sculptor: H.Fischer
2-D Original: H 448
1995 Retail: $30

Trends in Selling TM7: $25-30

THE HUMMEL CALENDARS

While they haven't been around as long as the figurines, the annual Hummel calendars represent a much longer tradition than most realize. The first calendar, published only in the German language, was for the year 1951. An English-language calendar followed in 1952, and the series has continued uninterrupted ever since.

CHAPTER ELEVEN

Old Names and Pseudonyms

With many of the M.I. Hummel figurines having been around for more than 50 years, it's only natural that some of the original old names have been changed through the years and that some pseudonyms have been acquired.

The following is provided as a cross-reference to the currently used name. No list like this can be complete. However, it should prove helpful to those who cannot locate a particular figurine in the alphabetical references which are part of this book.

Old Name or Pseudonym = Current Name

Afraid = Retreat to Safety
Angel Bridge = Angel Lights Candleholder
Angel Devotion = Angel Shrine Font
Angel Trio = Angel w/Accordion, Angel w/Lute, Angel w/Trumpet
Angel w/Flowers Font = Child w/Flowers Font
Angelic Care = Watchful Angel
Angelic Concern = Searching Angel Plaque
Angelic Prayer Font = White Angel Font
Angel's Joy = Angelic Sleep Candleholder
Apple Thief = Culprits
At the Dentist = Boy with Toothache
At the Wayside = Worship
Ave Maria = Adoration
Baby Ring w/Ladybug = Child in Bed Plaque
Banjo Betty = Joyful
Boss (The) = Hello
Brother and Sister = To Market
Butterfly Plaque = Flitting Butterfly Plaque
Carrier of Light = Candlelight Candleholder
Celestial Messenger = Heavenly Angel
Chef of Service = Waiter
Child in Hammock = Swaying Lullaby Plaque
Child Jesus = Holy Child
Children Trio = Boy w/Horse, Girl w/Doll, Girl w/Nosegay
Christ Child Font = Child Jesus Font
Christmas = Whitsuntide
Christmas Night = Christ Child
Congratulatory Visit = Begging His Share
Country Boy = Village Boy
Cradle Song = Lullaby Candleholder
Critic = Singing Lesson
Delivery Angel = Christmas Angel

Devotion = Worship
Difficult Problems = School Boys
Diligent Betsy = Little Helper
Doe at Shrine = Forest Shrine
Doll Doctor = Doctor
Drummer = Little Drummer
Duet (The) = Surprise
Errand Girl = Little Shopper
Evensong = Wayside Devotion
Fall = Apple Tree Boy
Father's Joy = For Father
First Shopping (The) = Sister
Flower Angel = Child w/Flowers Font
Flutist (The) = Serenade
Friends = Good Friends
Friendship = Friends
Goat Boy = Little Goat Herder
Goebel Dealer Plaque = Store Display Plaque
Good Bye = Auf Wiedersehen
Good Friends = Friends
Good Friends = Max and Moritz
Good Luck = Chimney Sweep
Good Shepherd (The) = Shepherd's Boy
Greetings From = With Loving Greetings
Gretel = Little Shopper
Guardian Angel = Watchful Angel
Hansel and Gretel = Surprise
Happy Bugler = Tuneful Good Night Plaque
Happy-Go-Lucky = Little Hiker
Happy-Go-Lucky Fellow = Farm Boy
Happy Harriet = Mother's Darling
Happy Holidays = Vacation Time Plaque
Happy Traveller = Globe Trotter
Hero of the Village = Brother
High Tenor = Soloist
Holy Communion = Angelic Song
Hummel Ring = Ba-Bee-Ring
I Congratulate = Congratulations
In Safety = Umbrella Boy
In Safety = Umbrella Girl
In the Crib = Blessed Child
Infant of Krumbad = Blessed Child
Joyful Adventure = Gay Adventure
Just Friends = Playmates
Just Sittin'—Boy = Wayside Harmony
Just Sittin'—Girl = Just Resting
Knitter = Happy Pastime

Ladybug Plaque = Child in Bed Plaque
Leader = Band Leader
Little Band = Boy w/Accordion, Girl w/Sheet Music, Girlw/Trumpet
Little Book Worm = Book Worm
Little Gooseherd = Goose Girl
Little Guardian = Heavenly Angel
Little Heavenly Angel = Angel w/Accordion, Angel w/Lute, Angel w/Trumpet
Little Homemakers = Chicken Licken, Little Shopper, Stitch in Time, Wash Day
Little Messenger = Meditation
Little Mothers of the Family = Going to Grandma's
Little Music Makers = Band Leader, Little Fiddler, Serenade, Soloist
Little Musician = Trumpet Boy
Little Scholar = School Boy
Little Shepherd (The) = Wayside Devotion
Little Sister (The) = Little Helper
Little Skier = Skier
Little Violinist = Puppy Love
Madonna w/Blue Cloak = Madonna Holding Child
Mail Coach = Mail Is Here
Master Piece = School Girls
Meg = Little Shopper
M.I. Hummel Plaque = Dealer Display Plaque
Mother of Ducks = Be Patient
Mother's Helper = Little Sweeper
Musician = Little Cellist
Night Watchman = Hear Ye, Hear Ye
On Holiday Plaque = Vacation Time Plaque
On the Alpine Pasture = Accordion Boy
Our Hero = Brother
Playing Soldiers = Volunteers
Playing to the Dance = Sweet Music
Primer Boy = School Boy
Primer Girl = School Girl
Psalmist = Angel Serenade with Lamb
Scandal = Signs of Spring
School Days = School Boy
Secret (The) = Telling Her Secret
Seven Swabians = Adventure Bound
Shoemaker = Boots
Shopper (The) = Sister
Sitting Angel = Angel w/Bird Font
Sitting Madonna w/Child = Flower Madonna
Smoky = Chimney Sweep
So Long = Farewell
Soloist = Street Singer
Spring = Apple Tree Girl
Spring Flowers = Spring Cheer

Tenderness = Bird Watcher
Three Pals = Farm Boy
Timid Hunter = Sensitive Hunter
Tired Little Traveler = Weary Wanderer
Toothache = Boy with Toothache
Traveller's Song = Happiness
Under One Roof = Stormy Weather
Urchin = March Winds
Violinist = Little Fiddler
Virgin With Flowers = Flower Madonna
Wanderer = Happy Traveller
Wandering Fiddler = Little Fiddler
Wandersong = Happiness

BIBLIOGRAPHY

Ehrmann, Eric. Hummel. *The Complete Collector's Guide and Illustrated Reference*. Huntington, New York: Portfolio Press Corporation, 1976.

Ehrmann, Eric. *M.I. Hummel. The Golden Anniversary Album*. New York: Portfolio Press Corporation, 1984.

Hunt, Dick. *The Goebel Miniatures of Robert Olszewski. An Authoritative Reference & Price Guide*. Satellite Beach, Florida: Collectibles Reference Press, 1989.

INSIGHTS. The Exclusive Journal for Members of the M.I. Hummel Club®. Volumes 1 through 17, 1977-1994.

Luckey, Carl F. *Luckey's Hummel Figurines & Plates. A Collector's Identification and Value Guide*. Florence, Alabama: Books Americana, Inc., 1994.

M.I. Hummel®. The Fascinating World of M.I. Hummel Figurines. Germany: Goebel, 1991.

Miller, Robert L. *The No. 1 Price Guide to M.I. Hummel® Figurines, Plates, Miniatures, & More...* Huntington, New York: Portfolio Press, 1992.

Schwatlo, Wolfgang. *M.I. Hummel® Collector's Handbook. Part I: Rarities and Collector Pieces*. Niedernhausen, Germany: Schwatlo GmbH, 1994.

The M.I. Hummel Album. Portfolio Press Corporation, 1992.

The Official Price Guide to Hummel Figurines & Plates. New York: The House of Collectibles, 1986.

Wonsch, Lawrence L. *Hummel Copycats with Values. A Guide to Those Other Hummels*. Lombard, Illinois: Wallace-Homestead Book Company, 1987.

ALPHABETICAL INDEX

Hummel Name	Mold No.:	Ref. No.	Pg. #
1991 Annual Plate, Just Resting	287	317	60
1991 Christmas Bell, Hear Ye, Hear Ye	777	206	60
1991 Mini Plate, Chicken-Licken	748	208	60
1992 Annual Bell, Whistler's Duet	714	187	61
1992 Annual Ornament, Light Up the Night	622	185	61
1992 Annual Plate, Wayside Harmony	288	316	61
1992 Christmas Bell, Harmony in Four Parts	778	186	61
1992 Friends Forever Plate, Meditation	292	188	62
1993 Annual Ornament, Herald on High	623	153	62
1993 Annual Plate, Doll Bath	289	157	62
1993 Christmas Bell, Celestial Musician	779	155	62
1993 Friends Forever Plate, For Father	293	156	63
1994 Annual Plate, Doctor	290	110	63
1994 Christmas Bell, Festival Harmony w/Mandolin	780	108	63
1994 Friends Forever Plate, Sweet Greetings	294	109	63
1995 Annual Plate, Come Back Soon	291	048	64
1995 Christmas Bell, Festival Harmony w/Flute	781	046	64
1995 Friends Forever Plate, Surprise	295	n.a.	64
1995 Mini Christmas Plate, Festival Harmony w/Flute	693	027	64
A Budding Maestro	477	292	65
A Fair Measure	345	773	65
A Free Flight	569	160	65
A Gentle Glow Candleholder	439	445	65
A Nap	534	213	65
A Story from Grandma	620	025	66
A Sweet Offering	549 3/0	144	66
Accompanist (The)	453	295	66
Accordion Boy	185	849	66
Accordion Boy Miniature	266-P	37225	219
Adoration	23/I	568	67
Adoration	23/III	567	67
Adventure Bound	347	771	68
An Apple A Day	403	272	68
Angel Cloud Font	206	522	68
Angel Duet	261	546	68
Angel Duet Candleholder	193	536	69
Angel Duet Font	146	513	69
Angel Facing Left Font	91A	507	69
Angel Facing Right Font	91B	506	69
Angel Lights Candleholder	241/B	548	70
Angel Serenade with Lamb	83	540	70
Angel Shrine Font	147	512	70
Angel Sitting Font	22/0	520	70
Angel with Accordion	238/B	551	71
Angel with Accordion Candleholder	39/0	532	71
Angel with Bird Font	167	509	72
Angel with Cloud Ornament (White)	585	131	223
Angel with Lute	238/A	552	71
Angel with Lute Candleholder	38/0	534	71
Angel with Lute Ornament (White)	580	134	223
Angel with Trumpet	238/C	550	71
Angel with Trumpet Candleholder	40/0	530	71
Angel with Trumpet Ornament (White)	586	130	223
Angelic Sleep Candleholder	25	499	72
Angelic Song	144	476	72
Angler (The)	566	052	72
Apple Tree Boy	142 3/0	879	73

Hummel Name	Mold No.:	Ref. No.	Pg. #
Apple Tree Boy	142/I	878	73
Apple Tree Boy	142/V	877	73
Apple Tree Boy	142/X	876	73
Apple Tree Boy & Girl Bookends	252/A&B	705	73
Apple Tree Boy Lamp	230	642	74
Apple Tree Boy Miniature	257-P	37219	219
Apple Tree Girl	141 3/0	883	74
Apple Tree Girl	141/I	882	74
Apple Tree Girl	141/V	881	74
Apple Tree Girl	141/X	880	74
Apple Tree Girl (Crystal Hummel)	n.a.	85010	214
Apple Tree Girl Lamp	229	643	74
Art Critic	318	798	75
Artist	304	811	75
Artist Figurine Plaque Museum Commemorative	756	093	75
At Grandpa's	621	051	76
Auf Wiedersehen	153/0	866	76
Auf Wiedersehen	153/I	865	76
Autumn Harvest	355	763	77
Ba Bee Ring-Boy Plaque	30/A	691	77
Ba Bee Ring-Girl Plaque	30/B	692	77
Baker	128	892	77
Baker Miniature	262-P	37222	219
Baking Day	330	425	78
Band Leader	129	891	78
Band Leader	129 4/0	398	78
Barnyard Hero	195 2/0	844	78
Barnyard Hero	195/I	843	78
Bashful	377	749	78
Bath Time	412	258	79
Be Patient	197 2/0	840	79
Be Patient	197/I	839	79
Begging His Share	9	978	79
Berlin Airlift Memorial (Auf Wiedersehen)	153/0	n.a.	76
Big Housecleaning	363	759	79
Bird Duet	169	545	80
Bird Watcher	300	814	80
Birthday Cake Candleholder	338	779	80
Birthday Candle	440	403	80
Birthday Present	341 3/0	098	80
Birthday Serenade	218 2/0	826	81
Birthday Serenade	218/0	825	81
Birthday Serenade-Boy (Doll)	n.a.	718	216
Birthday Serenade-Girl (Doll)	n.a.	717	216
Birthday Serenade Lamp	231	641	81
Birthday Serenade Lamp	234	639	81
Blessed Child	78/I/83	495	82
Blessed Child	78/II/83	492	82
Blessed Child	78/III/83	489	82
Blessed Child	78/II 1/2	n.a.	82
Blessed Child	78/V	n.a.	82
Blessed Child	78/VI	n.a.	82
Blessed Child	78/VIII	n.a.	82
Blessed Child	78/0	n.a.	82
Blessed Event	333	784	82
Book Worm	3/I	992	83
Book Worm	3/II	991	83

Hummel Name	Mold No.:	Ref. No.	Pg. #
Book Worm	3/III	990	83
Book Worm	8	979	83
Book Worms Bookends	14/A&B	715	83
Boots	143/0	875	84
Boots	143/I	874	84
Botanist	351	767	84
Botanist (Crystal Hummel)	n.a.	85020	214
Boy & Girl Wall Vase	360/A	662	84
Boy Wall Vase	360/B	661	84
Boy with Accordion	390	734	85
Boy with Bird Ashtray	166	671	85
Boy with Horse	239/C	820	85
Boy with Horse Candleholder	117	635	85
Boy with Toothache	217	827	86
Brother	95	911	86
Builder	305	810	86
Bust Of Sister Hummel	n.a.	HU1	86
Bust Of Sister Hummel	n.a.	HU2	86
Bust Of Sister Hummel	n.a.	HU3	86
Busy Student	367	757	87
Busy Student Miniature	268-P	37226	220
Call To Glory	739/I	103	87
Call To Worship Clock	441	300	88
Candlelight Candleholder	192	537	88
Carnival	328	789	88
Carnival (Doll)	n.a.	465	216
Celestial Musician	188/0	524	89
Celestiai Musician	188/I	523	89
Celestial Musician	188 4/0	154	89
Celestial Musician Miniature Ornament	646	152	89
Celestial Musician Ornament (White)	578	136	223
Chapel Time Clock	442	420	90
Cheeky Fellow	554	172	90
Chick Girl	57 2/0	417	90
Chick Girl	57/0	943	90
Chick Girl	57/I	942	90
Chick Girl Candy Box	III/57	667	91
Chick Girl Music Box	324	6434	92
Chicken Licken	385 4/0	216	92
Chicken Licken	385	741	92
Child In Bed Plaque	137	689	92
Child Jesus Font	26/0	519	93
Child Jesus Font	26/I	n.a.	93
Child with Flowers Font	36/0	515	93
Child with Flowers Font	36/I	n.a.	93
Chimney Sweep	12 2/0	975	93
Chimney Sweep	12/I	974	93
Christ Child	18	502	94
Christmas Angel	301	561	94
Christmas Song	343	547	94
Cinderella	337	780	94
Cinderella Miniature	264-P	37223	220
Close Harmony	336	781	95
Club Member Plaque (White)	n.a.	n.a.	95
Coffee Break	409	470	95
Come Back Soon	545	054	95
Confidentially	314	802	96

Hummel Name	Mold No.:	Ref. No.	Pg. #
Congratulations	17/0	964	96
Congratulations	17/2	n.a.	96
Coquettes	179	852	96
Crossroads	331	786	96
Crossroads Berlin Wall Commemorative	331	197	97
Crossroads Military Commemorative	331	787	96
Culprits	56/A	945	98
Culprits Lamp Base	44/A	653	98
Daddy's Girls	371	753	98
Daisies Don't Tell	380	746	98
Daisies Don't Tell Plate	736	302	99
Dealer Display Plaque	187	238	99
Dealer Display Plaque	187/A	845	99
Dealer Display Plaque, "The Tally"	460	402	99
Dealer Display Plaque Miniature	280-P	37229	220
Doctor	127	893	100
Doll Bath	319	797	100
Doll Bath Miniature	252-P	37214	220
Doll Mother	67	934	100
Duet	130	890	100
Easter Greetings	378	748	101
Easter Greetings (Doll)	n.a.	444	216
Easter Time	384	742	101
Evening Prayer	495	191	101
Eventide	99	906	101
Farewell	65	936	102
Farewell	65/I	n.a.	102
Farewell	65/0	n.a.	102
Farm Boy	66	935	102
Favorite Pet	361	761	102
Feathered Friends	344	774	103
Feeding Time	199/0	836	103
Feeding Time	199/I	835	103
Festival Harmony with Flute	173/0	542	104
Festival Harmony with Flute	173/II	541	104
Festival Harmony with Flute	173 4/0	045	104
Festival Harmony with Flute Miniature Orn.	648	043	104
Festival Harmony with Flute Orn. (White)	577	137	223
Festival Harmony with Mandolin	172/0	544	105
Festival Harmony with Mandolin	172/II	543	105
Festival Harmony with Mandolin	172 4/0	107	105
Festival Harmony with Mandolin Miniature Orn.	647	106	105
Festival Harmony with Mandolin Orn. (White)	576	138	223
Flitting Butterfly Plaque	139	688	106
Flower Girl	548	240	106
Flower Madonna	10/I/W	592	106
Flower Madonna	10/III/W	590	106
Flower Madonna	10/III	591	106
Flower Madonna	10/I	593	106
Flower Vendor	381	745	107
Flying Angel	366/0	275	156
Flying Angel	366/I	525	156
Follow The Leader	369	755	107
For Father	87	916	108
For Keeps	630	102	108
For Mother	257 2/0	414	108
For Mother	257/0	816	108

Hummel Name	Mold No.:	Ref. No.	Pg. #
For Mother (Crystal Hummel)	n.a.	165104	214
Forest Shrine	183	564	108
Friend or Foe?	434	461	109
Friend or Foe? (Doll)	514	n.a.	217
Friends	136/I	885	109
Friends	136/V	884	109
Friends Together	662/0	104	109
Friends Together	662/I	094	109
Gay Adventure	356	762	110
Gentle Song Ornament (White)	582	132	223
Gift From a Friend	485	198	110
Girl Wall Vase	360/C	660	84
Girl with Doll	239/B	821	85
Girl with Fir Tree Candleholder	116	636	85
Girl with Nosegay	239/A	822	85
Girl with Nosegay Candleholder	115	637	85
Girl with Sheet Music	389	735	110
Girl with Trumpet	391	733	110
Globe Trotter	79	926	111
Going Home	383	423	111
Going To Grandma's	52/0	948	111
Going To Grandma's	52/I	947	111
Good Friends	182	851	112
Good Friends & She Loves Me, She Loves Me Not Bookends	251/A&B	708	112
Good Friends Lamp	228	644	112
Good Hunting	307	808	113
Good Night	214/C/I	631	156
Good Night	260/D	608	160
Good Shepherd	42	477	113
Good Shepherd Font	35/0	516	113
Good Shepherd Font	35/I	n.a.	113
Goose Girl	47 3/0	961	114
Goose Girl	47/0	960	114
Goose Girl	47/II	959	114
Goose Girl (Doll)	517	n.a.	217
Goose Girl (White)	47/II	165	114
Goose Girl Miniature	283-P	37238	221
Goose Girl & Farm Boy Bookends	60 A&B	702	114
Grandma's Girl	561	211	115
Grandpa's Boy	562	210	115
Guardian (The)	455	214	115
Guardian Angel Font	29/I & 29/0	n.a.	115
Guardian Angel Font	248/0	511	115
Guiding Angel	357	528	116
Happiness	86	917	116
Happy Birthday	176/0	857	116
Happy Birthday	176/I	856	116
Happy Days	150 2/0	873	116
Happy Days	150/0	872	116
Happy Days	150/I	871	116
Happy Days Lamp	232	640	117
Happy Days Lamp	235	638	117
Happy Pastime	69	931	117
Happy Pastime Ashtray	62	672	118
Happy Pastime Candy Box	III/69	664	118
Happy Traveller	109/0	905	118

Hummel Name	Mold No.:	Ref. No.	Pg. #
Happy Traveller	109/II	904	118
Harmony In Four Parts	471	286	119
Hear Ye! Hear Ye!	15 2/0	418	119
Hear Ye! Hear Ye!	15/0	969	119
Hear Ye! Hear Ye!	15/I	968	119
Hear Ye! Hear Ye!	15/II	967	119
Hear Ye! Hear Ye! (White)	15/II	166	119
Heavenly Angel	21/0	560	120
Heavenly Angel	21/0 1/2	559	120
Heavenly Angel	21/I	558	120
Heavenly Angel	21/II	557	120
Heavenly Angel (White)	21/II	163	120
Heavenly Angel Font	207	521	120
Heavenly Angel Ornament (White)	575	139	225
Heavenly Angel Tree Topper	755	099	121
Heavenly Lullaby	262	497	121
Heavenly Protection	88/I	539	121
Heavenly Protection	88/II	538	121
Heavenly Song Candleholder	113	n.a.	122
Hello	124/0	895	122
Hello	124/I	894	122
Hello World	429	399	122
Herald Angels Candleholder	37	553	123
Holy Child	70	472	123
Holy Family Font	246	504	123
Home From Market	198 2/0	838	123
Home From Market	198/I	837	123
Homeward Bound	334	783	124
Honey Lover	312	804	124
Honey Lover Pendant	n.a.	826022	124
Horse Trainer	423	256	125
Hosanna	480	265	125
I Brought You A Gift	479	n.a.	125
I Didn't Do It	626	142	125
I Wonder	486	241	126
I'll Protect Him	483	266	126
I'm Carefree	633	112	126
I'm Here	478	285	126
In D Major	430	287	127
In the Meadow	459	408	127
In Tune	414	724	127
In Tune Music Box	66202	6935	127
Is It Raining?	420	268	128
It's Cold	421	722	128
It's Cold Plate	735	281	128
Joyful	53	946	128
Joyful Ashtray	33	674	129
Joyful Candy Box	III/53	668	129
Joyous News	27/III	555	129
Joyous News Candleholder	27/I	n.a.	130
Jubilee	416	421	130
Just Dozing	451	056	130
Just Fishing	373	424	130
Just Resting	112 3/0	899	131
Just Resting	112/I	898	131
Just Resting Lamp	225/I	647	131
Just Resting Lamp	225/II	646	131

Hummel Name	Mold No.:	Ref. No.	Pg. #
Just Resting Lamp	II/112	n.a.	131
Kindergartner	467	409	132
Kiss Me	311	805	132
Knit One, Purl One	432	720	132
Knitting Lesson	256	817	132
Land in Sight	530	190	132
Latest News	184/0	850	134
Let's Sing	110/0	903	134
Let's Sing	110/I	902	134
Let's Sing Ashtray	114	675	135
Let's Sing Candy Box	III/110	669	135
Let's Tell The World	487	254	136
Letter To Santa Claus	340	777	136
Little Architect	410/I	162	136
Little Band	392	732	137
Little Band Candleholder	388	738	137
Little Band with Candle Music Box	388/M	737	137
Little Band without Candle Music Box	392/M	731	137
Little Bookkeeper	306	809	138
Little Cellist	89/I	915	138
Little Cellist	89/II	914	138
Little Cellist (White)	89/II	164	138
Little Drummer	240	819	138
Little Fiddler	2 4/0	426	138
Little Fiddler	2/0	996	138
Little Fiddler	2/I	995	138
Little Fiddler	2/II	994	138
Little Fiddler	2/III	993	138
Little Fiddler	4	989	138
Little Fiddler (Doll)	513	n.a.	217
Little Fiddler Miniature	250-P	37211	221
Little Fiddler (White)	2/I	169	138
Little Fiddler Plaque	93	676	139
Little Gabriel	32 or 32/0	554	140
Little Gabriel	32/I	n.a.	140
Little Gardener	74	927	140
Little Gardener 1992 Special Event Piece	74	171	140
Little Goat Herder	200/0	834	140
Little Goat Herder	200/I	833	140
Little Goat Herder & Feeding Time Bookends	250/A&B	711	141
Little Guardian	145	475	141
Little Helper	73	928	141
Little Hiker	16 2/0	966	142
Little Hiker	16/I	965	142
Little Nurse	376	750	142
Little Pair (The)	449	239	142
Little Pharmacist	322	793	143
Little Scholar	80	925	143
Little Shopper	96	910	143
Little Sweeper	171 4/0	305	144
Little Sweeper	171/0	860	144
Little Sweeper (Crystal Hummel)	n.a.	84980	214
Little Sweeper Miniature	253-P	37212	221
Little Tailor	308	807	144
Little Thrifty	118	663	144
Little Tooter	214/H/0	203	156
Little Tooter	214/H/I	626	156

Hummel Name	Mold No.:	Ref. No.	Pg. #
Little Tooter	260/K	602	160
Little Troubadour	558	101	145
Little Visitor	563/0	100	145
Lost Sheep	68 2/0	933	145
Lost Sheep	68/0	932	145
Lost Sheep (Doll)	n.a.	443	217
Lost Stocking	374	752	146
Lucky Fellow	560	174	146
Lullaby Candleholder	24/I	501	146
Lullaby Candleholder	24/III	500	146
Madonna & Child Font	243	514	147
Madonna Holding Child	151/II	572	147
Madonna Holding Child (White)	151/W	571	147
Madonna Plaque	48/0	575	148
Madonna Plaque	48/II	574	148
Madonna Plaque	48/V	n.a.	148
Madonna with Halo	45/0	589	148
Madonna with Halo	45/0/W	588	148
Madonna with Halo	45/I	586	148
Madonna with Halo	45/I/W	585	148
Madonna with Halo	45/III	584	148
Madonna with Halo	45/III/W	583	148
Madonna without Halo	46/0	582	149
Madonna without Halo	46/0/W	581	149
Madonna without Halo	46/I	579	149
Madonna without Halo	46/I/W	578	149
Madonna without Halo	46/III	577	149
Madonna without Halo	46/III/W	576	149
Mail Is Here (The)	226	823	150
Mail Is Here Plaque	140	687	150
Make a Wish	475	267	150
March Winds	43	962	150
March Winds (Crystal Hummel)	n.a.	84960	214
Max & Moritz	123	896	150
Meditation	13 2/0	973	151
Meditation	13/0	972	151
Meditation	13/II	971	151
Meditation	13/V	970	151
Meditation (Crystal Hummel)	n.a.	85120	215
Meditation (White)	13/V	167	151
Merry Christmas Plaque	323	556	151
Merry Wanderer	7/0	984	152
Merry Wanderer	7/I	983	152
Merry Wanderer	7/II	982	152
Merry Wanderer	7/III	981	152
Merry Wanderer	7/X	980	152
Merry Wanderer	11 2/0	977	152
Merry Wanderer	11/0	976	152
Merry Wanderer (Crystal Hummel)	n.a.	85110	215
Merry Wanderer (Doll)	516	n.a.	217
Merry Wanderer Miniature	254-P	37213	221
Merry Wanderer (White)	7/I	168	152
Merry Wanderer Pendant	n.a.	n.a.	153
Merry Wanderer Plaque	92	677	153
Mischief Maker	342	775	153
Morning Concert	447	427	154
Morning Concert Mini with Display	n.a.	030	154

Hummel Name	Mold No.:	Ref. No.	Pg. #
Morning Stroll	375 3/0	114	154
Mother's Darling	175	858	154
Mother's Helper	133	887	155
Mountaineer	315	801	155
My Wish Is Small	463/0	176	155
Nativity Set 214/0	214/0	618	156
Nativity Set 214/I	214/I	619	156
Nativity Set 260	260	595	160
Not For You!	317	799	161
On Holiday	350	768	161
On Holiday (Doll)	n.a.	716	218
On Our Way	472	175	162
On Secret Path	386	740	162
One For You, One For Me	482	282	162
One Plus One	556	129	163
Ooh, My Tooth	533	053	163
Out of Danger	56/B	944	163
Out of Danger Lamp Base	44/B	652	98
Parade of Lights	616	159	163
Photographer	178	853	164
Pixie	768	029	164
Playmates	58 2/0	416	164
Playmates	58/0	941	164
Playmates	58/I	940	164
Playmates & Chick Girl Bookends	61/A&B	699	165
Playmates Candy Box	III/58	666	165
Pleasant Journey	406	448	166
Poet (The)	397/I	113	166
Postman	119 2/0	269	166
Postman	119	897	166
Postman (Crystal Hummel)	n.a.	85130	215
Postman (Doll)	n.a.	719	218
Postman Miniature	255-P	37217	221
Prayer Before Battle	20	963	167
Prayer of Thanks Ornament (White)	581	133	225
Professor (The)	320/0	195	167
Puppy Love	1	997	167
Puppy Love Figurine Plaque	767	047	168
Quartet Plaque	134	690	168
Retreat to Safety	201 2/0	832	168
Retreat to Safety	201/I	831	168
Retreat to Safety Plaque	126	694	168
Ride Into Christmas	396 2/0	727	169
Ride Into Christmas	396/I	726	169
Ride into Christmas (Doll)	519	n.a.	218
Ride Into Christmas Music Box	396	6433	169
Ring Around The Rosie	348	770	170
Rock-A-Bye	574	111	170
Run-A-Way (The)	327	790	170
Saint George	55	474	171
Scamp	553	189	171
School Boy	82 2/0	922	171
School Boy	82/0	921	171
School Boy	82/II	920	171
School Boy Miniature	281-P	37236	221
School Boys	170/I	862	172
School Boys	170/III	861	172

Hummel Name	Mold No.:	Ref. No.	Pg. #
School Girl	81 2/0	924	172
School Girl	81/0	923	172
School Girls	177/I	855	173
School Girls	177/III	854	173
Searching Angel Plaque	310	535	173
Sensitive Hunter	6 2/0	419	173
Sensitive Hunter	6/0	987	173
Sensitive Hunter	6/I	986	173
Sensitive Hunter	6/II	985	173
Serenade	85 4/0	413	174
Serenade	85/0	919	174
Serenade	85/II	918	174
Serenade Miniature	265-P	37228	222
She Loves Me, She Loves Me Not	174	859	175
She Loves Me, She Loves Me Not Lamp	227	645	112
Shepherd's Boy	64	937	175
Shining Light	358	527	175
Signs Of Spring	203 2/0	830	176
Signs Of Spring	203/I	829	176
Signs of Spring (Doll)	n.a.	446	218
Silent Night Candleholder	54	498	176
Sing Along	433	447	176
Sing with Me	405	422	177
Singing Lesson	63	938	177
Singing Lesson Ashtray	34	673	177
Singing Lesson Candy Box	III/63	665	178
Sister	98 2/0	908	178
Sister	98/0	907	178
Sister (Crystal Hummel)	n.a.	85340	215
Skier	59	939	178
Sleep Tight	424	255	179
Smart Little Sister	346	772	179
Smiling Through	408/0	459	179
Smiling Through Plaque	690	n.a.	179
Soldier Boy	332	785	180
Soloist	135 4/0	407	180
Soloist	135/0	886	180
Soloist (Crystal Hummel)	n.a.	85100	215
Song of Praise	454	294	180
Song of Praise Ornament (White)	579	135	225
Sound the Trumpet	457	303	180
Sounds of the Mandolin	438	304	180
Spring Cheer	72	929	181
Spring Dance	353/0	765	181
Spring Dance	353/I	764	181
Standing Boy Plaque	168	678	182
Star Gazer	132	888	182
Stitch in Time	255 4/0	259	182
Stitch in Time	255/I	818	182
Stormy Weather	71 2/0	415	182
Stormy Weather	71/I	930	182
Stormy Weather Miniature	251-P	37215	222
Storybook Time	458	193	183
Street Singer	131	889	183
Strike Up The Band	668	050	183
Strolling Along	5	988	184
Supreme Protection	364	570	184

Hummel Name	Mold No.:	Ref. No.	Pg. #
Wayside Harmony	111/I	900	197
Wayside Harmony Lamp	224/I	649	131
Wayside Harmony Lamp	224/II	648	131
Wayside Harmony Lamp	II/111	n.a.	131
Wayside Harmony Miniature	282-P	37237	222
We Come in Peace	754	044	197
We Congratulate	220	824	197
We Congratulate Miniature	267-P	37227	222
We Wish You The Best	600	209	198
Weary Wanderer	204	828	198
Welcome Spring	635	158	198
What Now?	422	721	199
What Now? Pendent	n.a.	n.a.	199
What's New?	418	257	199
Which Hand?	258	815	200
Whistler's Duet	413	194	200
White Angel Font	75	508	200
Whitsuntide	163	473	201
Winter Song	476	293	201
With Loving Greetings	309	806	201
Worship	84/0	563	202
Worship	84/V	562	202
Worship Font	164	510	202

MOLD NUMBER INDEX

Mold No.:	Hummel Name	Ref. No.:	Pg. #
24/III	Lullaby Candleholder	500	146
25	Angelic Sleep Candleholder	499	72
26/0	Child Jesus Font	519	93
26/I	Child Jesus Font	n.a.	93
27/I	Joyous News Candleholder	n.a.	130
27/III	Joyous News	555	129
28/II	Wayside Devotion	566	196
28/III	Wayside Devotion	565	196
29/0	Guardian Angel Font	n.a.	115
29/I	Guardian Angel Font	n.a.	115
30/A	Ba Bee Ring-Boy Plaque	691	77
30/B	Ba Bee Ring-Girl Plaque	692	77
30/I	Ba Bee Ring Plaque	n.a.	209
31	Silent Night Candleholder	n.a.	209
32 or 32/0	Little Gabriel	554	140
32/I	Little Gabriel	n.a.	140
33	Joyful Ashtray	674	129
34	Singing Lesson Ashtray	673	177
35/0	Good Shepherd Font	516	113
35/I	Good Shepherd Font	n.a.	113
36/0	Child with Flowers Font	515	93
36/I	Child with Flowers Font	n.a.	93
37	Herald Angels Candleholder	553	123
38/0	Angel with Lute Candleholder	534	71
39/0	Angel with Accordion Candleholder	532	71
40/0	Angel with Trumpet Candleholder	530	71
41	Singing Lesson without Base	n.a.	209
42	Good Shepherd	477	113
42/I	Good Shepherd	n.a.	209
43	March Winds	962	150
44/A	Culprits Lamp Base	653	98
44/B	Out Of Danger Lamp Base	652	98
45/0	Madonna with Halo	589	148
45/0/W	Madonna with Halo	588	148
45/I	Madonna with Halo	586	148
45/I/W	Madonna with Halo	585	148
45/III	Madonna with Halo	584	148
45/III/W	Madonna with Halo	583	148
46/0	Madonna without Halo	582	149
46/0/W	Madonna without Halo	581	149
46/I	Madonna without Halo	579	149
46/I/W	Madonna without Halo	578	149
46/III	Madonna without Halo	577	149
46/III/W	Madonna without Halo	576	149
47 3/0	Goose Girl	961	114
47/0	Goose Girl	960	114
47/II	Goose Girl	959	114
48/0	Madonna Plaque	575	148
48/II	Madonna Plaque	574	148
48/V	Madonna Plaque	n.a.	148
49 3/0	To Market	958	187
49/0	To Market	957	187
49/I	To Market	956	187
50 2/0	Volunteers	955	194
50/0	Volunteers	954	194
50/I	Volunteers	953	194
51 2/0	Village Boy	951	193

Mold No.:	Hummel Name	Ref. No.:	Pg. #
51 3/0	Village Boy	952	193
51/0	Village Boy	950	193
51/I	Village Boy	949	193
52/0	Going To Grandma's	948	111
52/I	Going To Grandma's	947	111
53	Joyful	946	128
III/53	Joyful Candy Box	668	129
54	Silent Night Candleholder	498	176
55	Saint George	474	171
56/A	Culprits	945	98
56/B	Out Of Danger	944	163
57 2/0	Chick Girl	417	90
57/0	Chick Girl	943	90
57/I	Chick Girl	942	90
III/57	Chick Girl Candy Box	667	91
58 2/0	Playmates	416	164
58/0	Playmates	941	164
58/I	Playmates	940	164
II/58	Playmates Candy Box	666	165
59	Skier	939	178
60 A&B	Goose Girl & Farm Boy Bookends	702	114
61/A&B	Playmates & Chick Girl Bookends	699	165
62	Happy Pastime Ashtray	672	117
63	Singing Lesson	938	177
III/63	Singing Lesson Candy Box	665	178
64	Shepherd's Boy	937	175
65	Farewell	936	102
65/I	Farewell	n.a.	102
65/0	Farewell	n.a.	209
66	Farm Boy	935	102
67	Doll Mother	934	100
68 2/0	Lost Sheep	933	145
68/0	Lost Sheep	932	145
69	Happy Pastime	931	117
III/69	Happy Pastime Candy Box	664	118
70	Holy Child	472	123
71 2/0	Stormy Weather	415	182
71/I	Stormy Weather	930	182
72	Spring Cheer	929	181
73	Little Helper	928	141
74	Little Gardener	927	140
75	White Angel Font	508	200
76	Doll Mother Bookend	n.a.	209
77	Cross with Doves Font	n.a.	209
78/I/83	Blessed Child	495	82
78/II/83	Blessed Child	492	82
78/III/83	Blessed Child	489	82
78/II 1/2	Blessed Child	n.a.	82
78/V	Blessed Child	n.a.	82
78/VI	Blessed Child	n.a.	82
78/VIII	Blessed Child	n.a.	82
78/0	Blessed Child	n.a.	82
79	Globe Trotter	926	111
80	Little Scholar	925	143
81 2/0	School Girl	924	172
81/0	School Girl	923	172
82 2/0	School Boy	922	171

Mold No.:	Hummel Name	Ref. No.:	Pg. #
82/0	School Boy	921	171
82/II	School Boy	920	171
83	Angel Serenade with Lamb	540	70
84/0	Worship	563	202
84/V	Worship	562	202
85 4/0	Serenade	413	174
85/0	Serenade	919	174
85/II	Serenade	918	174
86	Happiness	917	116
87	For Father	916	108
88/I	Heavenly Protection	539	121
88/II	Heavenly Protection	538	121
89/I	Little Cellist	915	138
89/II	Little Cellist	914	138
90	Eventide & Adoration Bookends	n.a.	209
91A	Angel Facing Left Font	507	69
91B	Angel Facing Right Font	506	69
92	Merry Wanderer Plaque	677	153
93	Little Fiddler Plaque	676	139
94 3/0	Surprise	913	184
94/I	Surprise	912	184
95	Brother	911	86
96	Little Shopper	910	143
97	Trumpet Boy	909	188
98 2/0	Sister	908	178
98/0	Sister	907	178
99	Eventide	906	101
100	Shrine Lamp	n.a.	209
101	To Market Lamp	n.a.	188
102	Volunteers Lamp	n.a.	209
103	Farewell Lamp	n.a.	209
104	Eventide Lamp	n.a.	209
105	Adoration w/Bird	n.a.	209
106	Merry Wanderer Plaque w/Wooden Frame	n.a.	209
107	Little Fiddler Plaque w/Wooden Frame	n.a.	209
108	angel wall decoration	n.a.	209
109/0	Happy Traveller	905	118
109/II	Happy Traveller	904	118
110/0	Let's Sing	903	134
110/I	Let's Sing	902	134
III/110	Let's Sing Candy Box	669	135
111 3/0	Wayside Harmony	901	197
111/I	Wayside Harmony	900	197
II/111	Wayside Harmony Lamp	n.a.	131
112 3/0	Just Resting	899	131
112/I	Just Resting	898	131
II/112	Just Resting Lamp	n.a.	131
113	Heavenly Song Candleholder	n.a.	122
114	Let's Sing Ashtray	675	135
115	Girl with Nosegay Candleholder	637	85
116	Girl with Fir Tree Candleholder	636	85
117	Boy with Horse Candleholder	635	85
118	Little Thrifty	663	144
119 2/0	Postman	269	166
119	Postman	897	166
120	Joyful & Let's Sing Bookends	n.a.	209
121	Wayside Harmony Bookend	n.a.	209

Mold No.:	Hummel Name	Ref. No.:	Pg. #
122	Puppy Love & Serenade w/Dog Bookends	n.a.	209
123	Max & Moritz	896	150
124/0	Hello	895	122
124/I	Hello	894	122
125	Vacation Time Plaque	695	191
126	Retreat to Safety Plaque	694	168
127	Doctor	893	100
128	Baker	892	77
129	Band Leader	891	78
129 4/0	Band Leader	398	78
130	Duet	890	100
131	Street Singer	889	183
132	Star Gazer	888	182
133	Mother's Helper	887	155
134	Quartet Plaque	690	168
135 4/0	Soloist	407	180
135/0	Soloist	886	180
136/I	Friends	885	109
136/V	Friends	884	109
137	Child In Bed Plaque	689	92
137/A	Child in Bed Plaque	n.a.	210
138	Baby in Crib Plaque	n.a.	210
139	Flitting Butterfly Plaque	688	106
140	Mail Is Here Plaque	687	150
141 3/0	Apple Tree Girl	883	74
141/I	Apple Tree Girl	882	74
141/V	Apple Tree Girl	881	74
141/X	Apple Tree Girl	880	74
142 3/0	Apple Tree Boy	879	73
142/I	Apple Tree Boy	878	73
142/V	Apple Tree Boy	877	73
142/X	Apple Tree Boy	876	73
143/0	Boots	875	84
143/I	Boots	874	84
144	Angelic Song	476	72
145	Little Guardian	475	141
146	Angel Duet Font	513	69
147	Angel Shrine Font	512	70
148	Farm Boy without Base	n.a.	210
149	Goose Girl without Base	n.a.	210
150 2/0	Happy Days	873	116
150/0	Happy Days	872	116
150/I	Happy Days	871	116
151/II	Madonna Holding Child	572	147
151/W	Madonna Holding Child (White)	571	147
152/A/0	Umbrella Boy	868	190
152/A/II	Umbrella Boy	870	190
152/B/0	Umbrella Girl	867	190
152/B/II	Umbrella Girl	869	190
153/0	Auf Wiedersehen	866	76
153/I	Auf Wiedersehen	865	76
154/0	Waiter	864	195
154/I	Waiter	863	195
155	Madonna w/Child	n.a.	210
156	Sitting Woman & Child Plaque	n.a.	210
157	Town Boy w/Flower Basket	n.a.	210
158	Town Girl w/Dog	n.a.	210

Mold No.:	Hummel Name	Ref. No.:	Pg. #
159	Town Girl w/Flowers	n.a.	210
160	Town Girl in Evening Dress	n.a.	210
161	Town Girl w/Hands in Pocket	n.a.	210
162	Town Girl w/Handbag	n.a.	210
163	Whitsuntide	473	201
164	Worship Font	510	202
165	Swaying Lullaby Plaque	686	185
166	Boy with Bird Ashtray	671	85
167	Angel with Bird Font	509	72
168	Standing Boy Plaque	678	182
169	Bird Duet	545	80
170/I	School Boys	862	172
170/III	School Boys	861	172
171 4/0	Little Sweeper	305	144
171/0	Little Sweeper	860	144
172 4/0	Festival Harmony with Mandolin	107	105
172/0	Festival Harmony with Mandolin	544	105
172/II	Festival Harmony with Mandolin	543	105
173/0	Festival Harmony with Flute	542	104
173/II	Festival Harmony with Flute	541	104
173 4/0	Festival Harmony with Flute	045	104
174	She Loves Me, She Loves Me Not	859	175
175	Mother's Darling	858	154
176/0	Happy Birthday	857	116
176/I	Happy Birthday	856	116
177/I	School Girls	855	173
177/III	School Girls	854	173
178	Photographer	853	164
179	Coquettes	852	96
180	Tuneful Good Night Plaque	696	189
181	Old Man Reading Newspaper	n.a.	210
182	Good Friends	851	112
183	Forest Shrine	564	108
184/0	Latest News	850	134
185	Accordion Boy	849	66
186	Sweet Music	848	186
187	Dealer Display Plaque	238	99
187/A	Dealer Display Plaque	845	99
188 4/0	Celestial Musician	154	89
188/0	Celestial Musician	524	89
188/I	Celestial Musician	523	89
189	Old Woman Knitting	n.a.	210
190	Old Woman Walking to Market	n.a.	210
191	Old Man Walking to Market	n.a.	210
192	Candlelight Candleholder	537	88
193	Angel Duet Candleholder	536	69
194/I	Watchful Angel	478	196
195 2/0	Barnyard Hero	844	78
195/I	Barnyard Hero	843	78
196/0	Telling Her Secret	842	186
196/I	Telling Her Secret	841	186
197 2/0	Be Patient	840	79
197/I	Be Patient	839	79
198 2/0	Home From Market	838	123
198/I	Home From Market	837	123
199/0	Feeding Time	836	103
199/I	Feeding Time	835	103

Mold No.:	Hummel Name	Ref. No.:	Pg. #
200/0	Little Goat Herder	834	140
200/I	Little Goat Herder	833	140
201 2/0	Retreat to Safety	832	168
201/I	Retreat to Safety	831	168
202	Old Man Reading Newspaper Lamp	n.a.	210
203	Umbrella Girl Music Box	6936	210
203 2/0	Signs Of Spring	830	176
203/I	Signs Of Spring	829	176
204	Weary Wanderer	828	198
205	Store Display Plaque in German	n.a.	210
206	Angel Cloud Font	522	68
207	Heavenly Angel Font	521	120
208	Store Display Plaque	n.a.	210
209	Store Display Plaque	n.a.	210
210	Store Display Plaque	n.a.	210
211	Store Display Plaque	n.a.	210
212	Store Display Plaque	n.a.	210
213	Store Display Plaque	n.a.	210
214/C/I	Good Night	631	156
214/H/0	Little Tooter	203	156
214/H/I	Little Tooter	626	156
214/I	Nativity Set 214/I	619	156
214/0	Nativity Set 214/0	618	156
215	Child Jesus w/Lamb	n.a.	210
216	Joyful Ashtray	n.a.	210
217	Boy with Toothache	827	86
218 2/0	Birthday Serenade	826	81
218/0	Birthday Serenade	825	81
219	Little Velma	n.a.	210
220	We Congratulate	824	197
221	Happy Pastime Candy Box	n.a.	210
222	Madonna Plaque w/Metal Frame	n.a.	210
223	To Market Lamp	650	188
224/I	Wayside Harmony Lamp	649	131
224/II	Wayside Harmony Lamp	648	131
225/I	Just Resting Lamp	647	131
225/II	Just Resting Lamp	646	131
226	Mail Is Here (The)	823	150
227	She Loves Me, She Loves Me Not Lamp	645	112
228	Good Friends Lamp	644	112
229	Apple Tree Girl Lamp	643	74
230	Apple Tree Boy Lamp	642	74
231	Birthday Serenade Lamp	641	81
232	Happy Days Lamp	640	117
233	Boy Feeding Birds	n.a.	210
234	Birthday Serenade Lamp	639	81
235	Happy Days Lamp	638	117
236/A	Angel in Tree	n.a.	210
236/B	Angel in Tree	n.a.	210
237	Star Gazer Plaque	n.a.	210
238/A	Angel with Lute	552	71
238/B	Angel with Accordion	551	71
238/C	Angel with Trumpet	550	71
239/A	Girl with Nosegay	822	85
239/B	Girl with Doll	821	85
239/C	Boy with Horse	820	85
240	Little Drummer	819	138

Mold No.:	Hummel Name	Ref. No.:	Pg. #
279	1986 Annual Plate, Playmates	405	54
280	1975 Anniversary Plate, Stormy Weather	n.a.	49
280-P	**Dealer Display Plaque Miniature**	37229	220
281	1980 Anniversary Plate, Ring Around The Rosie	n.a.	52
281-P	**School Boy Miniature**	37236	221
282	1985 Anniversary Plate, Auf Wiedersehen	n.a.	54
282-P	**Wayside Harmony Miniature**	37237	222
283	1987 Annual Plate, Feeding Time	321	55
283-P	**Goose Girl Miniature**	37238	221
284	1988 Annual Plate, Little Goat Herder	320	56
285	1989 Annual Plate, Farm Boy	318	57
286	1990 Annual Plate, Shepherd's Boy	319	59
287	1991 Annual Plate, Just Resting	317	60
288	1992 Annual Plate, Wayside Harmony	316	61
289	1993 Annual Plate, Doll Bath	157	62
290	1994 Annual Plate, Doctor	110	63
291	1995 Annual Plate, Come Back Soon	048	64
292	1992 Friends Forever Plate, Meditation	188	62
293	1993 Friends Forever Plate, For Father	156	63
294	1994 Friends Forever Plate, Sweet Greetings	109	63
295	1995 Friends Forever Plate, Surprise	047	64
300	**Bird Watcher**	814	80
301	**Christmas Angel**	561	94
302	**Concentration**	n.a.	211
304	**Artist**	811	75
305	**Builder**	810	86
306	**Little Bookkeeper**	809	138
307	**Good Hunting**	808	113
308	**Little Tailor**	807	144
309	**With Loving Greetings**	806	201
310	**Searching Angel Plaque**	535	173
311	**Kiss Me**	805	132
312	**Honey Lover**	804	124
313	**Sunny Morning**	n.a.	211
314	**Confidentially**	802	96
315	**Mountaineer**	801	155
316	**Relaxation**	n.a.	211
317	**Not For You!**	799	161
318	**Art Critic**	798	75
319	**Doll Bath**	797	100
320/0	**Professor (The)**	195	167
321 4/0	**Wash Day**	288	195
321/0	**Wash Day**	795	195
322	**Little Pharmacist**	793	143
323	**Merry Christmas Plaque**	556	151
324	**Chick Girl Music Box**	6434	92
324	**At the Fence**	n.a.	211
325	**Helping Mother**	n.a.	211
326	**Being Punished Plaque**	n.a.	211
327	**Run-A-Way (The)**	790	170
328	**Carnival**	789	88
329	**Off to School**	n.a.	211
330	**Baking Day**	425	78
331	**Crossroads**	786	96
332	**Soldier Boy**	785	180
333	**Blessed Event**	784	82
334	**Homeward Bound**	783	124

Mold No.:	Hummel Name	Ref. No.:	Pg. #
335	Lucky Boy	n.a.	211
336	Close Harmony	781	95
337	Cinderella	780	94
338	Birthday Cake Candleholder	779	80
339	Behave!	n.a.	211
340	Letter To Santa Claus	777	136
341 3/0	Birthday Present	098	80
342	Mischief Maker	775	153
343	Christmas Song	547	94
344	Feathered Friends	774	103
345	A Fair Measure	773	65
346	Smart Little Sister	772	179
347	Adventure Bound	771	68
348	Ring Around The Rosie	770	170
349	Florist	n.a.	211
350	On Holiday	768	161
351	Botanist	767	84
352	Sweet Greetings	766	186
353/0	Spring Dance	765	181
353/I	Spring Dance	764	181
354/A	Angel with Lantern Font	n.a.	211
354/B	Angel with Trumpet Font	n.a.	211
354/C	Angel with Bird Font	n.a.	211
355	Autumn Harvest	763	77
356	Gay Adventure	762	110
357	Guiding Angel	528	116
358	Shining Light	527	175
359	Tuneful Angel	526	189
360/A	Boy & Girl Wall Vase	662	84
360/B	Boy Wall Vase	661	84
360/C	Girl Wall Vase	660	84
361	Favorite Pet	761	102
362	I Forgot	n.a.	211
363	Big Housecleaning	759	79
364	Supreme Protection	570	184
365	Littlest Angel	n.a.	211
366/0	Flying Angel	275	156
366/I	Flying Angel	525	156
367	Busy Student	757	87
368	Lute Song	n.a.	211
369	Follow the Leader	755	107
370	Companions	n.a.	211
371	Daddy's Girls	753	98
373	Just Fishing	424	130
374	Lost Stocking	752	146
375 3/0	Morning Stroll	114	154
376	Little Nurse	750	142
377	Bashful	749	78
378	Easter Greetings	748	101
379	Don't Be Shy	n.a.	211
380	Daisies Don't Tell	746	98
381	Flower Vendor	745	107
382	Visiting An Invalid	744	194
383	Going Home	423	111
384	Easter Time	742	101
385 4/0	Chicken Licken	216	92
385	Chicken Licken	741	92

Mold No.:	Hummel Name	Ref. No.:	Pg. #
386	On Secret Path	740	162
387	Valentine Gift	739	192
388	Little Band Candleholder	738	137
388/M	Little Band with Candle Music Box	737	137
389	Girl with Sheet Music	735	110
390	Boy with Accordion	734	84
391	Girl with Trumpet	733	110
392	Little Band	732	137
392/M	Little Band without Candle Music Box	731	137
394	Timid Little Sister	729	187
395	Shepherd Boy	n.a.	211
396	Ride Into Christmas Music Box	6433	169
396 2/0	Ride Into Christmas	727	169
396/I	Ride Into Christmas	726	169
397/I	Poet (The)	113	166
398	Spring Bouquet	n.a.	211
399	Valentine Joy	725	193
400	Well Done	n.a.	211
401	Forty Winks	n.a.	211
402	True Friendship	n.a.	211
404	Sad Song	n.a.	211
403	An Apple A Day	272	68
405	Sing with Me	422	177
406	Pleasant Journey	448	166
407	Flute Song	n.a.	212
408/0	Smiling Through	459	179
409	Coffee Break	470	95
410/I	Little Architect	162	136
411	Do I Dare?	n.a.	212
412	Bath Time	258	79
413	Whistler's Duet	194	200
414	In Tune	724	127
415	Thoughtful	723	187
416	Jubilee	421	130
417	Where Did You Get That?	n.a.	212
418	What's New?	257	199
419	Good Luck!	n.a.	212
420	Is It Raining?	268	128
421	It's Cold	722	128
422	What Now?	721	199
423	Horse Trainer	256	125
424	Sleep Tight	255	179
425	Pleasant Moment	n.a.	212
426	Pay Attention	n.a.	212
427	Where Are You?	n.a.	212
428	I Won't Hurt You	n.a.	212
429	Hello World	399	122
430	In D Major	287	127
431	Surprise (The)	307	185
432	Knit One, Purl One	720	132
433	Sing Along	447	176
434	Friend or Foe?	461	109
435	Delicious	n.a.	212
436	An Emergency	n.a.	212
437	Tuba Player	271	188
438	Sounds Of The Mandolin	304	180
439	A Gentle Glow Candleholder	445	65

Mold No.:	Hummel Name	Ref. No.:	Pg. #
440	Birthday Candle	403	80
441	Call To Worship Clock	300	88
442	Chapel Time Clock	420	90
443	Country Song Clock	n.a.	212
447	Morning Concert	427	154
448	Children's Prayer	n.a.	212
449	Little Pair	239	142
450	Will It Sting?	n.a.	212
451	Just Dozing	056	130
452	1988 Annual Ornament, Flying High	296	56
453	Accompanist (The)	295	66
454	Song Of Praise	294	180
455	Guardian (The)	214	115
456	Sleep, Little One, Sleep	n.a.	212
457	Sound The Trumpet	303	180
458	Storybook Time	193	183
459	In the Meadow	408	127
460	Dealer Display Plaque, "The Tally"	402	99
461	In the Orchard	n.a.	212
462	Tit for Tat	n.a.	212
463/0	My Wish Is Small	176	155
464	Young Scholar	n.a.	212
465	Where Shall I Go?	n.a.	212
466	Do Re Mi	n.a.	212
467	Kindergartner	409	132
468	Come On	n.a.	212
469	Starting Young	n.a.	212
470	Time Out	n.a.	212
471	Harmony In Four Parts	286	119
472	On Our Way	175	162
473	Father Christmas	n.a.	212
474	Gentle Care	n.a.	212
475	Make a Wish	267	150
476	Winter Song	293	201
477	A Budding Maestro	292	65
478	I'm Here	285	126
479	I Brought You A Gift	n.a.	125
480	Hosanna	265	125
481	1989 Annual Ornament, Love From Above	283	57
482	One For You, One For Me	282	162
483	I'll Protect Him	266	126
484	1990 Annual Ornament, Peace On Earth	243	58
485	Gift From a Friend	198	110
486	I Wonder	241	126
487	Let's Tell The World	254	136
493	Two Hands, One Treat	192	189
495	Evening Prayer	191	101
512	Umbrella Girl (Doll)	n.a.	218
513	Little Fiddler (Doll)	n.a.	217
514	Friend or Foe? (Doll)	n.a.	217
516	Merry Wanderer (Doll)	n.a.	217
517	Goose Girl (Doll)	n.a.	217
518	Umbrella Boy (Doll)	n.a.	218
519	Ride into Christmas (Doll)	n.a.	218
530	Land in Sight	190	132
533	Ooh, My Tooth	053	163
534	A Nap	213	65

Mold No.:	Hummel Name	Ref. No.:	Pg. #
541	Sweet As Can Be	143	185
545	Come Back Soon	054	95
548	Flower Girl	240	106
549 3/0	A Sweet Offering	144	66
553	Scamp	189	171
554	Cheeky Fellow	172	90
556	One Plus One	129	163
558	Little Troubadour	101	145
560	Lucky Fellow	174	146
561	Grandma's Girl	211	115
562	Grandpa's Boy	210	115
563/0	Little Visitor	100	145
566	Angler (The)	052	72
569	A Free Flight	160	65
571	1991 Annual Ornament, Angelic Guide	202	60
574	Rock-A-Bye	111	170
575	Heavenly Angel Ornament (White)	139	225
576	Festival Harmony w/Mandolin Orn. (White)	138	223
577	Festival Harmony w/Flute Orn. (White)	137	223
578	Celestial Musician Ornament (White)	136	223
579	Song Of Praise Ornament (White)	135	225
580	Angel with Lute Ornament (White)	134	223
581	Prayer of Thanks Ornament (White)	133	225
582	Gentle Song Ornament (White)	132	223
585	Angel with Cloud Ornament (White)	131	223
586	Angel with Trumpet Ornament (White)	130	223
600	We Wish You The Best	209	198
616	Parade Of Lights	159	163
620	A Story from Grandma	025	66
621	At Grandpa's	051	76
622	1992 Annual Ornament, Light Up the Night	185	61
623	1993 Annual Ornament, Herald on High	153	62
626	I Didn't Do It	142	125
630	For Keeps	102	108
633	I'm Carefree	112	126
635	Welcome Spring	158	198
646	Celestial Musician Miniature Ornament	152	89
647	Festival Harmony with Mandolin Minature Ornament	106	105
648	Festival Harmony with Flute Minature Ornament	043	104
662/0	Friends Together	104	109
662/I	Friends Together	094	109
668	Strike Up The Band	050	183
690	Smiling Through Plaque	n.a.	179
693	1995 Mini Christmas Plate, Festival Harmony w/Flute	027	64
700	1978 Annual Bell, Let's Sing	n.a.	50
701	1979 Annual Bell, Farewell	n.a.	51
702	1980 Annual Bell, Thoughtful	n.a.	52
703	1981 Annual Bell, In Tune	n.a.	52
704	1982 Annual Bell, She Love Me, She Loves Me Not	658	52
705	1983 Annual Bell, Knit One, Purl One	657	53
706	1984 Annual Bell, Mountaineer	656	53
707	1985 Annual Bell, Sweet Song	411	54
708	1986 Annual Bell, Sing Along	404	54
709	1987 Annual Bell, With Loving Greetings	397	55
710	1988 Annual Bell, Busy Student	306	55
711	1989 Annual Bell, Latest News	279	57
712	1990 Annual Bell, What's New?	248	58

REFERENCE NUMBER INDEX

Ref. No.:	Hummel Name	Mold No.:	Pg. #
265	Hosanna	480	125
266	I'll Protect Him	483	126
267	Make a Wish	475	150
268	Is It Raining?	420	128
269	Postman	119 2/0	166
270	1989 Christmas Bell, Ride Into Christmas	775	58
271	Tuba Player	437	188
272	An Apple a Day	403	68
275	Flying Angel	366/0	156
279	1989 Annual Bell, Latest News	711	57
280	1989 Mini Plate, Wash Day	746	58
281	It's Cold Plate	735	128
282	One For You, One For Me	482	162
283	1989 Annual Ornament, Love From Above	481	57
296	1988 Annual Ornament, Flying High	452	56
285	I'm Here	478	126
286	Harmony In Four Parts	471	119
287	In D Major	430	127
288	Wash Day	321 4/0	195
292	A Budding Maestro	477	65
293	Winter Song	476	201
294	Song of Praise	454	180
295	Accompanist (The)	453	66
300	Call to Worship Clock	441	88
301	1988 Mini Plate, Little Sweeper	745	57
302	Daisies Don't Tell Plate	736	99
303	Sound the Trumpet	457	180
304	Sounds of the Mandolin	438	180
305	Little Sweeper	171 4/0	144
306	1988 Annual Bell, Busy Student	710	55
307	Surprise (The)	431	185
315	1987 Mini Plate, Band Leader	742	55
316	1992 Annual Plate, Wayside Harmony	288	61
317	1991 Annual Plate, Just Resting	287	60
318	1989 Annual Plate, Farm Boy	285	57
319	1990 Annual Plate, Shepherd's Boy	286	59
320	1988 Annual Plate, Little Goat Herder	284	56
321	1987 Annual Plate, Feeding Time	283	55
397	1987 Annual Bell, With Loving Greetings	709	55
398	Band Leader	129 4/0	55
399	Hello World	429	78
402	Dealer Display Plaque, "The Tally"	460	99
403	Birthday Candle	440	122
404	1986 Annual Bell, Sing Along	708	54
405	1986 Annual Plate, Playmates	279	54
406	Valentine Gift Plate	738	192
407	Soloist	135 4/0	180
408	In The Meadow	459	127
409	Kindergartner	467	132
411	1985 Annual Bell, Sweet Song	707	54
412	1985 Annual Plate, Chick Girl	278	54
413	Serenade	85 4/0	174
414	For Mother	257 2/0	108
415	Stormy Weather	71 2/0	182
416	Playmates	58 2/0	164
417	Chick Girl	57 2/0	90
418	Hear Ye! Hear Ye!	15 2/0	119

Ref. No.:	Hummel Name	Mold No.:	Pg. #
419	Sensitive Hunter	6 2/0	173
420	Chapel Time Clock	442	90
421	Jubilee	416	130
422	Sing with Me	405	177
423	Going Home	383	111
424	Just Fishing	373	130
425	Baking Day	330	78
426	Little Fiddler	2 4/0	138
427	Morning Concert	447	154
443	Lost Sheep (Doll)	n.a.	217
444	Easter Greetings (Doll)	n.a.	216
445	A Gentle Glow Candleholder	439	65
446	Signs of Spring (Doll)	n.a.	218
447	Sing Along	433	176
448	Pleasant Journey	406	166
449	Valentine Joy Plate	737	193
459	Smiling Through	408/0	179
461	Friend or Foe?	434	109
465	Carnival (Doll)	n.a.	216
466	1984 Mini Plate, Little Fiddler	744	53
467	1986 Mini Plate, Soloist	743	55
469	1985 Mini Plate, Serenade	741	54
470	Coffee Break	409	95
472	Holy Child	70	123
473	Whitsuntide	163	201
474	Saint George	55	171
475	Little Guardian	145	141
476	Angelic Song	144	72
477	Good Shepherd	42	113
478	Watchful Angel	194/I	196
489	Blessed Child	78/III/83	82
492	Blessed Child	78/II/83	82
495	Blessed Child	78/I/83	82
497	Heavenly Lullaby	262	121
498	Silent Night Candleholder	54	176
499	Angelic Sleep Candleholder	25	72
500	Lullaby Candleholder	24/III	146
501	Lullaby Candleholder	24/I	146
502	Christ Child	18	94
504	Holy Family Font	246	123
506	Angel Facing Right Font	91B	69
507	Angel Facing Left Font	91A	69
508	White Angel Font	75	200
509	Angel with Bird Font	167	72
510	Worship Font	164	203
511	Guardian Angel Font	248/0	115
512	Angel Shrine Font	147	70
513	Angel Duet Font	146	69
514	Madonna & Child Font	243	147
515	Child with Flowers Font	36/0	93
516	Good Shepherd Font	35/0	113
519	Child Jesus Font	26/0	93
520	Angel Sitting Font	22/0	70
521	Heavenly Angel Font	207	120
522	Angel Cloud Font	206	68
523	Celestial Musician	188/I	89
524	Celestial Musician	188/0	89

Ref. No.:	Hummel Name	Mold No.:	Pg. #
525	Flying Angel	366/I	156
526	Tuneful Angel	359	189
527	Shining Light	358	175
528	Guiding Angel	357	116
530	Angel with Trumpet Candleholder	40/0	71
532	Angel with Accordion Candleholder	39/0	71
534	Angel with Lute Candleholder	38/0	71
535	Searching Angel Plaque	310	173
536	Angel Duet Candleholder	193	69
537	Candlelight Candleholder	192	88
538	Heavenly Protection	88/II	121
539	Heavenly Protection	88/I	121
540	Angel Serenade with Lamb	83	70
541	Festival Harmony with Flute	173/II	104
542	Festival Harmony with Flute	173/0	104
543	Festival Harmony with Mandolin	172/II	105
544	Festival Harmony with Mandolin	172/0	105
545	Bird Duet	169	80
546	Angel Duet	261	68
547	Christmas Song	343	94
548	Angel Lights Candleholder	241/B	70
550	Angel with Trumpet	238/C	71
551	Angel with Accordion	238/B	71
552	Angel with Lute	238/A	71
553	Herald Angels Candleholder	37	123
554	Little Gabriel	32 Or 32/0	140
555	Joyous News	27/III	129
556	Merry Christmas Plaque	323	151
557	Heavenly Angel	21/II	120
558	Heavenly Angel	21/I	120
559	Heavenly Angel	21/0 1/2	120
560	Heavenly Angel	21/0	120
561	Christmas Angel	301	94
562	Worship	84/V	202
563	Worship	84/0	202
564	Forest Shrine	183	108
565	Wayside Devotion	28/III	196
566	Wayside Devotion	28/II	196
567	Adoration	23/III	67
568	Adoration	23/I	67
570	Supreme Protection	364	184
571	Madonna Holding Child (White)	151/W	147
572	Madonna Holding Child	151/II	147
574	Madonna Plaque	48/II	148
575	Madonna Plaque	48/0	148
576	Madonna without Halo	46/III/W	149
577	Madonna without Halo	46/III	149
578	Madonna without Halo	46/I/W	149
579	Madonna without Halo	46/I	149
581	Madonna without Halo	46/0/W	149
582	Madonna without Halo	46/0	149
583	Madonna with Halo	45/III/W	148
584	Madonna with Halo	45/III	148
585	Madonna with Halo	45/I/W	148
586	Madonna with Halo	45/I	148
588	Madonna with Halo	45/0/W	148
589	Madonna with Halo	45/0	148

Ref. No.:	Hummel Name	Mold No.:	Pg. #
590	Flower Madonna	10/III/W	106
591	Flower Madonna	10/III	106
592	Flower Madonna	10/I/W	106
593	Flower Madonna	10/I	106
595	Nativity Set 260	260	160
602	Little Tooter	260/K	160
608	Good Night	260/D	160
618	Nativity Set 214/0	214/0	156
619	Nativity Set 214/I	214/I	156
626	Little Tooter	214/H/I	156
631	Good Night	214/C/I	156
635	Boy with Horse Candleholder	117	85
636	Girl with Fir Tree Candleholder	116	85
637	Girl with Nosegay Candleholder	115	85
638	Happy Days Lamp	235	117
639	Birthday Serenade Lamp	234	81
640	Happy Days Lamp	232	117
641	Birthday Serenade Lamp	231	81
642	Apple Tree Boy Lamp	230	74
643	Apple Tree Girl Lamp	229	74
644	Good Friends Lamp	228	112
645	She Loves Me, She Loves Me Not Lamp	227	112
646	Just Resting Lamp	225/II	131
647	Just Resting Lamp	225/I	131
648	Wayside Harmony Lamp	224/II	131
649	Wayside Harmony Lamp	224/I	131
650	To Market Lamp	223	188
652	Out Of Danger Lamp Base	44/B	98
653	Culprits Lamp Base	44/A	98
656	1984 Annual Bell, Mountaineer	706	53
657	1983 Annual Bell, Knit One, Purl One	705	53
658	1982 Annual Bell, She Love Me, She Loves Me Not	704	52
660	Girl Wall Vase	360/C	84
661	Boy Wall Vase	360/B	84
662	Boy & Girl Wall Vase	360/A	84
663	Little Thrifty	118	144
664	Happy Pastime Candy Box	III/69	118
665	Singing Lesson Candy Box	III/63	178
666	Playmates Candy Box	III/58	165
667	Chick Girl Candy Box	III/57	91
668	Joyful Candy Box	III/53	129
669	Let's Sing Candy Box	III/110	135
671	Boy with Bird Ashtray	166	85
672	Happy Pastime Ashtray	62	118
673	Singing Lesson Ashtray	34	177
674	Joyful Ashtray	33	129
675	Let's Sing Ashtray	114	135
676	Little Fiddler Plaque	93	139
677	Merry Wanderer Plaque	92	153
678	Standing Boy Plaque	168	182
682	1984 Annual Plate, Little Helper	277	53
683	1983 Annual Plate, Postman	276	53
684	1982 Annual Plate, Umbrella Girl	275	53
685	1981 Annual Plate, Umbrella Boy	274	52
686	Swaying Lullaby Plaque	165	185
687	Mail Is Here Plaque	140	150
688	Flitting Butterfly Plaque	139	106

Ref. No.:	Hummel Name	Mold No.:	Pg. #
770	Ring Around the Rosie	348	170
771	Adventure Bound	347	68
772	Smart Little Sister	346	179
773	A Fair Measure	345	65
774	Feathered Friends	344	103
775	Mischief Maker	342	153
777	Letter to Santa Claus	340	136
779	Birthday Cake Candleholder	338	80
780	Cinderella	337	94
781	Close Harmony	336	95
783	Homeward Bound	334	124
784	Blessed Event	333	82
785	Soldier Boy	332	180
786	Crossroads	331	96
787	Crossroads Military Commemorative	331	96
789	Carnival	328	88
790	Run-A-Way (The)	327	170
793	Little Pharmacist	322	143
795	Wash Day	321/0	195
797	Doll Bath	319	100
798	Art Critic	318	75
799	Not For You!	317	161
801	Mountaineer	315	155
802	Confidentially	314	96
804	Honey Lover	312	124
805	Kiss Me	311	132
806	With Loving Greetings	309	201
807	Little Tailor	308	144
808	Good Hunting	307	113
809	Little Bookkeeper	306	138
810	Builder	305	86
811	Artist	304	75
814	Bird Watcher	300	80
815	Which Hand?	258	200
816	For Mother	257/0	108
817	Knitting Lesson	256	132
818	Stitch in Time	255/I	182
819	Little Drummer	240	138
820	Boy with Horse	239/C	85
821	Girl with Doll	239/B	85
822	Girl with Nosegay	239/A	85
823	Mail Is Here (The)	226	150
824	We Congratulate	220	197
825	Birthday Serenade	218/0	81
826	Birthday Serenade	218 2/0	81
827	Boy with Toothache	217	86
828	Weary Wanderer	204	198
829	Signs of Spring	203/I	176
830	Signs of Spring	203 2/0	176
831	Retreat to Safety	201/I	168
832	Retreat to Safety	201 2/0	168
833	Little Goat Herder	200/I	140
834	Little Goat Herder	200/0	140
835	Feeding Time	199/I	103
836	Feeding Time	199/0	103
837	Home From Market	198/I	123
838	Home From Market	198 2/0	123

Ref. No.:	Hummel Name	Mold No.:	Pg. #
839	Be Patient	197/I	79
840	Be Patient	197 2/0	79
841	Telling Her Secret	196/I	186
842	Telling Her Secret	196/0	186
843	Barnyard Hero	195/I	78
844	Barnyard Hero	195 2/0	78
845	Dealer Display Plaque	187/A	99
848	Sweet Music	186	186
849	Accordion Boy	185	66
850	Latest News	184/0	134
851	Good Friends	182	112
852	Coquettes	179	96
853	Photographer	178	164
854	School Girls	177/III	173
855	School Girls	177/I	173
856	Happy Birthday	176/I	116
857	Happy Birthday	176/0	116
858	Mother's Darling	175	154
859	She Loves Me, She Loves Me Not	174	175
860	Little Sweeper	171/0	144
861	School Boys	170/III	172
862	School Boys	170/I	172
863	Waiter	154/I	195
864	Waiter	154/0	195
865	Auf Wiedersehen	153/I	76
866	Auf Wiedersehen	153/0	76
867	Umbrella Girl	152/B/0	190
868	Umbrella Boy	152/A/0	190
869	Umbrella Girl	152/B/II	190
870	Umbrella Boy	152/A/II	190
871	Happy Days	150/I	116
872	Happy Days	150/0	116
873	Happy Days	150 2/0	116
874	Boots	143/I	84
875	Boots	143/0	84
876	Apple Tree Boy	142/X	73
877	Apple Tree Boy	142/V	73
878	Apple Tree Boy	142/I	73
879	Apple Tree Boy	142 3/0	73
880	Apple Tree Girl	141/X	74
881	Apple Tree Girl	141/V	74
882	Apple Tree Girl	141/I	74
883	Apple Tree Girl	141 3/0	74
884	Friends	136/V	109
885	Friends	136/I	109
886	Soloist	135/0	180
887	Mother's Helper	133	155
888	Star Gazer	132	182
889	Street Singer	131	183
890	Duet	130	100
891	Band Leader	129	78
892	Baker	128	77
893	Doctor	127	100
894	Hello	124/I	122
895	Hello	124/0	122
896	Max & Moritz	123	150
897	Postman	119	166

Ref. No.:	Hummel Name	Mold No.:	Pg. #
898	Just Resting	112/I	131
899	Just Resting	112 3/0	131
900	Wayside Harmony	111/I	197
901	Wayside Harmony	111 3/0	197
902	Let's Sing	110/I	134
903	Let's Sing	110/0	134
904	Happy Traveller	109/II	118
905	Happy Traveller	109/0	118
906	Eventide	99	101
907	Sister	98/0	178
908	Sister	98 2/0	178
909	Trumpet Boy	97	188
910	Little Shopper	96	143
911	Brother	95	86
912	Surprise	94/I	184
913	Surprise	94 3/0	184
914	Little Cellist	89/II	138
915	Little Cellist	89/I	138
916	For Father	87	108
917	Happiness	86	116
918	Serenade	85/II	174
919	Serenade	85/0	174
920	School Boy	82/II	171
921	School Boy	82/0	171
922	School Boy	82 2/0	171
923	School Girl	81/0	172
924	School Girl	81 2/0	172
925	Little Scholar	80	143
926	Globe Trotter	79	111
927	Little Gardener	74	140
928	Little Helper	73	141
929	Spring Cheer	72	181
930	Stormy Weather	71/I	182
931	Happy Pastime	69	117
932	Lost Sheep	68/0	145
933	Lost Sheep	68 2/0	145
934	Doll Mother	67	100
935	Farm Boy	66	102
936	Farewell	65	102
937	Shepherd's Boy	64	175
938	Singing Lesson	63	177
939	Skier	59	178
940	Playmates	58/I	164
941	Playmates	58/0	164
942	Chick Girl	57/I	90
943	Chick Girl	57/0	90
944	Out Of Danger	56/B	163
945	Culprits	56/A	98
946	Joyful	53	128
947	Going To Grandma's	52/I	111
948	Going To Grandma's	52/0	111
949	Village Boy	51/I	193
950	Village Boy	51/0	193
951	Village Boy	51 2/0	193
952	Village Boy	51 3/0	193
953	Volunteers	50/I	194
954	Volunteers	50/0	194

Ref. No.:	Hummel Name	Mold No.:	Pg. #
955	Volunteers	50 2/0	194
956	To Market	49/I	187
957	To Market	49/0	187
958	To Market	49 3/0	187
959	Goose Girl	47/II	114
960	Goose Girl	47/0	114
961	Goose Girl	47 3/0	114
962	March Winds	43	150
963	Prayer Before Battle	20	167
964	Congratulations	17/0	96
965	Little Hiker	16/I	142
966	Little Hiker	16 2/0	142
967	Hear Ye! Hear Ye!	15/II	119
968	Hear Ye! Hear Ye!	15/I	119
969	Hear Ye! Hear Ye!	15/0	119
970	Meditation	13/V	151
971	Meditation	13/II	151
972	Meditation	13/0	151
973	Meditation	13 2/0	151
974	Chimney Sweep	12/I	93
975	Chimney Sweep	12 2/0	93
976	Merry Wanderer	11/0	152
977	Merry Wanderer	11 2/0	152
978	Begging His Share	9	79
979	Book Worm	8	83
980	Merry Wanderer	7/X	152
981	Merry Wanderer	7/III	152
982	Merry Wanderer	7/II	152
983	Merry Wanderer	7/I	152
984	Merry Wanderer	7/0	152
985	Sensitive Hunter	6/II	173
986	Sensitive Hunter	6/I	173
987	Sensitive Hunter	6/0	173
988	Strolling Along	5	184
989	Little Fiddler	4	138
990	Book Worm	3/III	83
991	Book Worm	3/II	83
992	Book Worm	3/I	83
993	Little Fiddler	2/III	138
994	Little Fiddler	2/II	138
995	Little Fiddler	2/I	138
996	Little Fiddler	2/0	138
997	Puppy Love	1	167
6433	Ride Into Christmas Music Box	396	169
6434	Chick Girl Music Box	324	92
6935	In Tune Music Box	66202	127
6936	Umbrella Girl Music Box	203	191
37211	Little Fiddler Miniature	250-P	221
37212	Little Sweeper Miniature	253-P	221
37213	Merry Wanderer Miniature	254-P	221
37214	Doll Bath Miniature	252-P	220
37215	Stormy Weather Miniature	251-P	222
37217	Postman Miniature	255-P	221
37218	Visiting An Invalid Miniature	256-P	222
37219	Apple Tree Boy Miniature	257-P	219
37221	Waiter Miniature	263-P	222
37222	Baker Miniature	262-P	219

INDEX OF ORIGINALS

H-No.	English Name	German Name	Translation of German Name If Different than English Name	Figurines Produced from Original, and Mold No.
101	Hello There!	Hummelbaby	Hummel Baby	Ba-Bee Rings M 30/A&B
102	Blessed Event	Das grosse Ereignis	The Big Event	Blessed Event M 333 and Rock-A-Bye M 574
103	Good Morning	Guten Morgen		None
104	What's New	Das Ungeheuer	The Monster	Child in Bed Plaque M 137
105	Loves Laughing	Baby im Körbchen	Baby in the Basket	None
106	My Baby Bumblebee	's Hummele	It is the Little Bumble Bee	None
107	Nature's Child	Vom Himmel gefallen	Fell Out of the Sky	None
108	Sunflower Shade	Kind in der Wiege	Child in the Cradle	None
109	Baby and the Spider	Die Spinne	The Spider	Friend or Foe? M 434 and Friend or Foe? Doll M 514
110	Baby and the Bee	Hui, die Hummel!/I	Wheee, the Bumble Bee	None
111	Innocence	Aufgewacht	Awakened	None
112	The Unexpected Guest	Treue Freundschaft	True Friendship	None
113	Friend of the Flowers	Der Blumenfreund		None
114	Sleepy Time	Nur ein Viertelstündchen	Only a Quarter Hour ("Naptime")	Just Dozing M 451
115	The Candy Kiss	Schleckerlein	Little Sweet Tooth	None
116	Honey Lovers	Der Honigschlecker		Honey Lover M 312 and Honey Lover Pendant
117	Tastes Great!	Stiller Geniesser	Quiet Indulger	An Apple a Day M 403
118	The Song Birds	Ziwitt—sing mit!	Sing Along with Me!	None
119	I've Lost My Stocking	In Lauterbach hab'i...		Lost Stocking M 374
120	Slumber Time	Er träumt von besseren Zeiten	He Dreams of Better Times	Swaying Lullaby Plaque M 165
121	Wishing Time	Ward ein Blümlein mir geschenkt	A Flower Was Given to Me	None

H- No.	English Name	German Name	Translation of German Name If Different than English Name	Figurines Produced from Original, and Mold No.
122	Morning Light	Auf sonniger Höh'	On Sunny Heights	None
123	Daisy Duet	Für Dich	For You	None
124	Sunrise Shepherd	Hirtenlied/II	Shepherd's Song	None
125	Springtime Joys	Blumenkinder	Flower Children	None
126	She Loves Me?	Glücksklee	Lucky Clover—Lucky One	She Loves Me, She... M 174; She Loves Me... Lamp M 227; 1982 Annual Bell, She Loves Me, She... M 704; and She Loves Me, She... Bookend M 251/B
127	He Loves Me?	Er liebt mich		None
128	Daisy	Mädchen mit Margariten	Girl with Daisies	In the Meadow M 459
129	New Found Friends	Streng vertraulich	Strictly Confidential	Hello World M 429
130	Lily of the Valley	Maiglöckchen		None
131	Buttercup	Was gibt's da zu lachen?	What's So Funny?	Sing with Me M 405
132	Dandelion	Pusteblume		Make a Wish M 475
133	My Wish Is Small	Mein Wunsch ist klein		My Wish is Small M 463
134	Heidi	Anneliese	Anneliese	None
135	First Portrait	Hänschen	Little John	None
136	Portrait of a Little Girl	Warum nicht lustig?	Why Are You Not Happy?	None
137	Curiosity	Da schau her!	There, Look Here!	None
138	Discovery	Wer hat die Blumen all erdacht?	Who Imagined All the Flowers?	None
139	Spring Basket	Ein schwerer Geschenkkorb	A Heavy Basket of Presents	None
140	The Flower Girl	Blumenmädchen		None
141	Out of Tune	Musikanten	Musicians	In D Major M 430
142	Child of the Heart/I	Glücksherz/I	Lucky Heart	1989 Annual Ornament, Love From Above M 481

H-No.	English Name	German Name	Translation of German Name If Different than English Name	Figurines Produced from Original, and Mold No.
143	Young Crawler	Guck in die Welt	Loock in the World (Child's Pet Name)	None
144	Meeting in the Meadow	Sorglos	Without Worry	In Tune M 414, In Tune Music Box, 1981 Annual Bell, In Tune M 703
145	Meeting on the Mountain	Bub mit Edelweiss	Boy with Edelweiss	Whistler's Duet M 413 and 1992 Annual Bell, Whistler's Duet M 714
146	The Opinion/I	's stimmt net/I	It Is Not Right—Out of Tune	Singing Lesson and Singing Lesson Candy Box M 63; Sing Along M 433; and 1986 Annual Bell, Sing Along M 708
147	Tit-for-Tat	Wie du mir, so ich dir!	As You Treat Me, So I Treat You!	None
148	Dreamland	Mal Ausspannen	Relax Once—Take a Break	None
149	Mother's Darling	Mutters Liebling		None
150	Carefree	Was frag ich viel	What More Could I Ask?	I'm Carefree M 633
151	Grandma's Story	Grossmutter erzählt	Grandmother Tells Stories	A Story from Grandma M 620 and Storybook Time M 458
152	Grandpa's Helper	Beim Grossvaterle	At Granddaddy's	At Grandpa's M 621
153	On the Other Side	Hui, die Hummel!/II	Wheee, the Bumble Bee	None
154	Cinderella	Aschenbrödel		Cinderella M 337 and Cinderella Miniature M 264-P
155	Goose Girl	Gänseliesl		Goose Girl M 47; 1974 Annual Plate, Goose Girl M 267; Goose Girl Bookend M 60/A; Goose Girl Doll M 517; and Goose Girl Miniature M 283-P

H-No.	English Name	German Name	Translation of German Name If Different than English Name	Figurines Produced from Original, and Mold No.
156	Hold Your Head High and Swallow Hard	Kopf hoch—u. schlucken		None
157	Feathered Friends	Schwanenmutter	Swan Mother	Feathered Friends M 344
158	Retreat to Safety	Der Held	The Hero	Barnyard Hero M 195, Retreat To Safety M 201 and Retreat To Safety Plaque M 126
159	On Tiptoes	Was gibt's da drüben	What's Going on Over There	None
160	Behind the Fence	Blick über den Zaun	View Over the Fence	None
161	Summertime	Herzmädel	Heart Girl	None
162		Gute Erholung!	Good Recovery—Happy Vacation	None
163	Little Thrifty	Für die Armen	For the Poor	Little Thrifty M 118
164	Doll Mother	Gebet fürs kranke Püppchen	Prayer for a Sick Dolly	Doll Mother M 67 and Evening Prayer M 495
165	Prayer Before Battle	Gebet vor der Schlacht		Prayer Before Battle M 20
166	The Golden Rule	Quäle nie ein Tier zum Scherz	Never Hurt an Animal for a Joke	None
167	Let's Sing/I	Ich hab mich ergeben/I	I Have Given Myself	Let's Sing and Let's Sing Candy Box M 110; Let's Sing Ashtray M 114; and 1978 Annual Bell, Let's Sing M 700
169	Why So Sad?	Warum so traurig?		None
170	Girl with Music Sheet	Singendes Mädchen mit Notenblatt	Singing Girl with Sheet Music	None
171	The Tuba Player	Der grosse Bass	The Big Bass	Tuba Player M 437
172	Boy with Lute	Bub mit Laute		None
173	Big Housecleaning	Der Grossputz	Big Cleanup	Big Housecleaning M 363
174	Phillip	Phillip		None
175	Child with Bluebells	Kind mit Enzian		None

H-No.	English Name	German Name	Translation of German Name If Different than English Name	Figurines Produced from Original, and Mold No.
176	Child of the Heart/II	Glücksherz/II	Lucky Heart	Love From Above M 481
177	Child of the Heart/III	Glücksherz/III	Lucky Heart	Love From Above M 481
178	The Opinion/II	's stimmt net/II	It is Not Right—Out of Tune	Singing Lesson M 63; 1979 Annual Plate, Singing Lesson M 272; Sing Along M 433; and 1986 Annual Bell, Sing Along M 708
179	Let's Sing/II	Ich hab mich ergeben/II	I Have Given Myself	Let's Sing and Let's Sing Candy Box M 110; Let's Sing Ashtray M 114; and 1978 Annual Bell, Let's Sing M 700
182	Girl on a Fence/II	Mädchen auf dem Zaun/II		None
183	The Little Dreamer	Der kleine Träumer		None
184	Bärbel	Bärbel	Barbara	None
185	Rolf	Rolf		None
186	Irmgard	Irmgard		None
187	The Break	Der erste Einkauf	The First Purchase	None
188	Going to Grandma's	Für die Hungernden	For the Hungry	Going to Grandma's M 52
189	Starting Young	Früh übt sich	Early Practice	None
190	Two Schoolgirls	Zwei Schulmädchen		None
191	School Girl	Jetzt kann's losgehen!	Now it Can Start!	School Girl M 81 and 1980 Annual Plate, School Girl M 273
192	Little Scholar	Hauptprobe	Main Test	Little Scholar M 80
193	Little Brother's Lesson	Das kluge Schwesterlein	The Smart Little Sister	Smart Little Sister M 346; Busy Student M 367; Busy

H-No.	English Name	German Name	Translation of German Name If Different than English Name	Figurines Produced from Original, and Mold No.
194	School Chums	Frisch gewagt ist halb gewonnen	A Fresh Approach is Half the Battle	Student Miniature M 268-P; and 1988 Annual Bell, Busy Student M 710 School Boy M 82 and School Boy Miniature M 281-P
195	Knit One, Purl Two	Der erste Strumpf	The First Stocking	Knit One, Purl One M 432; and 1983 Annual Bell, Knit One, Purl One M 705
196	The Book Worm	Der Gelehrte	The Scholar	Book Worm M 3 and M 8; Book Worms Bookends M 14A&B (Pair); Thoughtful M 415; and 1980 Annual Bell, Thoughtful M 702
197	School Girls	's Meisterstück	The Masterpiece	School Girls M 177; Stitch In Time M 255; 1990 Mini Plate, Stitch in Time M 747; Knitting Lesson M 256; and Two Hands, One Treat M 493
198	School Boys	Schwieriges Problem	Difficult Problem	School Boys M 170, Dealer Display Plaque M 460 and One Plus One M 556
199	The Reader	Bücherwurm	Book Worm	To Keep You Warm M 759; What's New? M 418; 1990 Annual Bell, What's New? M 712
200	Captive	Arrest	Arrest—Detention	None
201	Mother's Helper	Mutters Stütze		Mother's Helper M 133

H-No.	English Name	German Name	Translation of German Name If Different than English Name	Figurines Produced from Original, and Mold No.
202	Little Bookkeeper	Stellvertretung	Substitute Teacher	Little Bookkeeper M 306
203	The Mountaineer	I habs erreicht	I Made it!	Mountaineer M 315 and 1984
				Annual Bell, Mountaineer M 706
204	Ring Around the Rosie	Ringelreihen	Ring Around	Ring Around The Rosie M 348;
				1980 Anniversary Plate, Ring
				Around The Rosie M 281; and
				Spring Dance M 353
205	The Goat Girl	Mädchen mit Zicklein	Girl with Little Goats	Good Friends M 182, Good Friends
				Bookend M 251/A and Good
				Friends Lamp M 228
206	Vacation time	Ein froher Gruss	A Happy Greeting	Vacation Time Plaque M 125
207	Rosebud	Röslein	Little Rose	None
208	The Flower Vendor	Ein frohes Fest!	A Joyful First	Flower Vendor M 381
209	Blue Belle	Mädchen mit Enzian	Girl with Enzian	Botanist M 351 and Botanist
				(Crystal Hummel)
210	Bye-Bye!	Auf Wiederseh'n/II	Till I See You Again!	Auf Wiedersehen and Berlin
				Airlift Memorial (Auf
				Wiedersehen) M 153; 1985
				Anniversary Plate, Auf
				Wiedersehen M 282; 1995 Annual
				Plate, Come Back Soon M 291;
				and Come Back Soon M 545
211	Traveling Musician	Der kleine Bassgeiger	The Little Bass Violinist	None
213	Scolding	Wir gehen spazieren	We Go Walking	None
214	Adventure Bound	Die sieben Schwaben	The Seven Swabians	Adventure Bound M 347 and
				Lucky Fellow M 560

H-No.	English Name	German Name	Translation of German Name If Different than English Name	Figurines Produced from Original, and Mold No.
215	The First Outing	Erste Ausfahrt		Morning Stroll M 375
216	The Globetrotter	Mit frohem Mut und heiterm Sinn!	With Happy Courage and Clear Mind	Globe Trotter M 79; 1973 Annual Plate, Globe Trotter M 266; and Happy Traveller M 109
217	Hansel and Gretel	Wir wollen gratulieren	We Want to Congratulate	Mother's Darling M 175, Going Home M 383, Grandma's Girl M 561, and Grandpa's Boy M 562
218	The Runaway	Wem Gott will recht Gunst erweisen	Whomever God Will Favor	The Run-A-Way M 327
219	The Well-Wishers/Girls	Gratulanten, Mädchen	Congratulators, Girls	To Market M 49, To Market Lamp M 101 and M 223, Sister M 98, Sister (Crystal Hummel), Daddy's Girls M 371 and Little Visitor M 563
220	The Well-Wishers/Boys	Gratulanten, Buben	Congratulators, Boys	To Market M 49, To Market Lamp M 101 and M 223, Village Boy M 51, and Village Boy (Crystal Hummel)
221	The Winged Visitor	Fliegerabwehr	Aerial Defence	None
222	The Locust Hunter	Heuschreckenbub	Locust Boy	Sensitive Hunter M 6
223	Timid Little Sister	Hansl und Gretl	Hansel and Gretel	Timid Little Sister M 394
224		Schulweg	School Path	Is it Raining? M 420
225		Auf heimlichen Wegen	On Secret Path	On Secret Path M 386
226		Unser Festlied stimmt	Our Holiday Song is in Harmony	Visiting an Invalid M 382, Visiting an Invalid (Crystal Hummel) and Visiting an Invalid Miniature

H-No.	English Name	German Name	Translation of German Name If Different than English Name	Figurines Produced from Original, and Mold No.
227		Drei im Glück	Three in Luck	Home From Market M 198
228		Wanderbulb	Hiker Boy	Merry Wanderer M 7 & M 11, Merry Wanderer (Crystal Hummel), Merry Wanderer Doll M 516, Merry Wanderer Miniature M 254-P, Merry Wanderer Plaque M 92, Merry Wanderer Pendant, Dealer Display Plaque M 187, Dealer Display Plaque Miniature M 280-P, Signs of Spring M 203 and Club Member Plaque
229		Geigerlein	Violin Player	Little Fiddler M 2 and M 4; Little Fiddler Doll M 513; Little Fiddler Plaque M 93; 1984 Mini Plate, Little Fiddler M 744; Little Fiddler Miniature M 250-P; Puppy Love M 1; and Puppy Love Display Plaque M 767
230	Doll Bath	Puppenbad		Doll Bath M 319; 1993 Annual Plate, Doll Bath M 289; and Doll Bath Miniature M 252-P
231	Kiss Me	Puppenmütterchen	Little Doll Mother	Kiss Me M 311
232	Washday	Grosse Wäsche	Big Laundry	Wash Day M 321 and 1989 Mini Plate, Wash Day M 746
233	At Your Service	Zu Befehl, Herr Leutnant!	Your Orders, Mr. Leutnant	Soldier Boy M 332

H-No.	English Name	German Name	Translation of German Name If Different than English Name	Figurines Produced from Original, and Mold No.
234	The Little Sweeper	Ordnung muss sein!	There Must be Order!	Little Sweeper M 171; Little Sweeper (Crystal Hummel); 1988 Mini Plate, Little Sweeper M 745; and Little Sweeper Miniature M 253-P
235	The Little Goat Herder	Erbhofbauer	Father's Heir/Boy	Little Goat Herder M 200; Little Goat Herder Bookend M 250/A; 1988 Annual Plate, Little Goat Herder M 284; and For Keeps M 630
236	Feeding Time	Erbhofbäuerin	Father's Heir/Girl	Be Patient M 197; Feeding Time M 199; Feeding Time Bookend M 250/B; and 1987 Annual Plate, Feeding Time M 283
237	The Fisherman	Der Fischer		Just Fishing M 373
238	Good Hunting	Weidmanns Heil!		Good Hunting M 307
239	The boss	Der Chef		Hello M 124
240	The Professor	Der Professor		The Professor M 320
241	Little Pharmacist	Der Apotheker	The Pharmacist	Little Pharmacist M 322
242	The Stargazer	Der neue Stern	The New Star!	Star Gazer M 132
243	The Baker	Mhm...., wie fein	Mhm..., How Fine	Baker M 128 and Baker Miniature M 262-P
244	The Waiter	Hab' die Ehre	'Have the Honors	Waiter M 154 and Waiter Miniature M 263-P
245	Latest News	Das Allerneueste		Latest News M 184 and 1989 Annual Bell, Latest News M 771

H-No.	English Name	German Name	Translation of German Name If Different than English Name	Figurines Produced from Original, and Mold No.
246	The Postman	Dringend	Urgent	Postman M 119; Postman (Crystal Hummel); Postman Miniature M 255-P; and 1983 Annual Plate, Postman M 276
247	Too Short to Read	Morgenkonzert	Morning concert	Morning Concert M 447 and Morning Concert Mini w/Display
248	The Conductor/I	Der Dirigent/I		Band Leader M 129 and 1987 Mini Plate, Band Leader M 742
249	The End of the Song	Das Ende vom Lied		None
250	Little Cellist	Der grosse Kontrabass	The Big Contrabass	Little Cellist M 89
251	The Artist	Der Kunstmaler		Artist M 304 and Artist with Plaque Museum Commemorative M 756
252	The Art Critic	Der Kunstkritiker		Art Critic M 318
253	The Poet	Der Poet		The Poet M 397
254	Confidentially	Zwiegespräch	Two Way Conversation	Confidentially M 314
255	Little Boots	Schusterbub	Shoemaker Boy	Boots M 143
256	The Doctor	Schwieriger Fall	Difficult Case	Doctor M 127 and 1994 Annual Plate, Doctor M 290
257	The Toothache	Bloss weil's sein muss	Only Because It Has to Be	Boy with Toothache M 217
258	The Little Tailor	Schneiderlein	Tailor	Little Tailor M 308
260	The Photographer	Bitte recht freundlich!	Please Smile!	Photographer M 178
261	Chimney Sweep	Ich bring dir Glück	I Bring You Luck!	Chimney Sweep M 12
262	The Draftsman	Schulausreisser	Truant	Little Architect M 410
263	The Little Flower Girl	Blumenkind	Flower Child	None
264	The Skier	Ski Heil	Good Luck Wish in Skiing	Skier M 59
265	Carnival Boys	Februar	February	Carnival M 328 and Parade Of

H-No.	English Name	German Name	Translation of German Name If Different than English Name	Figurines Produced from Original, and Mold No.
				Lights M 616
266	Safe Shelter	April	April	None
267	Wayside Worship	Mai	May	Worship M 84 and Worship Font M 164
268	Happiness	Juli	July	Happiness M 86
269	All Soul's Day	November	November	None
270	The Haystack Sleeper	August	August	Coffee Break M 409
271	Just for You	Ich gratuliere/I	I Congratulate	Spring Cheer M 72
273	Mountain's Peace	Waldfrieden	Forest Peace	Forest Shrine M 183
276	Prayer Time	Abendläuten	Evening Bell Ringing— Evening Prayer Time	
278	Resting	Kleine Rast	Brief Rest	None
282	Spring's Return	Frühlingstanz	Spring Dance	None
283	The Birthday Gifts	Wir gratulieren	We Congratulate	Welcome Spring M 635
				Happy Birthday M 176, Little Visitor M 563, Sweet As Can Be M 541 and We Wish You the Best M 600
284	Quartet	Vier Strassensänger	Four Street Singers	Harmony in Four Parts M 471; 1992 Christmas Bell M 778; Duet M 130; Quartet Plaque M 134; Soloist M 135; Solist (Crystal Hummel); 1986 Mini Plate, Soloist M 743; and Street Singer M 131
285	The Conductor/II	Der Dirigent/II		Band Leader M 129 and 1987 Mini Plate, Band Leader M 742

H-No.	English Name	German Name	Translation of German Name If Different than English Name	Figurines Produced from Original, and Mold No.
286	Boy with Lamb	Trachtenbub mit Schäfchen	Costumed Boy with Sheep	None
287	Sunny Weather	Schön-Wetter	Nice Weather	None
288	Stormy Weather	Hunde-Wetter	Dog weather	Stormy Weather M 71; Stormy Weather Miniature M 251-P; and 1975 Anniversary Plate, Stormy Weather M 280
289	Wayside Harmony	Vaters G'scheitster	Father's Smartest	Wayside Harmony M 111; Wayside Harmony Lamp M 224; Wayside Harmony Miniature M 282-P; and 1992 Annual Plate, Wayside Harmony M 288
290	Just Resting	Der Mutter Liebste	Mother's Dearest	Just Resting M 112; Just Resting Lamp M 225; and 1991 Annual Plate, Just Resting M 287
291	Telling Her Secret	Die grosse Neuigkeit	The Big News	Telling Her Secret M 196 and Which Hand? M 258
292	Not for You!	Nix für dich	Nothing for You!	Not for You! M 317
293	Shepherd's Boy	Bub mit Schäflein	Boy with Lamb	Shepherd's Boy M 64; 1990 Annual Plate, Shepherd's Boy M 286; and Lost Sheep M 68
294	Have the Sun in Your Heart	Hab' Sonne im Herzen/I		Umbrella Boy M 152/A; Umbrella Boy Doll M 518; and 1981 Annual Plate, Umbrella Boy M 274
296	Umbrella Girl	Ja ich bin zufrieden	Yes, I Am Content	Umbrella Girl M 152/B; Umbrella Girl Music Box M 203; Umbrella

H-No.	English Name	German Name	Translation of German Name If Different than English Name	Figurines Produced from Original, and Mold No.
				Girl Doll M 512; and 1982 Annual Plate, Umbrella Girl M 275
297	Apple Tree Boy	Sitzt ein Büblein auf dem Baum	A Little Boy Sits in the Tree	Apple Tree Boy M 142; Apple Tree Boy Lamp M 230; Apple Tree Boy Bookend M 252/A; 1987 Annual Plate, Apple Tree Boy M 270; and Apple Tree Boy Miniature M 257-P
298	Apple Tree Girl	's Lieserl sitzt im Blütenbaum	It Is Lieserl Sitting in the Flowering Tree	Apple Tree Girl M 141; Apple Tree Girl (Crystal Hummel); Apple Tree Girl Lamp M 229; Apple Tree Girl Bookend M 252/B; and 1976 Annual Plate, Apple Tree Girl M 269
299	Girl on a Fence/I	Mädchen auf dem Zaun/I		None
300	Boy on a Fence	Bub auf dem Zaun		Mischief Maker M 342
301	For Mother	Fürs Mutterle!		None
302	For Father	Fürs Vaterle!		For Father M 87 and 1993 Friends Forever Plate, For Father M 293
303	Off to Town	I geh in d' Stadt	I'm Going to Town	None
304	Looks Like Rain	Glück auf!	Good Luck!	None
305	His Happy Pastime	Kommt a Vogerl geflogen	A Bird Comes Flying	Singing Lesson and Singing Lesson Candy Box M 63; Singing Lesson Ashtray M 34; and 1979 Annual Plate, Singing Lesson M 272

H-No.	English Name	German Name	Translation of German Name If Different than English Name	Figurines Produced from Original, and Mold No.
306	Her Happy Pastime	Ist mir alles eins	It Is Not Important	Happy Pastime and Happy Pastime Candy Box M 69; Happy Pastime Ashtray M 62; and 1978 Annual Plate, Happy Pastime M 271
307	Happy John	Hans Im Glück	John in Luck	Little Hiker M 16
308	Coquettes	So zwei wie wir zwei	Two Like We Two	Coquettes M 179
309	The Little Hiker	Hänschen will gratulieren	Little John Wants to Congratulate	None
310	Farewell	Auf Wiederseh'n!/I	Goodbye (Till I See You Again)	Farewell M 65 and 1979 Annual Bell, Farewell M 701
311	Evening Tide	Abendstimmung	Evening Mood	None
312	Twilight Tune	Abendlied	Evening Song	None
313	The Work Is Done	Feierabend		Lamb M 214/0
314	Homeward Bound	Heimkehr	Homecoming	Homeward Bound M 334
316	Winter Fun	Fahrt in die Weihnacht	Ride Into Christmas	Ride Into Christmas and Ride Into Christmas Music Box M 396; Ride Into Christmas Doll M 519; 1975 Annual Plate, Ride Into Christmas M 268; and 1989 Christmas Bell, Ride Into Christmas M 775
317	March Winds	'S wird kalt!	It's Getting Cold!	March Winds M 43 and March Winds (Crystal Hummel)
318	Letter to Santa Claus	Brief ans Christkind	Letter to the Christ Child	Letter To Santa Claus M 340 and 1990 Christmas Bell, Letter To Santa Claus M 776
319	The Witch	Die Hexe		None

H- No.	English Name	German Name	Translation of German Name If Different than English Name	Figurines Produced from Original, and Mold No.
330	Culprits/Boy	Der Apfeldieb	The Apple Thief	Culprits M 56/A and Culprits Lamp Base M 44/A
331	Blue Heart Baby	Viel Glück!/III	Much Luck!	Tuneful Good Night Plaque M 180
332	Red Heart Baby	Viel Glück!/IV	Much Luck!	None
333	This Heart is Mine	Valentine, Bub	Valentine, Boy	None
334	Catch My Heart	Valentine, Mädchen	Valentine, Girl	None
335	I Like You/Boy	I hab di gern, Bub	I Love You, Boy	Valentine Joy M 399, Valentine Joy Plate M 737 and Standing Boy Plaque M 168
336	I Like You/Girl	I hab di gern, Mädchen	I Love You, Girl	Valentine Gift M 387 and Valentine Gift Plate M 738
337	Take Me Along	Viel Freud zum Fest!	Much Joy for the Holders	None
338	The Strummers	Ständchen	Serenade	Happy Days M 150, Happy Days Lamp M 232 and M 235, and Little Troubadour M 558
339	To Market, To Market	Viel Glück im neuen Jahr!	Much Luck in the New Year!	None
340	Little Helper	Herzlichen Ostergruss!	Heartfelt Easter Greetings!	Little Helper M 73 and 1984 Annual Plate, Little Helper M 277
341	My Dolly	Herzlichen Glückwunsch!/I	Heartfelt Congratulations!	None
342	Serenade	Ein frohes, neues Jahr!	A Happy New Year!	Serenade M 85, Serenade Miniature M 265-P and 1985 Mini Plate, Serenade M 741
345		Kind mit Brief	Child with Letter	Meditation M 13; Meditation (Crystal Hummel); and 1992 Friends Forever Plate, Meditation M 292

283

H-No.	English Name	German Name	Translation of German Name If Different than English Name	Figurines Produced from Original, and Mold No.
346	Boys Ensemble	Viel Glück!/II	Much Luck!	Sound the Trumpet M 457 and Strike Up the Band M 668
347	Girls Ensemble	Herzlichen Glückwunsch!/IV	Congratulations!	Close Harmony M 336, Birthday Cake Candleholder M 338 and Birthday Present M 341
348	Special Gift	Herzlichen Glückwunsch!/II	Congratulations!	Jubilee M 416
349	Special Delivery	Herzlichen Glückwunsch!/III	Congratulations!	Jubilee M 416
350	Bashful	Viel Glück!/I	Much Luck!	Bashful M 377
351	Follow the Leader	Lach mit	Laugh with Me	Follow the Leader M 369 and Flower Girl M 548
352	Max and Moritz	Max und Moritz		Max and Moritz M 123, Scamp M 553 and Cheeky Fellow M 554
353	Pleasant Journey	Frohe Fahrt		Pleasant Journey M 406 and Pixie M 768
354	A Smile Is Your Umbrella	Hab' Sonne im Herzen/II	Have the Sun in Your Heart	Smiling Through M 408 and Smiling Through Plaque M 690
355	Begging His Share	Und viele, viele Jahre noch!	And Many, Many Years to Come	Begging His Share M 9
357	Wee Three	I bring viel Lieb	I Bring Much Love	On Holiday M 350; Sweet Greetings M 352; and 1994 Friends Forever Plate, Sweet Greetings M 294
358	Utterly Absorbed	Versunken	Absorbed	None
367		Auf zum Fest	Off to the Festival	On Holiday M 350
368		Bildstöckle	Wayside Shrine	Adoration M 23
369		Zwei Kinder beim Bildstöckle	Two Children at Wayside Shrine	None
370		Der richtige Osterhase	The Real Easter Bunny	Easter Time M 384

H-No.	English Name	German Name	Translation of German Name If Different than English Name	Figurines Produced from Original, and Mold No.
371	Chick Girl	...und haben einander so lieb	...and we love one another so much	Chick Girl and Chick Girl
				Candy Box M 57; Chick Girl
				Bookend M 61/B; Chick Girl
				Music Box M 324; and 1985
				Annual Plate, Chick Girl M 278
372	Playmates	Wir sitzen so fröhlich beisammen	We're Sitting So Happy Together	Playmates and Playmates Candy
				Box M 58; Playmates Bookend
				M 61/A; and 1986 Annual
				Plate, Playmates M 279
373	First Interview	Erstes Interview		None
374	A Little Hare	Häslein im Grünen	Bunny in the Grass	None
375	Favorite Pet	Froher Ostergruss!	Happy Easter Greetings!	Favorite Pet M 361 and 1991
				Annual Bell, Favorite Pet M 713
376	Chicken-Licken	Mädchen mit Kücken	Girl with Chick	Chicken-Licken M 385 and 1991
				Mini Plate, Chicken-Licken M 748
377	Children on the Church Road	Osterkirchgang	Easter Churchwalk	Chapel Time Clock M 442
378	The Shepherd's Tune	Flötender Hirtenbub	Flute-Playing Shepherd Boy	None
379	Easter Playmates	Ostergruss, Bub	Easter Greetings, Boy	Easter Greetings M 378
380	Easter Basket	Ostergruss, Mädchen	Easter Greetings, Girl	Autumn Harvest M 355
381	And One Makes a Dozen	Der Festtags-Strauss	Holiday Bouquet	For Mother M 257 and For
				Mother (Crystal Hummel)
382	Return to the Fold	Bub mit Lamm	Boy with Lamb	None
383	In Full Harmony	Hirtenlied/I	Shepherd's Song	Wayside Devotion M 28 and
				Eventide M 99
384	Praise to God	Ostersonntag	Easter Sunday	1992 Annual Ornament, Light Up
				The Night M 622

H-No.	English Name	German Name	Translation of German Name If Different than English Name	Figurines Produced from Original, and Mold No.
385	Alleluja	Alleluja		Angel with Lute M 238/A, Angel w/Lute Candleholder M 38/0, Herald Angels Candleholder M 37, Joyful and Joyful Candy Box M 53, Joyful Ashtray M 33
386	The Easter Lamb	Fröhliche Ostern	Happy Easter!	Angel Serenade w/Lamb M 83 and Angel Duet Font M 146
387	Who Has the Sweetest Lamb?	Wer hat die schönsten Schäfchen?	Who Has the Prettiest Lamb?	The Accompanist M 453
388	Life Is to Treasure	Freut euch des Lebens		None
389	Sunshine	O Sonnenschein	Oh, Sunshine	The Guardian M 455
399	On Our Way	Bald sind wir drüben	We Are Almost on the Other Side	On Our Way M 472
400	Safe Crossing	September	September	On Our Way M 472
401	In Guardian Arms	Schlaf nun selig und süss	Sleep Peaceful and Sweet	None
402	Deliver Us from Evil	Schutzengel	Guardian Angel	None
404	The Guardian Angel	Der Schutzengel		None
405	Guardian Angel Preserve Us	Schutzengel halte treue Wacht	Guardian Angel Keep Diligent Watch	None
406	The Renewal	Margritchen	Little Daisy	None
407	Boy's Communion	Jesu, komm zu mir	Jesus, Come to Me	None
408	Girl's Communion	Lieber Heiland, bleib bei mir	Dear Jesus, Stay with Me	None
409	Angel/Trumpet	Hosanna!	Hosanna!	None
410	Tender watch	Krippenwacht		1990 ARS Christmas Plate, Tender Watch
411	Angel Duet	O, du fröhliche	O, You Merry Christmas Time	Angel Duet Candleholder M 193; Angel Duet M 261; 1988 ARS Christmas Plate, Angel Duet
412	Candle Light	Das Licht in der Nacht	The Light in the Night	Candlelight Candleholder M 192

286

H-No.	English Name	German Name	Translation of German Name If Different than English Name	Figurines Produced from Original, and Mold No.
413	Angel/Prayer	Englein, betend	Little Angel Praying	None
414	Angel/Light	Hell strahlt das Licht	Bright Shines the Light	None
415	Heavenly Duo	Singt Fried den Menschen	Sing of Peace for Mankind	Angel w/Cloud Ornament (White) M 585 and Angel w/Trumpet Ornament (White) M 586
416	Searching the Heavens	Seid stille, ihr Wind	Be Still, You Wind	1991 Annual Ornament, Angelic Guide M 571
417	Trumpeting from Clouds	Mit süssem Jubelschall	With Sweet Triumphant Song	None
418	Christmas Tree Bearer	Engel mit Christbaum	Angel with Christmas Tree	1988 Annual Ornament, Flying High M 452
419	The Christ-Child	Christkind		None
420	The First Christmas Tree	Der erste Christbaum		A Gentle Glow C'hldr M 439
421	Corpus Christi	Fronleichnam		Angelic Song M 144
422	Three Little Cherubs	Drei Engelbuben	Three Little Angel Boys	None
423	Angelic Sleep	Zur Ruhe singendes Englein	Lullaby Singing Little Angel	Angelic Sleep C'hldr M 25
424	Heavenly Lullaby	Laute spielendes Englein	Lute-Playing Little Angel	Lullaby Candleholder M 24 and Heavenly Lullaby M 262
425	Heavenly Angel	Adventsengel	Advent Angel	Heavenly Angel M 21; Heavenly Angel Ornament (White) M 575; Heavenly Angel Tree Topper M 755; Heavenly Angel Font M 207; and 1971 Annual Plate, Heavenly Angel M 264
426	Sieglinde's First Tree	Sieglindes erster Christbaum		None
431	Christmas Angel	Engel mit Adventskranz	Angel with Advent Wreath	None
432	Little Gabriel	Engel mit Trompete	Angel with Trumpet	None

H-No.	English Name	German Name	Translation of German Name If Different than English Name	Figurines Produced from Original, and Mold No.
433	Angel with Deer	Engel mit Reh		None
434	Prayer of Adoration	Die Freude der Weihnacht	The Joy of Christmas	1990 Annual Ornament, Peace On Earth M 484
435	Angel/Horn	Ein gutes Neues Jahr!	A Happy New Year!	Joyous News and Joyous News Candleholder M 27; Little Gabriel M 32, Herald Angels Candleholder M 37, Angel w/Trumpet M 238/C, and Angel w/Trumpet Candleholder M 40/0
436	Angelic Care	Frohe Weihnacht	Merry Christmas	Watchful Angel M 194
437	Light of the World	Licht der Welt		Merry Christmas Plaque M 323
438	Guiding Angel	Mein Laternlein sternlichtklar	My Little Lantern as Bright as the Stars	None
439	The Angel's Prayer	Lobgesang	Song of Praise	None
440	Heavenly Messenger	Himmelsbote		None
441	Celestial Musician	Geigenengel	Violin Angel	Celestial Musician M 188; Angel Ornament M 578; Celestial Musician Miniature Ornament M 646; 1987 ARS Christmas Plate, Celestial Musician; and 1993 Christmas Bell, Celestial Musician M 779
442	Bearing Christmas Gifts	Der Weihnachtsengel	The Christmas Angel	Christmas Angel M 301
444	The Littlest Candle	Allerseelen	All Soul's Day	Angel Shrine Font M 147, Angel Lights Candleholder M 241/B and Shining Light M 358

H-No.	English Name	German Name	Translation of German Name If Different than English Name	Figurines Produced from Original, and Mold No.
448	Angel/Harp	Engel mit Harfe	Angel with Harp	Song of Praise M 454 and Song of Praise Ornament (White) M 579
449	Angel/Mandolin	Engel mit Mandoline	Angel with Mandolin	Angel w/Lute Ornament (White) M 580
451	Watchful Angel	Was ist denn da drunten los?	What Is Going on Down There?	Searching Angel Plaque M 310
452	Star Bethlehem	Stern der Liebe	Star of Love	Hosanna M 480
453	Guiding Light	Viel Glück und Segen	Much Love and Many Blessings	Christmas Song M 343; 1989 ARS Christmas Plate, Guiding Light
454	Angel and Birds	Ich gratuliere/I	I Congratulate	Congratulations M 17
457	Bath Time	Lass dich waschen kleiner Wicht	Let Me Bathe You, Little One	Bath Time M 412
458	Festival Harmony/Mandolin	Engel mit Laute	Angel with Lute	Festival Harmony w/Mandolin M 172; Festival Harmony w/Mandolin Orn. (White) M 576; 1994 Christmas Bell M 780; and 1994 Mini Orn., Festival Harmony w/Mandolin M 647
459	Festival Harmony/flute	Engel mit Flöte	Angle with Flute	Festival Harmony with Flute M 173; Festival Harmony w/Flute Ornament (White) M 577; 1995 Mini Ornament Festival Harmony w/Flute M 648; 1995 Mini Christmas Plate, Festival Harmony w/Flute M 693; 1995 Christmas Bell, Festival Harmony w/Flute M 781; and Gentle Song Ornament (White) M 582

H-No.	English Name	German Name	Translation of German Name If Different than English Name	Figurines Produced from Original, and Mold No.
460	Bon Voyage!	Glückliche Fahrt		Land in Sight M 530
470	Windplayers	Turmbläser	Tower Musicians	None
471	Trinity	Krippenkind	Manger Child	None
472	The Old Shepherd	Hirt an der Krippe	Shepherd by the Manger	None
473	The Wise Men	Die heiligen drei Könige	The Three Holy Kings	None
474	Christmas Child	Das Christkind	The Christ Child	None
475	Alleluja Angel	Alleluja Engel		None
477	Silent Night, Holy Night	Stille Nacht, heilige Nacht		Whitsuntide M 163 and Call to Worship Clock M 441
478	Let's Tell the World	Sturmläuten	Stormbells	Winter Song M 476 and Let's Tell The World M 487
479	Joyous Christmas	Fröhliche Weihnacht	Merry Christmas	None
480	Flying Angel	Dezember	December	Flying Angel M 366
481	Jubilation	In dulce jubilo		None
482	Prince of Peace	Friede den Menschen	Peace for Mankind	None
483	Merry Christmas	Fröhliche Weihnachten		Moorish King M 214/L and M 260/N, King Kneeling on One Knee M 214/M and King Standing M 260/O
484	Love and Luck	All Glück und Heil	Much Luck and Love	None
485	Glory to God in the Highest	Ehre sei Gott in der Höhe		None
486	Bless Your Soul on Christmas	Glückselige Weihnacht	Blissful Christmas	Good Night M 214/C and M 260/D
487	Joyous Holidays	Wir wünschen ein glückselig Jahr	We Wish You a Blissful New Year	None
488	Good Luck in the New Year	Ins neue Jahr viel Glück		None
489	We Wish the Very Best	Wir wünschen Euch für Leib und Seel'	Our Good Wishes for Body and Soul	A Budding Maestro M 477, I'm Here M 478 and I Brought

H-No.	English Name	German Name	Translation of German Name If Different than English Name	Figurines Produced from Original, and Mold No.
491	For All Men	Friede den Menschen auf Erden	Peace for All Mankind on Earth	You A Gift M 479
493	God Is Born	Gnadenreiche Weihnacht	Most Gracious Christmas	None; Donkey M 214/J and M 260/L; Cow M 214/K and M 260/M
495	May You Sing	Mag einer singen oder klagen	Either Sing or Complain	Gay Adventure M 356
497	Town Crier	Glück zum Neuen Jahr!	Luck for the Coming New Year	Hear Ye, Hear Ye M 15; 1972 Annual Plate, Hear Ye, Hear Ye M 265; and 1991 Christmas Bell, Hear Ye, Hear Ye M 777
498	The Holy Child	Christkindlein	Little Christ Child	Child Jesus Font M 26
499	Little Good Shepherd	Kleiner guter Hirte		Good Shepherd M 42
500	The Good Shepherd	Der gute Hirte		None
501	Help Me Be Good	Mach ein frommes Kind aus mir!	Help Me to Be a Good Child	Friends Together M 662
502	Eternal Light	Das ewige Licht leuchte ihnen	May the Eternal Light Shine on Them	None
503	Do No Creature Harm	Keinem Tierlein tu ein Leid!		None
504	Save the Flowers	Was Blümlein spricht	What Little Flower Tells You	None
505	O Come, Holy Ghost	Komm Heiliger Geist		None
506	Little Jesus the Gardener	Jesuskind als Gärtner		None
520	Queen of May	Madonna im Rosenhag	Madonna in the Rosegarden	Sounds of the Mandolin M 438 and Song of Praise M 454
521	Mary, Queen of May	Majenkönigin		None
522	Fruit of the Vine	Madonna mit der Weintraube	Madonna with Grapes	None
523	Mother of God	Magd Gottes	Maid of God	None
524	Mary Mother, Queen Maid	Maria, Mutter, reine Maid!	Mary, Mother, Virgin Maid	None
525	Immaculata	Immaculata/II		None
526	Mother at the Window	Madonna vor dem Fenster		None

H-No.	English Name	German Name	Translation of German Name If Different than English Name	Figurines Produced from Original, and Mold No.
527	Mother of Christ	Mutter Christi		None
528	Queen of the Rosary	Rosenkranzkönigin		None
529	Nativity	Und hat ein Blümlein bracht	And Bore a Flower for Us	Madonna M 214/A/M and M 260/A; Infant Jesus M 214/A/K and M 260/C
530	At Mary's Knee	Du liebliche Mutter	Your Loving Mother	None
531	Mary Take Us into Your Care	Maria breit' den Mantel aus!	Mary, Spread Your Guardian Cloak!	None
532	Madonna in Green	Mutter Gottes	Mother of God	None
533	Loving Mother and child	Maria hilf	Mary Help Us	Madonna & Child Font M 243
534	The Holy Family/II	Heilige Familie/II		None
536	Virgin and Child	Weihnacht	Christmas	None
537	Born in Bethlehem	Liebliche Mutter	Sweetest Mother	None
538	Blessings	Jungfrau Mutter	Virgin Mother	None
539	Virgin Mother	Liebreich holdseligste	Loving Most Gracious	None
540	Christ Child Sleeping	Still, weil's Kindlein schlafen will!	Still, the Baby Wants to Sleep!	None
543	Christ Is Born	Christ ist geboren		None
544	Mother of Sorrows/II	Maria mit Schwertern/II	Mary with Swords	None
545	Madonna in Red	Madonna in Rot		Madonna Plaque M 48
546	The Holy Family/I	Heilige Familie/I		Holy Family Font M 246
547	Madonna with Child	Madonna mit Kind		None
548	Madonna in the Meadow	Wiesenmadonna		Flower Madonna M 10
549	Madonna with the Blue Cloak	Schutzmantelmadonna	Guardian Coat Madonna	Supreme Protection M 364
615	Crossroads	Drei Wanderburschen	Three Hiking Boys	Crossroads, Crossroads Berlin Wall Commemorative and Crossroads Military Commemorative M 331

H-No.	English Name	German Name	Translation of German Name If Different than English Name	Figurines Produced from Original, and Mold No.
616	Teach Me to Fly	Sing mir ein Lied	Sing Me a Song	Boy with Bird Ashtray M 166
617	Mail Is Here	Trari-trara–die Post ist da!	Trari-Trara the Mail is Here	The Mail is Here M 226 and Mail is Here Plaque M 140
619	Sunrise	Sonnenaufgang		None
620	Sing to the Mountains	Sonntag	Sunday	None
622	Hard Letters	Ein lieber Gruss!	A Sweet (Dear) Greeting	None
623	Easy Letters	Ein dicker Gruss!	A Big Greeting	With Loving Greetings M 309 and 1987 Annual Bell, With Loving Greetings M 709
624	Gift Bearers	Beim Christkindlein	By the Christ Child	What Now? M 422, What Now? Pendant and Sleep Tight M 424
625	Angel's Music	Engelsmusik		Angel Serenade M 214/D and M 260/E
626	A Gift for Jesus	Jesus ist unser Bruder	Jesus is Our Brother	It's Cold M 421, It's Cold Plate M 735 and Horse Trainer M 423
627	O Dearest Infant Jesus	O du liebes Jesulein	Oh, You Dear Baby Jesus	Silent Night Candleholder M 54, Heavenly Song Candleholder M 113 and We Come in Peace M 754
628	Mother and Child	Madonna mit der Rosenknospe	Madonna with the Rosebud	None
629	Hail, O Favored One	Gegrüsset seist Du, Maria!	Greeted Be You, Mary	None
630	The Birth of Jesus Christ	Christi Geburt		None
631	The Flight to Egypt	Flucht nach Aegypten		None
632	In Nazareth	In Nazareth		Joseph M 214/B and M 260/B
633	Jesus in the Crib	Krippe mit Jesuskind	Manger with Baby Jesus	None
650	June	Juni		None

H-No.	English Name	German Name	Translation of German Name If Different than English Name	Figurines Produced from Original, and Mold No.
651	St. Francis	St. Franziskus		None
652	Good Friday	Karfreitag		None
653	With All My Heart	Jesuslein, ich hab dich so lieb!	Baby Jesus, I Love You So Much!	I Wonder M 486
654	The Secret	Das Geheimnis		None
655	Volunteers	Lieb' Vaterland, magst ruhig sein!	Dear Fatherland, May You Be Peaceful!	Volunteers M 50 and Little Drummer M 240
656	Wrongdoing	Peter, das war nicht recht!	Peter, That Was Not Right!	None
657	The Sulky Child	Trotzköpfchen	Little Sulky Child	None
658	Reconciliation	Versöhnung		None
659	You Can Count on Me	Kannst dich verlassen!	Count on Me!	None
660	Little Nurse	Hansel, merk dir das	John, Remember This	Little Nurse M 376
661	January	Januar		None
662	March	März		None
663	Lakeside	Seelandschaft		None
664	October	Oktober		None
665	Sailboats on the Shore	Segelboote am Ufer		None
666	It Is Finished	Es ist vollbracht!		None
667	Immaculate Mother	Immaculata/I	Immaculata	Madonna with Halo M 45 and Madonna without Halo M 46
668	Divine Love	Göttliche Liebe		None
669	Mother of Us All	Unser aller Mutter		None
670	Francis of Assisi	Franz von Assisi		None
672	The Saviour	Die Erlösung	The Redemption	None
673	St. Francis at the Crib	St. Franziskus an der Krippe	St. Francis at the Manger	None
674	Mother of the Creator	Mutter des Schöpfers		None
675	St. Joseph	St. Joseph		None

H-No.	English Name	German Name	Translation of German Name If Different than English Name	Figurines Produced from Original, and Mold No.
677	Mary's Gentle Child	Maria mit dem Kinde lieb	Mary with the Child So Dear	None
678	Mary in Mourning	Die Schmerzensmutter	The Mother of Pain	None
679	Mother's Joy	Mutterglück		None
680	Abide in My Love	Bleibet in meiner Liebe		None
682	Madonna in the Mountains	Madonna vor den Bergen		Madonna Holding Child M 151
683	The Lord Is My Shepherd	Guter Hirte	Good Shepherd	None
700	Pet-Loving	Tierliebe	Animal Love	None
701	On the Way to School	Auf dem Schulweg		Kindergartner M 467
702	Assistance	Beim Lernen	At Study	None
703	Sharing	Beim Essen	At Dinner	None
704	Child's Prayer	Beim Beten	At Prayer	None
705	Making Repairs	Beim Spielen	At Play	None
706	Protection	Beschützt/Die Tollkirsche	Protected	None
707	Madonna of the Missions	Missionsmadonna		None
708	Our Lady of Sorrows	Schmerzensmutter		None

295